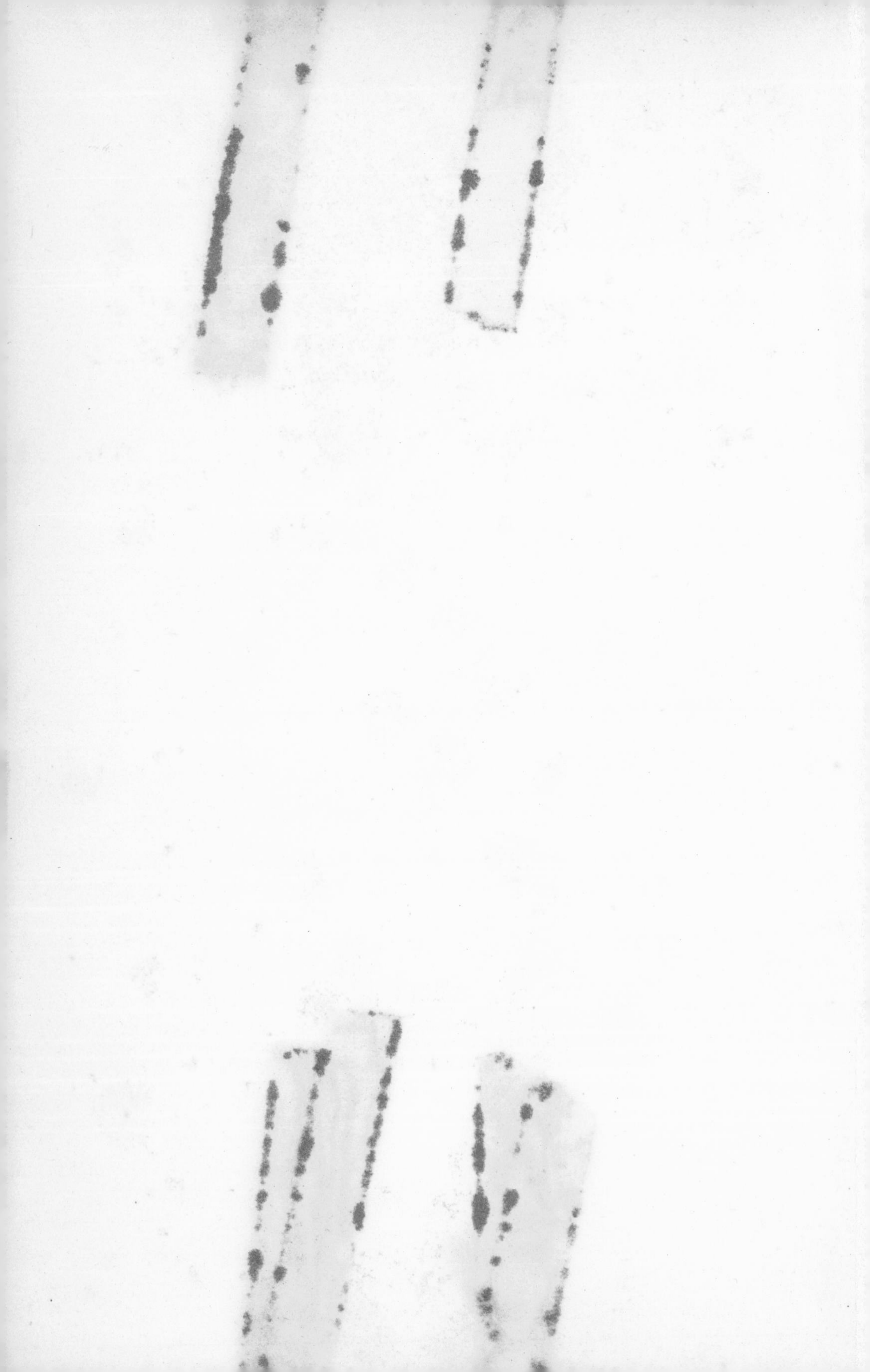

A HISTORY OF FLORIDA BAPTISTS

A HISTORY OF FLORIDA BAPTISTS

By

Edward Earl Joiner

Edward Earl Joiner

This volume is affectionately

dedicated

to

Florida Baptists

L. C. Card Number: 78-185685

Printed by Convention Press, Inc.
Jacksonville, Florida

CONTENTS

MAPS

LIST OF PHOTOGRAPHS

Preface

The interest of Florida Baptists in making a record of their history appears to be as old as their organized Convention life. In 1854, the same year the Florida Baptist Convention was organized, J. R. Graves reported in his paper, *The Tennessee Baptist,* that William B. Cooper had been appointed to prepare a history of Florida Baptists.[1] Graves planned to publish it in several installments, but apparently it never was produced.

The next suggestion that a history be written came through the request of the Alachua Association in 1894 that the State Convention make plans for the writing of a history, and for the organization of a historical society. The Convention responded to this suggestion by appointing during the same year a historical secretary, E. H. Rennolds, who reported in 1895 that he was diligently gathering historical materials, sending some to J. F. Forbes, president of Stetson, and some to the American Baptist Historical Society, in Philadelphia, Pennsylvania, and Hamilton, New York.[2] For the next three years Rennolds reported his progress in collecting records at each annual session, but no action was taken on appointing someone to write a history. In 1899, the Convention appointed E. H. Rennolds, S. L. Laudermilk, and C. S. Farris as members of a committee to make recommendations to the Convention for writing the history.[3] Since a similar committee was recommended again in 1901, however, we assume that nothing concrete had been accomplished toward writing and publishing a history.[4] In 1903 E. H. Rennolds reported as historical secretary that

[1]December 16, 1854.

[2]Florida Baptist Convention, *Annual,* 1895, p. 3.

[3]Florida Baptist Convention, *Annual,* 1899, p. 15.

[4]*Ibid.,* 1901, p. 57.

while nothing had been done about publishing a history, he was continuing to collect materials. At the same session, the Convention passed a motion that the Florida Baptist Historical Society be organized for the purpose of having a history of Florida Baptists written and funds raised for its publication.[5] The 1904 *Annual* indicates that another committee to draft plans for preparation of the history had been appointed consisting of L. B. Warren, J. H. Tharp and C. S. Farris, but that the historical society had not been organized.[6] Perhaps the main driving force for the historical interest between 1894 and 1904 was E. H. Rennolds, because after 1912 when Rennolds died, the subject of the history was not mentioned again until the Convention of 1920 when another motion was passed calling for the creation of a historical society, and a committee was appointed to create the society, the committee consisting of A. J. Holt, H. C. Peelman, C. V. Waugh, and W. A. Hobson. The committee did not bring back a report to the Convention until 1923, but their report indicates that the historical society had been organized, and that the idea of writing a history had not been forgotten. The report also called attention to the need for churches to write their own histories, and referred to the First Baptist Church of Arcadia as the only church that had done so.[8] In 1925 when the Convention celebrated what was believed to be the 100th anniversary of the beginning of Baptist church life in Florida, S. B. Rogers produced a brief *History of Florida Baptists,* only 25 pages. After that, the historical society and interest in the history seems to have died again since no further mention of them is found in the records until 1931, when the Convention passed a resolution introduced by W. A. Hobson, again calling for the writing of a history of Florida Baptists.[9] Again, a committee was appointed, and efforts to collect materials at Stetson renewed, but no concrete action effected to produce the history.

In 1938, Gordon C. Reeves produced the first documented "History of the Florida Baptist Convention" in the form of a Master's thesis at Stetson University. Reeves also tried to revive the Convention's interest in collecting historical records.[10] In 1939, the Conven-

---

[5]*Ibid.,* 1903, pp. 56-57.
[6]*Ibid.,* 1904, p. 23.
[7]Florida Baptist Convention, *Annual,* 1920, p. 62.
[8]*Ibid.,* 1923, p. 86.
[9]*Ibid.,* 1931, p. 66.
[10]Florida Baptist Convention, *Annual,* 1938, p. 119.

tion passed another motion that a historical society be formed.[11] Again, nothing appears to have been done, for in 1940, and again in 1941, plans were reported for the formation of the society.[12] In 1941 the first suggestion was made and approved for a historic marker in Madison County commemorating the organization of the Florida Baptist Convention. In 1942 the interest in the history became more intense and concrete when the Convention passed a resolution by W. D. Nowlin again calling for the history to be written and suggesting C. M. Brittain as the author.[13] Brittain declined for reasons of health and time, and the committee formed to seek an author and financing for the project was still unsuccessful in 1944.[14] In 1945, the committee on Baptist history reported that Dr. John L. Rosser, pastor of Ancient City Baptist Church in St. Augustine had been asked to write the history and he had agreed. Dr. Rosser immediately began work on the project, and by 1947, the manuscript was near completion.[15] In 1949 Rosser's *History of Florida Baptists* was published by Broadman Press.

In 1950 a Florida Baptist historical society was formed again, and has been in operation to the present (1970). Two years later, in 1952, Jack Dalton completed his doctoral dissertation at the University of Florida on "A History of Florida Baptists."

In 1962, James Semple completed his doctoral dissertation at Southwestern Baptist Theological Seminary, the title of which was "A History of the Florida Baptist Convention, 1865 to 1918." The same year, Dr. Harry C. Garwood's book, *Stetson University and Florida Baptists* was published.

I have read all the works mentioned above, and am greatly indebted to all of them. However, I have done my own research, and most of my conclusions are based on my own research. These other authors cannot therefore be blamed for my mistakes. They are to be praised for the help they gave to me by way of information, ideas, and guidelines in finding source materials. I am grateful to the Florida Baptist Convention and to Dr. Edgar R. Cooper for the motion at the 1967 session which initiated the action and resulted in the writing of this history.

I was asked by the historical society to write this history in the

---

[11]*Ibid.*, 1939, pp. 152-153.
[12]*Ibid.*, 1940, p. 128, and 1941, p. 158.
[13]*Ibid.*, 1942, p. 108.
[14]*Ibid.*, 1944, p. 77.
[15]Florida Baptist Convention, Annual, 1947, pp. 113-114.

spring of 1968. With the approval of the State Board of Missions, research was begun in the Fall of 1968, and with a sabbatical leave generously provided by Stetson University, writing of the first draft was begun and completed in the spring of 1970. Several months of editing and revising delayed completion of preparation for publication until early 1971.

The writer feels some regret that so little attention was given to Negro Baptist history but limitations of space, responsibility, and source materials made the restriction necessary. Their history needs to be written and deserves a separate volume. It seems unfortunate also that limitations of space and time necessitates omission of extensive biographical sketches of many important individuals, and histories of many local churches. More individual biographies and histories need to be produced, and hopefully some of these will be published or reported later.

I owe a debt of gratitude to many people, more than I can name. Among the many, I am particularly grateful to my colleague in the Department of Religion, Dr. Rollin Armour, for much encouragement and help. Many thanks to Dr. Byron Gibson, chairman of the department of English at Stetson, who read the manuscript and offered many valuable suggestions. Much help has been given by several student assistants in research and editing. They include: Willie Mae Andrews, Gregg Padgett, and Al Felty. To several secretaries and assistants who typed parts of the manuscript at various stages I am particularly grateful for their patient reading of my longhand and editing notes. They include: Mrs. Jocelyne Mires Wimer, Mrs. Mark Weaver, and Miss Jakay Jarvis, who typed the final draft. To Dr. O. LaFayette Walker, chairman of the Department of Religion I am indebted for his thoughtful consideration in lightening my responsibilities in the department while the project was in process. To Dr. Harold Bennett, executive secretary-treasurer of the Florida Baptist Convention, and his staff of workers, I am greatly indebted for granting graciously and efficiently every request I made for assistance. A special word of thanks goes to John V. Hays, a Stetson student, who gave many, many hours to preparing the associational maps and statistical charts. Thanks also to Charles Peterson, Director of Promotion for the Florida Baptist Convention, for preparing numerous photographs and the map locating Florida Baptist Institutions. I am grateful also to a great host of people from E. H. Rennolds in 1894 to John Maguire in 1968, who supplied historical information to the writer through documents contributed to the Stetson Baptist Historical

Collection or through personal conversations. I am particularly grateful to the Florida Baptist Convention for the generous financial assistance that made this work possible.

Finally, I owe a special debt of gratitude to the following persons who read the manuscript in the final stages and made many important corrections and valuable suggestions: Rollin S. Armour, professor of religion at Stetson University and curator, secretary-treasurer of the Florida Baptist Historical Society; Edgar R. Cooper, editor of the *Florida Baptist Witness;* James A. Haskins, pastor of Azalea Park Baptist Church, Orlando, and president of the Florida Baptist Historical Society; John H. Maguire, executive secretary-treasurer emeritus of the Florida Baptist Convention; Jack A. Shaw, vice-president of the Florida Baptist Historical Society; W. G. Stracener, retired editor of the *Florida Baptist Witness* and president of the Florida Baptist State Convention; and Carolyn Weatherford, director of the Woman's Missionary Union Department of the Florida Baptist Convention.

The writer cannot claim to be complete or entirely objective in what follows in this book. Much writing has to be produced from written records, and not all that is important in history is written. Therefore, the historian, when he is honest, knows he does not have the last word. I have tried to be fair, and that is difficult because limitations of space and cost required selectivity in using materials and information. What follows is my best understanding of the main events in Florida Baptist Convention history from the sources I have examined.

E. Earl Joiner

Stetson University
DeLand, Florida

CHAPTER ONE

Roots and Foundations of Florida Baptists; to 1854

Baptists were among the first Americans to bear witness for the Christian faith in the area of Florida before statehood was achieved, and they were to become the largest Christian group in the State. However, the Territory of Florida had a long, political and religious history before it achieved statehood, and before the coming of the early Baptist settlers who organized the Florida Baptist Convention. Thus, before plunging into the main story of Florida Baptists, it seems appropriate to examine briefly the religious and political background of the territory into which early Baptists came.

The first efforts to establish some form of Christian witness in what came to be known as Florida were made not by Baptists but by Spanish Roman Catholics and French Huguenots. This religious interest, though genuine among some members of both groups, was subordinate to the political and economic concerns which dominated both the Spanish and the French. The military clashes between the French and the Spanish, however, soon resulted in the end of the Huguenot community.[1]

Spanish explorers had made several attempts at establishing some kind of foothold on the Florida peninsula between 1513 and 1560, and although all of them were abortive, the Spanish still maintained that

[1]Michael V. Gannon, *The Cross in the Sand: The Early Catholic Church in Florida.* (Gainesville, University of Florida Press, 1965), p. 28. Gannon says there were no clergy among the Huguenots; however, since the Huguenot movement was a relatively young Protestant movement, one can hardly conclude that the religious element was not present in the group.

Florida belonged to them. Accordingly, they readily assumed the right to destroy the French Huguenot adventurers who began building a fort (Fort Caroline) near the mouth of the St. Johns River in 1564. With a sense of military and religious responsibility Pedro Menendez de Aviles volunteered to go and remove the French threat and convert the Indians. Leading an expedition of ships loaded with armed men and taking with him several priests, he arrived at Fort Caroline in 1565 and engaged in battle four French warships which had come to defend the fort. The battle was a draw, and Menendez then sailed to what came to be named St. Augustine, landing on September 6, 1565.[2] Shortly thereafter, Menendez and a task force of soldiers marched overland and destroyed the fort, killing all the men and leaving a sign saying, "I do this not to Frenchmen but to Lutherans."[3] Later, a French expedition made a raid on the Spanish settlement, and after killing a number of Spaniards left a sign saying, "We did this, not because these people were Spanish or even because they were Catholics, but because they were murderers and thieves." Although some of the early priests are reported to have ministered only to Spanish soldiers, those who came with Menendez and those with later Spanish expeditions were seriously concerned for the salvation of the Indians. Menendez established a chain of military outposts from Parris Island, South Carolina, to the Gulf Coast of Florida, and later a chain of Spanish outposts was established along the northern border of Florida between St. Augustine and what is now Pensacola.

Successful but short lived missionary activities were established in connection with some of these military outposts. Temporary successes were achieved during the 17th century, for example, among three groups of Indians: the Timucuans, the Guales, and the Appalachees. These missionary efforts were often hampered, and sometimes ended, however, by three factors. First, the religious purposes of the priests were often misinterpreted by being identified with the more economic and political interests of the Spanish military men. Second, the priests could not adjust their missionary efforts to the migratory nature of many of the Indians. Third, the priests had great difficulty in imposing their concepts of Christian morality on the Indian converts.[4] Ultimately, the English exploited the Spanish weaknesses and turned many of the Indians in the missions against the Spanish. In addition,

---

[2] *Ibid.*, p. 27.

[3] See Marjory S. Douglas, *Florida: The Long Frontier* (New York: Harper and Row, 1967), p. 74.

[4] Gannon, *op. cit.*, pp. 34, 40-41.

according to Gannon, James Moore, former governor of Carolina, carried many of the mission Indians away as slaves.[5] Gannon adds, however, that many of the missionaries lost their fervor before the missions died. By 1708 the Spanish Catholic missions were no more. Their failure appears to have reflected the general Spanish decay of the time.[6] In 1740 General Oglethorpe tried to take St. Augustine for England, but failed. His efforts, however, were prophetic of more to come, for the English were soon to be in control of Florida.

The Environment Into Which the Earliest Florida Baptists Came

English

Under the terms of the Treaty of Paris, Florida was ceded to England in 1763, and was under British domination until 1783. According to Gannon, within a year all Catholics were gone from Florida except eight laymen.[7] During the twenty years of English rule, the Anglican Church was established,[8] and Catholicism survived, though greatly weakened. There is no clear evidence that any Baptists came to Florida during these twenty years of British domination, but since Georgia was in process of settlement and since Baptists came to Georgia very early, it is possible that some Baptists then lived on what is now Florida territory. Boundary lines were not so precisely drawn then as they are now. Moreover, the main Spanish strength in Florida was centered in the garrisoned towns of St. Augustine and Pensacola, whose collective purpose was to protect shipping between Spain and her colonies further south. The English immediately began building real colonies. The American Revolution, furthermore, drove many Tory refugees from the Southern Colonies to settle in Florida.

Second and Final Spanish Rule — 1783-1821

In 1783, when without warning, England ceded Florida back to Spain, almost all the English settlers departed. The resulting Spanish rule was very weak, however, because the main Spanish garrisons of Pensacola and St. Augustine were so poorly supplied with men and materials that about all they could do was defend themselves. They

---

[5]*Ibid.,* p. 50.

[6]Clifton E. Olmstead, *History of Religion in the United States.* (Englewood Cliffs, N. J.: Prentice-Hall, Inc., 1960), p. 28.

[7]Gannon, *op. cit.,* p. 83.

[8]John L. Rosser, *A History of Florida Baptists* (Nashville: Broadman Press, 1949), p. 2.

could not maintain control over the rest of the peninsula.[9] As Spanish relations with the Indians deteriorated, moreover, the Spanish increased their problems further by giving asylum and freedom to slaves escaping from Georgia and other places.[10] While the freedom they knew under the domination of the Spanish was still a form of servitude, it held a promise of hope to those who dared to make a break for freedom. However, the Spanish offer of asylum for slaves so infuriated the Georgia farmers that many of them raided Indian and Spanish territory, taking land, timber, and slaves, and enslaving some who had been born free in Florida.[11]

At the beginning of the last period of Spanish rule, Indians dominated a great deal of the land territory of Florida and they were viewed as a threat to all of it. Although many of the Timucuans and Appalachees along the North Florida border had either been killed in battle or died of white man's diseases, in Central and South Florida the Calusas and the Seminoles were strong. To gain any help they could get in controlling the Indians, the Spanish offered land to the hungry Southern settlers. Thus, gradually much land came to be occupied by Americans, most of whom were eager to bring Florida into the United States.[12] Their desires were effected by the Treaty of 1819 in which the Territory of Florida was formally ceded to the United States.

The Earliest Baptists in Florida

Runaway Slaves

No one knows for certain exactly when the first Baptists set foot on Florida soil, but it would appear possible, even probable, that some of the first Baptists in Florida were Southern slaves who had escaped to promised freedom under the second and last period of Spanish rule (1783-1821). Some of those Negro Baptists who held the earliest known meetings in St. Augustine in 1784 undoubtedly were former slaves who had accepted the faith of their masters in Georgia or South Carolina.[13] Unfortunately, we cannot identify any of these slaves who may have found in their Baptist faith a spiritual freedom which proved an added stimulus to gain political freedom as well.

---

[9]Douglas, *op. cit.*, p. 117.

[10]*Ibid.*, p. 119.

[11]*Ibid.*

[12]*Ibid.*

[13]L. B. Lassiter, *On This Foundation.* (Jacksonville, Florida: Convention Press, 1961), p. 4.

Adventurers, Patriots, and Migrants from Neighboring Southern States

Since Florida was one of the last sections on the eastern seaboard to be settled by Americans, it was natural that many of those moving into Florida during the latter part of the Spanish dominion were transplanted frontiersmen, mainly from Georgia and South Carolina. Some of them were land-hungry adventurers who violated Spanish domain the same way the Spanish had earlier violated the domain of the Indians. Others were men of integrity who unknowingly crossed the rather uncertain boundaries.

Some of these adventurers, moreover, anticipated the eventual domination of this territory by the United States. Europeans, however, avoided settlement in Florida during the early years of the Republic because they did not expect the weak, new nation to last. Thus, during much of the last period of Spanish rule, most of the newcomers to Florida were transplanted Southern adventurers. One of the most significant events among many actions of those Southerners who crossed into Spanish territory was one with which the coming of *Wilson Conner,* the *first known Baptist minister,* was associated. Wilson Conner came to Florida, not on a preaching mission, but rather on a political and military mission. He was part of a movement initiated by General Matthews, a former Governor of Georgia, who had secret indications from President Madison and some members of the Congress that if he could capture Amelia Island (now Fernandina) and offer it to the United States it would be accepted. Forming a group of men and securing help from Colonel John McIntosh, who had a great plantation on the St. Johns River, and obtaining nine American gunboats, Conner easily captured the island. The group then elected John McIntosh as governor and proclaimed the "Republic of East Florida." A provisional government was set up, and Conner was selected as delegate to the Continental Congress. The President, however, under pressure from England and Spain, refused to recognize the venture, and Conner returned to Florida and later to Georgia, by 1815. Thus, *one of the first efforts to gain statehood for Florida was led by a Baptist minister.*[14]

Wilson Conner had been ordained to the ministry in 1803 in Georgia, but we have no evidence that he did any preaching during his adventure in Florida. Since, however, among ministers in early American Baptist life, the lines between the minister and the laity

---

[14]Douglas, *op. cit.,* p. 124; Rosser, *op. cit.,* p. 5.

were not so clearly drawn as they are now, this is not surprising. Commonly, a farmer would be ordained to the ministry and continue farming, sometimes preaching and sometimes not. Conner was described as being in a "backslidden" state during much of his life as a political and military adventurer. Later, he did return to the ministry and in fact died preaching, when in the summer of 1844 he preached at Hawkinsville, Georgia, on the text, "Verily, I say unto you, the hour is coming, and now is, when the dead shall hear the voice of the Son of God, and they that hear shall live." At the end of the sermon he sat down and died, probably of a heart attack.[15] Unfortunately, *if any Baptists other than escaped slaves settled in Florida during the time of Spanish dominion, their names are not known.* It is clear, however, that when Florida was ceded to the United States in 1821, Georgia and South Carolina were heavy contributors to the settlement of the State, especially along the northern border.

Seafaring Migrants from Northern Areas along Coastal Settlements

The settlers who came by boat were more diverse in geographical origin than those who came over land, and they came to be distributed very rapidly over a very wide area. Along the coast they came to Jacksonville, St. Augustine, Key West, Tampa, Pensacola. Up the rivers they came, mainly to those places which had military protection. Many Northern states were represented among the new settlers who came by water. It was through the instrumentality of some of these seafaring migrants that the first Sunday school in Florida was established, at Key West in 1844.[16] Although in many instances Northerners and Southerners were intermingled in the same communities, a greater concentration of Southerners was found in the most heavily settled areas along the northern border during the early years of the 19th century. In other areas Northerners were more common. Thus *it seems safe to assume that early Florida Baptists were both Northerners and Southerners who lived for a long time in the same state with little awareness of one another.*

---

[15]Jesse H. Campbell, *Georgia Baptists: Historical and Biographical* (Richmond: H. K. Hilyson, 1847), pp. 11-13.

[16]Rosser, *op. cit.*, p. 121.

First Churches and Ministers

Pigeon Creek

Although some preaching and organized worship may have occurred earlier, *the first established Baptist church in Florida was the Pigeon Creek Baptist Church, organized on January 7, 1821, in Nassau County near what is now Callahan.* The Spanish flag still waved over Florida. Some interesting facts about this first Baptist church in Florida, organized near the border of Georgia, are worth reviewing because it seems typical of the early Baptist churches in Florida and in other Southern states. It was organized by Isom Peacock and Fleming Bates with twelve members including Bates, who is listed in the minutes of the church as the first Pastor.

A *Calvinist type theology* was implied in the statement of faith, along with a *strict code of discipline.* When the question of *footwashing* arose, it was discussed and readily accepted as an appropriate part of the observance of the Lord's Supper. Moreover, no hesitation or discussion is indicated in the minutes when on July 20, 1822, "a black man of Brother Lopers by the name of Peter" is reported to have come forward for membership in the church. Thus, the first Baptist church to be organized in Florida was *integrated.*[17]

---

[17]Pigeon Creek Baptist Church, *Minutes,* January 7, 1821, p. 1.

Fleming Bates appears to have been the first Baptist minister to do anything like extensive work as a *missionary in organizing churches.* He served as pastor at Pigeon Creek until he moved to Alachua County, where he became pastor of the New Zion Church, near Gainesville. He labored with and was survived by another pioneer preacher in northeast Florida named John Tucker, who came to Florida in 1832. Together they organized several churches in northeast Florida, and after Bates' death Tucker was the only Baptist minister in that area for several years.[18]

Campbellton

Toward the western end of the settled northern strip of Florida, near Marianna in Jackson County three miles from the Alabama line, the *second* Baptist church in Florida was organized on *March 12, 1825,* as *Bethlehem* Church, the name being changed in 1861 to Campbellton Baptist Church. This church was constituted by Jeremiah Kembril and E. H. Calloway, itinerant ministers from Alabama, with 19 members. When organized, the church then opened its doors for membership, three members were received, and E. H. Calloway

[18]Rosser, *op. cit.*, p. 6.

was called as pastor.[19] Bethlehem Church was *the first Baptist church in Florida to have a woman's missionary organization.* It is still an active church.[20]

Sardis

The next church to be organized was the Sardis *Church, also in Jackson County,* only a few months after Bethlehem, *1825.* Since no minutes of the original organization meeting are available, the size and circumstances of the original organization are not known.[21]

Ebenezer

The fourth Baptist church to be established in the 1820's was the *Ebenezer* Church, constituted in *1829,* on the plantation of Mr. Joseph White in *Jefferson County.* It began with 10 members and Benjamin Manning, Sr., was pastor.

---

[19] R. W. Weaver, "Centennial Address," *Florida Baptist Witness,* Mar. 19, 1925, p. 11.

[20] Lassiter, *op. cit.,* p. 7.

[21] West Florida Baptist Association, *Minutes,* 1849, pp. 7, 12. Sardis is mentioned regularly in the minutes of this association from 1849 until 1888, when it was granted a letter of dismission. It is now extinct.

Indian Springs

The next church to be organized was the *Indian Springs* Church, just west of Ebenezer in *Leon County*. This church was constituted, also in 1829, by Henry Miller and Theophilus Hardee. There were 10 members, and Hardee was called as pastor.

Providence and others

In 1832 Providence Baptist Church was organized in Columbia County, under the leadership of John Tucker, John Prevatt and Elias Knight. Tucker was called as pastor. The following year, 1833, saw the organization of New River Church in Columbia County. No knowledge of the details is available. In 1834 two other churches were organized: Elizabeth Church in Jefferson County and Hickory Hill (later known as Orange Hill) in Washington County. The *last church in the 1830's* to be organized was Bethel Church, in 1838, in Jacksonville, making a *total of 10 churches.*

In the 1840's the rate of organization increased rapidly with *36 churches being organized by the end of 1849.* By 1854, when the Florida Baptist Convention was organized, 19 more had been added to the list. The churches organized in the 1840's and the 1850's reflect the increase in the population of the new state and the geographical spread of settlers down the center of the state and along coastal areas as far south as Key West.

ASSOCIATIONS

Suwanee

The first Baptist associational organization was developed in Florida in 1835, and while it did not include the first church, Pigeon Creek,[22] it did include most of the churches organized in the 1830's, namely Bethlehem, Sardis, Ebenezer, Indian Springs, Providence, New River, Orange Hill, and Elizabeth. The *Suwanee Association* was organized at Providence Church in *Columbia* County. Ten years later the *anti-missionary movement became dominant* among the leadership of the association, and the missionary churches, including most of the original churches, were excluded. *In 1847 the association changed its name to the Suwanee River Primitive Baptist Association.*

---

[22]This church joined the Piedmont Association in Georgia and later became a Primitive Baptist Church. It is now extinct.

Florida Association

Most of the original churches forming the Suwanee Association had apparently left that association before 1845, for in 1843 they left the Ocklockne Association in Georgia because it had become dominated by the anti-missionary movement,[23] and *formed the Florida Association.* The churches originally in Suwanee Association participating in the organization of this association included Ebenezer, Indian Springs, Providence, Bethlehem, and Sardis. Other churches included were Elizabeth, Concord, Monticello, and Aenon.[24]

West Florida

The third association to be organized was the West Florida Association which came into being in 1847 when representatives from churches in several counties in Florida,[25] and some in Alabama met and organized.

Alachua

In the same year, 1847, was formed the Alachua Association, organized at Fort Clark. It was composed of twelve churches having a *membership of 500, of whom 230 were Negro.* In theory, at least, it represented an area extending from the Suwannee River east to the Atlantic Ocean, north to the Georgia line and south to Key West.[26] Obviously, in 1847, great segments of this area had no settlers and greater segments had no churches. Furthermore, geographical boundaries were not firmly established as determining associational affiliation. Therefore, the lines dividing the associations on the maps represent only rough approximations.[27]

Religious Leaders, Life and Problems Among Pioneer Florida Baptists

It is with great reservation that one selects men to describe as leaders among Baptists since Baptists have become what they are in part due to democratic participation of many laymen. Thus, one can

---

[23]Obviously, the anti-missionary movement was strong in southern Georgia and therefore threatened or divided many of the early churches along the northern border of Florida.

[24]Rosser, *op. cit.,* pp. 27-28.

[25]The Florida counties represented were Gadsden, Franklin, Jackson, Washington, Holmes and Walton.

[26]S. B. Rogers, *A. Brief History of Florida Baptists, 1825-1925,* pp. 8-9.

[27]See Map 2, p. 34.

easily exaggerate the function and contribution of leaders. However, it is very clear that certain men have played an extraordinary role in leading and stimulating other men. The pioneer leaders among early Florida Baptists deserve special praise because, like Baptist pioneers in other states, they were often uneducated and unpaid men who combined their work as ministers with their regular vocation. Those few who were paid received very little. At the risk of neglecting other important men, it seems necessary to name as pioneer leaders those who are described in the paragraphs which follow.

Fleming Bates

While nothing is known of his early life, it is clear that Fleming Bates came from the Sardis Church in southeast Georgia around 1820 to participate in the organization of Pigeon Creek Church and to become its first pastor, as mentioned above. Apparently, he was the only minister working in northeast Florida for some years until the coming of John Tucker. He served as pastor of Pigeon Creek for several years, but eventually moved to Alachua County, where he continued his labors. Bates became ensnared by the anti-missionary movement near the end of his life and gave most of his energies to that movement, perhaps being partly responsible for the loss of Pigeon Creek to the Primitive Baptists.[28]

John Tucker

Tucker was born in Georgia in 1785, and began work as a Methodist minister in 1806. In 1828, however, he was baptized by a Georgia Baptist district missionary, and after coming to Florida in 1832, he was ordained as a Baptist minister in 1833.[29] Apparently Tucker was greatly inspired by Fleming Bates and maintained affection for him despite their disagreement over the anti-missionary movement.[30] The continuing affection of John Tucker for Fleming Bates indicates the greatness of his heart because the anti-missionary movement was very strong and made Tucker's work very hard. When the Seminole War came, 1834-1842, John Tucker continued to minister in Alachua County at the risk of his life, after ministers of other denominations had left for safer territory. He went from fort to fort, leading wor-

---

[28]*Florida Baptist Witness,* Feb. 15, 1906, p. 8.

[29]G. W. S. Ware, article in *Florida Baptist Witness,* Feb. 15, 1906, p. 8.

[30]Tucker, letter to editor of *Index,* dated Feb. 28, 1845, in *Christian Index,* Mar. 21, 1845, p. 1.

ship, preaching funerals, comforting the suffering and the fearful.[31] Although he received some help from William Friar who came in 1840, and from William Cooper, who came when the Seminole War ended, Tucker had to do much of his work alone, sustained and driven by a great sense of purpose. In 1843-1844 he was employed as a missionary by the American Baptist Home Missionary Society. He traveled over a wide area during those years (2,000 miles in 1844, an astounding feat for that time) but concentrated his activities in Hernando County, where in 1844 he baptized J. M. Hayman, who was to become a significant leader in that section.[32] During those years, he wrote, "I am a missionary, and I must travel."[33]

When the Southern Baptist Convention was organized in 1845, John Tucker was appointed by the Home Mission Board as the only missionary to Florida. During that year he apparently concentrated his energies on a large area in the center of the State, and until August of 1845 he found no other Baptist ministers in that area. In August he gained the help of Daniel Edwards, from Georgia. Later, he notes that Edwards moved to Florida.[34] He traveled, preached, baptized white and colored people, organized many churches (the exact number is not known) and pastored as many as six churches while ministering to still others at the same time. One of his last letters includes the very understandable statement, "I need much help."[35] The date of his death is not known, but one story indicates that he carried to his grave a bullet from an Indian rifle.[36]

William B. Cooper

Born in South Carolina in 1807, and educated at Columbia College in Washington, D.C., Cooper came to Florida in 1838 in hopes that the warm climate would improve his health. He began his Florida ministry at the Hickstown church, near Madison, and did much missionary work throughout Madison, Leon, and Jefferson counties in Florida, and Lowndes and Thomas counties in Georgia. When the anti-missionary movement made inroads among some Florida Baptists, he became a champion defender of missions. The organization of the

[31] *Ibid.*, p. 2.

[32] *Report of the American Baptist Home Mission Society, 1844,* p. 53.

[33] *Ibid.*

[34] "Home Mission Report," Southern Baptist Convention, *Minutes,* 1846, p. 33.

[35] *Southern Baptist Missionary Journal,* June, 1848, p. 22; Oct., 1848, p. 114.

[36] Ware, *op. cit.,* p. 8.

Florida Association was due in part to his efforts, and he was elected as its moderator sixteen times. Also, he served three terms as president of the Florida Baptist Convention. No wonder when he died the Florida Association voted to erect a monument in his memory.[37]

Richard Johnson Mays

Born in Edgefield County, South Carolina, Richard Mays migrated to north Florida from around 1832 in search of better cotton land. He settled in the gentle rolling hills near Madison and built a ten-room mansion called "Clifton." Mays owned thousands of acres of land and several hundred slaves, and soon established a reputation as a distinguished citizen. He established Mays Academy on his plantation. No detailed information on the Academy is available, but it is probably safe to assume that it was a small private school established mainly for the education of the children of the Mays family.

An active churchman, Mays served as clerk in the Hickstown Church (later to be named Madison), and helped to organize Concord Church, where he was first ordained as a deacon in 1841, and later that year was licensed and ordained to preach. He served at various times as pastor of the Concord church and other churches in the area, was moderator of Florida Association three times, and was the first president of the Florida Baptist Convention. Mays died at his home near Concord on July 18, 1864, and is buried in the church cemetery.[38]

Joshua Mercer

Despite the meager information available on his work, Joshua Mercer deserves recognition among the early Florida Baptist pioneers. Born in 1788, the brother of the Jesse Mercer for whom Mercer University was named, he apparently came to Florida first in 1835,[39] and settled here in 1841.[40] He began as a home missionary for the Georgia Baptist Convention and continued as a working minister on his own. Though wounded by Indians in the battle of Calabee, he survived to serve pioneer Florida Baptists for more than twenty-five years, first in the area of Orange Hill (earlier known as Hickory Hill) and later in Washington County in West Florida. In 1851 he established

---

[37]The records do not indicate whether or not the monument was ever erected. Rosser, *op. cit.*, pp. 9-10.

[38]Rosser, *op. cit.*, pp. 12-13.

[39]Thomas Muse, letter in *Florida Baptist Witness,* Mar. 26, 1925, p. 8.

[40]Rosser, *op. cit.*, p. 7.

what may have been the first school in Florida to be operated by a Baptist, the Orange Hill Academy, at Orange Hill.[41]

O. T. Hammond

Appointed as missionary to Florida by the American Baptist Home Mission Society, Hammond came with his wife to the area near Tallahassee in June, 1837. Apparently, from the North and well educated, the Hammonds were struck by the beauty of Florida on the one hand and by the ignorant, primitive quality of many of the people, including ministers, on the other hand. Hammond's area of responsibility obviously included more than one state, for later reports (a year or two later) from him indicated that he was then in Alabama, where he died. Though his work in Florida was brief, and difficult to evaluate,[42] it was clearly an unselfish work because since his wife taught school, Hammond returned his salary to the American Baptist Home Mission Society.[43] When he died, the Society was slow to appoint a successor, perhaps because of the Indian War.

James MacDonald

Born in Scotland of distinguished ancestry in 1798, James MacDonald came to America in 1818 at the age of 20 and settled in Burke County, Georgia. Reared a Roman Catholic, MacDonald developed a burning desire to read the Bible despite the rules of his church against it. He migrated to Cuba seeking to escape from his troubled mind, and was arrested. While in prison there he read the New Testament and had a profound experience of conversion. Pledging to become a missionary when released, he returned to Georgia where he was baptized into a Baptist church. In 1835 he began preaching in Florida. From that time until his death in 1869 he carried the Gospel faithfully, traveling extensively and facing the same problems of loneliness and danger during the Indian War that John Tucker knew. Like Tucker, however, he had great courage and dedication. In July, 1838, he organized four white citizens and two Negro slaves as Bethel (later the First Baptist Church) Baptist Church in Jacksonville.

In 1841, MacDonald was appointed by the American Baptist Mis-

---

[41] R. W. Weaver, "Centennial Address," *Florida Baptist Witness,* Mar. 19, 1925, pp. 8-9. More details about the academy will be given in Chapter Two.

[42] His correspondence hints that the rough pioneer Florida life may have been too much for him.

[43] *Report of the American Baptist Home Mission Society,* 1838, pp. 21, 28, 44, 45.

sion Society to replace O. T. Hammond,[44] and he worked with him until the slavery controversy, when his connection with him threatened to limit the effectiveness of his work. Then he resigned and worked for the Florida Association for about two years—from 1842. When the Southern Baptist Convention was organized in 1845, he was appointed by the Home Mission Board, serving the Board for two years. MacDonald often ministered to a mixed and unresponsive population of Spanish Catholics, universalists, skeptics, moral renegades, and Negroes. Often he received the greatest response from Negroes, whom he baptized freely and admitted to membership in the churches. MacDonald led in establishing the Alachua Association in 1847, and published in 1848 the first Baptist newspaper in Florida. He called it *The Baptist Telegraph and Florida Emigrant.* Though he was able to continue publication only a few months, the effort he made reflects his awareness of the need for a paper to advance the work of missions.

Toward the end of his labor in Florida MacDonald lamented that in all east Florida in an area 200 miles long there were no more than five ministers.[45] In 1853 he resigned as pastor of the Sharon Baptist Church in Nassau County and returned to Georgia, where he died on April 25, 1869.

J. M. Hayman

Born in Georgia in 1822, Hayman came to Florida with his father in 1843. During the same year young Hayman was converted and baptized by John Tucker. Almost immediately he felt the call to preach, and preached his first sermon in Hillsborough County on June 8, 1851. His subsequent ministry was to be spent in DeSoto, Hillsborough, Manatee, Hernando, Polk and Pasco Counties. Traveling 38,000 miles through difficult terrain he ministered sacrificially to hundreds of isolated areas and established churches in Bartow (originally called Peas Creek—1854), in Tampa (1860) and in Plant City (1866).[46]

Other Pioneer Baptist Leaders

Four men are discussed together because of their connection with the founding of Baptist work in Key West. Key West was settled in 1823 by merchants who came from Rhode Island, Virginia, and North

---

[44] *Southern Baptist Missionary Journal,* 1849, p. 19.
[45] *Ibid.*
[46] Rosser, *op. cit.,* p. 12-13.

Carolina to develop among other things, a lucrative salvage business. The first Baptist minister to come to Key West was Charles C. Lewis, a sea captain who had been converted in 1842 back in Connecticut. Seeing the great need for a Baptist work in Key West, he exchanged the title of "Captain" for that of "Reverend." Going from house to house, he soon assembled a congregation and after being licensed to preach by a Baptist church in Connecticut, he organized a small group into the Key West Baptist Church in 1843. The congregation then proceeded to call him as pastor and to ordain him. By 1843, the congregation had 23 members.

Lewis returned to Connecticut in 1843, and in *1844* G. G. Tripp became pastor and *organized the first Sunday school in Florida,* but he appears to have stayed only a few months, and the Sunday school died. In October, 1845, H. D. Doolittle brought together the scattered Key West flock, consisting of whites and blacks. Interestingly, he observed better discipline and faithfulness among the blacks than among the whites. During the period when the church was without a pastor, the blacks had continued to hold prayer meetings each week and had heard preaching by Austin Smith, a slave who had earlier been licensed to preach by Lewis. With the help and support of these faithful blacks, Doolittle re-organized in 1845 the Sunday school begun earlier by Tripp, with about 100 members.[47] Despite the great hurricane of 1846 which destroyed the church building and despite the temporary absence of Pastor Doolittle, who had gone north, the fire of spiritual zeal was not quenched. When Doolittle returned, the Key West Baptists worshipped again in the Monroe County Courthouse, as they had done in the beginning.

When appointed by the American Baptist Home Mission Society to replace Doolittle in 1847, J. H. Breaker found the Baptist fellowship still without a building.[48] In 1850, Breaker reported that despite a malicious attack by an Episcopal minister, who published a tract calling the Baptists heretics,[49] the work was flourishing, religious interest requiring three services a day.

---

[47]J. H. Breaker, letters in *Southern Baptist Missionary Journal,* Sept. 1850, pp. 90, 94-96; also *Report of American Baptist Home Mission Society,* May, 1846, p. 46.

[48]*Report of American Baptist Home Mission Society,* 1849, p. 188.

[49]*Ibid.* The name of the minister is not given.

Hardship in the Wilderness

From the preceding discussion, it should be clear that the pioneers who labored to establish Baptist work in Florida between 1800 and 1854 faced great difficulties, frustrations and dangers, but a few men had the courage to face the challenges of one of the last sections of the eastern frontier.

From numerous descriptions may be painted a picture of the beginnings and difficulties of a typical frontier Baptist church. A missionary would come into an area where there were a few houses in reasonable proximity to one another, and going from house to house, he would gather a small group for preaching. Together they would agree on another home to meet for the next preaching services some weeks later when the preacher returned. Thus churches would be organized and often would continue for years before constructing a building. Many of the early buildings were crude structures built by the members themselves, who cut the logs, rived out boards, hewed puncheons or planks and put them together for a church. Often those who came to church would travel long distances, bringing their guns and hunting dogs, hunting on the way to church and back. Sometimes during the services there would be several deer hanging up near the church.[50]

Theology, Polity and Discipline

Despite the freedom and variety one finds among Florida Baptist pioneers, the prevailing theology, if one judges from numerous statements of faith by churches and associations, was Calvinistic.[51] Although Calvinistic theology produced widely different interpretations among Florida Baptists, it provided a basis for strict moral discipline. What may appear to Florida Baptists today as a rather extreme standard of discipline instead must be viewed as a natural response to the loose and untamed morality of frontier men. Most early missionaries and associational histories witness to the great difficulties experienced in maintaining discipline.[52] Mrs. Peaslee's history, for example, states that a common topic of discussion in early association meetings was how to raise moral standards in the churches. The typical answer was to advocate Bible study and church discipline. This history reports, moreover, that members excommunicated from one church would often move to another church where they were frequently taken in without question. However, demands were very strict. For example, one association even advised, "That all light literature such as novels, romances, plays, etc., be banished from the house of the brethren of the Association, as pernicious to the morals and spiritual welfare of themselves and children."[53]

A major theological controversy which split many churches and affected the practice of church life during the pioneer period was the anti-mission question. While it was not a long lasting problem, it threatened the struggling Baptist movement where and when it began, along the border of north Florida in the 1830's and 1840's. The removal of most of the original churches forming the Suwanee Association when it became dominated by anti-mission leadership in 1845,

---

[50]I. C. S. Sheffield, W. E. Yearly, Graham Carter, and W. H. Tucker, *History of Harmony Baptist Association Since Organization, Comprising Parts of Levy, Gilchrist and Alachua Counties* (N.D., Garwood Historical Collection, Stetson University Library), p. 2.

[51]Alachua Baptist Association, *Minutes,* 1848, p. 3, for a typical statement.

[52]For example, Mrs. Herbert R. Peaslee, Jr., *A Century of Witnessing in South Florida Baptist Association, 1867-1967.* (Published by the South Florida Baptist Association, 1967), p. 4.

[53]*Ibid.,* pp. 5-7.

however, was symbolic of the direction in which most Florida Baptists were to move. *For, by 1850, the anti-missionary groups had formed their own churches and associations and were no longer a threat to the inner structure of early Florida Baptist organizations.*

Education

Although many of the pioneer Baptist ministers had little or no formal training, the presence of a few educated and cultured men among them helped to create very early an awareness of need for education. References in the reports of early representatives of the American Baptist Home Mission Society to the gross ignorance of many of the early settlers, including ministers, were very soon paralleled by similar expressions of concern for education by Southern leaders from Georgia, Alabama and South Carolina. Not only was this interest expressed in the establishment of *Orange Hill Academy* (mentioned earlier) which opened in December, 1851, and taught English, Latin, Greek, mathematics, and music,[54] but it was expressed also *as early as 1850 in a move to establish a college.*[55] Although Florida Baptists were not ready to take such a step at that time, the existence of strong interest in such a venture is a very significant index to the kind of vision early Florida Baptist leaders had. However, the absence of educational requirements for the ministry was in some cases an advantage among pioneer Baptist churches. For example, it meant that many Baptists produced their own ministerial leadership. Some churches might have two or three farmer-preachers among their members, though others had none.

Tension over Missions and Slavery

In the early years of Florida Baptist history one finds little trace of the hostility over sectionalism and race which was soon to divide the country. Representatives of the American Baptist Home Mission Society, often *Northerners,* as indicated earlier, had no *serious problems in working with Southerners. Integration* in the churches, moreover, *was the rule rather than the exception.* Negroes held membership in most Baptist churches in all areas, often outnumbering white members. Comparatively speaking, however, there was a greater concentration of Southerners along the northern border in the first half

[54]R. W. Weaver, *Centennial Address, Florida Baptist Witness,* March 19, 1925, pp. 8-9.

[55]Doak S. Campbell, *The Florida Baptist Association; The First Hundred Years, 1842-1942.* (Published by the Florida Baptist Association, no date), p. 7.

of the 19th century, and more diverse groups including Northerners along the inland waterways and the coasts. Moreover, although Florida Baptists had no unified self-identity, the prevailing tendency in 1845 was to identify with the thinking of the neighboring Southern states of Georgia, Alabama, and South Carolina, from which many of the early settlers along the northern border had migrated. It is probably safe to assume, furthermore, that some of them joined in the Southern criticism which developed shortly after the American Baptist Home Mission Society was formed in 1832, especially since Florida was one of the areas neglected by the Society.[56]

Apparently, Jesse Mercer, whose work was well known among some early Florida Baptists, held some hope for a time that the American Baptist Home Mission Society would respond to Southern needs.[57] Therefore, an interesting ambivalence came to exist among Florida Baptists in the 1840's toward the Southern Baptist Convention and the American Baptist Home Mission Society with its headquarters in the North. For example, by 1845, the Florida Association was recommending that churches and ministers, when they received new ministers, should require not only that they present satisfactory credentials, but that they define their position on the great question which had divided the Baptists of the North from those of the South.[58] At the same time, in the other areas of the State, mission work was being done by Baptist missionaries from the North, and the question of their views on slavery was never raised.

From the preceding pages several facts are clear. First, Baptists were on Florida soil from its beginning as a United States territory, and by the time Florida achieved statehood they were firmly established in every geographical area of the state, even though they had not developed their own state organization. The main concentration, however, was along the northern border and along a few coastal areas. Second, early Baptists in Florida were a widely scattered and heterogeneous group which included Negroes, Northerners and Southerners, in some cases with little communication with one another. Third, communication and missionary activity was established among many of these scattered groups, leading to the first organized churches and associations. Much credit for those early organizations must go to the

---

[56]W. W. Barnes, *The Southern Baptist Convention.* (Nashville: Broadman Press, 1954), p. 13.

[57]*Ibid.,* p. 14.

[58]Campbell, *op. cit.,* p. 4.

courageous missionaries, some from Georgia, and others from the American Baptist Home Mission Society. Fourth, pioneer Florida Baptists *early demonstrated two of the basic concerns which have been given preeminence among Florida Baptists ever since; namely missions and education.*

Associational Development and Growth

1842

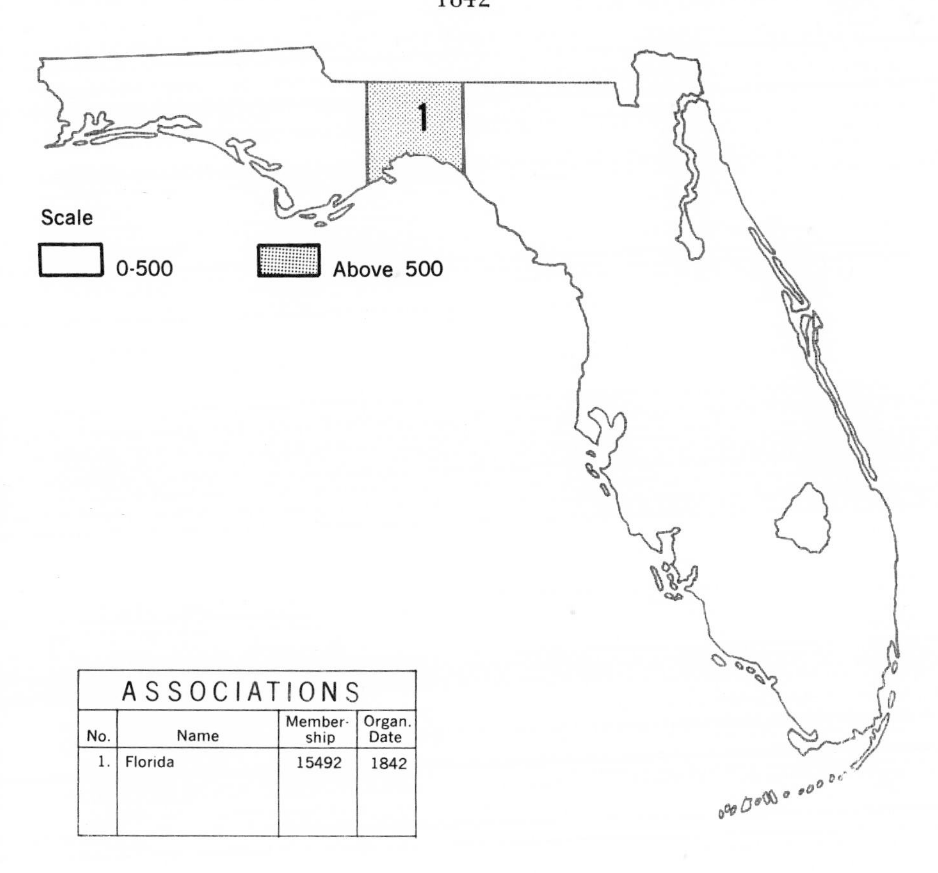

ASSOCIATIONS			
No.	Name	Member-ship	Organ. Date
1.	Florida	15492	1842

Associational Development and Growth

1850

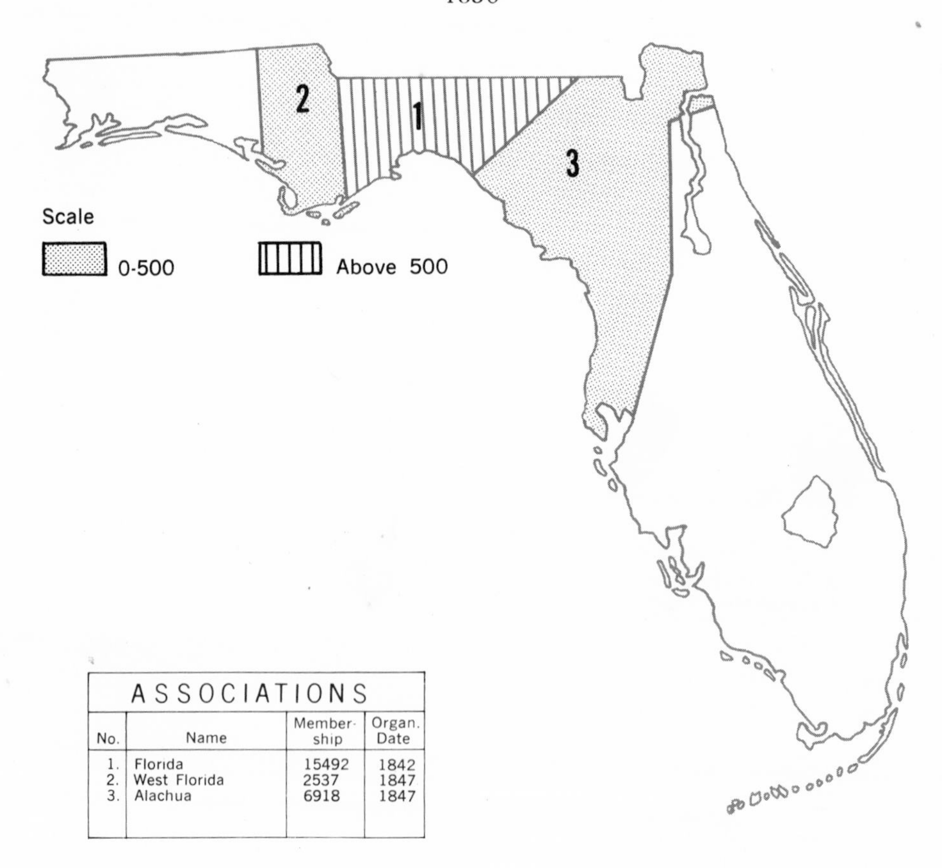

ASSOCIATIONS			
No.	Name	Member-ship	Organ. Date
1.	Florida	15492	1842
2.	West Florida	2537	1847
3.	Alachua	6918	1847

CHAPTER TWO

Convention, Catastrophe, and Survival: 1854-1880

While many Florida Baptists were still recovering from the wounds and insecurity created by the Seminole wars, and others were already apprehensive of tensions which would soon split the nation as they had already split most denominations, a few Florida Baptists had sensed the need for a state convention. Between 1830, when the population was estimated to be about 34,730 including Indians, and by 1845 the population had increased to 57,951.[1] Statehood, just achieved in 1845, meant that Florida was the youngest of the 31 states then established, and since economic opportunity seemed great, many settlers and adventurers came. By 1850 the population was 87,445.[2] Reflecting elements of settled and landed Southern aristocracy and rough pioneers, the Baptist leaders in the three existing associations (Florida, West Florida, and Alachua) saw and responded to the need for organizing for more effective work of the Kingdom of God in Florida.

I. Organization of the Convention

Although the name of the person who originally conceived the idea is not known, the suggestion that a Florida Baptist convention be organized was first made in the Florida Association annual meeting in 1853, at Olive Church, Thomas County, Georgia.[3] At this meeting a resolution was introduced and approved which called for the orga-

[1]Douglas, *op. cit.,* pp. 143, 158.

[2]Article on "Florida," *Encyclopedia Brittanica,* (Chicago: Encyclopedia Brittanica Co., 1965), Vol. IX, p. 473.

[3]Florida Association at this time included a number of churches in south Georgia.

nization of a Florida Baptist convention. Immediately, committees were appointed to contact the other two associations to determine their interest in the venture. William B. Cooper and W. Blewett were requested to communicate with the West Florida Association. S. W. Baker and W. H. Goldwire were to contact the Alachua Association.[4] Both the committees were to report at the next annual session of the Florida Association. Clearly, the next annual meeting of the association proved to be also a convention organization meeting. While the Florida Association was meeting in the Concord Baptist church, near Madison, the delegates (as they were then called) from the three associations assembled only a short distance from the church in the parlor of Richard Johnston Mays to organize the convention. They probably met there instead of the Church for three reasons. First, the associational meeting was in session at the church. Second, since the church was small, it probably would not have held all the local association delegates and those from the other associations who had come for the convention organization meeting. Furthermore, to conserve time for those involved in the Florida Association and the convention organization it may have been thought necessary to hold both meetings at the same time rather than ask delegates involved in both meetings to stay an extra day. Finally, since the convention organization meeting occurred on November 20, 1854, the weather probably required a meeting inside a building, and the large home of R. J. Mays was the most appropriate place. Also, Browning reports that many of the delegates stayed at Mays' ten room home, which was larger than the church building.[5]

Seventeen delegates participated in this organization meeting. Representing the West Florida Association were Josh Mercer, D. P. Everett, and G. W. Underwood. Representing the Alachua Association were J. M. Hayman, Daniel Edwards, J. H. Breaker, and William Connell. From the Florida Association, representatives were R. J. Mays, William B. Cooper, B. S. Fuller, W. H. Goldwire, W. Blewett, D. G. Daniel, H. Z. Ardis, S. C. Craft, T. W. Terrell, and John Cason.[6]

---

[4]*Proceedings of the Florida Baptist State Convention,* 1854, p. 1. Hereafter, although the exact title varies from year to year, the title Florida Baptist Convention, *Minutes,* will be used.

[5]Edwin B. Browning, "The Early History of Concord Missionary Baptist Church, 1841-1866," mimeographed, 1946, Garwood Baptist Historical Collection, Stetson University Library, pp. 2 ff.

[6]Florida Baptist Convention, *Minutes,* 1854, p. 1.

THIS MEMORIAL
COMMEMORATES THE
ORGANIZATION OF THE
FLORIDA BAPTIST CONVENTION
IN THIS COUNTY, WHICH WAS
A PART OF THE
FLORIDA BAPTIST ASSOCIATION
NOVEMBER 20, 1854
FLORIDA BAPTIST
CONVENTION 1946
SITE OF THE
ORGANIZATION OF THE
BAPTIST CONVENTION
MILES NORTHWEST OF
SPOT ON LOVETT

R. J. Mays was asked to preside over the organization meeting, and D. G. Daniels was appointed secretary. The first item of business was the adopting of a constitution, modeled, according to Rosser,[7] after that of the Georgia Baptist Convention, which had been organized in 1822. However, brief comparison of the two constitutions leads to a different conclusion. Indeed, what strikes the reader first and most forcefully is the contrast with rather than the similarity between the original constitutions of the Georgia Baptist Convention and the Florida Baptist Convention. In fact the only prominent similarity in form or content is the proportionate church member representation.[8] There are similarities in form and content between the original constitution of the Georgia Baptist Convention and those of the Alachua, Florida, and West Florida Baptist Associations.[9] Those associations perhaps borrowed directly from the original Georgia Baptist constitution. The conclusion is obvious, however, that the model used by the framers of the original constitution of the Florida Baptist Convention must be sought elsewhere. Similarities in form and content between Florida Baptists' original constitution and those of both the Triennial Convention of 1814 at Philadelphia and the Southern Baptist Convention, adopted in 1845, suggest that they were the main models used.[10] However, distinctive elements in the Florida Baptist Convention constitution suggest also that either another source was used or that those who drew up the Florida constitution thought for themselves.

One of the most striking elements that all three of these constitutions have in common is the reference to "societies" and their representation through financial contributions. The inclusion of this section in the constitutions of both the Southern Baptist Convention and the Florida Baptist Convention is most remarkable in view of the contention of Barnes, a notable Southern Baptist historian, that one of the differences between Northern and Southern Baptist leaders was over the question of membership through societies based on finances. Barnes

---

[7]*Op. cit.*, p. 37.

[8]Jesse Mercer, *A History of the Georgia Baptist Association.* (Washington, Ga., 1838), pp. 29-34.

[9]Alachua Baptist Association, *Minutes,* 1848, pp. 3-4; West Florida Baptist Association, *Minutes,* 1850, p. 14; and Florida Baptist Association, *Minutes,* 1860, pp. 6-7.

[10]W. W. Barnes, *The Southern Baptist Convention, 1845-1953.* (Nashville: Broadman Press, 1954), p. 6. Cf. Southern Baptist Convention, *Annual,* 1845, pp. 3-5.

offers the explanation that the continued power of anti-mission groups throughout the Convention forced the framers of the constitution to compromise to get the constitution adopted. Then the first task the Southern Baptist Convention leaders had to perform was to effect a practical change from the traditional society method of supporting denominational causes to a more centralized method.[11] Barnes' explanation may also account for the presence of the "societies" representation section in the Florida Baptist constitution, but the presence, contribution and influence of J. R. Graves, the famous Landmark leader, suggests another possibility.[12] It is strange that his presence is not mentioned in the records of the organization meeting. Is it possible that J. R. Graves was present and assisted in the writing of the Florida Baptist Convention constitution, but left Florida before the organization meeting assembled?[13] The great influence of J. R. Graves among some Florida Baptists at the time would suggest an affirmative answer.[14] However, distinctive elements in the Florida constitution suggest that those who drew up that document were not determined in the process, either by Graves, or any other influence, but by their own vision of Baptist tradition and the needs of their day.[15]

Because the constitutional structure of the Florida Baptist Convention has changed so radically, significant features of that first constitution are worth reviewing.[16] The first article is what one informed of Baptist tradition would expect. It reads, significantly: "This body is constituted upon the New Testament Scriptures as acknowledged and held, generally, by the Baptist Denomination."[17]

---

[11]*Ibid.,* p. 33. The society method, which prevailed in the Northern Baptist Convention and was common among Baptists in the South before 1845, involved several organizations that were dedicated to the support of various and benevolent enterprises, but were independent of denominational control.

[12]Article signed "G," "Florida Association," *Christian Index,* December 14, 1854, p. 198, where the author says: "J. R. Graves was present, and contributed not a little to the interest and success of the occasion." The occasion of course was the organization of the Florida Baptist Convention.

[13]*The Southern Witness,* February 22, 1906.

[14]West Florida Baptist Association, *Minutes,* 1859, p. 3, where it is stated that D. P. Everett, one of the editors of the *Landmark Banner and Cherokee Baptist,* praised that paper before the Association and that the Association adopted the paper as its medium of communication. D. P. Everett had been one of the delegates representing the West Florida Association at the organization meeting.

[15]Graves' influence is more obvious in other ways, as will be shown later.

[16]Appendix I.

[17]*Ibid.*

The second article, however, which regulates membership in the Convention, exhibits distinguishing elements. This article indicates, for example, that the Convention would consist first, of associations in Florida or sister states. Thus, no geographical boundaries were defined. Second, it would include those associations whose constitutions were approved by the Convention and which should contribute to the Convention. Third, it would include those auxiliary societies which should contribute to the Convention. Fourth, the Convention would include individuals who should contribute to the Convention according to the prescribed rules. Membership, moreover, was to be representative, the associational membership being determined by the total membership in the association.[18] The number of representatives from the auxiliary societies was to be determined by the amount of money given, one member for each $50.00 given annually. Finally, each individual giving $10.00 annually was entitled to membership. Thus, two factors, membership and money, determined power in the Convention, and they tended to counterbalance each other.

Four officers were to be elected by ballot at each annual meeting —a president, a secretary, an assistant secretary, and a treasurer. An executive committee, also elected by ballot at each annual meeting, was to attend to Convention business between sessions, including the filling of vacancies when they occurred.

The purposes of the Convention as stated were the following five:

1. To unite the influence and pious intelligence of the Baptists within its bounds, and thusly to facilitate their union and co-operation,

2. To form and encourage plans for the revival of experimental and practical religion in the state and elsewhere,

3. To aid in giving effect to useful plans of the several associations,

4. To afford an opportunity to those who may conscientiously think it to be their duty to form a fund for the education of pious young men who may be called by the spirit and their churches, to the Christian ministry,

5. And to promote pious and useful education in the Baptist Denomination.

---

[18]Although the form and understanding of representation has changed, this principle of proportionate representation is reflected in the present constitution.

The constitution was adopted on November 20, 1854, and the Convention elected R. J. Mays as president. D. G. Daniels was elected secretary; S. C. Craft, assistant secretary; and John Cason, treasurer. H. Z. Ardis, S. C. Craft, William B. Cooper, B. S. Fuller, W. H. Goldwire, and W. Blewett were elected as an executive committee for the following year. The Convention adjourned after laying plans to hold the next convention on Friday before the first Sunday in December, 1855, at Union Academy Church in Jackson County. Later records indicate a change of plans and that the Convention of 1855 was held in Concord Church instead. No minutes of that convention are available. Union Academy Church changed its name to Greenwood, and did host the Convention in 1856, though again the minutes have been lost.

In 1857 the Convention met in Thomasville, Georgia, with representatives from all the existing associations. Two features of convention life described in the minutes of this convention are interesting because they are typical of many of the early conventions. One common feature of these early conventions was the custom of receiving and appointing correspondents with neighboring conventions and associations as a means of communication. In a day when newspapers were few and many other present-day communication media nonexistent, the significance of this custom was greater than can be appreciated today. The second noteworthy feature was the creation and perpetuation of a board of trustees which acted for the Convention between sessions. Apparently, the creation of a board of trustees followed efforts at securing a charter of incorporation, and the board was a forerunner of the State Board of Missions.[19]

Church and Denominational Life Before the Civil War

Church, association, and convention life, activity, and organization had hardly got under way before the Civil War brought to a halt most of what was being done. Although some churches continued holding worship services uninterrupted throughout the war, others closed, and association and convention sessions were suspended until the war ended. Some basic patterns of action and areas of concern developed, however, indicating that Florida Baptists were moving toward achieving a basic identity which related them to what was going on elsewhere in the Southern Baptist Convention. These basic patterns also indicate that Florida Baptists added to the foundations on which they are still building.

---

[19]Florida Baptist Convention, *Minutes,* 1857, p. 6.

One of those foundations was the work of the association. That unit of denominational organization, which was later to draw great praise for Southern Baptists from outsiders, developed its distinctive functions among Florida Baptists before the Civil War.[20] The first of these functions was to unify the churches. The association brought together representatives and groups of churches in close geographical proximity to discuss and share common interests and problems, and to organize for implementing those goals and purposes on which they agreed. Second, the association very early came to be a means by which churches and church leaders could take council with one another. Some churches and church leaders wanted the association to become an agent of discipline and to act as an arbiter in cases of church discipline or conflict. Very early, however, the associations developed the policy of refusing to serve as arbiter. They did, however, often take counsel and offer opinions in response to the many inquiries which came to them from individuals and churches.[21] A third function of the association meeting is really inherent in the two already mentioned; namely, the provision of an opportunity for fellowship, which was a great source of strength for many isolated groups, especially in that early period when Florida was still predominantly rural and sparsely settled. Finally, the association very early became the organized means by which areas needing churches were given help and by which weak churches could receive adequate pastoral care. As early as 1860, the Florida Association had four men serving as missionaries in the large territory the association sought to cover.[22] The four men were R. Frier, W. F. Duval, Z. G. Wheeler, and G. W. Bostick. The association was also at first the only organized means through which the concerns developed in discussion became realized in action or in movements which hopefully would lead to some kind of action.

At the beginning of the Civil War there were in Florida only four associations: Florida, Alachua, and West Florida, discussed in Chapter One, and the Santa Fe Association, which was formed in 1857 from churches in the Alachua Association.

A second foundation laid among Florida Baptists before the Civil War was the development of solid conviction on the value of educa-

---

[20]Charles G. Hamilton, "What Makes Southern Baptists Tick," article by an Episcopalian, originally published in the *Christian Century,* Oct. 3, 1951, and reprinted in the *Baptist and Reflector,* Oct. 11, 1951, p. 4.

[21]West Florida Baptist Association, *Minutes,* 1853, p. 8.

[22]Florida Baptist Association, *Minutes,* 1860, pp. 2-5.

tion. Along with missions, education was a prime concern from the beginning of church, association, and convention life among Florida Baptists. In a real sense, the pre-war victory of Florida Baptists over the anti-missionary movement both guaranteed and determined the commitment of Florida Baptists to education.[23] This concern for education was very early expressed in three forms. First, it was expressed in those efforts to establish and make effective the education functions inherent in a proper understanding of the local church. Notable illustrations are in the call for more Sunday School work,[24] and a most remarkable resolution by Joshua Mercer calling for a revision of the King James version of the Bible which would put the Bible in modern English.[25]

The second form in which this early interest in education was expressed was in efforts to establish schools. The Orange Hill Academy, established by Joshua Mercer in 1851, is an instructive example of early Baptist interest in fostering education in general as a Christian responsibility. In that academy, English, Latin, Greek, mathematics, modern languages, and music were taught.[26] Although Orange Hill lasted only a few years,[27] the establishing of Orange Hill and other such academies led to a firm determination to establish a college. It is significant in this connection that as early as 1850, the *Minutes* of the Florida Association record a move to begin a college.[28] Also, in 1857 the Convention record notes that two fiscal items were on hand in the treasury, $35.00 for missions and $35.00 for an educational fund. Perhaps someone considered them of equal importance.[29]

A third form in which early Florida Baptists expressed interest in education is in the sale of good books. Often referring to this work as "colportage work," the Convention appointed a depository agent who presided over the shipment and sale of these books. Missionaries and ministers helped in selling these books. In a day when Sunday schools were still rare and in many areas where public schools were non-exis-

---

[23]*Southern Baptist Missionary Journal,* March, 1850, p. 257. Missionary letters printed here show how under the leadership of Joshua Mercer, victory over the anti-missionary forces in the West Florida Association was achieved and how the association organized to educate the churches in missions.

[24]West Florida Baptist Association, *Minutes,* 1856, p. 10.

[25]*Ibid.,* 1855, p. 7.

[26]*Florida Baptist Witness,* March 19, 1925, p. 9.

[27]It did not develop into a college, but died like most of the early academies.

[28]Campbell, *op. cit.,* p. 7.

[29]Florida Baptist Convention, *Minutes,* 1857, p. 6.

tent, this practice immeasurably helped the cause of religious and general education.[30]

A third foundation laid in Florida Baptist life before the Civil War was the implicit emphasis on the freedom and the responsibility of the local church. Individual churches not only created the associations, but they felt their own individual responsibility for the work of missions and they nourished the growth of individuals among them who were concerned about missions. For example, the First Baptist Church of Fernandina, which had been established in 1859, encouraged the ministry of W. F. Wood, who later went in 1886 to do mission work in Cuba.[31] As indicated earlier, although associational and area missionaries had a part in the organization of many Baptist churches, once organized, the churches were free, autonomous local units, to whom the association could not dictate. This freedom contributed to the growth of the churches and to the development of denominational life.

Although the rate of organizing churches slowed down somewhat in the 1850's as compared with the 1840's, some new churches were still being organized up to the outbreak of the Civil War. In 1854 there were 65 churches.

Unsolved Problems Before the Civil War

It has been customary to refer to the spiritual vacuum which followed the Civil War, and indeed desperate conditions did come to exist in church and community life during that period. Careful scrutiny of the contemporary records of church and community life in Florida, however, indicates that while the Civil War inflicted death, injuries, and sufferings on hundreds of thousands of people in the North and the South, in Baptist matters in Florida it only worsened conditions which were already bad. In other words, one may easily be tempted to blame more of the post-war spiritual drought on the war than an accurate picture will justify. Clearly, despite the economic prosperity between the achievement of statehood and the Civil War, that prewar period was marked by spiritual decay and moral turpitude.

The fact that the Florida Baptist Convention was organized several years before the Civil War began means that Florida Baptists had

---

[30] *Ibid.*, pp. 6-7.

[31] *History of First Baptist Church, Fernandina.* (Printed, no author, no date), p. 12.

faced and overcome some very serious problems. Moreover, their disposition on the conflict between Baptists in the North and Baptists in the South had been determined long before the war by their close relations with the Southern states from which many of the early settlers had migrated. Indeed, the anti-slavery movement, strong earlier in the South, had largely died before Florida Baptists developed any sense of corporate identity. It is clear, however, that many years before the war, Florida Baptists had faced certain problems which they were not prepared to solve. Some of these problems are considered in the paragraphs that follow.

First, Florida Baptist pioneers were not able to solve the problem of ministerial leadership. On the one hand, enough ministers could never be found. Many early Florida Baptists apparently lacked something that was characteristic of earlier pioneer Baptists in other frontier areas. One of the reasons Baptists were generally so effective on the frontier, according to Sweet, was that they produced their own ministers on the spot.[32] While Florida Baptist pioneers demonstrated the power to do this in part,[33] they were never able to produce enough. The result was that the few ministers who were available were overworked and were underpaid when paid at all. The struggling frontier churches, therefore, without ministerial leadership and unable to produce it among themselves, in many instances died almost as soon as they were born.[34]

Complicating the problem, many of the ministers produced on the Florida frontier and many who migrated to Florida from other states were inadequately qualified in training and moral character to provide the kind of leadership desperately needed. Thus, it is to the everlasting glory of comparatively few leaders that pioneer Florida Baptists did as well as they did.[35]

A second problem which became obvious before the Civil War was the increasing immorality among church members. Dueling, drinking, gambling and stealing, for a time characteristic of the frontier areas of the new state, appear to have affected the moral life of many church members.[36] The moderator of the Alachua Association, in his circular letter of 1856, cited the spiritual and moral dearth

---

[32]William Warren Sweet, *The Story of Religion in America* (New York: Harper and Brothers, 1950), p. 215.

[33]R. J. Mays is a notable example.

[34]West Florida Baptist Association, *Minutes,* 1852, pp. 10-11.

[35]*Ibid.,* 1850, p. 1.

[36]Douglas, *op. cit.,* pp. 154-155.

in the land, and suggested two approaches to the problem. First, he suggested a high standard of Gospel morality in the churches, which in his judgment would raise the respect unchurched people had for the church. Second, he suggested that the pastors could do more than they were doing to cooperate with one another and supplement the work of the associational missionary, who often had a very wide area of responsibility.[37]

Despite strict discipline which was administered in some churches, the cold, gloomy, and sad state of religion which prevailed in the Alachua Association in 1857 was attributed to the low morality and inner strife in the churches.[38] An example may be typical of the difficulty frontier Baptist churches had in dealing with moral problems. Although on the frontier and among church members drinking and alcoholism became increasingly common near mid-19th century, many Baptists knew nothing to do except condemn it, and at first many were reluctant to do even that. The *Minutes* of Concord Church, for instance, record that in June, 1854, Francis McCall moved that a rule be added to the Church discipline against strong drink as a beverage. Action on his motion was postponed several times as he repeatedly made the suggestion, and in September, 1854, it was postponed indefinitely. In January, 1857, the Minutes record that brother McCall was excommunicated for withdrawal from and contempt to the church.[39] Moreover, resolutions condemning drinking are very hard to find in Baptist church or associational minutes before the Civil War.[40]

A third problem pioneer Florida Baptists encountered but did not solve before the Civil War was the place and plight of Negro slaves in general and in the Baptist churches in particular. The institution of slavery was readily accepted with no transition from early condemnation to gradual acceptance among pioneer Florida Baptists.[41] However, slaves were readily accepted in Florida Baptist churches. As indicated already, both the first Baptist church to be organized in Florida and the church where the Convention was organized had

---

[37]Alachua Baptist Association, *Minutes,* 1856, p. 6.

[38]*Ibid.,* 1857, p. 8.

[39]Browning, *op. cit.,* pp. 23-24.

[40]West Florida Baptist Association, *Minutes,* 1853, p. 8. Here it is recorded that an inquiry had been directed to the association about the propriety of a Baptist selling liquor. The answer of the association was a firm no. However, the answer included no comment on the propriety of a Baptist drinking liquor.

[41]Of course in areas along the coast and inland central Florida where more Northerners lived exceptions could be found to this general judgment.

Negro slaves as members.[42] However, uncertainty existed in the minds of some church leaders as to what status slaves should have as members of Baptist churches. In some churches they were treated just as were other members, and the quality of their contribution to the life of the church was not only recognized, but praised. Concern was often expressed for their welfare. Nonetheless they were generally relegated to a status in the church which could not be described as equal, despite the fact that in many Florida Baptist churches Negroes were in the majority. An excellent example of the uncertainty of some churches over the Negro's place in the church is seen in an inquiry directed by the Apalachicola church to the West Florida Association about how much freedom to conduct their own affairs should be allowed the Negro members of the congregation. Presumably, the Negro members had expressed interest in some kind of religious autonomy, and the white leaders wondered what was proper. The answer of the association, although indecisive in some respects, clearly shows that in the opinion of the association the Negro members were not to be accorded the same freedom and equality in the church enjoyed by whites. The answer was as follows:

> We do not regard the colored portion of the church formally a branch, but only as constituting a part of the Apalachicola church; yet owing to their great disproportion of members and means, and in view of the intelligence and piety they manifest, we approve of their holding separate conferences and translating such business as belongs peculiarly to themselves, *yet always under the supervision of the white brethren, one of whom should act as moderator.* (Emphasis mine) We would also advise that the colored portion of the church keep a separate account of their benevolent contributions which with the amount they send up to the association, may be stated in their regular church letter, or be presented through some white brother, whom they may choose, that the result of their efforts may appear in our minutes.[43]

Florida Baptists and the Civil War

If any political uncertainty existed in the Florida Baptist Convention during the last decade before the war, it had largely disappeared

---

[42] It may strike some people as a surprise to know that segregation among Baptist churches was a phenomenon which developed after the Civil War and then by choice of the free Negroes. More will be said on this subject later.

[43] West Florida Baptist Association, *Minutes,* 1854, p. 11.

and opinion was solidified by 1860, when the Convention fully approved a resolution by F. C. Johnson expressing sympathy for the Southern cause and supporting the destruction of all political ties with the Union. The resolution also expressed great concern for the welfare of the population, and especially of the slaves.[44]

At the beginning of the War the disposition of Florida Baptist leaders toward the Southern cause is best illustrated by examples. First, the great plantation of R. J. Mays, first president of the Convention, was turned to producing food and clothing and other supplies for the Confederate cause. Moreover, five of Mays' sons served in the Confederate Army. Second, many ministers who also were laymen became soldiers, and for a brief time money intended for the salaries of associational missionaries accumulated in the Florida Association since there were no ministers to employ. In fact some of the mission money gathered for the association was sent to various forms of war effort. For example, the Florida Association used $500.00 in their treasury to buy a Confederate bond, supposed to bear interest at 8%.[45] The West Florida Baptist Association organized a group of farmers who agreed to sell food at reduced price to the families of Confederate soldiers.[46]

Although a great part of the Florida peninsula was not directly involved in the war, the settled areas along the coast that were dependent on shipping were blockaded, and the inland areas and northern borders were affected directly both by the war itself and by the political, economic, military and spiritual conditions created by the secession of Florida from the Union on January 11, 1861.[47]

In 1860, the population of Florida totaled 144,024, almost half of whom were slaves. Only 14,373 men were of voting age. Five west coast counties had a total population of 8,500, and the state boasted of only eight cities of more than 1,800 people.[48] In 1850, Florida had been classified as 100% rural.[49] It was still largely rural in 1860. Its circumstances and resources for participating in a war

[44]Of course, the slaves were the property of Southerners. See Florida Baptist Convention, *Annual,* 1860, p. 7.

[45]Campbell, *op. cit.,* p. 12.

[46]John E. Johns, *Florida During the Civil War.* (Gainesville: University of Florida Press, 1963), p. 185.

[47]Florida seceded before Georgia, which withdrew on January 19, 1861. See Douglas, *op. cit.,* pp. 166-168.

[48]*Ibid.,* p. 172.

[49]"Florida," *Encyclopedia Brittannica,* Vol. 9, p. 473.

were therefore meager. Nonetheless, fighting groups filled with enthusiasm were organized in all heavily populated areas, where the frontier spirit, even among the wealthy, was still strong. Even though the Baptists of Florida numbered only about 5,529 in 1859, they generally shared the enthusiasm for the Southern cause.

Unfortunately, the shortage of church and denominational records during the Civil War makes impossible an accurate description of the relation of Florida Baptist churches to the war during the conflict itself. The brief references that do exist suggest influential effects of the war.

First, it appears certain that many churches were left without ministerial leadership because some ministers were also laymen and became soldiers, as indicated above. Others left their posts as pastors and went as chaplains to the spiritual needs of the men on the battlefields. The departure of so many leaders forced a number of churches to close their doors,[50] some never to be re-opened.

Other churches were adversely affected by the war itself and by occupation by military authorities. The First Baptist Church of Jacksonville, for example, was badly disrupted.

> The day of the Battle of Olustee February 20, 1864 the church was taken possession by the Federals and used as a hospital for wounded soldiers. The floors were strewn with hay and the wounded, both negro and white, laid out in rows. From this time until the troops left Jacksonville, the church was occupied as a military hospital by the Federal Army. The building was left greatly damaged. From a member who was an eyewitness came this report; "The church was left in a deplorable condition, when vacated by the troops. Scarcely a pane of glass was left in the windows and very little plastering on the walls."[51]

Despite the victories of the Confederates in the two major battles fought in Florida, at Olustee and Tallahassee, the presence of Union troops in other areas and the general disorder and confusion which accompanied the progress of the war in Florida together resulted in very great damage.[52] Tampa, for instance, was burned by Federal troops. Many homes, churches, and schools were destroyed. In some areas schools and churches closed until the war ended.

---

[50]Barnes, *op. cit.*, p. 48.

[51]"130th Anniversary: Pastors and People, 1838-1968, Bethel Baptist Institutional Church-First Baptist Church, Jacksonville, Florida," printed program, p. 3. Cf. *Florida Times Union,* July 6, 1968, p. A-12.

[52]Douglas, *op. cit.*, p. 195.

However, many churches continued to hold services throughout the war with little or no interruption. In fact, from the minutes of some of these churches one would have difficulty learning that a war was in process.[53] In other cases references to the war are made, but mainly as an event which interfered with the work of missions and further increased the shortage of ministers.[54] Florida Baptists, like Southern Baptists generally, while committed to the Southern cause, were very reluctant to engage in official critical discussion of the moral issues involved in the war. They appear to have been influenced by the view that political matters should be left to political leaders and that church leaders should attend to church affairs.

Formation of Negro Churches

One of the most significant and in some ways tragic events occurring among Florida Baptists during this period was the formation of Negro Baptist churches and associations. This separation of the races for worship was significant because it reflected a special sense of responsibility and self-identity emerging among Negro Baptists. It was a tragic event because in many ways it resulted in a weakening of both groups, Negro Baptists and white Baptists.

Whether any Florida Baptist churches that were exclusively Negro existed before the Civil War is not known. It is certain that some Negro Baptist churches existed in Georgia before the Civil War.[55] It is also apparent that many Negroes were beginning to feel uncomfortable in the same churches with their white masters. One explanation for this discomfort, given by a Negro writer, is that worship in the white churches did not allow adequate opportunity for full expression of the Negroes' deep feelings.[56]

After the Civil War the desire for separate churches grew among Florida Negro Baptists until it came to be expressed in the formation of their own churches. Several factors explain the growing sense of need among Negro Baptists for their own separate churches. First, it became quickly apparent that although many white Baptists were genuinely concerned for their spiritual and moral welfare, they were

---

[53]Browning, *op. cit.*, p. 26, for example.

[54]Florida Baptist Convention, *Annual,* 1866, pp. 7-11.

[55]Edward A. Freeman, *The Epoch of Negro Baptists and the Foreign Mission Board* (Kansas City, Kansas: The Central Seminary Press, 1953), p. 27.

[56]Ira D. Reid, *The Negro Baptist Ministry: An Analysis of its Profession, Preparation and Practices* (A report of a survey by the Joint Survey Commission of the Baptist Inter-Convention Committee, 1951, mimeographed), p. 13.

not willing to give Negroes full freedom and equality in the life of the denomination.[57] Second, even if they had been given full equality in the churches, Negro Baptists could not feel completely free. As long as they were in the same churches with their masters, they felt psychologically dependent. Thus, at the first opportunity, many Negro Baptists moved to establish their separate churches.[58] In other instances lawsuits over property were necessary. Bethel Church in Jacksonville experienced such disagreement. The courts awarded the property to the Negroes because they were in the majority. In exchange for a cash settlement, the white members retained possession of the old church property, and the Negro members bought a lot at another location. Thus, in 1868 a Negro Baptist church was organized in Jacksonville.[59] Other churches must have been organized in other places the same year or earlier, for, according to Pegues, the Bethlehem Baptist Association was organized by Negroes in 1868. Immediately, this association took steps to organize an institution of learning. A site was selected at Live Oak, Florida, and after much difficulty and the receipt of some aid from the American Baptist Home Mission Society, the Live Oak Institute was finally opened in October, 1880, with Rev. J. L. Fish, a Negro, as president.[60] As late as 1883, however, statistical reports in the *Minutes* of the Florida Baptist Convention still included Negro churches and membership totals.

Church and Associational Life After the Civil War

The most notable feature of church, association, and convention life for several years following the Civil War was widespread poverty, both economic and spiritual, and the critical shortage of ministers.[61] Conditions were desperate, but ministers were urged not to preach to congregations which did not give them support.[62] In these desperate circumstances a sense of close fellowship with other denominations

---

[57]For example, Florida Baptist Association, *Minutes,* 1867, p. 15, where it was noted that only white membership would be represented in the Association. Cf. Browning, *op. cit.,* p. 29, who reports that shortly after the War two recently freed Negroes had asked for license to preach. The church appointed a time for them to try out their talents. They had their try, but the brethren were not satisfied. Later, one of them was allowed to "exhort."

[58]Dalton, *op. cit.,* p. 357.

[59]*Florida Times Union,* July 6, 1968, p. A-12.

[60]A. W. Pegues, *Our Baptist Ministers and Schools* (Springfield, Mass.: Willey & Co., 1892), pp. 602-603.

[61]Florida Baptist Convention, *Annual,* 1866, pp. 7-11.

[62]*Ibid.,* 1867, pp. 5-6.

was manifested, suggesting awareness of common conditions. At the annual sessions during this period, the Convention often used the facilities of Methodist and Presbyterian Churches, and Convention leaders often preached to Methodist and Presbyterian congregations during the Convention.[63] The shortage of ministers was so lamentable, indeed, that in 1871 when the committee on ministerial education reported that they had found one man who was studying for the ministry, the report appears to have given the Convention new hope.[64]

A second feature of post Civil War Florida Baptist life is all the more remarkable in view of the economic and spiritual destitution mentioned above; namely, renewed interest in education. In 1866, when the annual convention sessions were renewed, a committee on education was appointed and heard. Then the *Minutes* also record that after interesting remarks made by several people, the report of the committee was adopted.[65] The nature of these remarks is not clear. One very real possibility is that while the desirability of establishing a college was acknowledged, the impossibility of concrete convention action at that time was admitted.

By 1869 the interest in education was still growing and had by then combined with the concern for ministerial supply. The committee on education at that time expressed a deep need for a ministerial school, though they clearly did not have in mind a theological seminary as one thinks of such today, but rather a good college. They reported: "The time is drawing nigh, when, in many of our communities, no ministers except those who shall exhibit a good degree of mental culture will be able to secure respectful attention.[66]

As late as 1876, however, it is clear that the Convention was still unable to do more than talk about establishing a college. At this convention the committee on education brought a recommendation that an agent be employed to canvass the state and raise money for a school to be established. After discussing the recommendation at great length, the Convention concluded that the time was not yet ripe for such an effort.[67]

A third feature of Florida Baptist life following the Civil War was associational growth. Not many new associations came into being immediately after the war, but by 1867 there was developed a special

---

[63]*Ibid.,* pp. 5-6.
[64]*Ibid.,* 1871, p. 10.
[65]*Ibid.,* 1866, p. 4.
[66]*Ibid.,* 1869, p. 17.
[67]*Ibid.,* 1876, p. 36.

form of associational activity which not only marked a transition from the few to the many associations, but also was to serve as a supplement to associational life for many years to come. Reference here is made to the union meeting, which began apparently as an effort to bring some associational experience to the reach of many who could not attend the annual meeting because of distance. An association would be divided into districts, and churches in those districts would come together quarterly for one or two days of discussion and sharing of mutual problems and hopes. These union meetings also served to foster communication between the local churches and the association and the state convention.[68] Very likely some new associations grew out of these union meetings. In any case, by 1879, to the original list of associations, consisting of Florida, Alachua, West Florida, and Santa Fe River Associations, were added the following: South Florida (1867),[69] Wekiwa (1869),[70] New River (1882),[71] Elim and Suwanee (1873),[72] Peace River (1876),[73] St. Johns River (1877),[74] Beulah (1879),[75] Harmony (1879),[76] and St. Marys (1879).[77]

Despite the spiritual and economic poverty and despite continued lamentations, Florida Baptists not only maintained their denominational distinctives and their pride in them,[78] but they also began as early as 1869 to see some hope and to make some plans for the future.[79]

---

[68]Florida Baptist Association, *Minutes,* 1867, p. 14.

[69]Dalton, *op. cit.,* p. 228.

[70]*Ibid.,* p. 240.

[71]*Ibid.,* p. 176.

[72]Elim did not survive. The organization of the Suwanee Association came from a group of churches which wanted to preserve the name of the original Suwanee Association. In addition to these, the 1873 *Annual* refers to another association called the Missionary Baptist Association which was admitted to the Convention. See Florida Baptist Convention, *Annual* 1873, p. 21. Some objected to admitting the association because of the indefiniteness of the name and because of the lack of articles of faith. Since the name never appears in later *Annuals,* however, this association apparently did not survive.

[73]Dalton, *op. cit.,* p. 246.

[74]*Ibid.,* p. 178.

[75]*Ibid.,* p. 181.

[76]*Ibid.,* p. 188.

[77]Later named Jacksonville Association. *Ibid.,* p. 192.

[78]In 1866 the Convention, informed that F. C. Johnson had been admitted to a seat in Presbyterian session of the Florida Presbytery, stated that Florida Baptists were not responsible for what he said and that he did not represent the Convention. Florida Baptist Convention, *Annual,* 1869, p. 17.

[79]*Ibid.,* 1870, p. 2.

Those feeble hopes and tentative plans were greatly strengthened in the 1870's by help and promises of continued aid from the American Baptist Home Mission Society and the Home Mission Board of the Southern Baptist Convention. Although the disposition of the Florida Baptist Convention toward the American Baptist Home Mission Society was cool, Florida Baptists had benefited from the Society's help before the war, and they were now too desperate to refuse assistance. Thus, it is no wonder that P. P. Bishop, for some time a general agent for the American Baptist Home Mission Society, was elected secretary of the Convention in 1869.[80] He was elected president in 1870 and was re-elected in 1871. He offered help to the Convention from the American Baptist Home Mission Society, and for a brief time the help was received.[81] Although cautious, the Convention accepted an arrangement in which the executive board of the Convention nominated missionaries who would be paid by the American Baptist Home Missionary Society.[82] The only requirement of the Society was that whatever money the missionaries raised would go to the American Baptist Home Missionary Society. This cooperative Convention arrangement was short-lived, however, as the fear grew among Florida Baptists that relations with the American Baptist Home Mission Society might strain relations with Southern Baptists.[83]

In 1872 W. N. Chaudoin was received at the Convention annual session as a guest. He was then serving as District Secretary of the Domestic Mission Board of the Southern Baptist Convention, for the States of Georgia, Florida, and South Carolina.[84] Apparently encouraged by his presence and the possibility of help from the Home Mission Board, the Convention immediately authorized the Board of Trustees to employ a state evangelist.[85] Kinsey Chambers was thus engaged, and made his first report to the Convention of 1873.[86]

One other event deserves mention among those desperate expressions of hope for the future that came in those first efforts to recover from the Civil War. This was the attempt to found a Florida Baptist paper. One of the first references in the Convention *Annual* to such

---

[80]*Ibid.,* 1869, p. 13.
[81]*Ibid.,* 1870, pp. 9-10.
[82]*Ibid.,* p. 11.
[83]*Ibid.,* 1872, p. 9.
[84]*Ibid.,* p. 16.
[85]*Ibid.*
[86]*Ibid.,* 1873, p. 24.

a potential venture was in 1872.[87] H. B. McCallum undertook the project sometime in 1873. He called this paper *The Florida Baptist*. Unfortunately, financial difficulties made it necessary to discontinue publication after only a few months.[88] Efforts to resume publication in 1876, moreover, were only temporarily successful,[89] but the idea of a paper had been born, and it was to be revived soon.

Another feature of Florida Baptist life in the period after the Civil War was the beginning of Convention concern for what was later to be viewed as a major moral issue: the liquor question. In 1872 the first Convention Committee on Temperance was appointed and prepared a report which was adopted only after several amendments, several substitute motions, and much discussion.[90] Changes introduced by the amendments and substitutes were in the direction of a milder statement; for example, the suggestion that the Convention withdraw fellowship from those who indulge in drink was changed to an admonition that the churches exert influence to eradicate the great evil.[91] In view of this reluctant beginning, it is not surprising that the list of committees appointed in 1873 did not include a temperance committee. However, the Convention of 1875 received a temperance report without comment,[92] as did subsequent conventions. For several years (until 1880) the Convention report was mildly stated. In 1877 the Florida Association's Temperance Report observed that the use of alcohol was increasing, and that to witness against it, Christians should abstain from drinking, selling, or buying it.[93]

A final issue which received increasing attention at this time as a moral question among Florida Baptists was the violation of the Sabbath. Standing committees on the Sabbath, along with missions and temperance committees, became increasingly common after the Civil War.[94]

---

[87]*Ibid.*, 1872, pp. 18-19.

[88]McCallum transferred his subscription list to the *Christian Index*, arranging that a part of the *Index* be devoted to a Florida Baptist department. See *History of the Baptist Denomination In Georgia*, compiled for the *Christian Index* (Atlanta, Ga.: The Index Publishing Co. 1881), p. 372.

[89]Florida Baptist Convention, *Annual*, 1876, p. 36.

[90]Some associations had such a committee earlier.

[91]Florida Baptist Convention, *Annual*, 1872, p. 16.

[92]*Ibid.*, 1875.

[93]Florida Baptist Association, *Minutes*, 1877, pp. 2-3.

[94]*Ibid.*

In this chapter it is clear that between 1854 and 1879 pioneer Florida Baptists used materials brought in earlier to lay foundations for both difficulties yet existing and for possibilities that are still being realized. The foundation for difficulties will be described in a later chapter. For the moment let it be noted that Florida Baptists early developed a missionary vision and organized themselves to implement that vision. They had dreams about such instruments as a college and a Baptist newspaper to help them carry out their plans. They made efforts, moreover, to make those plans a reality. And although many of their efforts were abortive, frustrated as they were by a catastrophic war and the tragic circumstances which accompanied it, the dreams would not die. And because they would not die, many of them were later to be realized.

Associational Development and Growth
1880

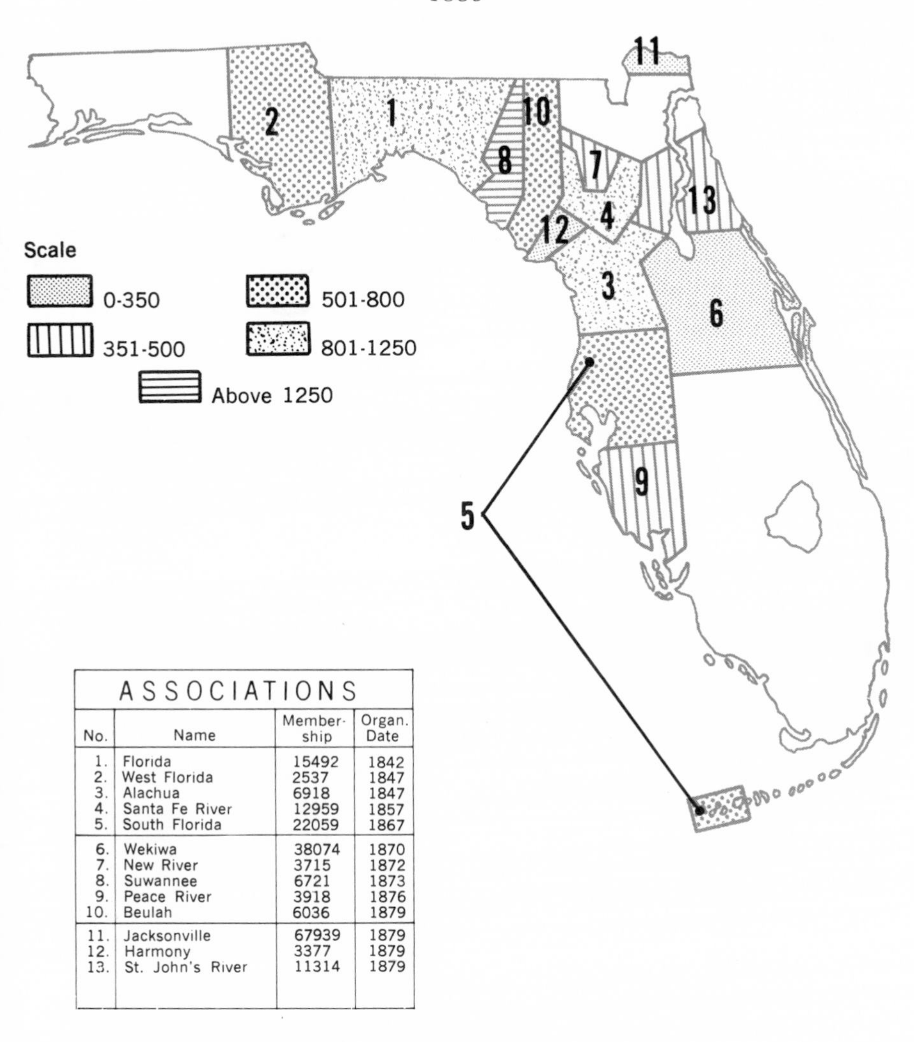

ASSOCIATIONS			
No.	Name	Member-ship	Organ. Date
1.	Florida	15492	1842
2.	West Florida	2537	1847
3.	Alachua	6918	1847
4.	Santa Fe River	12959	1857
5.	South Florida	22059	1867
6.	Wekiwa	38074	1870
7.	New River	3715	1872
8.	Suwannee	6721	1873
9.	Peace River	3918	1876
10.	Beulah	6036	1879
11.	Jacksonville	67939	1879
12.	Harmony	3377	1879
13.	St. John's River	11314	1879

CHAPTER THREE

New Life: The State Board, Stetson, and THE FLORIDA BAPTIST WITNESS: 1880-1900

Despite the birth of hope in the 1870's and the dreams that were significant because of their possibilities in the future, the last years in that decade were very gloomy. F. B. Moodie later recalled that in 1877, when the *Minutes* of the 1871-1876 conventions were published in one volume, no money was on hand to pay the expense. H. B. McCallum, personally, paid it. Attendance at the Convention became smaller and smaller until the effort was temporarily given up, from 1877 through 1879.[1]

The year 1880, however, marks a kind of rebirth for the Florida Baptist Convention. Although the size of the group meeting that year would be small by today's standards, with a total of twelve delegates, the spirit and vision were nonetheless good. The session was held in Madison, not far from the place where the Convention had been organized in 1854, and was marked by a spirit of enthusiasm and determination.

This new spirit was generated and encouraged by amazing growth in both population and industry in Florida. The introduction of Northern industrial capital brought visions of great economic prosperity,[2] and the immigration and migration of new people and ministers brought new hope and life to many weak churches. The lamentation over the shortage of ministers, heard often in the past, came to an end. E. H. Rennolds wrote in 1885 that Sumter County abounded

---

[1]Letter by F. B. Moodie, *Florida Baptist Witness,* February 24, 1910.
[2]Douglas, *op. cit.,* p. 234.

in Baptist ministers.[3] As they learned of the pleasant climate and economic possibilities available, many people, distinguished and obscure, came; some to visit, but many to stay.

The Convention: Developing a Sense of Identity

Between 1880 and 1900, the new spirit in the state was reflected among Florida Baptists in their growing awareness of a need to develop a sense of identity. Although the Convention is still attempting today to define its identity, the search for identity during this period found main expression in two broad purposes to which Florida Baptists are still committed. These purposes are missions and education. These purposes were implemented by several different means. First, the Convention maintained the custom of receiving corresponding delegates from various other state conventions and sending delegates to them, thus maintaining constant and fresh communication with other groups and learning from them.[4]

Second, as indicated in Chapter Two, the Florida Baptist Convention determined to resolve the problem of divided loyalties by generally rejecting aid from the American Baptist Home Mission Society in favor of the Home Mission Board of the Southern Baptist Convention.[5] Nevertheless, individual churches, missions, and Negro Baptist work continued to receive aid from the American Baptist Home Mission Society for several years.[6] The significant point of this decision by the Florida Baptist Convention, however, was that *it determined to be identified mainly with the Southern Baptist Convention.*

Third, Florida Baptists committed themselves to missions and education in the significant role they played in the founding of Stetson University. The details of this event will be discussed later in this chapter.

Fourth, this commitment was expressed in the organization of a pastors' conference, to assemble before each annual convention session, for the purpose of self-education through sharing. The idea for a pas-

---

[3]*Florida Baptist Witness,* March 19, 1885.

[4]Florida Baptist Convention, *Annual,* 1885, p. 41. Note that the representatives sent and received were called "delegates." Today they would be called "messengers."

[5]James H. Semple, "A History of the Florida Baptist Convention, from 1865 to 1918," unpublished Doctoral Dissertation, Southwestern Baptist Theological Seminary, 1962, pp. 24-25.

[6]For example: First Baptist Church, DeLand, Florida, *Minutes,* October 16, 1881, and September 23, 1883.

tors' conference or ministers' conference, as it sometimes has been called, appears to have originated with L. D. Geiger, who suggested the need in 1885. His suggestion was for a ministers' institute in which ministers could, like teachers, exchange ideas. In his Marion associational column he even suggested a date and place for such a meeting. The meeting was to be held the fifth Sunday in November, 1885, at Citra.[7] Whether or not such a meeting as he suggested occurred is uncertain, but it is certain that by 1889 the idea had caught the interest of many ministers, for at the annual convention, the pastors' conference was organized, a committee was appointed, and a program was prepared. The objects of the conference, as suggested in the constitution were (1) to awaken deeper interest in the study of the Scriptures, (2) to encourage mutual improvement, mental and spiritual, and (3) to devise methods for improving the work of the church.[8] Programs of the Conference consisted of prepared "position papers" (they would be called today), open discussion, and sermons, sometimes preached for purposes of criticism. Topics considered included such subjects as "Special Demands Upon Florida Baptists at this Present Juncture," or "Pastoral Authority: Its Nature and Abuse," and "What Constitutes a Call to the Ministry?" L. D. Geiger, who originated the idea, was often on the program, and often the discussions were very lively. For example, in 1896 when Geiger read a paper on "The Harmony between the Doctrines of Election and Missions," almost every pastor present participated in the discussion which followed.[9] One can hardly avoid observing how significantly the format and style of the pastors' conference of today has changed since its beginning in 1889.

Finally, these purposes were implemented in the organization of the State Board of Missions, to which special attention will now be given.

The Convention: Its Basic Agency

The State Board of Missions: Organization

Two most significant factors in the new spirit developing among Florida Baptists were the organization of the State Board of Missions in 1880 and the election of W. N. Chaudoin as corresponding secretary, a position equivalent today to executive secretary. Chaudoin was

---

[7]*Florida Baptist Witness,* Nov. 12, 1885.
[8]Florida Baptist Convention, *Annual,* 1889, pp. 7-8.
[9]*Ibid.,* 1896, p. 2.

E. N. CHAUDOIN, *Executive Secretary,*
1880 - 1901

to be a dominating factor in Florida Baptist life for 20 years.[10] Though frail of body, Chaudoin was strong of spirit, and according to many estimates, that was what the Convention needed most at that time. Moreover, spirit was virtually all that the Convention had at its disposal at the beginning of this period. Its economic resources were small, and the needs and challenges of these last two decades were to be larger than most people could imagine, with a population increase of 500% between 1850 and 1900.[11] In 1880 the population was estimated as 269,493. By 1885 it was estimated as 342,551, or a growth of 30% in only five years. The center of the population was shifting, moreover, for between 1880 and 1885 while Gadsden, Jefferson, Leon, Liberty, Madison, and Taylor counties along the northern border showed a decrease in population, Orange, Polk, Sumter, and Volusia counties in central Florida, more than doubled.[12]

While the newly organized State Board could not know the extensiveness of the staggering challenges confronting them and while they were aware of their limitations, they organized with faith and hope for the future. The first minutes of the board reported receipts totalling $104.11, and cash paid out $103.60, leaving a balance of 51 cents. However, with such small amounts they had employed two missionaries, a Dr. Robinson, and N. A. Bailey, paying each of them a salary of $25.00 a quarter. Also, they now had a full time executive, W. N. Chaudoin, whose salary, along with that of the missionaries, was to be supplemented for several years to come, by the Home Mission Board of the Southern Baptist Convention.[13] In 1886, the State Board was paying Chaudoin's salary, which was set then at $600.00 per year plus traveling expenses.[14]

Even with the remarkable growth of the Convention and with the help of the Home Mission Board, however, the State Board was plagued with financial difficulties during this period. For example, the church loan fund, ostensibly established in 1883 for financing much

---

[10]W. N. Chaudoin credited N. A. Bailey with the original proposal to form a State Board of Missions. See Florida Baptist Convention, *Annual,* 1898, p. 22. He also credited Bailey with the first suggestion for forming a Baptist Ministers Assurance Association (a forerunner of the Relief and Annuity Board) and with being one of the founders of women's work in Florida.

[11]"Florida," *Encyclopedia Brittannica,* 1965, IX, p. 473.

[12]*Florida Baptist Witness,* Jan. 14, 1885.

[13]State Board, *Minutes,* December 10, 1882. Cf. Florida Baptist Convention, *Annual,* 1881, p. 14.

[14]State Board, *Minutes,* January 3, 1883.

needed church buildings,[15] appeared in 1886 to be a useless venture because no money was available and no loans from banks were possible.[16] The only commitment viewed as absolute was to pay the salaries of the two corresponding secretaries. (W. N. Chaudoin, and Mrs. N. A. Bailey who was in charge of woman's work.) In 1887, optimism prevailed, for then the missionaries' salaries also were declared absolute.[17] In 1895, however, the missionaries' salaries were again declared relative to income.[18]

It is therefore remarkable that the State Board of Missions accomplished so much. Created by the Convention and ably led by Chaudoin the State Board came to perform two broad functions which it has served ever since. First, it formed the tradition of carrying out the wishes of the Convention. This tradition included the responsibility for coordinating and encouraging the work of the various agencies and special mission enterprises of the Convention, such as the Woman's Missionary Union and the Sunday School to be discussed later. Second, the Board came to stimulate and guide the Convention direction, serving often as an advisory body. The two major concerns which dominated the board in serving both these functions throughout this era were missions and education. Since a separate section will be given to education later, major attention will first be directed to the mission work of the Board.

The Function of the State Board of Missions

As financial resources increased, the State Board appointed other missionaries in addition to the two mentioned above, and it is difficult to exaggerate the significance of the work of these men. Like the pioneer missionaries before them, they often traveled long distances, preaching, organizing Sunday Schools, constituting churches, and helping erect buildings for them. Despite vain efforts to create a working loan fund for church buildings, Chaudoin was able by his own personal efforts to secure aid for the construction of a number of significant churches.[19]

In addition to appointing, helping and supervising State missionaries, the State Board also cooperated with associational missions and strengthened their work by doing much which they wanted to do but

---

[15]*Ibid.,* July 4, 1883.
[16]*Ibid.,* June 30, 1886. Cf. also *Minutes,* Dec. 14, 1884.
[17]*Ibid.,* January 5, 1887.
[18]*Ibid.,* March 21, 1895.
[19]Rosser, *op. cit.,* p. 66.

could not. An example is the appointment in 1885 of Alberto J. Diaz and Minnie Diaz as missionaries to Cuba.[20] This appointment had grown out of the work of W. F. Wood, minister at Fernandina, and later at Key West, who had gone to Cuba as a missionary.[21] W. L. Mahon wrote that Manatee Association had pledged $800.00 to send or support a missionary when there was not a single meeting house in the Association, except log shanties. Through the efforts of W. F. Wood and T. J. Sparkman, the interest and support of the Convention were gained.[22]

One area of mission responsibility which the State Board of Missions recognized but did not implement during this period was for work among the Florida Indians. Very early records of Florida Baptists show some interest in mission work among the Indians, but since the Indian War of 1835-42, enthusiasm for Indian missions had waned.[23] Neglect of the Indians reflects on the one hand the guilt Baptists shared with other Floridians for breaking treaties with the Indians by encroaching on their lands. On the other hand, even those who shared no guilt, because they had not been part of the problem, knew that great hostility toward the white man still existed among the few remaining humiliated Florida Indians.[24] Because of this hostility, mission work among the Indians was not to become a reality during this period. However, the dream and the concern which were to bear fruit in a later period came to life again.[25] The report of the State Board to the Convention in 1893 lamented the pitiful plight of the red man, but gave no indication that anything was being done for him.[26]

Another area of mission responsibility which the State Board recognized during this period received more attention than the plight of the Indians, but never received the attention needed or deserved, namely, the Negro Baptists. Some work with them was done but was complicated by hostilities still smouldering since the Civil War. Attention to specific work on their behalf will be discussed in a separate section.

---

[20]State Board, *Minutes,* Nov. 14, 1885.

[21]*Florida Baptist Witness,* Sept. 3, 1890, editorial by F. B. Moodie.

[22]W. L. Mahon, "Origin of Cuban Baptist Missions," *Florida Baptist Witness,* Mar. 2, 1898, p. 1.

[23]See Chapter One.

[24]Douglas, *op. cit.,* pp. 133-150.

[25]Florida Baptist Convention, *Minutes,* 1884, p. 5.

[26]*Ibid.,* 1893, p. 106.

One function which the State Board assumed and continues to serve was the receiving and handling of the Convention's property, in both money and real estate. For the purpose of performing this service, the Board began to seek incorporation in 1885, an event apparently first viewed as necessary when Stetson University was born.[27]

Finally, the State Board participated with the Convention in creating and directing or coordinating a number of agencies and instruments to achieve the broad purposes of missions and education.

The Convention: Developing A Style of Work

Women's Work

Florida Baptist women's awareness of their own unique function in the life of Florida Baptists goes back at least as far as the organization of the Campbellton Baptist Church in 1825, which probably had the first organized women's group.[28] Other women's groups soon followed, and by the time of the organization of the State Board of Missions, the significance of women's work in the church and the Convention was recognized by the Convention's action in 1881 in granting women seats in the Convention's annual session on an equal basis with men.[29] Shortly thereafter W. N. Chaudoin, executive secretary, on recommendation of the Mission Report, appointed Mrs. N. A. Bailey, of Micanopy, as Secretary of Women's Work. This action also reflected the fact that by 1881 there were many women's missionary societies.[30]

The main functions of these societies were (1) collecting money for missions, (2) encouraging young people to give their lives to mission work, (3) giving direct support to mission projects, and (5) cooperating with the work of the Convention in all its endeavors. Their alertness is reflected in their representation in the organization meeting of the southwide Women's Missionary Union in 1888.[31] When the Southern Baptist Convention in 1883 assigned Florida $400.00 to raise for foreign missions, the Florida Convention voluntarily raised it to $800.00. Chaudoin attributed this action to the work of the women.[32] Their commitment to the total program of Florida Bap-

---

[27]State Board, *Minutes,* April 1, 1885.

[28]Lassiter, *op. cit.,* p. 7.

[29]Florida Baptist Convention, *Minutes,* 1881, p. 4.

[30]Lassiter, *op. cit.,* p. 12. Cf. *Florida Baptist Witness,* March 12, 1885.

[31]Lassiter, *ibid.,* p. 21.

[32]Florida Baptist Convention, *Annual,* 1884, p. 6.

tist life is seen in the naming of four women in 1889 to the Committee on Sunday Schools.[33] From the time of her appointment as Corresponding Secretary of Women's Work, Mrs. Bailey engaged herself busily in encouraging existing missionary societies and in organizing new ones. Before her death, in 1886, Mrs. Bailey had seen organizational increase from four missionary societies and one children's missionary band, to 109 societies and bands. Mission giving had increased from $74.38 to $1,225.38. She had participated, moreover, in the organization of the oldest missionary society in the state, at Micanopy in 1881. Also, she had helped secure the appointment of Miss Adela Fales as missionary to the Cubans at Key West in 1886.[34]

On the death of Mrs. Bailey, Mrs. L. B. Telford, a former missionary to China, was elected to head the women's work. Her first report to the Convention in 1888 indicates that already she had helped to organize two associational missionary unions, had appointed 16 missionaries and had organized 25 children's bands.[35] At the convention in Ocala in 1889 Mrs. Telford was able to report that despite a yellow fever plague $1,118.91 had been raised for missions. Furthermore, money given to missions increased each year until her death. During her last year the Baptist women of Florida raised $2,295.00 for missions.[36] Long plagued with health problems, Mrs. Telford died in 1893. Miss J. L. Spalding, who had assisted Mrs. Telford for some time, was elected to replace her.

In 1894 a significant change occurred in the organizational relationship between the Women's Department and the Florida Baptist Convention. Whereas, women's work had been directly under the auspices of the executive secretary, W. N. Chaudoin, and the Convention, in 1894 women's work became fully autonomous. Making this change meant relieving Chaudoin of responsibility for women's work and accepting a pattern of organization common in other states. The supervision of women's work was placed in the hands of a central committee and the corresponding secretary, all elected by the women in their own meetings. Their organization now became Woman's Missionary Union, and this pattern of autonomy and cooperation was to continue until 1968, when something nearer to the old arrangement was reinstated. Undoubtedly, much credit for the

---

[33]*Ibid.*
[34]Lassiter, *op. cit.*, p. 11. *Florida Baptist Witness,* June 18, 1885.
[35]Lassiter, *ibid.*, p. 19.
[36]*Florida Baptist Witness,* Mar. 3, 1904, pp. 2-3.

stewardship habits of Florida Baptists must be given to these women, who organized themselves to promote the stewardship of giving to missions both in the local church and elsewhere. In 1900, the Florida Woman's Missionary Union rejoiced in the appointment of one of its young women, Miss Mary A. Taylor, by the Home Mission Board as a missionary to Havana, Cuba. She was the first native Florida woman to volunteer for mission service outside the United States.[37]

Sunday School

As indicated previously, the earliest known Sunday School organized in Florida was established at Key West in 1844 by G. G. Tripp, an employee of the American Baptist Home Mission Society.[38] Although at the beginning of Florida Baptist Convention life, Sunday Schools were very few and some opposition to them still existed, the Convention became immediately aware of the importance and possibilities of the Sunday School, appointing a committee on Sunday School in 1860.[39] From this time on, associational Sunday School committees became increasingly common, and their reports abound in exhortations to the churches to engage in Sunday School work. Obviously, many were slow to make the start. By 1880, however, Sunday Schools were increasing in number, the first Sunday School missionary was appointed, and the first reference to Sunday School literature was made. The Southern Baptist Convention as yet had no Sunday School literature; consequently most of the literature used was that published by the American Baptist Publication Society. When the *Florida Baptist Witness* came into being, it often carried Sunday School lesson materials in its columns. At the Convention in Ocala in 1881, a Sunday School Board was appointed.[40] In 1884, the first state Sunday School worker, G. W. Hall, was named and the first statistical reports appeared on Sunday School work[41]

Thus, although there was then no permanent full-time employee to supervise and promote Sunday School work, it is clear that before the end of the 19th century the Sunday School was already an established part of Florida Baptist educational and evangelistic life, plagued

---

[37]Florida Baptist Convention, *Annual,* 1900, p. 39. Also *Florida Baptist Witness,* Sept. 3, 1890. As indicated earlier mission work had been established in Havana by F. M. Wood.

[38]Rosser, *op. cit.,* p. 121.

[39]*Ibid.,* p. 122.

[40]*Ibid.,* p. 125.

[41]*Ibid.,* p. 142.

though it was by a shortage of literature and the continued refusal of some churches to participate.

Baptist Young People's Union

This organization, originating in Chicago, Illinois, in July, 1891, for the purpose of organizing societies for young people in Baptist churches, had followers among Florida Baptists in less than five years.[42] Among them, as among other Southern Baptists, however, it was not accepted readily. On the contrary, it was for a time a source of great controversy and misunderstanding. Obviously, it fulfilled a need, for despite the absence of Convention sanction,[43] it became an autonomous movement, holding its own annual meetings. Although it was commended to the churches by the Convention in 1896,[44] it was still a debated issue in 1899, for when L. D. Geiger spoke at that time to the ministers' conference on the subject "Should the Baptist Young People's Union Take Preference over the Christian Endeavor Societies in our Churches?" lively discussion followed and apparently no conclusion was reached.[45] By this time, nonetheless, it had gained considerable support in the Convention.[46]

The Orphanage

All that was achieved in establishing a home for homeless children during this era was a firm decision to do something concrete about a problem that often had been mentioned. This firm decision came in the Convention of 1899, when C. S. Farris, from Stetson University, read a resolution calling for a committee appointment to consider establishing a Baptist orphanage.[47] The committee was appointed, and reported in the Convention of 1900, recommending organizational procedures for establishing the home.[48] Trustees were named, and at the Convention of 1901, they reported their decision that the orphanage be located at Arcadia. Land and money had been given by the citizens of Arcadia and DeSoto County, with a combined total value of $5,450.00. Enthusiasm for the venture was great, and while

---

[42]*Ibid.*, p. 226.

[43]In 1895 the B.Y.P.U. was considered, but neither sanctioned nor condemned.

[44]Florida Baptist Convention, *Annual,* 1896, p. 30.

[45]Florida Baptist Convention, *Minutes,* 1899, p. 4.

[46]Rosser, *op. cit.,* pp. 228-230.

[47]Florida Baptist Convention, *Annual,* 1899, p. 20.

[48]Rosser, *op. cit.,* p. 248.

the opening of the home was not yet possible, it was soon to become a reality.

Beginning Interest in a Retirement System

First recorded interest in some kind of aid to the families of ministers in their old age came in the Florida Baptist Convention of 1884, when S. F. Gove introduced a resolution calling for a committee to plan some such aid. Nothing came of it immediately, but the idea was proposed in the Ministers' Conference in 1889, and in 1890 the Baptist Ministers' Life Association was formed. It could hardly be called a retirement system in the current understanding of the term, but it was a beginning. In brief, the constitution called for an annual membership fee (at first 50 cents and later $1.00) and an assessment of $1.00 on the death of any member. The proceeds accumulated were to be used in aiding elderly indigent ministers and their widows with doctor bills and actual burial expenses. Thus, it was an emergency fund rather than a retirement system, but it performed a needed function at a time when many ministers and their families paid for their sacrifice and dedication with great suffering and deprivation. By 1898 the organization had grown in membership from 31 to 159. Eighteen members had died and payments had reached $2,382.66.[49]

Associational Growth

At the beginning of this period many new associations had recently been formed,[50] and the union meetings, which had served earlier to supplement association life in remote, scattered areas, seemed to come to an end, for they are rarely mentioned. The multiplication of associations beginning near the end of the preceding period and accelerating rapidly during the 1880's and 1890's was in fact one of the distinguishing characteristics of this era. The number of associations increased for several reasons. First, there was in this period a phenomenal increase in population and in the number of churches, and these churches increasingly and justifiably wanted a center of associational life near where they were. Second, new associational organizations were sometimes created because of conflicts which developed within an established association. Third, transportation problems were very great in a day before automobiles, and in a state as long as Florida, when in 1875 one association covered an area as

---

[49] *Ibid.*, pp. 279-281.

[50] See map at the end of this chapter.

large as five today. Subdivision was a necessity. Fourth, sectional jealously not only led to formation of new associations, but, along with conflicts within an association, caused considerable migration of churches, which often changed associations without moving. In some cases a church would join an association outside what one would consider its appropriate territory. For this reason the geographical lines on the association maps are tentative estimates.

As indicated earlier, however, the association meeting during this period continued to perform very important functions in denominational life. During tense years, moreover, the associations developed a sense of identity and a growing awareness of their significance in Convention life. In this period, for example, many associations had their own columns in *The Florida Baptist Witness* for purposes of communication and public relations.

At the beginning of this period few associations were represented in the State Convention sessions. The 1880 Convention, for instance, had representatives from only seven associations, although at least 13 associations had held their own meetings that year.[51] By the end of the 19th century, however, associational representation at the State Convention had increased considerably.

While most associations did not change from their traditional functions described in Chapter Two, the sense of identity and power developing in the associations during this period did in some cases threaten to change tradition in associational function in one regard, namely, discipline. The traditional stance of the associations as described earlier was to give counsel to local churches and individuals where it was sought, but steadfastly to avoid putting any pressure on them. Because of the high incidence of discipline problems occurring in the churches, to be discussed in more detail later, it is understandable that associations would sometimes be tempted to overstep their bounds. A case in point is Marion Association, which voted in 1885 to withdraw fellowship from J. W. McNamara, whose preaching they regarded as contrary to Baptist doctrine.[52] They also voted to tell Equity Church,[53] where he held membership, that if they did not do the same the association would withdraw fellowship from them also.[54] It should be added that this type of attempt at associational discipline was apparently very rare.

---

[51]Florida Baptist Convention, *Annual*, 1880, pp. 10ff.

[52]In what way is not stated.

[53]The name is an ironic coincidence.

[54]Marion Association Column, *Florida Baptist Witness*, Nov. 12, 1885.

The associations had for the most part developed a strong sense of fellowship and had demonstrated a profound concern for missions which contributed to Convention life. For example, Manatee Association paid $800.00 to help send a missionary to Cuba, when most of the churches in its territory were worshipping in log shanties.[55] The associations had become an instrument for sharpening and giving expression to the moral sensitivities which were developing among them. In short, they developed activities which gave them power and significance for a long time to come.

The Great Step Forward in Education: Stetson University

All the developing organizations mentioned above, the Convention, the State Board, the associations, and many small groups and individuals, combined to share in the great strides Florida Baptists made in education during this period.

As indicated earlier, education was one of the first and continuing major concerns of pioneer Florida Baptists, and although very many of their ministers in earlier frontier days and in this era had little or no college training, their awareness of need for such became increasingly intense. Numerous efforts were made between 1850 and 1880 to begin some work in education beyond and outside the local church, and many academies were attempted which sought to provide basic elementary and high school education in a period when no public schools were available.[56] Many of these schools died, and no record of their achievements is available. Others were talked about and never begun. However, the allusions to those begun and to those conceived as possibilities in Florida Baptist records, give significant clues to continuing Baptist concern for education in this period.

Because of its significance for an understanding of later developments in Florida Baptist thought on education, it is important to elaborate on the nature of the basic concern of Florida Baptists as reflected in the early academies referred to above. This basic concern was for a school to serve the general public. Likewise, when they first began to think about a college, Florida Baptists did not think about it as an instrument of the denomination alone. This notion was to develop later. They tended to think, moreover, that while the state might

---

[55]W. L. Mahon, "Origin of Cuban Baptist Mission," *Florida Baptist Witness*, Mar. 2, 1898, p. 1.

[56]Harry C. Garwood, *Stetson University and Florida Baptists* (DeLand, Florida: Florida Baptist Historical Society, 1962), pp. 1-17.

contribute to higher education, the main responsibility for such was with the denominations.[57]

At the beginning of this period, though the enthusiasm for education was great, the possibility of establishing a college apparently was not envisioned. The hope probably still existed, but the conversation focused rather around two specific areas, first, aid for students preparing for the ministry and, second, support for existing schools in other states.[58] However, the Convention *Annual* of 1881 carries a list of trustees of State College, located at Madison, which suggests that the idea of a college still was then being promoted. State College apparently existed on paper only.

In 1882 Convention interest in a college was rekindled when the report of the committee on education reiterated the need for an educated ministry, and reported the interest of F. B. Moodie in establishing a female college. The Convention passed a resolution commending Moodie for his interest, but took no more concrete action.[59]

In 1883 the Convention *Annual* no longer listed trustees of State College in Madison, but rather listed a proposed committee to solicit funds for a female college.[60] The report of the committee indicates that F. B. Moodie was chairman and recommended that Dr. N. B. Wharton be requested to serve as general agent. Again in the 1884 Convention a committee to locate a female college is listed, including H. M. King, R. Bean, P. P. Bishop, T. W. Getzen, and A. E. Kitchen. Interestingly, Bishop had stated earlier that he never expected to live to see the day when Florida Baptists would have a college.[61] However, the committee brought a report that appears more optimistic. The committee brought several resolutions which were rejected in favor of a substitute set of resolutions offered by T. E. Langley. Langley's resolutions called for (1) establishing the college, (2) a board of nine trustees to be elected by the State Board of Missions as soon as the committee reported that it had located the college, (3) the Denomination in the state to provide $10,000.00 in order to secure pledges from the community where the college was to be located, and (4) the president of the Convention to appoint a committee of five to consider and rec-

[57]Editorial, "State Aid to Colleges," *Florida Baptist Witness,* Mar. 25, 1896.
[58]Florida Baptist Convention, *Annual,* 1880, p. 10.
[59]*Ibid.,* 1882, pp. 22, 26, 27.
[60]*Ibid.,* 1883, p. 2.
[61]*Ibid.,* 1884, p. 2.

ommend a location.[62] The resolution adopted was an amendment to the original motion and was adopted only after considerable discussion. The nature of that discussion is a mystery. Significantly, one of the members of Moodie's original committee on locating the college was H. A. DeLand, a former Baptist deacon and Sunday School superintendent from Fairport, New York. DeLand had spent each winter in Florida since 1876. He also founded the town of DeLand and had contributed liberally to the building of the first public school there.[63]

On November 5, 1883, DeLand employed Dr. J. H. Griffith, pastor of the DeLand Baptist Church, to teach a group of young people in the church subjects beyond those taught in the public school which he had helped to establish. This was the beginning of DeLand Academy, as it was later to be named by the trustees.[64] In 1884 DeLand erected a building costing $8,000, later named DeLand Hall, to house the new school. The existence of DeLand Academy was acknowledged in the report of the Convention's committee on education in 1884.[65]

Shortly after the December, 1884 Convention session, DeLand wrote to H. M. King, chairman of the above-mentioned committee of five and made a proposal to the Convention. In brief, DeLand proposed that if the Convention would establish its proposed college in DeLand, he would provide land, cash and pledges having a total value of $15,000.00. He pledged also to let the college use the existing DeLand Academy building for three years, assuming that by then it would be clear what other buildings would be needed. He also pledged more support in the future.[66]

---

[62]Two resolutions offered by the committee were rejected as premature. They called for articles of incorporation and rotation of trustees. See Florida Baptist Convention, *Annual,* 1884, pp. 30-31.

[63]Garwood, *op. cit.,* p. 18.

[64]*Ibid.*

[65]Florida Baptist Convention, *Annual,* 1884, pp. 25, 30-31.

[66]The letter to King read as follows: "My Dear Brother: In accordance with your suggestion, I herewith submit to your committee to locate the college, the proposal I made you when you were here, viz: $6,000.00 cash; a subscription from the citizens of DeLand and vicinity, of not less than $4,000.00 and lands from myself to the amount of $5,000.00, making a total of $15,000.00. In addition to this, I will agree to let the college have the use of rooms for recitations etc., in the Academy building (the college to provide the needful furniture) for a period not to exceed two or three years (three years at most) by which time it will become fully apparent what buildings will be needed,

On February 19, 1885, the "locating committee" made its report to the State Board of Missions. The committee indicated that they had considered three locations, Gainesville, Lake Wier, and DeLand, and recommended that DeLand's offer be accepted. It would appear that the State Board understood DeLand's offer to mean that the property would be deeded to the Convention, since the Board immediately voted to take steps for the incorporation of the Convention.[67] Here, however, was the root of a very serious and unfortunate misunderstanding, because no indication was given in DeLand's letter to H. M. King as to who should hold the deed to the property he was giving. The writer will later make a judgment as to what DeLand's intentions were.

Immediately the State Board of Missions nominated a temporary board of trustees for the proposed college consisting of the following: H. A. DeLand, David Moore, Walter Gwynn, Theodore Shotwell, F. B. Moodie, P. P. Bishop, J. S. Turner, J. H. Griffith, and H. M. King.[68] This temporary board of trustees met on April 31, 1885, and elected H. A. DeLand as President of the Board, Theodore Shotwell, treasurer, and J. H. Griffith, secretary.[69] They agreed to name the school DeLand College, and to make it a quality institution. They also appointed one committee to draw up a charter and another one to raise money for construction of a dormitory.[70] The institution was opened as DeLand College on October 15, 1885, with 33 students.[71] By that time Dr. J. F. Forbes had been named president.

Just before the 1885 State Convention assembled, an editorial appeared in the *Witness* which pointed out that the next step was for the Convention to raise the money they had promised in their initial offer of $10,000.[72] When the Convention of 1885 assembled, the report of the temporary board of trustees was read twice and discussed

---

and it is to be hoped that by or before that time the college will be in a financial condition to erect suitable buildings. I also desire your committee to bear in mind that which I have publicly signified, that with the blessing of God, what I offer to do is ONLY the beginning of my purpose. If, now your committee decide that the cause will be best promoted by locating the college at Lake Weir, no one will more heartily acquiesce than myself. Please let me hear from you as soon as practicable. Fraternally yours, H. A. DeLand."

[67]State Board, *Minutes,* Feb. 19, 1885.

[68]Garwood, *op. cit.,* pp. 22-23.

[69]*Ibid.,* p. 23.

[70]*Ibid.,* p. 24.

[71]*Ibid.,* p. 25.

[72]Editorial, *Florida Baptist Witness,* Nov. 5, 1885.

at some length before adoption. First, the trustees reported that the instructions to the interim board to prepare a charter had not been carried out because it had been judged better to have the college incorporated by a special act of the Legislature. Second, they recommended that a committee of three be elected to nominate a board of 15 trustees, who would then be charged with the responsibility of incorporating the institution. In the meantime the temporary trustees were to handle money and property. Third, they recommended that the Convention accept Mr. DeLand's offer which was to give *to the denomination* all the property belonging to DeLand Academy, provided the denomination in the State at large should raise the $10,000.00 they had earlier pledged.[73]

The committee of three, appointed to nominate 15 trustees for the College, consisted of J. H. Griffith, F. B. Moodie, and J. F. Forbes. At the same session this committee recommended the following to be elected trustees: H. A. DeLand, Theodore Shotwell, M. W. Sargent, J. F. Forbes, D. Moore, J. H. Griffith, J. S. Turner, F. B. Moodie, Whitfield Walker, G. F. Drew, P. P. Bishop, H. M. King, E. C. Hood, Elias Earle, and H. E. Osteen. Interestingly, this list includes all the men who had served on the interim board except Walter Gwynn, and Gwynn was later added when Hood resigned.[74] Great enthusiasm for the new college was very evident, and much talk and much writing were engaged in for promoting the raising of the Convention's pledge and the building of a dormitory. It would appear, however, that the Convention was about to run before it was able and that it was unable to count the cost of building a college against the measure of its own resources, for its resources at the time were meager. The State Board, for example, reported in April, 1886, that DeLand had promised to deed DeLand College to the Convention, though, as indicated earlier, the question of who would hold the deed to the property had *not* yet been that specifically stated by DeLand. This information is important to an understanding of the controversy which was later to develop. In June, 1886, the State Board *Minutes* indicate that no one would lend the Board money to start a church building fund.[75] Thus, the Board was hardly in any position to take over the support of a college. Moreover, it appears that H. A. DeLand had greatly overestimated the financial resources in the Convention, for he obviously expected the Convention to raise very soon the money it had prom-

[73]Florida Baptist Convention, *Annual,* 1885, pp. 35-36.

[74]Garwood, *op. cit.,* p. 28.

[75]State Board, *Minutes,* Apr. 7, 1886, and June 30, 1886.

ised.[76] It is also possible that serious commitment to higher education was something not yet shared by many Florida Baptists, but really only by a very few.

In any case, however, the State Board of Missions shared that commitment, for when Mr. DeLand set a deadline for the Convention's pledge to be paid before he would donate the property, several members of the State Board by their signatures made themselves liable for a note of $10,000.00.[77] That is, they took the Convention's responsibility on themselves as individuals, hoping (1) that this would satisfy Mr. DeLand's requirements, and (2) that the Convention would raise the money for which they made their personal pledges. In the May 4 meeting of the State Board, it was reported that Mr. DeLand was satisfied.[78]

In 1886 an editorial by J. H. Griffith appeared in the *Florida Baptist Witness* which continues the earlier outlook on establishing a Baptist college to serve the public. He wrote concerning the school, "It is for no denomination or section but for our community at large that the school exists. There is nothing sectarian. It is a literary institution. It is as broad as knowledge."[79] Earlier, J. F. Forbes had asked that no one send a child to DeLand College because it was Baptist, or under Baptist control, but because they wanted to send their children to the best school.[80] Of course Forbes and DeLand were at the time trying to stir up enthusiasm in the DeLand area for contributions from various groups, and these statements must in part be related to that fact. These statements appear also to show, however, that they still thought of DeLand College at least partly in terms of its benefits to Florida Baptists, not as Baptists, but as citizens.

In any case, residents in the area of DeLand gave very generously,

---

[76]*Ibid.,* Mar. 2, 1887, where J. W. Place, agent for DeLand College, reported to the Board that Mr. DeLand required the sum of $10,000.00 be raised by the *4th of May* (two months off) or his proposition to donate the property of the College *to the Denomination* would be withdrawn.

[77]The signatures included those of: N. A. Bailey, W. H. Lee, P. C. Drew, B. W. Becks, H. M. King, J. D. Harris, F. B. Moodie, W. M. Ines, John Vinzar, Jr., Thos. W. Getzen, Whitfield Walker, J. H. Goss, and G. W. Hall.

[78]State Board, *Minutes,* May 4, 1887. The minutes of this meeting show that the secretary, N. A. Bailey, in reporting this event, used the word *Convention* in referring to the future holders of the college property, not realizing any conflict between his use of that word and the word *denomination* which he accurately attributed to Mr. DeLand's agent, J. W. Place.

[79]*Florida Baptist Witness,* Feb. 4, 1886.

[80]*Ibid.,* Jan. 7, 1886.

but financial reverses experienced by DeLand created a financial crisis for him and therefore for the college, since, as chairman of the trustees and chief donor, he still carried a heavy responsibility. It is for this reason that he probably felt it necessary to put pressure on the Convention. However, the main sources of help for the first few years were to come not from the Convention but from Northern industrialists who became interested in Stetson through the influence of H. A. DeLand. At the beginning the Convention, aware of its own financial limitations, rejoiced over the generous aid DeLand College was receiving from these other sources. The report on education in 1885 specifically mentioned the generosity of H. A. DeLand, John B. Stetson, and C. T. Sampson, whose contributions, along with those of others, had then brought the total property value of the college to $35,000.00. The report also urged the Convention to complete payment of its part on the endowment.[81]

In January, 1886, the trustees decided to build a dormitory. Henry A. DeLand offered $1,000.00 toward the construction. During the winter of 1886, when John B. Stetson made his first visit to DeLand, he became interested in the school through the influence of Dr. Forbes and gave the largest amount to the construction of the dormitory. C. T. Sampson also contributed to the project. The dormitory was completed at a cost of between $6,000 and $7,000. It was named Stetson Hall, and until Chaudoin Hall was built later, it housed both men and women with walls and separate stairways dividing the men's and women's sections.[82]

The Convention ratified the 1887 action of the State Board in making a note for $10,000.00 to satisfy Mr. DeLand's requirement, at its annual session in 1890.[83] The note called for interest payments until the principal was paid in full. Thus, for several years, the Convention paid small amounts on both interest and principal, expressing the hope each year that it would pay off the endowment that year, but never quite achieving that hope.

In the meantime, however, on April 4, 1887, H. A. DeLand, apparently satisfied with the notes given by the State Board as reported above, conveyed the property of DeLand Academy to John B. Stetson, David Moore and John F. Forbes, as "trustees," legal representatives of the total board of 15 trustees until a legislative charter could be

---

[81]Florida Baptist Convention, *Annual,* 1885, pp. 9-10.

[82]Olga Bowen, "Buildings on Stetson Campus," unpublished manuscript, 1968, Stetson University Library.

[83]Florida Baptist Convention, *Annual,* 1890, pp. 10-16.

secured. This act was in accordance with the recommendation adopted by the Convention in the 1885 session.[84]

The next step was the securing of the charter, and that had to be done quickly because the new school, depending heavily on DeLand's continued support, was seriously threatened at its very birth when DeLand experienced financial disaster because of the disastrous freeze of 1886. Seeking larger support from John B. Stetson, DeLand was told that help would be given when a charter was secured. With the full approval of the trustees, J. F. Forbes and A. G. Hamlin, an attorney, went to work feverishly drawing up a charter to save the school from closing because of financial difficulty.[85] The charter was submitted to the Legislature and enacted into law in 1887, and the trustees held their first meeting under the new charter on January 18, 1888.

The charter called for not less than 18 or more than 24 trustees, three-fourths of whom should be Baptists. Some had wanted the requirement that the trustees hold membership in churches related to the Florida Baptist Convention, but the Convention had rejected that requirement. The president was also a trustee *ex officio,* and had to be a Baptist.[86] Within these limitations, the charter stated that the trustees would elect their own successors.[87] Also, the charter changed the name from DeLand College to DeLand University.[88]

The State Board *Minutes* of April 4, 1888, imply that almost immediately some misunderstanding over the charter was apparent, for they indicate that a special committee was appointed to confer with the DeLand University Trustees on the relation of the University to the Convention. The *Minutes* do not indicate what the difficulty was. Very likely the question was over the recommendations, originally made to the Convention and deleted, which called for (1) a rotating board of trustees and (2) the requirement that three-fourths of the trustees be Baptists holding membership in churches related to the Florida Baptist Convention. Anyway, the appointed committee reported to the State Board their findings on July 4, and their report was adopted. The *Minutes* say that the report was on file with the secre-

---

[84]*Ibid.,* 1885, pp. 35-36.
[85]Letter by A. G. Hamlin, *The Gospel Herald,* May 23, 1903.
[86]Garwood, *op. cit.,* p. 43.
[87]*Ibid.*
[88]Rosser, *op. cit.,* p. 172.

tary, but it does not appear in the *Minutes*. Whatever its contents, the Board apparently was satisfied.[89]

Although as early as 1888, some complaint was heard which questioned the wisdom of locating the college in DeLand, W. N. Chaudoin, executive secretary and past president of the Convention, and trustee of DeLand University, defended the location in editorials of the *Florida Baptist Witness,* Sept. 5, 1888, and Sept. 26, 1888. The complaints apparently did not stop, however, for in 1890, a letter from ministerial students at the University again defended the location.[90] Most reports on the University however, carried nothing but the highest praise, for despite its commitment to quality education, it was also committed to quality religion from the beginning. As the University grew and the reports of the trustees became more detailed, the reports came to include references to the number of students converted during the year, the number joining the church, and the prayer meetings held in the dormitories and in the chapel. In 1890 the total student enrollment was 100.[91] In March, 1898, world famous evangelist Dwight L. Moody came for a series of meetings,[92] and in December evangelist Sam Jones came.[93]

Because of John B. Stetson's generosity in taking the place of Henry DeLand as chief benefactor of the University, Mr. DeLand requested in 1889 that the name of the University be changed to John B. Stetson University. The change was effected without delay, and for several years, Mr. Stetson continued to be the chief supporter of the University.

In 1892, the Convention's note for its part in the endowment promised to Mr. DeLand was still not paid. For several years the income of the Convention had risen steadily, and its obligations and outlay had increased accordingly. Why was support for Stetson so slow in coming? Three possible explanations occur to the writer. First, in its early years Stetson was well financed by Northern capital (except for a brief crisis between H. A. DeLand's financial setback and John B. Stetson's involvement), and many of the trustee reports present only glowing accounts of prosperity and progress with no request for help. The messengers of the Convention quite naturally and easily designated their money therefore to other places they con-

---

[89]State Board, *Minutes,* April 4, and July 4, 1888.
[90]*Florida Baptist Witness,* Apr. 30, 1890.
[91]Florida Baptist Convention, *Annual,* 1890, pp. 16-17.
[92]Editorial, *Florida Baptist Witness,* Mar. 16, 1898.
[93]*Florida Baptist Witness,* Dec. 21, 1898.

sidered more needy. Second, although Stetson was first among Florida colleges, it was established later than most other Southern Baptist colleges, and many of the early Florida Baptists, migrants from other Southern states as they were, were already accustomed to giving as individuals to other schools. This is an important factor because Florida Baptists had no unified budget. All gifts were designated broadly, mostly to missions. It appears that education came to be no longer regarded as a mission project except where ministerial students were involved. Third, the Convention may have assumed that support for ministerial students was enough.

This issue of financial support became a more serious problem in the last decade of the 19th century, for as Stetson grew, its need for support increased. Thus by 1893, the trustees included a request for $5,000 from the Convention for completing a new dormitory. They also asked that the $10,000 endowment note be paid. The report was discussed by twelve different men.[94] Oddly enough, the report of the Convention committee on education, a separate committee, mentions Lakeside College in Lake City, and expressed hope that although it was a small, private enterprise in its infancy, it would become a great educational and spiritual force. While it paised Stetson, it said nothing about the endowment note.[95]

Difficulties besetting Stetson and driving the trustees to ask the Convention for help could not be met by the Convention which was also experiencing increasing financial problems.[96] In 1895, Stetson's trustees again gave glowing reports of progress,[97] while the State Board again reported increasing financial difficulty.[98] But in 1896, the trustees of Stetson not only asked the Convention for extensive help, but noted a decline in enrollment due to the increase in public grammar schools.[99] During the early years of Stetson's history the elementary and secondary schools were not only part of its work, but in fact accounted for the majority of its enrollment. For example, in 1897 the trustees reported 13 enrolled in the college and 36 in the grammar school.[100] Stetson was beginning to feel pinched financially for the first time since the crisis which had occurred at the very be-

---

[94]Florida Baptist Convention, *Annual,* 1893, p. 89.
[95]*Ibid.*, pp. 91-92.
[96]*Ibid.,* 1894, pp. 37-38.
[97]*Ibid.,* 1895, pp. 61-64.
[98]State Board, *Minutes,* March 21, 1895.
[99]Florida Baptist Convention, *Annual,* 1896, pp. 39-44.
[100]*Ibid.,* 1897, p. 34.

Elizabeth Hall, Stetson University

ginning. It would appear that its very progress in constructing needed dormitories and classrooms created additional financial responsibility because of increased staff and maintenance requirements. Through the generosity of John B. Stetson, C. T. Sampson, and others, five buildings had been constructed since DeLand Hall was built in 1884. These buildings included Stetson Hall, constructed in 1886; a gymnasium, constructed in 1891; Elizabeth Hall constructed in three sections in 1892, 1897 and 1898; Holmes Hall, constructed in the late 1880's; and the first two sections of Chaudoin Hall, constructed in 1892 and 1894.[101] However, it was becoming increasingly obvious that the kind of support needed for the best foundation for the future must come for the many rather than the few. Unfortunately, few men either in Stetson or in the Convention recognized this point. The 19th century came to an end and the 20th century was born with lengthy Convention discussion of the indebtedness to Stetson[102] and lamentation over inability to pay the salaries of Convention missionaries.[103] Stetson continued to construct new buildings,[104] planning still others. Much of its help was coming from sources less affected by the recent disastrous freezes than those sources supporting the Convention.

The Beginning of the State Paper

One of the most important events occurring among Florida Baptists during this period was the founding of the State paper, *The Florida Baptist Witness.* Efforts had been made before 1880 to establish some written means of communication and news among Florida Baptists. For example, in 1848 James McDonald began publication in Jacksonville of *The Baptist Telegraph and Florida Emigrant,* but was forced to discontinue it after only a short time.[105] During these early years the *Christian Index,* the Georgia Baptist paper, founded in 1821, served many Florida Baptists, giving generous space to news items about events among Florida Baptists and many Florida Baptists subscribed to it. However, as they grew and developed their own convention and other organizations, many Florida Baptists increasingly desired to have their own paper.

W. N. Chaudoin traces the origin of the *Florida Baptist Witness* to the abortive efforts in the 1860's of two young pastors, one at

---

[101]Bowen, *op. cit.,* p. 1-9.
[102]Florida Baptist Convention, *Annual,* 1899, p. 22.
[103]*Ibid.,* pp. 28-29.
[104]*Ibid.,* 1901, p. 38.
[105]Rosser, *op. cit.,* p. 143.

Thomasville, Georgia, and the other at Monticello, Florida.[106] They chose a name, *The Peninsular Pioneer and Florida Baptist,* and got up a subscription list, but the paper never materialized. In 1872 interest was generated in the Santa Fe River Association and the Florida Association in establishing a Baptist paper in Florida. The Convention, meeting in November, approved the suggested venture, and Hugh B. McCallum was named editor, and T. E. Langley and J. H. Tomkies were named assistant editors. Thus, in 1873, Hugh B. McCallum, pastor at Lake City and publisher of a newspaper, began publication also of *The Florida Baptist.* He was unable to get sufficient financial support, however, and had to discontinue it in 1875.[107] It was a generous effort on the part of McCallum, made largely at his own expense. Efforts made by the Convention in 1876 to revive and continue the paper were vain.[108] The editor apparently gave his subscription list to the *Christian Index,* for in 1880 an ad for that paper in the Florida Baptist Convention *Annual* described the *Index* as the successor to *The Florida Baptist,* with W. N. Chaudoin listed as the Florida editor.

In 1884, with the help and urging of F. B. Moodie, A. P. Ashurst of Columbia, Alabama began the publication of the paper which survived. The name, *The Florida Baptist Witness,* was provided by W. N. Chaudoin.[109] Moodie and Ashurst were editors, and W. N. Chaudoin and N. A. Bailey were associate editors. At the Convention that year the committee on periodicals commended the *Witness* as a necessity for Florida Baptists for three reasons. It was regarded necessary as (1) a medium of communication, (2) as an exponent of Baptist Bible principles and (3) as a medium to inform on religious and secular conditions in the state. Therefore, the paper was reported dedicated to four purposes; namely, (1) to raise the moral tone of the people of Florida, (2) to publicize New Testament principles, (3) to stimulate the missionary spirit, and (4) to rouse the people to the needs of their children in educational matters.[110]

The format and style of the *Witness* at its beginning present a striking contrast to the *Witness* of today. Published weekly, it abounded in patent medicine ads, no doubt an absolute necessity at that time

---

[106]Chaudoin does not mention their names.

[107]W. N. Chaudoin, "Origin of the Witness," *Florida Baptist Witness,* Jan. 9, 1895.

[108]Florida Baptist Convention, *Annual,* 1876, pp. 36 ff.

[109]*Florida Baptist Witness,* Jan. 9, 1895.

[110]Florida Baptist Convention, *Annual,* 1884, p. 24.

for its very survival. It included all kinds of news, religious, secular and scientific, both local, national and international. It was to contribute a great deal to Florida Baptist life.

In March, 1885, the editors, then A. P. Ashurst, W. N. Chaudoin, and C. C. Hill, announced that the paper would be removed to DeLand to be closer to south Florida (really central Florida), from which the bulk of their work came. H. A. DeLand promised to buy $1,000 worth of advertising.[111] The paper was still to be printed at Lake City.[112]

In June, 1885, Ashurst, sole owner of the paper, sold half interest to S. M. Provence, who then replaced C. C. Hill as one of the editors. Provence had recently come to Florida from a pastorate in Columbus, Georgia. Before the year was out a number of associations had regular (sometimes irregular) columns in the *Witness* in which they publicized news events and carried on discussions of current issues in the churches. Usually these columns were edited by the associational missionary.

By January, 1886, the *Witness* had come into the hands of J. H. Griffith, who was editor, and W. H. S. Northrup, who was business manager.[113] By June, however, Griffith had gone and N. A. Bailey and W. N. Chaudoin were listed as editors.[114]

In 1887 the *Witness* was sold by Northrup to L. B. Plummer of DeLand. Plummer then became business manager, and Bailey and Chaudoin were again listed as associate editors.[115] On September 1, P. C. Drew of Lake City was added as associate editor. During that year also "The Home Circle," written by J. H. Porter, became a regular feature column in the *Witness*. As one would expect, it dealt with various aspects of home life.

On October 6, 1887, the name *The Florida Baptist Witness* was shortened to *The Florida Witness*. An editorial explained that for economic reasons the editors had to reduce the size of the paper and it cost less simply to leave out the word *Baptist*. Further, the editors argued, anyone reading the paper would know it was Baptist. A later editor, W. D. Turnley, labeled Plummer's administration as short and weak and stated that the format Plummer had adopted was not popular. He added also that Plummer later became a Presbyterian.[116] On

---

[111]*Florida Baptist Witness,* Feb. 18, 1904.
[112]*Ibid.,* Mar. 26, 1885.
[113]*Ibid.,* Jan. 7, 1886.
[114]*Ibid.,* June 24, 1886.
[115]*Ibid.,* Aug. 4, 1887.
[116]*Ibid.,* Feb. 18, 1904.

November, 1887, a new feature appeared, a column called "University Notes."[117]

On March 29, 1888, the editors announced that the paper would shortly be moved to Ocala. The reason for the move was that Plummer had sold the paper to W. D. Turnley, an Ocala attorney, who now became managing editor. C. H. Nash, became editor-in-chief, and J. C. Porter became field editor. Bailey, Chaudoin and Drew were retained as associate editors.[118] The name *Baptist* was put back in the paper and the paper restored to its earlier size. By then it had 1500 subscribers. Toward the end of Turnley's ownership of the paper publication had to be suspended for several months because the yellow fever epidemic cut off the paper supply due to quarantine regulations.[119]

On November 7, 1888, Turnley sold the *Witness* to M. F. Hood, another attorney. Apparently, the other editors and associates were retained. By then the *Witness* regularly had a "Woman's Department," a "Temperance Column," a "Sunday School Lesson," and a children's section called "Uncle Hall's Corner."[120] In 1890, L. D. Geiger became associate editor, and J. C. Porter, pastor at Lake Weir, and N. A. Bailey of Orlando were listed as correspondents.[121] Interestingly, the "Woman's Department" at this time was not being edited by the State W. M. U. Secretary, Miss Jennie Spaulding, but Mrs. M. F. Hood.

By December, 1890, ownership of the paper came to be shared, for the proprietors were listed as E. C. Hood, M. F. Hood, S. H. Blitch, and J. C. Porter. Associate editors were L. D. Geiger and C. H. Nash.[122]

By January, 1893, Porter and Blitch were listed as publishers, and C. S. Farris, as editor. Issues from May 24, 1893, to January 2, 1895, are missing, but the January 9, 1895, issue shows that the *Witness* was still in Ocala, then in a new building recently dedicated with many speeches and a grand celebration. J. C. Porter was then the sole proprietor. J. F. Forbes, president of Stetson, spoke and W. N. Chaudoin reviewed the history of the *Witness*. Chaudoin's speech described the early history carefully but dismissed the more recent era of Hood with

[117]*Ibid.*, Nov. 17, 1887.
[118]*Ibid.*, Apr. 27, 1888.
[119]*Ibid.*, Feb. 18, 1904.
[120]*Ibid.*, Nov. 7, 1888.
[121]*Ibid.*, Feb. 19, 1890.
[122]*Ibid.*, Dec. 10, 1890.

one sentence. Hood, then living at Lake Weir, resented the neglect, and shortly gave expression to his resentment in the *Witness*.[123] By then Miss J. L. Spaulding, W. M. U. secretary, was in charge of the "Woman's Work Department," and the "Home Circle Department" was edited by Mrs. J. C. Porter. "Uncle Hall's Corner" had disappeared. Giving excellent coverage of all kinds of news and discussions of issues of interest to Florida Baptists, and despite financial problems, the *Witness* continued under J. C. Porter's direction until the end of the century.

Separation of Negro Baptists in Florida

Between 1880 and 1901 the process of separation between Negro and white Florida Baptists, begun earlier, was completed. It was a gradual process,[124] however, and although records describing the process are few, it appears generally to have proceeded peacefully and in friendly spirit. Here and there, however, occur hints that Negro and white Baptists were aware of the increasing hostility between the races toward the end of the century.

Recognition of the progress of separation is seen first in the formation of Negro associations. Not given equal recognition and representation in white Baptist associations, the Negro Baptist churches naturally developed their own. At first, having no state convention, the Negro associations continued with the Florida Baptist Convention. Thus, in 1880 Negro Baptist associations in the Convention included Bethlehem No. 1, Bethlehem No. 2, Jerusalem, and Nazarene Associations. Negro churches then had a total membership of 8,776. White membership at the time totaled almost as much, 8,410.[125] In 1883, however, listing of statistical information on Negro Baptist Churches in Florida is found in the Florida Baptist Convention *Annual* for the last time. At that time eight Negro Baptist associations were listed with a combined membership of 16,857. Compared with the white membership of 9,190 reported, it is obvious that Negro Baptists in Florida at the time were growing much more rapidly than their white Baptist brothers. Probably the growth of their churches

[123] *Ibid.,* Jan. 8, 1895 and Jan. 23, 1895.

[124] First Baptist Church of Sanford had one Negro member until 1891, when she moved her membership by her own choice to South Carolina. See *History of the First Baptist Church of Sanford* (No editor, no date, Stetson University Library), p. 6.

[125] Florida Baptist Convention, *Annual,* pp. 14-15.

was spurred not only by the freedom they found in them,[126] but also by migration to Florida of Negro Baptists from neighboring Southern states, especially as racial tensions increased during the last two decades of the 19th century.

Obviously, by 1883 or early in 1884 Negro Baptist leaders in Florida were laying plans for organizing their own state convention. In their efforts to establish their own autonomy and identity, Negro Baptists were helped and encouraged from the beginning by the Florida Baptist Convention and by the American Baptist Home Mission Society. The Florida Baptist Convention helped (1) by establishing friendly relationships with the "Colored Baptist Convention of Florida" (as it was then designated),[127] (2) by providing some help in the construction of Negro Baptist Churches,[128] (3) by holding institutes for Negro ministers and deacons,[129] (4) by sharing use of buildings with them,[130] and (5) by encouraging support for Negro schools.

The most substantial help received by the emerging Negro Baptist Convention, however, came from the American Baptist Convention. Although the Florida Baptist Convention had formally severed relations with the American Baptist Home Mission Society earlier in favor of the Home Mission Board of the Southern Baptist Convention, many white Baptist churches in Florida continued to receive help from American Baptists well into the period under consideration. Nonetheless, after the formal Convention rejection, most American Baptist aid in Florida was directed appropriately to helping the Negro churches. American Baptists employed missionaries to work among Negroes and gave great help in establishing The Live Oak Institute, which opened in 1880.[131] By 1883 the Live Oak Institute was going well with four teachers. This school continued for many years with moderate success. However, by the beginning of the last decade of the 19th century difficulties were evident, for in 1891 the American Baptist Home Mission Society threatened to withdraw support because they were not satisfied with the results being obtained. Moreover, the school was receiving some harassment from local whites.[132]

---

[126]The church was the only place they had real freedom.

[127]Florida Baptist Convention, *Annual,* 1885, pp. 7-8.

[128]State Board, *Minutes,* Jan. 5, 1886.

[129]*Ibid.,* Jan. 20, 1889.

[130]*Ibid.,* Apr. 8, 1891.

[131]*Florida Baptist Witness,* May 20, 1901; also *Baptist Home Mission Monthly,* Apr. 1883, pp. 87-88.

[132]*Baptist Home Mission Monthly,* Aug., 1892, pp. 277-278.

In the face of local opposition and threatened loss of help from the American Baptist Home Mission Society, Negro Baptists in Florida rallied to keep the school going. Leaders in the Negro Baptist Convention, however, saw only increasing difficulty for a school located in Live Oak. Therefore, they easily agreed to begin another school in Jacksonville, which they considered to be a much better location. By October 5, 1892, the proposed new school in Jacksonville was a reality. It was called Florida Baptist Academy, and was located temporarily in the Bethel Baptist Church.[133] Though still open in 1901 with 174 students, the school at Live Oak was eventually closed. Nonetheless the Live Oak Institute had proved a very significant venture. Its history shows that Negro Baptists in Florida had achieved success in an organized effort in education before their white brothers had. The Institute did not make the progress that Stetson University made because of the lack of financial backing.

Unfortunately, during the last decade of the 19th century relations between Negro and white Florida Baptists appear to have deteriorated. Their relationships probably were affected by racial tensions created by the increasing incidence of lynching in neighboring Southern states and in Florida as well.[134] In denominational life, in any case, the strained relationship between Negro and white Florida Baptists was reflected in the failure of a committee, appointed by the Florida Baptist Convention, to secure agreement by the Colored Baptist Convention to pay half the salary of a missionary (presumably white) to work among the Negroes. According to an editorial in the *Witness,* the Florida Baptist Convention had carried its proposal to the Colored Baptist Convention in Ocala, which was presided over by Rev. W. A. Wilkinson.[135] The committee reported that they were told that the Colored Convention would have to work out their own destiny, and that when they wanted advice and assistance they would ask for it.[136] It must have been extremely humiliating, therefore, when later W. A. Wilkinson was required by the American Baptist Home Mission Society to secure the approval of the Florida Baptist Convention in order to be appointed as a missionary.[137] In 1896 the Convention commended the American Baptist Home Mission Society for its help

[133] *Ibid.,* Aug., 1893, p. 271.

[134] Douglas, *op. cit.,* pp. 231-232.

[135] The term "colored" is used frequently in this section of the manuscript because it was the term most commonly used by Negroes and whites.

[136] *Florida Baptist Witness,* Feb. 11, 1891.

[137] Florida Baptist Convention, *Annual,* 1895, p. 73.

to the colored Baptists of Florida and asked that the help be continued.[138]

While Negro Baptists in Florida could not blame the Florida Baptist Convention for the increase in lynching, their leaders surely must have seen the moral deficiency of such editorials as appeared in the *Witness* in April 5, 1899. Here, the editors commented on a recent report of the lynching of four Negroes in Georgia. They condemned the lynchings of course, but they laid the blame on (1) the open barroom, (2) the quartering of low quality Northern Negro soldiers in the South following the Civil War, and (3) the slow judicial system.[139] Thus, the editors tended to tone down guilt for an unspeakable crime against humanity.

Growing Interest in Social and Moral Issues

As Florida Baptists developed a sense of identity during this period, a part of that identity was the awareness developed of their responsibility to speak out on numerous social, political, and moral questions which came to their attention.

Appropriately, moral concern was first and most extensively expressed among Florida Baptists during this period in efforts among local churches to discipline their own members. The custom of reporting the number of exclusions and restorations in the local church's report to the association developed during this period, and the totals were regularly printed in the State Convention *Annuals*. It is indeed rather shocking to contemporary eyes to see how many were excluded. For a time, nonetheless, the custom of church discipline may have been effective, because in 1890 while 301 were reported excluded, 194 were restored.[140] By 1899, however, the ratio was less favorable, when 648 were excluded and only 244 were restored. As the number excluded grew larger the percentage restored grew smaller, suggesting that at first, most of those excluded were shocked into a change of behavior by the judgment of the church and the community. As late as the 1880's and early 1890's, many Florida communities were very much like earlier frontier communities in other states, where to be condemned by the church was often a very effective means of church and community discipline.[141] It would appear, however, that toward the end of the 1890's the practice of excommunication was

---

[138]*Ibid.*, 1896, p. 35.

[139]Editorial, "Three Acts of Injustice," *Florida Baptist Witness,* Apr. 5, 1899; see also editorial of June 7, 1899.

[140]Florida Baptist Convention, *Annual,* 1889, p. 55.

[141]William Warren Sweet, *Religion on the American Frontier,* Vol. I (New

beginning to lose its effectiveness among Florida Baptist churches.[142] It seems also that some churches went rather far by today's standards in seeking to protect church members from the ways of the world. For example, the Bartow Church passed a resolution without a dissenting vote which threatened with excommunication anyone who engaged in such worldly amusements as saloons, pool rooms, bowling alleys, skating rinks, circuses, dancing, horse racing, card playing, or drinking.[143]

Coincident with the declining effectiveness of efforts at church discipline were increased interest in legislative efforts to control morality. Most significant among the problems envisioned by Florida Baptists as capable of solution by legislation during this era was the alcohol problem. Whereas, during earlier periods Florida Baptists were reluctant to condemn drinking completely, they not only came to do so rather generally between 1880 and 1901, but they became rather active in various movements leading first to control and finally to prohibition of alcohol by legislation.[144] While the main subject of the "Annual Temperance Report" was usually liquor, it sometimes included condemnation of the use of tobacco and snuff.[145]

Another issue which Florida Baptists saw as a moral problem requiring legislative action was Mormonism. The moral issue was polygamy, and the Convention sought an amendment to the Constitution which would prohibit any "polygamist" (Mormon) to hold office.[146] A third issue was sectarian appropriations to Catholic schools, which grew out of the fact that during the 19th century the Catholic church received much federal money for their mission schools to the Indians. Florida Baptist leaders condemned this practice with a strong resolution.[147] Their condemnation of this practice illustrates their early concern for separation of church and state. Their strong response may also reflect, however, some anti-Catholic feeling.[148]

York: Harper Brothers, 1931), pp. 145-146.

[142]Florida Baptist Convention, *Annual,* 1899.

[143]Letter from J. M. Hayman, *Florida Baptist Witness,* July 30, 1885.

[144]Florida Baptist Convention, *Annual,* 1882, p. 27.

[145]*Ibid.,* 1899, pp. 52-54.

[146]*Ibid.,* p. 15.

[147]State Board, *Minutes,* Apr. 4, 1894.

[148]Note, for example, that the budget voted by the State Board in 1894 included $1,200 for the salary of the pastor at St. Augustine. The writer cannot avoid the judgment that this amount ($200 more than Chaudoin received) reflects an interest in a predominantly Catholic town all out of proportion to the size of the community. *Ibid.,* Jan. 14, 1894.

Another moral issue which the Convention viewed as requiring executive action was prize fighting. The Convention supported the efforts of the governor to prevent a prize fight being promoted during the Florida State Fair in Jacksonville.[149]

Other moral issues which provoked some discussion among the churches included dancing, divorce and remarriage. No consensus was reached on these problems, but at least some sharing of thought was done.[150]

In addition, Florida Baptists became interested in politics during this period, and when the editors of the *Witness* declared their support for W. S. Jennings, cousin of the famed William Jennings Bryan, as gubernatorial candidate, many rejoiced.[151]

One other political issue caught the attention of Florida Baptists during the closing years of the 19th century: the conflict which led to the war with Spain. Although the editor urged caution in our political relations with Spain, his sympathies clearly lay with the people of Cuba and against Spain.[152]

Theological Diversity and Controversy

Between 1880 and 1901 Florida Baptists became theologically what they have been ever since: a widely mixed group from many places and representing wide theological variety within the broad stream of Baptist tradition. Theological discussion among Florida Baptists touched many issues during this period, but centered mainly around three; namely, Landmarkism, liberalism, and footwashing. Of these, the most significant and far reaching in its consequences was the Landmark controversy. This controversy, rooted in the convictions of J. M. Pendleton and J. R. Graves that Southern Baptists were falling away from their original doctrines (the old landmarks), had split the Southern Baptist Convention in the 1850's[153] The Landmarkers contended generally for four ideas. First, they contended that the church is only local and visible, that there is no such thing as "the" church. The Kingdom of God in their view is the sum total of all true Baptist churches. One practical conclusion they drew from this conviction was that such organizations as the Foreign Mission

---

[149]Florida Baptist Convention, *Annual,* 1894, p. 17.
[150]*Florida Baptist Witness,* Aug. 1, 1888 and Sept. 3, 1890.
[151]*Ibid.,* June 14, 1899.
[152]*Ibid.,* June 17, 1896, Mar. 2, 1898, and Apr. 6, 1898.
[153]Barnes, *op. cit.,* pp. 112-113.

Board or the Sunday School Board ought not to exist.[154] Second, the Landmarkers argued that valid baptism called for a valid administrator; namely, a properly ordained Baptist minister. They held any other baptism to be worthless. Third, the Landmarkers questioned the legitimacy of other denominations' referring to themselves as churches or their members considering themselves Christians, or their ministers being regarded as such. Finally, the Landmarkers argued that there had been a direct historic succession of true Baptist churches all the way back to the days of the Apostles.[155]

The Landmark movement was largely defeated in its efforts to change the structure of the Southern Baptist Convention and thus bring the Convention into line with its beliefs.[156] The Landmarkers continued their pressure on the Southern Baptist Convention, however, and among Florida Baptists J. R. Graves was a silent but strong influence at the very beginning as indicated in Chapter Two. Also, he was present and lectured twice at the Florida Baptist Convention of 1880. His doctrines were publicly endorsed, moreover, and Graves was praised as "defender of our faith" and worthy to be heard in all the churches.[157]

In 1889 L. D. Geiger wrote in the *Witness* that Southern Baptists were more indebted to J. R. Graves than to any other one man. The reason he gave for that statement was that J. R. Graves had put on the doctrinal brakes when they were needed.[158] Geiger's statement is significant, not only because it drew no opposition in the *Witness* but also because it helps to explain the paradox that while Landmarkism was officially condemned by the Southern Baptist Convention, many Southern Baptists were heavily influenced by some Landmark views.

Obviously, many Southern Baptists saw in Graves a sharp tool which served their own inclination to theological conservatism. Among Florida Baptists especially Landmarkism was a tool which moved some beyond conservatism to exclusivism and theological dogmatism.[159]

---

[154]*Ibid.*, p. 112.

[155]Frank S. Mead, *Handbook of Denominations in the United States* (Nashville: Abingdon Press, 1965), p. 47.

[156]Barnes, *op. cit.*, pp. 112-113.

[157]Florida Baptist Convention, *Annual,* 1880, p. 5.

[158]*Florida Baptist Witness,* May 29, 1889.

[159]C. S. Farris, "A Divided House," *Florida Baptist Witness,* Jan. 30, 1895, p. 69. Cf. R. T. Caddin, "Unbroken Succession of the True Church," *Florida Baptist Witness,* Jan. 5, 1898.

It is very important to observe, however, that while elements of Landmarkism appear here and there among Florida Baptists and indeed appear dominant at times, other views were represented among them also. There was often indeed a kind of fluidity of doctrine which some might find surprising. For example, the First Baptist Church of DeLand adopted a Landmark confession as its first statement of faith, only to replace it shortly with a more traditional statement. Not a word of debate is reported in the *Minutes.*[160]

A second theological issue discussed among some Florida Baptists was the issue centered in the famed Whitsitt controversy. This controversy arose over the claim of Dr. William H. Whitsitt, president of Southern Baptist Theological Seminary, that he was not able to demonstrate the "Baptist succession" theory by his research and that Baptists in England had revived immersion as the mode of baptism in 1641. These judgments, when published in 1896, raised questions about the validity of one of the widely popular tenets of Landmarkism. In the ensuing storm of controversy, Dr. Whitsitt resigned, but the debate continued.[161] J. C. Porter, editor of the *Witness* defended the integrity of Dr. Whitsitt, pointing out that the question was one of historical research and that since most people had not done the research, they were hardly qualified to speak. He claimed that many were guilty, therefore, of starting false rumors.[162]

A final theological issue which created brief discussion in 1889 was the question of whether footwashing was a necessary element in observing the Lord's Supper. The practice of footwashing, apparently widespread during the early anti-mission controversy, had largely died after the defeat of the anti-mission movement among pioneer Florida Baptists. Several notes printed in the August 7 and September 25, 1889, issues of the *Witness,* indicate, however, that in some areas the question of footwashing was still a debated issue. The tone of the discussion makes it clear, nonetheless, that the practice was fast being abandoned in the few areas where it still existed.

Continuation of Sectionalism

One other factor in Florida Baptist life during the last decade of the 19th century is important to present because it is a significant element in setting the stage for the dramatic controversy to be described

---

[160]First Baptist Church, DeLand, *Minutes,* Feb. 27, 1881.

[161]Barnes, *op. cit.,* pp. 137-138.

[162]Editorial, "Dr. Whitsitt Denies the Charge," *Florida Baptist Witness,* Aug. 19, 1896.

in the next chapter. This factor was the continuation or revival of sectionalism. The continuation of hostile feelings between the North and the South as reflected among some Florida Baptists has been mentioned already in connection with discussion of the increase in lynching in the South and the severing of formal relationships with the American Baptist Home Mission Society. In 1887 an editorial appeared in the *Witness* which referred to recent attacks on Southern Baptists by the *National Baptist*. The nature of the attacks was not clarified, but the *Witness* editor replied rather defensively that no white man should be called illogical.[163] The real exposure of the issue of sectionalism, however, came over the discussion of possible reunification of the Southern and the Northern Baptist Conventions. That question led to the reopening of the old wounds of the Civil War conflict. The editor of the *Witness* blamed L. D. Geiger for reopening the controversy among Florida Baptists.[164] Apparently, Geiger had defended the South's right to secede and the right of Confederate soldiers to pensioning equal to the pensioning of Union soldiers.[165] W. N. Chaudoin defended the continued separation between Southern and Northern Baptists, citing on the one hand the danger of centralization inherent in having only one large organization and, on the other hand, the danger of loss of efficiency in the multiplication of "societies" common in the Northern Baptist Convention. Chaudoin was a calming influence, but feelings on the subject were keen. The old spectre of sectionalism could still poison the air when the subject arose, and it was to rise again.[166]

Thus, the end of the 19th century marked the close of a very important era. Two of the most significant events which make this era important were the organization of the State Board of Missions and the establishing of Stetson University, agencies which gave expression to the two major concerns which have always been dominant among Florida Baptists; namely, missions and education.

Problems arising early in the 20th century were to threaten, but not destroy these agencies.

---

[163] *Ibid.*, Dec. 15, 1887.

[164] Editorial "No North and No South," *The Florida Baptist Witness*, June 1, 1888.

[165] *Florida Baptist Witness*, May 25, 1888.

[166] *Ibid.*, Aug. 22, 1888.

Associational Development and Growth

1895

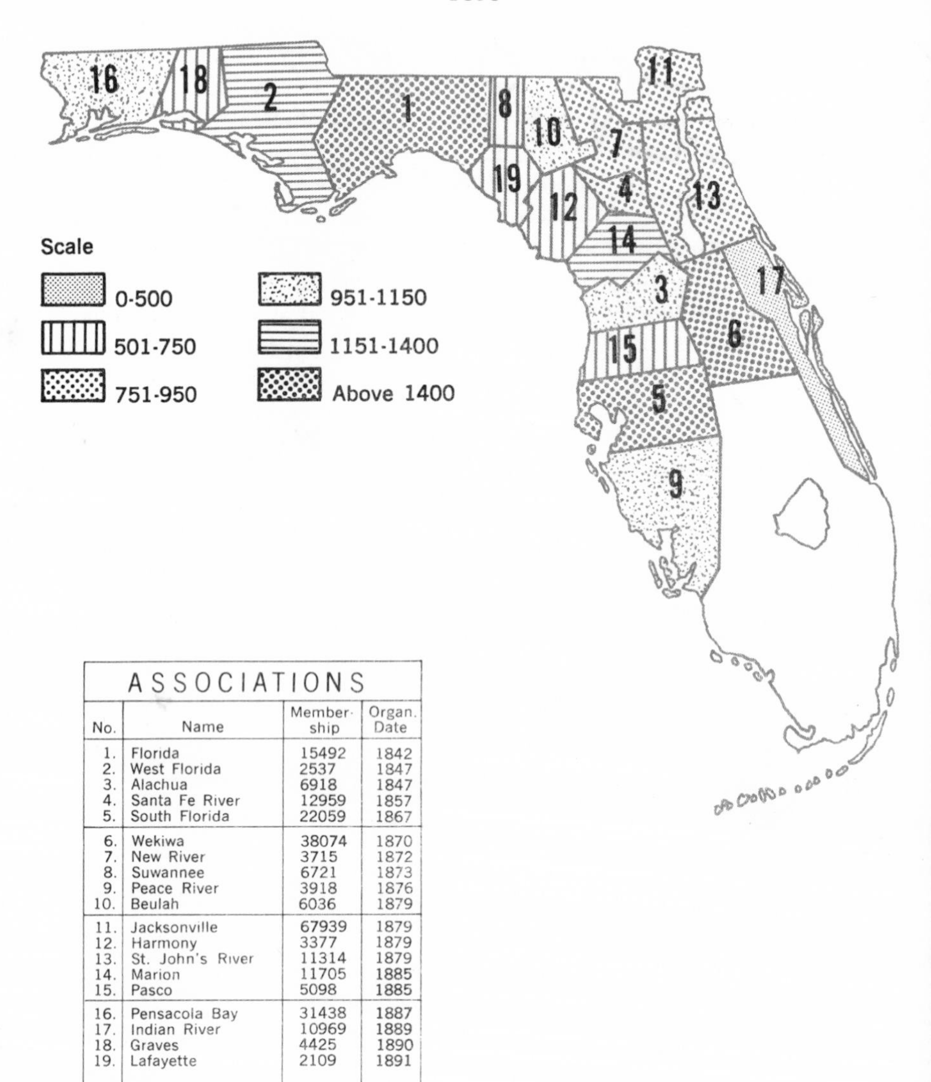

ASSOCIATIONS			
No.	Name	Member-ship	Organ. Date
1.	Florida	15492	1842
2.	West Florida	2537	1847
3.	Alachua	6918	1847
4.	Santa Fe River	12959	1857
5.	South Florida	22059	1867
6.	Wekiwa	38074	1870
7.	New River	3715	1872
8.	Suwannee	6721	1873
9.	Peace River	3918	1876
10.	Beulah	6036	1879
11.	Jacksonville	67939	1879
12.	Harmony	3377	1879
13.	St. John's River	11314	1879
14.	Marion	11705	1885
15.	Pasco	5098	1885
16.	Pensacola Bay	31438	1887
17.	Indian River	10969	1889
18.	Graves	4425	1890
19.	Lafayette	2109	1891

CHAPTER FOUR

Expansion, Recognition, and Controversy: 1901-1940

In a very real sense the birth of the 20th century was for Florida Baptists a premature one, for they were not ready for it. They were still feeling the pinch of financial distress which plagued the whole country, but especially Florida during the last few years of the 19th century. They began the new century therefore with a sense of frustration born, on the one hand, of the economic pessimism present everywhere, and on the other hand, of their awareness of the great needs and challenges which were to confront them in the new century.

These two decades were marked by a definite rise in the economic and social status of Florida Baptists despite the frequent financial difficulties they experienced in their denominational activities. Nowhere is this rise in the social status of Florida Baptists better illustrated than in the report by E. H. Rennolds, chaplain of the Florida Senate in 1911, that Baptists in the State Congress were second in number only to the Methodists in both houses.[1] The social status of Florida Baptists in Florida during this period may also have been reflected in the adoption by the legislature on May 12, 1913, of Florida's first official state song, "Florida, My Florida," written by a Baptist minister, C. V. Waugh, of Lake City, Florida. Waugh was born in Manchester, Virginia on June 8, 1848, and ordained as a Baptist minister in 1873. His first pastorate was the First Baptist Church of Gainesville, Florida, which he began in 1876. In 1893 he was named

[1]E. H. Rennolds, "Religious Census of the Legislature," *Florida Baptist Witness,* Apr. 6, 1911, p. 10.

professor of languages at Florida Agricultural and Mechanical College in Lake City. During that same year he wrote the poem, "Florida, My Florida," and used the German air "Der Tannenbaum," as the musical score.[2] The text of the song is as follows:

Land of my birth, bright sunkissed land,
    Florida, my Florida
Laved by the Gulf and Ocean grand,
    Florida, my Florida
Of all the States in East or West,
Unto my heart thou art the best;
Here may I live, here may I rest,
    Florida, my Florida.

In country, town, or hills and dells,
    Florida, my Florida
The rhythmic chimes of the school bells
    Florida, my Florida
Will call thy children day by day
To learn to walk the patriot's way,
Firmly to stand for thee for aye,
    Florida, my Florida.

Thy golden fruit the world outshines
    Florida, my Florida,
Thy gardens and thy phosphate mines,
    Florida, my Florida
Yield their rich store of good supply,
To still the voice of hunger's cry,
For thee we'll live, for thee we'll die,
    Florida, my Florida.

Th' oppressors rod can't rest on thee,
    Florida, my Florida
Thy sons and daughters free must be,
    Florida, my Florida
From North and South, from East and West,
From freezing blasts they come for rest,
And find in thee their earnest quest,
    Florida, my Florida

---

[2]Kenneth E. Crouch, "State Songs," unpublished manuscript, University of Virginia Library, 1970.

When ills betide and woes o'ertake,
Florida, my Florida
Thy sons and daughters quick will make,
Florida, my Florida
The sacrifice of loves and life
To save from woe, from ills and strife,
To fell thy foes in danger rife,
Florida, my Florida.

An article on "Florida" in the 1910 edition of *Encyclopedia Brittanica* says that in 1906, the Baptists were the strongest denomination in the state.[3] This rise in the numerical strength and social status of many Florida Baptists reflects the extensive migration and the growth of industry in the state. The population grew from 528,542 in 1900 to 968,470 in 1920. Between 1900 and 1910 the percentage increase was 42.4%. Between 1910 and 1920 the percentage rate slowed to 28.7%, still representing significant growth. Baptist growth not only reflected the general population increase, but it exceeded it. In 1901 there were 484 churches with a total membership of 60,874.

Despite significant growth in the general economic prosperity of Florida which was shared by Florida Baptists, there were also significant economic reverses, and these also affected Florida Baptists. Indeed, it would appear that many churches shared only in the economic difficulties which plagued Florida Baptists during this era, and were able, in fact, to survive only because of aid from the Home Mission Board of the Southern Baptist Convention.[4] Some churches did not survive.

Florida Baptists faced many serious crises during this period, and tensions arose often to threaten harmony. By the end of this era, nonetheless, some significant steps forward had been made, steps that have influenced the direction and character of Florida Baptists ever since.

The Character of the Convention

After serving as president of the Convention for a total of 21 years, W. N. Chaudoin stepped down for the last time in 1903. His calm and gentle spirit had guided the Convention and the State Board for more than two decades. No one since has served as president so many

[3] Vol. IX, p. 542.

[4] Victor I. Masters, "The Home Board and Florida Baptists," *The Southern Witness,* July 28, 1907.

times. Moreover, a pattern was broken, for no one since has served as president and executive secretary at the same time. In this period there were eight different presidents, with no one serving more than three terms in succession.

Upon Chaudoin's retirement a significant change in the Convention atmosphere is almost immediately discernible. Whether the shifts in Convention administration reflected the changed atmosphere or were the cause of it is not clear. However, the peace and harmony of the last decades of the 19th century and the beginning years of the 20th century were often interrupted by controversy, strife and economic difficulty. Nevertheless, by the end of this period, because of some excellent leadership, the Convention could look back on some great achievements, and it was prepared to meet some great challenges in the future.

One of the first significant events in the Convention during this period was the securing of a charter, a matter which had been discussed for some years without action.[5]

The growth in the number of churches, made possible in part by migration and in part by continued help from the Home Mission Board,[6] was reflected during this period in a great increase in the number of churches giving to State Missions.[7] This growth of mission interest in general, moreover, came to be expressed in two events which were overdue. First, it was expressed in the appointment in 1904 of the first foreign missionary from Florida. He was Frank J. Fowler, who was appointed along with his wife to serve in Argentina.[8]

Second, the growth of mission interest was expressed in the development of concern for the spiritual welfare of the Seminole Indians. In 1913, a special committee, chaired by Dr. A. J. Holt, who had served as a missionary among the Indians of the West, reported preliminary investigation of the possibilities of evangelism among the Seminole Indians of Florida. Unfortunately, the committee had to report that, due to the hostility among the Seminoles because of the white man's treatment of them, it would be unwise for a white missionary to go among them. They did conclude that the best approach would be made by working through the Home Mission Board to secure a Christian Indian from among the Seminoles in Oklahoma to work among

---

[5]Florida Baptist Convention, *Annual* 1903, p. 30.

[6]*Ibid.,* p. 17.

[7]*Ibid.,* 1905, p. 31.

[8]L. B. Warren, "Florida's First Missionary," *Southern Baptist Witness,* August 4, 1904, p. 6.

the Florida Seminoles.[9] In 1914 the Convention passed a resolution protesting the expropriation of Indian lands by the State of Florida and asking that the land be given back to the Seminoles for a home.[10] In 1916 the State complied with their request and the Federal government gave additional land.[11]

In 1915 the financial crisis in the country and among Florida Baptists was so great that the Convention annual session was not held.[12] By 1920, however, things were looking better, for the Convention made plans to pay all its debts and to give its assigned share of the Southern Baptist Convention Seventy-five Million Campaign, a campaign calculated to pay off Southern Baptist Convention debts and put all the institutions of Southern Baptists on a sound basis.[13]

One aspect of Convention life, the pastor's conference, continued very much as it began earlier. The annual meeting of ministers taking place usually just before the Convention continued with fair regularity during this period and performed a very useful function for the ministers. The conference continued to be centered in sharing insights into practical problems of pastoral ministry and in the discussion of current popular theological questions. Typical examples of the latter were such topics as "Baptist Principles and How Best to Educate the Masses in Them,"[14] and "When, Where and By Whom Was the first Baptist Church Set Up."[15] A paper was usually read, followed by free discussion, which was usually lively.

The State Board, Geiger and Rogers

As indicated earlier in Chapter Three, the State Board of Missions became very quickly the basic instrument through which the purposes and work of the Florida Baptist Convention were served. One of the first significant acts of the State Board at the beginning of this era was to accept executive secretary W. N. Chaudoin's resignation, which he tendered in 1901 because of ill health. Despite ill health throughout his leadership of Florida Baptists, he had served them well.

L. D. Geiger was elected to replace Chaudoin. Geiger was a native of Florida, born at Old Town in Marion County in 1854.

---

[9]Florida Baptist Convention, *Annual,* 1913, pp. 56-59.
[10]*Ibid.,* 1914, p. 50.
[11]Lassiter, *op. cit.,* p. 52.
[12]Florida Baptist Convention, *Annual,* 1916, p. 20.
[13]*Ibid.,* 1920, pp. 9, 17-19.
[14]*Ibid.,* 1903, pp. 6-7.
[15]*Ibid.,* 1906, pp. 6-7.

L. D. Geiger, *Executive Secretary,*
1901 - 1909

Having only a very limited country school education, he was first a Baptist, then became a "Campbellite" preacher for ten years, returning after that to the Baptist fold. Before he became executive secretary, he served a number of churches at various places including Micanopy, Leesburg, Ocala, Apopka, Brooksville and Lakeland.[16] He had served as vice-president of the Convention in 1896 and 1897 and was serving as Chaudoin's assistant at the time Chaudoin retired. By that time, moreover, his leadership and influence among Florida Baptists were widely recognized. In 1902 Stetson University conferred on him the honorary degree of Doctor of Divinity.

Among the first problems Geiger and the board faced were two which recurred often during the first two decades of the 20th century: the lack of money and the shortage of ministers. Both of these problems often impinged on each other, and great lamentation over wide spiritual destitution resulted. The State Board found it impossible to employ and pay much needed missionaries.[17] Some churches found it impossible to hold services. The State Board report to the Convention in 1901, for example, noted that several county seat towns, some with good houses of worship, had been unable to hold regular preaching services during the past year. Among them were Milton, DeFuniak Springs, Bronson and Inverness.[18] Not only were ministers in short supply in Florida, but the prospects of producing Baptist leadership for the future looked slim. In 1904, for instance, only two ministerial students enrolled at Stetson.[19] Moreover, although there apparently were ministers who wanted to come to Florida from other states, Florida Baptists possessed neither the mechanics nor the means for inducing them to come.[20] What is still worse, at least one editorial gently suggests that the quality of some ministers left something to be desired because they used sad, unbelievable stories which exalted eloquence rather than logic. The editor warned those ministers that soon thinking men would lose confidence in them.[21]

Despite economic difficulties in Florida, continued help by the Home Mission Board enabled the State Board to help many churches

---

[16]*Florida Baptist Witness,* Apr. 29, 1909, pp. 2-3.

[17]Editorial by L. D. Geiger, *Florida Baptist Witness,* June 27, 1905.

[18]Florida Baptist Convention, *Annual,* 1901, p. 29.

[19]Editorial, "Ministerial Education," *Florida Baptist Witness,* Mar. 10, 1904.

[20]*Florida Baptist Witness,* Nov. 15, 1903. Column on "Missions" by L. D. Geiger.

[21]Editorial, *The Southern Witness,* (temporary varied name for *Florida Baptist Witness*) Jan. 24, 1907.

and to employ several missionaries. Also, the Board defined the duties of the missionaries more specifically than ever before, thus helping to make the best possible use of their efforts. In 1906 the board began to require a signed statement by each missionary pledging to (1) do colportage work (sell and circulate books), (2) give special attention to Christian work among the colored people, (3) hold meetings for children as often as possible, (4) take, read and promote the State paper, and (5) take an offering for missions at least once each quarter.[22] Similarly, better definition of the work of the board and its agencies was sought in 1907 when W. A. Hobson moved that the Board be organized into departments or committees so that different things coming before them could be referred to a special committee dealing with that subject. The first such committees named were the following: evangelism, education, building, and Sunday School.[23]

In 1909 Dr. L. D. Geiger died. During his eight years as Executive Secretary of Florida Baptists, gifts to missions increased from $13,000 in 1901, the year he became secretary to $75,000 the last year of his work.[24] However, because the needs enlarged faster than the resources, the Board was in debt. S. B. Rogers, then pastor at Gainesville, was elected to replace Geiger.

S. B. Rogers was the first executive secretary of Florida Baptists with university education and theological training. Educated at Mercer University and the University of Chicago, Rogers had served pastorates at Marianna and Chipley before going to Gainesville. A great champion of the temperance cause, he was credited also with uniting a divided Convention, with moving Florida Baptist headquarters from Gainesville to Jacksonville, and with the construction of the Florida Baptist Building, later named the Rogers Building in his memory.[25]

Rogers was an excellent executive and businessman, and although the Board and Convention continued to have financial difficulty during his administration, from his first year in office he made significant moves in the direction of progress. For example, in 1910 he had the Board recommend to the Convention: (1) adoption of a more systematic plan of giving by the churches, (2) adoption of a percentage basis for all causes supported and fostered by the Board, (3) employment of a combination Sunday School and Baptist Young People's

---

[22]State Board, *Minutes,* Aug. 1, 1906.

[23]*Ibid.,* Apr. 11, 1907.

[24]*Florida Baptist Witness,* Apr. 29, 1909, pp. 2-3.

[25]Florida Baptist Convention, *Annual,* 1926, pp. 21-24.

S. B. Rogers, *Executive Secretary,*
1909 - 1926

Union Secretary, and (4) an increase of 20% for State Missions giving during 1910. These recommendations were adopted.[26] It would be difficult to exaggerate the significance of these recommendations. In order to appreciate the importance of the adoption of a systematic budget and percentage apportionment, one must realize that previously contributions were received by the State Missions Board in a rather haphazard manner and used as designated by the contributor. The result was that some mission needs were more than met while others were sadly neglected. The new plan was calculated to provide for a more equitable distribution of funds according to need.

To implement these plans further, the State Board suggested that the churches adopt budgets which stated amounts planned to be contributed to State Missions and to other causes.[27] Following the lead of the Southern Baptist Convention,[28] the State Board became so impressed with the southwide emphasis on efficiency that it recommended: (1) the appointment of a budget committee, (2) the elimination of the State office of associate evangelist, letting the pastors help each other with the evangelizing,[29] and (3) the employment of a combination Sunday School and enlistment man whose responsibility would include the promotion of efficiency in the churches. This concern for efficiency proved to be a controversial issue among Florida Baptists, as for Southern Baptists, at least for a time. One reason was that it appeared to some to set evangelism and efficiency ever against each other.[30] Fortunately, the employment of an efficiency man and better understanding of the purpose and results soon convinced many Florida Baptist churches of the worth of efficiency.[31] One practical result in the churches was the beginning of the every member canvas, a pledging campaign which brought more money into many churches than they had dreamed possible.

However, Rogers apparently suggested changes in the administrative structure of the board which provoked controversy not so easily settled. Rogers and others proposed a unit system of administration in which all work of Florida Baptists, State Missions, Stetson University, and the Florida Baptist Orphans Home would be placed under

---

[26] *Ibid.*, 1910, pp. 17-18.

[27] *Ibid.*, 1914, p. 18.

[28] Barnes, *op. cit.*, p. 177; cf. also Barnes, Chapt. XI.

[29] Florida Baptist Convention, *Annual*, 1914, pp. 25-26.

[30] W. A. Hobson, "Baptist Efficiency," *Florida Baptist Witness*, Feb. 4, 1915.

[31] S. B. Rogers, "Efficiency in the Country," *Florida Baptist Witness*, Apr. 29, 1915.

one board, consisting of one representative from each association, one other from each of four major cities, and an additional number from the area near the headquarters of the Board. The Board would then be divided into three committees, each entrusted with supervision of a department of the work, responsible, of course, to the larger board and through that to the denomination.[32] Obviously, this proposal would have done away with trustees of Stetson and of the Orphanage. C. W. Duke argued strenuously against the proposal along three lines. First, he denied that such a plan would promote efficiency. Second, he argued that the election of trustees by associations rather than by the Convention would widen the gulf between the Convention and its agencies and institutions because it would hide the committees behind a "board" fence and thus create a hierarchy. Finally, he argued that the proposed plan would be an experiment and that Florida Baptists were not yet strong enough to experiment.[33] Rogers tactfully pointed out, however, that the proposed plan was not really very different from the plan under which Florida Baptists were already operating.[34] Rogers had a point, but apparently the Convention was not willing to effect such broad changes in administration structure as the Rogers unit system plan proposed. Nonetheless, many of his suggestions which were carried out by the Board and the Convention greatly improved the administrative efficiency with which Florida Baptists did their work.[35] Because of the improved administrative and economic procedures, the State Board was able, despite frequent economic difficulty, to accomplish many things which would otherwise have been impossible.

Toward the end of this period, the new hope which developed in the Convention generally was reflected in the State Board's actions when in 1918 the Board began authorizing payment of expenses of Board members to attend the Board meetings. In exchange, the

---

[32]Florida Baptist Convention, *Annual,* 1916, pp. 44-45. The minutes show that G. W. Schofield introduced a resolution in which he suggested a committee to study the unit plan of State Board organization in order to promote more efficient administration.

[33]C. W. Duke, "The Unit System for Florida," *Florida Baptist Witness,* Nov. 7, 1916, p. 6. Cf. W. A. Hobson, "The Unit System in Florida," *Florida Baptist Witness,* Dec. 7, 1916. Hobson essentially agreed with Duke, adding that the unit system would involve a dangerous centralization of power. He further argued for changing the charter, which he agreed actually supported the unit system as Dr. Rogers suggested.

[34]*Florida Baptist Witness,* Nov. 16, 1916, p. 4.

[35]State Board, *Minutes,* Feb. 5, 1918.

Board members were then required to stay until the end of each meeting.[36] Also, the earlier skepticism of the enlistment-efficiency move disappeared, for in 1919 three enlistment men were employed as directed by the Convention.[37]

Convention Agencies and Work

Sunday School: Growth Despite Leadership Shortage

At the beginning of this era there were 202 Sunday Schools with a total enrollment of 9,709.[38] Since there were at that time 484 churches with a total membership of 28,139,[39] it is obvious that the Sunday Schools were still teaching only a minority of Florida Baptists. Leaders in Sunday School work realized the importance of the challenge, however, and began in 1903 to hold separate Sunday School conventions to discuss ways of enlarging and improving the teaching ministry. In 1909 the State Board and the Convention already concerned about the need for more Sunday Schools, authorized the employment of the first state secretary to further the work of Sunday Schools and the Baptist Young People's Union.[40] By that time the number of Sunday Schools had increased to 301, with total enrolment of 17,496.[41] With the number of churches then at 569, it is obvious that the percentage of Sunday Schools to churches was increasing.[42] In February, 1910, the State Board employed Louis Entzminger of Kathleen, Florida, as Sunday School and B.Y.P.U. secretary.[43] Under his leadership 28 new Sunday Schools were organized that year.[44] In 1911, however, Entzminger resigned, and in 1912 George Hyman was employed. Hyman worked hard, but progress was slow. In 1913 the first Sunday School encampment was held on the campus of Columbia College. Attendance was good, and enthusiasm high. During the same year Hyman resigned to become pastor at Sanford. For two years, the committee appointed to find someone to replace him, was unsuccessful, and the work was neglected. Enthusiasm for

---

[36] *Ibid.*

[37] *Ibid.* Jan. 16, 1919.

[38] Florida Baptist Convention, *Annual,* 1901, p. 68.

[39] *Ibid.,* p. 70.

[40] *Ibid.,* 1909, p. 78.

[41] P. T. L. Queen, "Sunday School Convention," *Florida Baptist Witness,* May 18, 1911, p. 4.

[42] Florida Baptist Convention, *Annual,* 1909, p. 114.

[43] *Ibid.,* 1910, p. 12.

[44] *Ibid.,* p. 16.

Sunday School did not die, however, for between 1913 and 1915 the number of Sunday Schools increased from 352 to 469, and enrollment climbed from 24,553 to 35,058. In 1914, the State Board employed T. F. Hendon as a combination Sunday School and enlistment man to promote efficiency along with the Sunday School. As mentioned earlier the efficiency work drew criticism, but in view of the continued progress of Sunday School work which followed his employment, one must conclude that he did not impede the work of the Sunday School but helped it.[45]

In 1916 W. W. Willian was elected Sunday School and B.Y.P.U. secretary. Immediately, he began a program of enlargement which was to bear much fruit in years to come. Details of his work will be described in Chapter Five.[46]

Baptist Young People's Union Becomes Accepted

This organization, debated as to its appropriateness in Florida Baptist Churches from its beginning to the end of the 19th century, came to be an accepted part of Florida Baptist life in the early years of the 20th century. In 1905 the first convention committee on B.Y.P.U. work was appointed.[47] The B.Y.P.U. was still a very small movement, however, and was to remain small for many years. District meetings came to be held during this period to discuss ways to enlarge the work among the churches. Dedicated to the training of children and young people for Christian service in the church, its leaders were diligent, but they were always overworked, trying to promote Sunday Schools and Baptist Young People's Unions at the same time. In 1920 there were only 111 senior unions with a total enrollment of 3,514 and 50 junior unions with an enrollment of 1,140. These statistics are more significant than they may appear, for they reflect a sizable increase in the number of young people involved in the total life and work of the church.

In 1920 O. K. Armstrong was elected to be the first B.Y.P.U. secretary. Unfortunately, he resigned after only a few months, and Dr. Willian had to resume the responsibility along with the Sunday School work.[48]

Woman's Missionary Union Enlarges its Work

Between 1901 and 1920 the Woman's Missionary Union continued

---

[45]State Board, *Minutes,* Dec. 8, 1913.

[46]*Ibid.,* Jan. 31, 1916.

[47]Rosser, *op. cit.,* p. 230. The abbreviated form B.Y.P.U. was commonly used to refer to this organization.

[48]*Florida Baptist Witness,* June 17, 1920, p. 9, and Sept. 13, 1921, p. 10.

and enlarged its work of educating for missions and collecting money to support mission work. In 1901 the first mission organization for young women in Florida was assembled in Palm Avenue Baptist Church in Tampa.[49] By 1904 when the Woman's Missionary Union celebrated its first decade as an independent auxiliary, the number of societies had increased from 55 in 1894 to 144 in 1904. Regretfully, the children's bands, without leadership, had declined from 33 to 22. Mission gifts assembled by the women's organization between 1894 and 1904 totaled $22,024.46.

In 1905 the Florida Woman's Missionary Union assumed support of recently appointed missionaries to Argentina, the Reverend and Mrs. Frank J. Fowler.[50] In 1906, Miss J. L. Spaulding's salary as corresponding secretary of Woman's Missionary Union was raised to $600, and she was asked to give full-time service as a traveling secretary rather than promoting the work only by correspondence. In 1909, she traveled a total of 6,396 miles by rail, boat and carriage.[51] In 1907, the name Young Woman's Auxiliary was applied to the 600 organizations for young women which had been established by the Woman's Missionary Union. This event was followed by the organization in 1909 of the first chapter of Royal Ambassadors, a mission organization for boys. This first chapter was organized in Riverside Church in Jacksonville.[52] In 1912, a product of the Florida Woman's Missionary Union, Miss Lulu Sparkman, became the first woman from Florida Baptists to be appointed a foreign missionary. With her husband, A. J. Terry, she served in Brazil for 44 years.

In 1911, having served as corresponding secretary and treasurer for 18 years, Miss Jennie Spaulding resigned.[53] She was succeeded by Mrs. H. C. Peelman, who had been assisting Miss Spaulding as field secretary for some time.[54] In 1914, at the request of the Home Mission Board, Mrs. Peelman went to Cuba and organized the Woman's Missionary Union of Cuba.[54] Also in 1914, the Florida Woman's Missionary Union produced a history of its organization. It was written by Mrs. Louise Porter Hood, of Ocala, and was published at a cost of $240.50[55]

---

[49]Lassiter, *op. cit.*, p. 36.
[50]*Ibid.*, p. 38.
[51]*Ibid.*, p. 39.
[52]*Ibid.*, pp. 40-41.
[53]*Ibid.*, p. 45.
[54]*Ibid.*, p. 46.
[55]*Ibid.*, p. 50.

At the end of this period the Woman's Missionary Union accepted its share of responsibility in the Seventy-five Million Campaign with zeal and enthusiasm.

The Layman's Movement: Forerunner of the Brotherhood

The Layman's Movement was the Baptist response to an inter-denominational Layman's Missionary Movement which sought to enlist men in the work of missions. At first Florida Baptists were as suspicious of this movement as they had been of earlier young people's movements. For a brief time the value of the movement was debated,[56] but by 1909 Ira C. Carter had been appointed by the Convention to promote the Layman's Movement.[57] By 1913, there was a standing committee on the Layman's Movement.[58] Each year through 1919 this standing committee reported to the Convention the progress of the movement. The general interests of various mission enterprises were promoted, but from time to time special projects were stressed. For example, the major project sponsored by the Layman's Movement between 1913 and 1919 was raising money for liquidation of the debts on the Home and Foreign Mission Boards.[59]

Ministerial Relief and the Relief and Annuity Board of the Southern Baptist Convention

The growth of the Baptist Minister's Assurance Association was very slow during this period, for despite the fact that membership was open to various denominational organizations, in 1914 after 30 years of existence the Association had as members only 128 ministers, 85 laymen, and 39 organizations.[60] Florida Baptists were not quite ready to pursue this kind of social responsibility alone. Already, however, they were learning to follow the leadership of the Southern Baptist Convention, and when the Relief and Annuity Board was established by the Southern Baptist Convention in 1918, the Florida Baptist Convention responded in 1919 by voting to cooperate with the Relief and Annuity Board. Thereafter, the work of the Baptist Ministers Assurance Association was to be gradually absorbed into the work of the

---

[56]Florida Baptist Convention, *Annual,* 1911, p. 121.

[57]Editorial, "The Layman's Movement," *Florida Baptist Witness,* Mar. 4, 1909.

[58]Florida Baptist Convention, *Annual,* 1913, p. 6.

[59]*Ibid.,* 1917, p. 46.

[60]Rosser, *op. cit.,* p. 281.

Relief and Annuity Board of the Southern Baptist Convention.[61]

Associational Growth and Complaints

Between 1900 and 1920, ten new associations were organized. These were Middle Florida in 1900, Central in 1903, Bethel in 1905, Santa Rosa in 1907, Miami in 1909, Tampa Bay in 1911, Smyrna in 1912,[62] Black Creek in 1913, Seminole in 1914, and Caloosa in 1916. Together with the older associations, they provided associational meetings in reasonable travel range of churches in most areas of the State by the end of this period. However, through most of this period, transportation was still very limited in many areas, and very slow in all areas by today's standards. Also some associations still represented widely separated areas. For example, Miami Association in 1912 was 262 miles long.[63] Moreover, in those large associations as settlements increased and the number of churches grew, the desire increased for more opportunity for more discussion and inter-church sharing than was possible in the annual association meeting. Thus, the custom of holding smaller district union meetings, which appears to have died in the preceding period, came to life again in the early 1900's. Despite the problem of distance which still existed in some areas, the revival of the union meeting appears to have been less related to the problem of distance than to the need for more discussion and sharing. As before, in the union meeting any problems of interest to the group might be discussed and often were discussed at such great length indeed that many of those attending the meetings came to tire of them.[64] In some cases they apparently became interdenominational meetings,[65] and it seems possible that their interdenominational character in a time when interdenominational conflict was increasing may have accounted for growing criticism of the meetings. Despite criticism, however, the union meeting had some defenders as late as 1919.[66]

---

[61]*Ibid.,* pp. 283-285.

[62]This one later died.

[63]Florida Baptist Convention, *Annual,* 1912, p. 27.

[64]Editorial, significantly entitled "Caught in a Trap," *Florida Baptist Witness,* July 7, 1910.

[65]P. T. L. Queen, "Jacksonville Union Meeting," *Florida Baptist Witness,* Feb. 9, 1911, p. 3. Here the writer praises the meetings, saying they "opened men's eyes to the possibility of world redemption."

[66]R. P. McPherson, "The Union Meeting Menace," *Florida Baptist Witness,* May 8, 1919. Despite the title of the article it is a defense of the union meeting.

The Orphanage: Beginning and Debt

The Florida Baptist Orphanage, long in the planning stage between 1880 and 1900, became a reality in 1904. By 1901, trustees had been elected and the town of Arcadia had been chosen as the location.[67] In 1904, the first building was erected on an 80-acre tract of land and the Orphanage was opened to receive its first child.[68] B. M. Bean was elected to serve as superintendent. Much of the acreage owned by the Orphanage was utilized as farm land and was used to provide part of the food for the Orphanage. In 1905 there were 23 children in the home.[69] When Superintendent Bean died in 1912 the home was in good condition and 75 children were receiving care.[70]

In 1912, J. E. Trice became the superintendent. The number of children receiving care continued to increase, but by 1914 the home reported a deficit of $962.57.[71] Economic adversity in the State accounted in part for the failure of contributions to keep up with the expanding needs of the Orphanage. Unfortunately two other factors may have affected the economic status of the Home. For one thing Trice was sometimes accused of being a poor manager. Also, the scandal which developed raising questions about the character of Trice almost certainly affected the confidence many had in the administration of the Home and thus hurt its support. It appears that anonymous letters were received by notable Florida Baptist leaders which questioned the character of Trice. Able leaders investigated the charges in the letters, and judging them without basis, defended Trice.[72] Rumors continued to spread, nonetheless, and on January 3, 1916, an attempt was made on his life in the form of a shotgun blast through a window. He turned just in time to escape death.

By 1917, the debt was $1,378.48, and the State Board authorized a special campaign.[73] It was to be a long, long campaign, not ending until 1932. Thus, although the Orphanage survived, it was to see many lean years in the next decade.

---

[67]Florida Baptist Convention, *Annual,* 1901, p. 56.

[68]*Ibid.,* 1904, pp. 28-29.

[69]*Ibid.,* 1905, p. 65.

[70]*Ibid.,* 1912, p. 60.

[71]*Ibid.,* 1914, p. 49.

[72]W. A. Hobson, "The Trice Trouble," *Florida Baptist Witness,* Dec. 16, 1915.

[73]State Board, *Minutes,* Jan. 11, 1917.

Education: Stetson Crisis and Conflict

As indicated in Chapter Three, during the first twenty years of its existence, Stetson University received very little financial help from the Convention. The Convention, of course, had little to give, and because through most of those beginning years Stetson appeared to prosper on gifts from other sources, the Convention made little effort to increase its giving. For the most part the Florida Baptist Convention and Stetson University enjoyed friendly relations during those first twenty years. However, as indicated in Chapter Three, some seeds of misunderstanding and discord had already been sown. Around the turn of the century additional tensions developed, and a conjunction of events created serious conflicts between Stetson and the Convention which resulted in a tragic break lasting from 1907 to 1919. This break was without parallel in the history of Southern Baptist State Conventions and their colleges.[74] The crisis reached its climax, and for many appeared to be centered on a controversy over Stetson's charter. Misunderstanding over the nature of the charter had developed several years before the turn of the century, but the conflict had been settled, if only temporarily. In brief, the charter called for a self-perpetuating board of trustees, three-fourths of whose members would be Baptists. The charter also required that the president be a Baptist. Earlier dissatisfaction in the State Board of Missions had been relieved by the explanation by the trustees of the reasons for the charter being framed as it was. By 1907, however, the dissatisfaction with the charter was not only revived, but feeling became so intense that the Convention voted to go to court to get the charter changed.[75] W. S. Jennings, former governor, and Convention president, initiated the move.[76] On the advice of attorneys consulted for the Convention, Jennings went to the Legislature to secure the change. Stetson President Lincoln Hulley also went, however, and defended the charter, successfully, for the Legislature refused to change the charter.[77] The main issue continued to be disagreement over the charter, with some members of the Convention desiring rotation of trustees and direct Convention participation in their election. Without doubt, this conflict was a significant factor and "the straw that broke the camel's

---

[74]It did have an earlier parallel in the break between the American Baptist Convention and Columbian College in Washington, D. C.

[75]Florida Baptist Convention, *Annual,* 1907, pp. 49-51.

[76]Jennings was a cousin of the famed William Jennings Bryan, who later spoke at Stetson.

[77]It is rumored that W. S. Jennings and Lincoln Hulley had a fist fight over the matter.

back." However, a number of other underlying and inter-related factors contributed to the heat and tragedy of the controversy over the charter.

The first of these factors was the Forbes controversy of 1903. It appears that President Forbes' moral character was vigorously attacked,[78] and a terrible scandal broke out in DeLand and around the state over the accusation. The Stetson trustees, the State Board, and the Convention investigated the rumors, and finding no basis for them,[79] completely exonerated President Forbes. Nevertheless, the affair reflected and caused further conflict among Stetson's trustees and heightened the tension between Stetson and the Convention.[80] In 1904, the Convention adopted without discussion a committee report which called for limited and staggered terms for Stetson's trustees, the inclusion of the Convention's president and secretary as ex-officio members of the board, and the changing of the charter to affirm these regulations.[81] President Forbes resigned, and Lincoln Hulley was elected as president.

A second factor contributing to the controversy was a kind of reductivism, common in scientific thought around the turn of the century, which appears to have influenced the thinking of Florida Baptists as they engaged in debate over the charter. It took the form of attempting to solve the charter controversy by reducing it to the question of who owned Stetson University. A kind of either-or, one-cause thinking led many to reason that if the Convention started Stetson, then the Convention should be able to change the charter because the Convention owned it. At the 1907 Convention W. S. Jennings offered resolutions which claimed that the Convention owned Stetson.[82] The resolutions were adopted. The tragedy is that these resolutions were emotionally supported opinions on technical, legal questions of fact, and debate was not the best way to solve the problem. Even the State Board's lawyers were trapped by this kind of thinking.[83] On the other side, some of Stetson's representatives argued that the school was begun independently of the Convention and im-

---

[78]He was accused of being indiscreet with a woman teacher.

[79]One local explanation of the rumor is that Dr. Forbes fired a kitchen employee for mishandling food supplies and the employee got revenge by starting the rumor.

[80]Florida Baptist Convention, *Annual,* 1903, pp. 55-56.

[81]*Ibid.,* 1904, pp. 75-76.

[82]*Ibid.,* 1907, p. 49.

[83]State Board, *Minutes,* Apr. 11, 1970.

plied that the Convention therefore had no say in the matter.[84] The tragedy is that both groups once the controversy got under way, overlooked the simple fact of the complexity of events, persons, and forces which made it possible for Stetson to come into being and to become what it was. Moreover, some of the contending parties failed to recognize that they both wanted the same thing, namely a school that would be controlled by Baptists. Ironically, the charter and some of the property deeds guaranteed that. The real disagreement and misunderstanding, therefore, was over the question of how Baptist control could best be guaranteed. The differences between the contending parties, moreover, reflected their background more than it did their insight into the problem. Convention leaders argued that Baptist control was best guaranteed by Convention control because that was the kind increasingly becoming common among Southern Baptists. DeLand, on the other hand, seems to have preferred control by a board of Baptist trustees because he had concluded that such control worked best in the American Baptist Convention, from which he came. Many Florida Baptists, however, were not satisfied with Baptist control. They wanted Florida Baptist control, and under the circumstances existing then, they did not feel that they had it.

A third factor in the background of the charter controversy consists of the changes which began to take place in Baptist thought about education, changes which were bound to create tension between Stetson and Convention. It is difficult to define these changes precisely, but, in general, early in the 20th century Florida Baptists came to think of their college as now primarily private rather than public,[85] as committed to indoctrination rather than free inquiry, and as committed to development of religion and moral character rather than to the development of the intellect.[86] In short, the college was now expected to share in greater measure burdens previously borne primarily by the churches. It seems very clear that Stetson had already shouldered some of this burden, but was not willing to shoulder more of it, and the Convention was not willing to wait. What accounts for these changes in Florida Baptist thought about education? One cause appears to be the continued influence of Landmarkism, exalted earlier by L. D. Geiger,[87] a former Campbellite preacher who was executive

---

[84] A. G. Hamlin, "Reply to George T. Leitner and Others," *Florida Baptist Witness,* June 14, 1906, pp. 1-2.

[85] Florida Baptist Convention, *Annual,* 1910, p. 55.

[86] *Ibid.,* 1907, pp. 39-40.

[87] See Chapter III.

secretary of the Convention at the time of the break between Stetson and the Convention. Geiger personally made the earliest suggestion the writer could find that the Convention take over the abandoned college property at Lake City and establish a college owned by the Florida Baptist Convention.[88] Landmark influence would of necessity condemn critical investigation in favor of a dogmatic, logical, reductivistic approach to truth in religious matters.[89] In reality this approach was not only contradictory to that which was prominent at Stetson, but to Baptist tradition as well, an approach which emphasized a free and fresh investigation of the truth in Biblical and spiritual study as in other studies. Old convictions were to be exposed to fresh study of the Bible rather than to be used as a mold into which to force the Bible. But many Southern Baptists in general and Florida Baptists in particular were influenced by this narrowing approach to the use of the Bible, and they expected their college to accept that influence.

Another cause of these changes appears to have been the growing apprehensions of some Florida Baptists over the creation of public colleges. They feared that the skepticism they saw in the public colleges would result in neglect of moral training. This fear quite naturally intensified their interest in this element in denominational schools.[90] A third cause of these changes was an increase in interdenominational conflict between Baptists and others which resulted in a kind of Baptist self-centeredness, not without parallel among other denominations, one might add.[91] A final cause of these changes may have been an address by Dr. P. T. Hale at the Southern Baptist Convention. He was reported in the *Witness* as saying, "If our Baptist colleges are not different from those of other denominations and of the state there is no reason why they should exist at all. I believe that the professors of our Baptist institutions should be Baptists."[92] The author who quoted Hale apparently did not intend to knock Stetson, yet he did argue that (1) Stetson should emphasize theology more

---

[88]State Board, *Minutes,* Apr. 11, 1907. However, the idea very likely originated earlier than this earliest suggestion at a meeting of the State Board.

[89]Chapter III, discussion on Landmarkism.

[90]Florida Baptist Convention, *Annual,* 1903, pp. 61-62; 1907, pp. 39-40; and *Annual,* 1910, pp. 55-57.

[91]F. C. Edwards, "The War Renewed," *The Southern Witness,* Nov. 21, 1907.

[92]Southern Baptist Convention, *Annual,* 1907, pp. 25-27.

than law, and (2) Stetson should be more sectarian.[93] For more than 20 years Stetson's President Forbes had boasted that while Stetson was Baptist controlled and profoundly Christian, it was not narrowly sectarian, and no significant complaint was heard. One should of course understand that this boasting in Stetson's early history was calculated to get students and financial help from every honorable source possible. After the turn of the century when other Southern Baptists moved toward a more sectarian view of their colleges and a new sound was heard among Florida Baptists also, the old boasting that Stetson was non-sectarian became very offensive, regardless of the reason.

Hale's address caused a fourth and quite different factor also in the developing conflict between Stetson and the Florida Baptist Convention. It is remarkable that at the very time some Florida Baptists were considering abandoning Stetson and taking over the property of the Florida Agricultural and Mechanical College at Lake City, Hale proposed at the Southern Baptist Convention that a great Baptist university be established in the South. No doubt some Florida Baptists dreamed immediately that the proposed college at Lake City could become that university.[94]

A fifth underlying factor which increased hostility between Stetson and the Convention was the development of inter-collegiate athletics. In 1906, the Convention passed a resolution by F. B. Moodie strongly condemning intercollegiate athletics and asking Stetson to stop such competition.[95] Stetson obviously declined to end such competition, and the Convention did not press the matter. However, as late as 1920, some opposition was still voiced. Here the focus was on football. The editor of the *Witness,* noting a recent football game between Stetson and Mercer, lamented that he was not opposed to athletics, but stated that football was *so deadly* that he had to oppose it.[96]

A sixth factor in the background of the Stetson-Convention charter controversy may have been the continuation of sectionalism, which had become prominent around the turn of the century. Hostility between the North and the South was still not dead in the South, includ-

---

[93]C. R. Pattison, "What Do the Baptists of Florida Need in Their Educational Institution," *The Southern Witness,* Nov. 8, 1906.

[94]F. B. Moodie, "The New Baptist University at Lake City and What it Aspires to Be," *The Southern Witness,* July 4, 1907.

[95]*The Southern Witness,* Jan. 25, 1906, p. 2.

[96]Editorial, "Another Deadly Amusement," *Florida Baptist Witness,* Nov. 26, 1920, p. 2.

ing Florida. This hostility was colored by a peculiar incongruity in Florida in the fact that while Stetson continued to build with cash from generous donors, frequently from the North, the State Board was in debt and having difficulty paying its missionaries. Embarrassment, jealousy and hostility grew out of this combination of facts. Numerous articles in the *Witness* during the early 1900's refer critically and enviously to the acceptance of Northern money by Stetson. In 1912 this criticism found expression in a statement approved by the Convention.[97] This statement, while intended to exalt denominational control of denominational colleges, really exposed the problem of economic support, especially against today's perspective. In particular, the statement warned against the accepting of grants from wealthy corporations. The statement correctly reiterated the need for denominational connection, and suggested that receiving large amounts from wealthy corporations was worse than depending on tax support, since the government could always be called to account. This economic factor was complicated emotionally for Stetson and Florida Baptists also by mutual embarrassment over the Convention's long delay in paying the principal on the $10,000 endowment note pledged as the Convention's part in establishing the college. When the charter controversy began, the note still was not paid.[98] Moreover, Stetson was now feeling the economic pinch, and President Hulley tactfully implied in 1905 that, paradoxically, at the very time of the University's economic need what it got was not money, but criticism.[99] The mutual embarrassment over this issue created mutual hostility, which contributed to high feeling over the charter controversy.

Finally, the controversy may have been abetted by the decline in the number of ministerial students at Stetson since a major interest of Florida Baptists had always been helping ministerial students. An editorial in the *Witness* laments the small number of ministerial students at Stetson in 1902. However, the editor added that the decline was general in other colleges also, and had been in process for 10 years.[100] An editorial in 1904 noted that there were only two ministerial students at Stetson.[101]

Unfortunately as the rift between Stetson and the Convention widened, Stetson's trustees did little to help the situation because clear-

---

[97]Florida Baptist Convention, *Annual,* 1912, pp. 36-37.
[98]*Ibid.,* 1904, p. 60; 1905, p. 32.
[99]*Ibid.,* 1905, pp. 87-90.
[100]*Florida Baptist Witness,* Oct. 22, 1902.
[101]*Ibid.,* Mar. 10, 1904.

ly they were having their own problems and were preoccupied with those problems. They demonstrated less sensitivity to the Convention's committee than was appropriate. In 1906 members of the Committee on Closer Relations with Stetson reported to the Convention that when they appeared before the trustees to voice the Convention's concerns they were treated discourteously and told that the trustees had more pressing problems to attend to at the time. This response suggests also some division between the trustees and the administration of the university since Dr. Farris, a member of the Convention committee, was also Dean of the University. Later, in 1907, the committee reported being received courteously by the trustees, who heard their request for changing the charter so that the Convention would have greater voice in electing trustees. They were told by the trustees, however, that it would be unwise to grant their request, and that since thirteen of the trustees were also in the Convention, the Convention had a clear majority.[102] Furthermore, when the break became imminent and was effected, President Hulley drove the wedge deeper by his vigorous attack on the Convention in *The Gospel Herald,* a paper which he established, and used to present his views on the controversy.

His attack was directed along four main lines. First, he questioned the Convention's claim to the ownership of Stetson.[103] Second, he argued that the Convention's acceptance of money and property from Lake City was a violation of separation of church and state.[104] Third, he debated the economic wisdom of the Convention's attempting to start a new college.[105] Fourth, he disputed the Convention's theory of denominational work, claiming it ignored the sovereignty of the local church.[106] In these arguments Hulley was essentially correct, but in view of the situation and the vituperation in his arguments, Hulley could accomplish nothing but the increased loss of his influence in the Convention.

Despite the break between Stetson and the Convention, Stetson was able to survive because President Hully and the trustees were able to get help from various other sources, including Andrew Carnegie,

---

[102]Florida Baptist Convention, *Annual,* 1907, p. 45.

[103]"The Stetson University Charter," *Gospel Herald,* Apr. 25, 1907, May 16, 1907.

[104]"An Open Letter to Florida Baptists," *Gospel Herald,* Nov. 14, 1907.

[105]Editorial, "Real Estate Values," *Gospel Herald,* Oct. 31, 1907; also "Who Will Pay the Bill," *Ibid.,* Nov. 14, 1907. Here, Hulley, predicted the death of the new school.

[106]"Florida Baptist Convention Issue," *Gospel Herald,* Jan. 30, 1908.

Mrs. Stetson, C. T. Sampson, J. B. Conrad and J. Howell Cummings. Moreover, Stetson continued to grow and added a number of new buildings, including Science Hall (later named Flagler Hall) in 1902, Sampson Hall in 1907 (for a library), Conrad Hall in 1909, and Cummings Gymnasium in 1910.[107]

THE BEGINNING AND THE END OF COLUMBIA COLLEGE

The possibility for the establishing of Columbia College was created by the moving of the State-supported Florida Agricultural and Mechanical College from Lake City to Gainesville. The State gave the abandoned college property and the $15,000 in the treasury to Lake City. The citizens of Lake City, missing the cultural advantages of having a college, offered the money and property to any group that would establish a college there.

After being rebuffed by Stetson trustees in 1906, L. D. Geiger suggested that the State Board consider acquiring the abandoned property at Lake City for the purpose of establishing a Baptist College.[108] By June, 1907, the Education Commission, acting on behalf of the State Board, reported having reached an agreement with the city council of Lake City. The Board then agreed to call a special session of the Convention at Lake City for July 24, 1907.[109] The idea of a new college created great excitement and enthusiasm. Only one dissonant note was sounded in the *Witness*.[110] Albert Carlton of Wauchula advanced three arguments against establishing the new college. First, he questioned whether a convention which would not pay off a $10,000 debt in more than 20 years would in the foreseeable future be able to deal with its annual deficit. Second, he said he saw no change in the nature of Stetson to justify the rash condemnations then rampant. Third, he predicted that in a few years the same ones now condemning Stetson as non-Baptist would return to calling it our Baptist University.[111] Carlton was a true prophet, but his voice was not heard amidst the roar of enthusiasm for the new college. The special session in Lake City was the largest in the Convention's history, with 1500 messengers. Almost $50,000 was pledged towards an endowment goal of $250,000. The completeness of the break with

---

[107]Bowen, *op. cit.*, pp. 9-13.

[108]State Board, *Minutes*, Apr. 11, 1907.

[109]*Ibid.*, June 18, 1907.

[110]"Bro. Carlton Opposes the New College," *The Southern Witness*, July 18, 1907, p. 5.

[111]*Ibid.*

Stetson was symbolized in a debate in 1908 on whether or not to include the annual report of Stetson University in the program. When the program committee read its report and W. A. Hobson noted the omission of the Stetson report, considerable debate followed in which no less than ten messengers spoke, and the report was returned to the program committee for reconsideration. Then, ironically, the people sang "Come, Ye That Love the Lord." Later, the revised program included the report from Stetson. It was to be given on Thursday evening. The *Minutes* however, make no mention of the report from Stetson, though other reports were printed as scheduled.[112]

The new school was named Columbia College, and G. A. Nunnally, of Georgia, was selected as president. With a faculty of eleven the college was opened in October, 1907, and in January, 1908, when the Convention met it had an enrollment of 163.[113] The faculty was able and dedicated, and morale among the students was good. From the beginning, however, the college was plagued with financial difficulties. In 1909, the Columbia trustees reported that although the college had received $3000.00 from the Convention, that amount was not enough to cover expenses.[114] Often more pledges than cash were received, pledges in many instances never to be paid.

At the end of the scholastic year G. A. Nunnally resigned, and Dr. H. W. Tribble was elected president. Despite his noble efforts and increased Convention support, economic pressures mounted. In 1912, Dr. Tribble died after serious injuries received in an accident. After S. B. Rogers declined the invitation to become president, Dr. A. P. Montague, president of Howard College in Alabama, was elected president.[115] Despite his sacrificial efforts, however, the debts increased by 1913 to almost $30,000.00.[116] By 1917, the debt had climbed to $49,559.23.[117] Despite several campaigns and varied efforts to reduce the indebtedness, only small dents were made in it. Before the fall session in 1918, the trustees of Columbia College decided not to reopen the college because of the debt and the lack of students.[118] The property was returned to the city of Lake City. The

---

[112]Florida Baptist Convention, *Annual,* 1908, p. 7.

[113]Rosser, *op. cit.,* pp. 212-213.

[114]Florida Baptist Convention, *Annual,* 1910, pp. 19, 31-32.

[115]Rosser, *op. cit.,* pp. 216-217.

[116]Florida Baptist Convention, *Annual,* 1913, pp. 42-43.

[117]Rosser, *op. cit.,* p. 218.

[118]Florida Baptist Convention, *Annual,* 1919, p. 52. Two factors caused the difficulty in getting students. First, since many colleges were established in the

$15,000 cash had long been spent. The Convention pledged to pay off the remaining indebtedness, and eventually did so by the end of 1920.[119]

Why did the Convention, so full of enthusiasm in 1907 for this new college, fail so miserably in supporting it? Several conclusions seem clear. First, the Convention had again run before ready. Some leaders obsessed with the idea of getting something for nothing let their enthusiasm obscure their foresight. Second, some evidence suggests that the Convention, despite initial enthusiasm, was not really united. It is rather remarkable, for example, that in 1909, when L. D. Geiger read the proposed Convention program as prepared by the executive committee, it was only partially adopted after lengthy discussion and many amendments.[120] The messengers even dispensed with the Convention sermon. A third conclusion is that serious commitment to anything beyond ministerial education was still shared by only a few leaders. Furthermore, the school did not have the support necessary for survival, even from Convention leaders. For example, C. C. Carroll lamented that the Education Commission, created to guarantee the permanency of the school, was never able to get a quorum present at a meeting.[121] Similarly, throughout the life of Columbia College, notable Convention leaders, including trustees of Columbia, continued to send their children to Stetson. Finally, and perhaps most significantly, while it is clear that the Convention still had its dual interests in missions and education, during this period the Convention simply took on more than it could handle. Although the overall financial resources of the Convention increased substantially between 1900 and 1920, its commitments increased even more. For example, in 1913, which was a record year for the Convention with $97,241.93 in receipts, Columbia College was $30,000 in debt. Two facts seem clear. First, the Convention was giving to Columbia more generously than ever. For example between 1908 and 1918, the Convention gave to Columbia College over $90,783.00, which was more than the Convention had ever given to Stetson. Second, the Conven-

---

early 1900's, competition for students became very keen. During these years, the *Witness* carried many advertisements for schools all over the country. Second, and most significant was World War I, which took many students from all colleges. Thus, the competition for those who could continue in college became even greater, and a small, new college like Columbia had little chance of survival.

[119]*Ibid.*, 1920, p. 22.

[120]*Ibid.*, 1909, p. 7.

[121]Garwood, *op. cit.*, p. 145.

tion employed 81 missionaries that year, a very large obligation in itself.

Stetson-Convention Relationship Renewed

It is very clear from the report of the Convention's education committee in 1919 that interest in education had not died among Florida Baptists.[122] Immediately after the closing of Columbia College, exploration of ways to renew relationships with Stetson University began.[123] Stetson had remained committed to Christian education throughout the break, and President Hulley apparently held no grudges. When the Convention met in DeLand in 1911, he invited the messengers into his home for tea. Obviously, the leaders of the Convention were also interested in healing the breach. Both they and President Hulley were willing to give a little. Thus a new agreement was reached.[124] The Convention and Stetson's trustees agreed on the following points: (1) that a majority of Stetson trustees should be resident Florida Baptists, affiliated with Florida Baptist churches and with the Convention and that movement to implement this goal should be made immediately, (2) that only those trustees should be elected who had first been approved by the Florida Baptist Convention, and (3) that the Convention would give the full weight of its influence to the moral, religious, and financial support of Stetson.[125]

Unfortunately, the differences between Stetson and the Convention were not completely solved. Some of the causes of tension were forgotten completely, as they should have been, but others were glossed over temporarily only to be raised again. The charter controversy was one of them. For the next few years, however, relations between Stetson and the Convention were very good.

The State Paper: Migration and Metamorphoses of the *Florida Baptist Witness*

At the beginning of the 20th century, the *Florida Baptist Witness* was still being published in Ocala by J. C. Porter. In 1902 W. N. Chaudoin was listed as associate editor. When the Forbes controversy of 1903 arose, John B. Stetson and some of his friends apparently were not pleased with the action of the Convention in exonerating

---

[122]Florida Baptist Convention, *Annual,* 1919, pp. 53-56.

[123]*Ibid.,* p. 56.

[124]*Ibid.,* 1920, pp. 18-19.

[125]*Ibid.,* pp. 13-24.

Dr. Forbes. To publicize their version of the controversy, J. B. Holly began a new paper, the *Southern Baptist,* first published in Jacksonville in April, 1903. Before he died in 1904 J. C. Porter sold the *Florida Baptist Witness* to a company represented by W. L. C. Mahon. Then W. A. Hobson, pastor of the First Baptist Church in Jacksonville, and one of his church members, D. H. McMillan, bought the *Florida Baptist Witness* from Mahon and prepared to publish it in Jacksonville. Hobson, convinced that the competing papers could cause only greater harm, persuaded Mr. Stetson to discontinue the *Southern Baptist* and to throw his weight behind the *Florida Baptist Witness.* Thus, in February of 1904 the two papers were merged under the name, *The Florida Baptist Witness.* Hobson was to serve as editor and Holly as business manager and field representative. The policy of the consolidated paper was (1) to work for all denominational interests, (2) to uphold Stetson University and the Orphanage, and (3) to unify the Baptist people in all denominational enterprises.[126]

Disagreements among the owners of the paper, however, made harmony impossible, and to solve the problem Mr. Stetson agreed to buy out the other parties and convey ownership of the paper to the Convention.[127] Mr. Stetson required that it be moved to Orlando, where a better bid for printing had been found. F. C. Edwards became managing editor with C. S. Farris and C. H. Nash as editors. Thus, the *Florida Baptist Witness* was to be published exclusively by the Convention. It was to be directed for the Convention by a publication board consisting of A. A. Murphree, B. B. Tatum, and E. O. Painter.[128] By March, 1905, the name had been changed to *The Southern Witness,* and with the new name came a new format and location. It was a smaller paper with larger type and was being printed in DeLand.[129] Still beset with economic difficulties, the paper was able to continue with help from Mr. Stetson.[130]

At the end of 1906, Edwards resigned as managing editor and J. H. Tharp, pastor at Arcadia, was named editor.[131] The paper

---

[126]*Southern Baptist Witness,* June 2, 1904.

[127]Rosser, *op. cit.,* pp. 149-151. Also Florida Baptist Convention, *Annual,* 1905, p. 51.

[128]*The Florida Baptist,* Feb. 1, 1905.

[129]*The Southern Witness,* Mar. 2, 1905.

[130]Rosser, *op. cit.,* p. 152.

[131]*Ibid.*

moved to Ocala to obtain lower printing prices.[132] In 1908 the *Witness* was moved to Arcadia, and the name was changed back to the *Florida Baptist Witness*. Still having financial problems, editor Tharp warned his readers against the false claims of medical ads in the paper, explaining that he had to take them in order to make expenses.[133] Yet he eliminated all medical ads before he resigned, in January, 1909.[134]

The Publication Board of the Convention then secured C. M. Brittain, pastor at Lake City, and Frank Edwards, pastor at Starke, to serve as editors, with Miss S. D. Fannin as field editor.[135] In March, 1909, the paper moved again, this time to Jacksonville, keeping the same staff. In April, 1910, the editors announced another move, this time to Lakeland, and W. J. Sullivan was then listed as field editor.[136] In September, 1910, the editors bewailed their economic woes and begged people to pay up their subscriptions.[137]

In 1911, the Publication Board announced plans to release Brittain and Edwards from their contracts as editors and to employ E. Z. Golden, of West Point, Georgia, as editor and business manager.[138] The continued economic difficulties caused many to become dissatisfied with the existing arrangement now that the Convention, always beset with its own financial difficulties, was responsible for the deficit. Thus, at the 1911 Convention a motion was made to abolish the Publication Board. It lost by a close vote,[139] but in 1912, when the same suggestion came from the State Board, it passed, and the State Board took charge of publishing the *Witness*.

On March 13, 1912, the State Board sold the *Witness,* then printed in Arcadia, to W. D. Nowlin, pastor at Lakeland, for $2,000, and Nowlin became editor.[140] Not able to make the paper profitable, Nowlin kept it only two years and in 1914 sold it to Dave Scott, J. L. Livingston and J. E. Trice, of Arcadia. The new owners employed A. J. Holt to serve as editor. Although others assisted in the writing

[132]*The Southern Witness,* Mar. 7, 1907.

[133]*Florida Baptist Witness,* Mar. 26, 1908, p. 4.

[134]Florida Baptist Convention, *Annual,* 1909, p. 25.

[135]*Florida Baptist Witness,* Feb. 11, 1909.

[136]*Ibid.,* Apr. 14, 1910.

[137]*Ibid.,* Sept. 8, 1910, p. 1.

[138]Brittain was serving as editor without pay, and was able to live only by supplying in pulpits and by holding revival meetings. Edwards had continued his pastorate. Rosser, *op. cit.,* p. 153.

[139]Florida Baptist Convention, *Annual,* 1911, p. 72.

[140]*Ibid.,* 1912, pp. 19-20.

at times, Holt continued as editor until February, 1918, while also serving as pastor at Arcadia. The paper continued to operate at a loss. In 1918, the State Board decided to buy the paper, did so, and employed J. W. Mitchell from Parkersburg, West Virginia, as editor and manager. Dr. Mitchell was an experienced journalist and a good businessman. The *Witness* was moved back to Jacksonville, hopefully its permanent home.

Despite the frequent movement, the continuing changes in administration, and the recurring economic problems which plagued the *Florida Baptist Witness* between 1900 and 1920, the paper served its purposes well in the life of Florida Baptists. With great fairness, the editors reported significant events and gave space to diverse points of view. Moreover, they generally tried to maintain balanced perspectives on points of controversy and were sensitive to what was going on in the world. The denominational paper, like the denominational schools, deserved more support than Florida Baptists were able or willing to give.

Theological Developments and Diversity

Despite the continued influence of Landmarkism mentioned above, it would be an error to classify Florida Baptists during this period as predominantly Landmark in basic theological orientation. Undoubtedly, Landmark ideas did continue to affect the thinking of many Florida Baptists in some areas.[141] However, the diversity of theological ideas affecting the thinking of many Florida Baptists would probably have amazed many Florida Baptists had they been able to recognize those ideas for what they were. For example, many Florida Baptists would have been amazed at the extent to which liberalism, which reached its height in American Protestant thought between 1890 and 1910, affected their thinking during this period. The central feature of Protestant liberalism reflected among Florida Baptists was the optimism concerning the Kingdom of God and its possibilities for the future here on earth. With this optimism was combined a simplistic, reductivistic approach to the solution of problems, also a characteristic of liberalism. Nowhere can these combined liberal elements better be seen than in Florida Baptist thought on the temperance movement.[142] In brief, the many social problems of the country, for

---

[141]W. G. Patterson, "More about Landmarkism," *The Southern Witness*, Feb. 21, 1907.

[142]The temperance movement itself will be discussed in more detail in a later section.

many Florida Baptists as for other Southern Baptists, could be related or reduced to one; namely, the alcohol problem. Solve that, they thought, and the country would move toward a perfect civilization. Florida Baptist Convention temperance reports, for example, viewed the growth of support for the temperance movement as symbolic of the movement of the country "toward a higher and more perfect civilization."[143] The same optimism, moreover, was applied to other areas. For example, an editorial in 1919, discussing the social problems of the day, suggested that the golden rule and brotherly love would solve all labor-capital problems and all war-peace problems.[144]

Another example of the influence of liberalism among Florida Baptists is to be seen in the pessimism sometimes expressed concerning the place and future of evangelism. Reflective of the influence of Horace Bushnell's emphasis on growth and his critique of traditional evangelism, the "Report of the State Board of Missions" in 1919 observed "that evangelism which has for its ambition a great ingathering into the churches has passed its day of usefulness, if it ever had one."[145] The report went on, as Bushnell would have done, to call for a balance between evangelism and mature growth.[146]

However, these liberal elements in Florida Baptist thought were more than matched by reactions against liberalism also found among Florida Baptists. Although liberalism affected the thought of many Florida Baptists, it was never praised. On the contrary, it produced or contributed to a number of reactionary movements or tendencies among Florida Baptists. One of these reactionary tendencies was expressed in the condemnation of church unionism (not to be confused with the union meetings among Florida Baptists, described earlier). The ecumenical movement, like liberalism, was centered generally in the North and was not well understood by Florida Baptists, though they knew about it and recognized their own need for unity. They condemned the ecumenical movement, however, because they viewed it as requiring compromise in doctrine and practice.[147] Moreover,

---

[143]Florida Baptist Convention, *Annual,* 1906, p. 39.

[144]J. W. Mitchell, editorial, "Our Labor Troubles," *Florida Baptist Witness,* Dec. 4, 1919.

[145]Florida Baptist Convention, *Annual,* 1918, pp. 16-17.

[146]*Ibid.*

[147]Editorial, "Concerning Unionism," *Florida Baptist Witness,* Feb. 20, 1919. Cf. editorial, "Inter-church World Movement," *Ibid.,* Apr. 22, 1920, p. 7.

they warned Negro Baptists against the movement,[148] and even asked churches not to call pastors who had sympathy with it.[149]

Another reactionary tendency was expressed in the condemnation of Northern liberals by name. Washington Gladden was particularly singled out in connection with his attack on the Congregational Board of Missions for accepting money from John D. Rockefeller, whose business methods Gladden criticized. The editors of the *Witness* defended Rockefeller and condemned Gladden.[150]

A third example of Florida Baptist reaction to liberalism was a growing tendency to theological dogmatism. An editorial in 1911 is a typical example of this tendency. It read as follows:

> . . . The fundamentals of Christianity are set forth in certain great dogmas. An attempt to understand, leaves Christianity no certain foundations. Strict so-called scientific methods in the study of the tenets of Christianity will always lead toward infidelity . . .[151]

The mixture of theological elements one finds among Florida Baptists during this era indicates that although they were making some progress in their educational development, Florida Baptists still had a long way to go. Nothing is more suggestive of this judgment than the fact that S. B. Rogers was the first executive secretary of Florida Baptists to have formal theological training. Furthermore, even those who were generally well educated sometimes lacked the theological sophistication to recognize significant differences in theological viewpoints. Editor Mitchell's comment on Landmarkism is typical of this lack of theological awareness. Concerning the Landmarkers, he wrote: "They are good folks, and there is not much difference, in fact, if they were stood up side by side with us, no one could distinguish between us."[152] Nonetheless, the very theological diversity reflected among Florida Baptists during this period is indicative of a growing sensitivity to what was going on in the theological world outside their own circle.

---

[148]State Board, *Minutes,* Feb. 24, 1920.

[149]*Ibid.*

[150]Other Florida Baptists, however, sometimes condemned Northern industrialists rather generally, as did the social-ethics-minded Northern liberals. See section on Stetson earlier in this chapter.

[151]"Dogma and Fidelity," *Florida Baptist Witness,* Mar. 9, 1911, p. 6.

[152]Editorial, "The Final Word," *Florida Baptist Witness,* June 5, 1919, p. 2.

Social, Moral Concern and Legislation

In the area of social concern some Florida Baptists made their greatest progress, while others stood still. Significantly the prevailing tendencies in Florida Baptist thought reflected sensitivity and awareness of insights into the social meaning of the Christian faith being reached by Christians in other parts of the country. Florida Baptists became particularly responsive to the progress of the leadership of the Southern Baptist Convention in social-ethical questions. In some of their social criticisms Florida Baptists reflected the influence of Northern liberals, but most often reflected their own growing social consciousness.

While Florida Baptists were interested in a broad social-ethical issues, the one movement which evoked the greatest and most enduring concern was the temperance movement. Although Florida Baptists were reluctant at first to join the movement condemning drinking,[153] they became passionately committed during this period to doing away with the manufacture and sale of alcoholic beverages. However, there sometimes appeared in the midst of strong prohibition statements, reflections of an older, more tolerant attitude. The following excerpt from a 1912 temperance report is a classic example:

> . . . Time was when a man could drink whiskey to excess and defy the laws of God and man by living out his alloted span of life, but not today. For the whiskies and brandies and wines and beers of today are not those that our forefathers once kept in their decanters and gave to their guests and drank themselves. By no means no. Those beverages were made from wholesome grain and apples and pears and peaches. But the intoxicating drinks of today are blends and decoctions, forged with the liquid fires of torment and into them go the deadly night shade and aqua fortis and capudine and capesam and cayenne pepper, and the poisonous fusil oil. Into the lighter drinks of wine and beer there go the fumes of sulphuric and carbolic acid. The consequence is that men today do not know the comparatively harmless drink of ancient times, but when they become intoxicated on these fiery beverages they turn loose whole menageries of wild and tormented beasts into their maddened brains.[154]

Obviously, the author of this report had read the labels on the bottles

---

[153]See Chapters II and III.

[154]Florida Baptist Convention, *Annual,* 1912, pp. 69-70.

carefully, and his conclusion was that they do not make wine as they once did.

Shortly after the turn of the century, the temperance report calling for prohibition became a regular part of each session of the Convention. The Convention supported and followed the progress of various kinds of legislation which prepared the way for the prohibition amendment, and many members rejoiced when it was finally passed.[155] Though the temperance report recognized that the fight was not over, many Florida Baptists equated the progress of the temperance movement with the progress of the kingdom of God.[156] Political candidates moreover, were increasingly evaluated by their views toward prohibition.[157]

What is perhaps most significant about the temperance movement among Florida Baptists is that it reflects their sensitivity to the social awakening among Southern Baptists and Protestants generally. An editorial in 1909 reflected contemporary thinking of many Florida Baptists when the editor defended the right of Baptists to bring all Christian influence to bear on the moral and civic conditions in which men live.[158] In the case of temperance as well as other issues this right came to be interpreted as the right to use legislation to regulate the conditions under which men live. Among the issues for which Florida Baptists saw legislative control as appropriate were Sunday laws and Mormons serving in public office.[159] A resolution called for laws prohibiting Sunday baseball, football, horse racing because such practices were corrupting the morals of the people of the State.[160] On another occasion the editor said Mormonism was far more destructive than liquor ever was.[161]

Apparently, Florida Baptists saw no infringement on the religious liberty of anyone in calling for Sunday laws and for legal restrictions on Mormonism, since the one area of social concern that evoked the most comment, next to temperance, was religious liberty. The comments on religious liberty were aroused during World War I when many Southern Baptists received word that restrictions had been placed on J. B. Gambrell by a military officer when Gambrell and

---

[155]*Ibid.*, 1920, p. 72.
[156]*Ibid.*, 1906, p. 29.
[157]*Florida Baptist Witness,* June, 1908, p. 5.
[158]*Ibid.*, Mar. 18, 1909, p. 4.
[159]Florida Baptist Convention, *Annual,* 1905, pp. 82-83.
[160]*Ibid.*, 1918, p. 44.
[161]*Florida Baptist Witness,* Feb. 6, 1919, p. 3.

others from the Home Mission Board sought to hold revival meetings among the military troops in Texas. The Convention protested this action, accusing the officer of censoring religious teaching.[162] The many articles protesting this restriction of religious liberty which appeared in the *Witness* indicate that Florida Baptists were not only alert to what was going on, but were especially sensitive to the basic concern that had made their history most distinctive, namely, religious liberty.[163]

World War I did not produce only protest among Florida Baptists, however. It also aroused their patriotism, with which was combined a deep concern for the spiritual welfare of the soldiers. Nowhere is the patriotism aroused better expressed than in an editorial by Dr. A. J. Holt. He said that citizens owe the government three things: (1) taxes, (2) loyalty, and (3) service, and that if the government calls young men should go.[164] Spiritual concern for the soldiers brought two kinds of volunteers from Florida Baptists. Some became military chaplains. Among them was George Hyman who had served the Convention as Sunday School secretary.[165] Others left their churches for brief periods to become camp pastors in military posts near their churches. Frequently, these camp pastors would secure leaves of absence from their churches, and being subsidized by the Home Mission Board, would set up something like a temporary mission near a military post. Many outstanding Florida pastors, including W. A. Hobson of First Church of Jacksonville, gave themselves sacrificially to this work. For a time the military authorities gave freedom of movement to these camp pastors, but before the end of the war their liberties began to be curtailed, as indicated above, and when the war ended the War Department prohibited further camp mission work. Under the leadership of S. B. Rogers, the State Board decided to honor the restriction of the War Department.[166] By 1920 the swing to pacifism had begun and the editor of the *Witness* was reflecting the changing style of Christian thought when he stated that all Christians should condemn war.[167]

---

[162]Florida Baptist Convention, *Annual,* 1917, p. 68.

[163]For example, C. W. Duke, "General Funston and Religious Liberty," *Florida Baptist Witness,* Nov. 30, 1916, p. 2.

[164]"Render Unto Caesar the Things that are Caesar's," *Florida Baptist Witness,* Apr. 26, 1917, p. 6.

[165]*Florida Baptist Witness,* May 18, 1919, where he was honored for his service by a picture on the front page of the *Witness.*

[166]State Board, *Minutes,* Feb. 4, 1919.

[167]Editorial, "The God of War," *Florida Baptist Witness,* Nov. 4, 1920, p. 2.

Three other areas of social concern caught the attention of some Florida Baptists during this period. One was the question of woman suffrage. Oddly enough, although the Convention in 1881 had recognized the equality of women with men as Baptists by voting them full status as messengers, the Convention of 1919 was not quite ready to accord them equal status with men as voting citizens, for the Convention tabled a resolution calling for support of woman suffrage.[168] Another area of social concern which caught the attention of some Florida Baptists was the praise heaped on notable industrialists who became known for their philanthropy. Though these philanthropists were occasionally praised by Florida Baptists, their ethics were sometimes questioned, and the editor of the *Witness* wisely warned against equating Christianity with philanthropy, as some did.[169] A final area of social concern which developed among Florida Baptists during this era was for a ministry to the sick. From time to time in earlier periods, resolutions expressing concern for a ministry to the sick had been passed, but the first concrete plans for establishing a hospital appear to have developed during this period. In 1907, the Convention authorized a committee to plan for establishing a hospital.[170] Unfortunately, it was a concern which produced no action at the time, for like the initial concern for education, it had to wait.[171]

Race Relations and Negro Baptists in Florida

The organizational separation between Negro and white Baptists in Florida after the Civil War was followed by increasing racial tensions in the State, and at times that tension appears to have affected relations between members of the Florida Baptist Convention and their Negro Baptist brethren. Indeed, a peculiar ambivalence marked this relationship during the early decades of the twentieth century. On the one hand, Florida Baptists were acutely aware of the increasing incidence of lynching in the South. From the time of the Civil War to the end of this period the Negro population in Georgia, South Carolina, Alabama and Mississippi steadily declined, whereas in Florida it increased.[172]

---

[168]Florida Baptist Convention, *Annual,* 1919, p. 75.

[169]Editorial, "What Makes a Christian," *Florida Baptist Witness,* Mar. 2, 1911, p. 6; cf. "Blood Money in Education," *Ibid.,* where Harvard is condemned for accepting money from Adolphus Busch.

[170]Florida Baptist Convention, *Annual,* 1907, p. 55.

[171]*Ibid.,* and 1917, p. 50.

[172]Ira D. Reid, "The Negro Baptist Ministry: An Analysis of its Profession,

Between 1900 and 1931 at least 170 Negroes were lynched in the state of Florida, which was more lynchings in Florida than in either Alabama, Arkansas, South Carolina, North Carolina or Tennessee.[173] The lynchings were generally condemned by the editors of the *Witness* when they commented on them, and Florida Baptists were warned against generalizations which assumed that all Negroes were lawless and dangerous.[174] Occasionally, however, the editors got on the defensive, arguing that the lynching in the South was no worse than what was done in the North,[175] and that much of the trouble with the Negroes in the South resulted from Northerners confusing their thinking following the Civil War.[176] Thus, Florida Baptists seem to have lacked insight into the depth of evil symbolized in the many lynchings that took place. Some of them were blind, moreover, to their own prejudices concerning Negroes. For example, some interpreted Genesis 9 (which alludes to a curse placed on Noah's grandson Canaan) as condemning the Negro to servitude and inferiority forever, and as destined to accept his lot as the ward of the white people.[177] Another example is provided in editorials in 1906 which favored education for the Negro, but argued that the basic need of the Negro was for character, not intellectual education, and that Southerners understood that need best.[178] Finally, jokes sometimes printed in the *Witness* presented the Negro as lazy, stupid and irresponsible by nature. Ironically, for a time such Negro jokes were carried in a "Sunshine Column."[179]

On the other hand, relationships between the Florida Baptist Convention and the Negro Baptist Convention appear to have become less

---

Preparation and Practices," a report of a survey by the Joint Survey Commission of the Baptist Inter-Convention Committee, 1951 (Mimeographed ms., Southern Baptist Historical Commission Library, Nashville, Tennessee), p. 2.

[173]C. Eric Lincoln, *The Negro Pilgrimage in America* (New York: Bantam Books, 1967), p. 81.

[174]Editorial, "Our Brother in Black," *Florida Baptist Witness,* Nov. 8, 1906, p. 6.

[175]Editorial, "The South and 'The Independent'," *Florida Baptist Witness,* Nov. 1, 1906, p. 6.

[176]Editorial, "Liberty, Unity, Fraternity," *Florida Baptist Witness,* Aug. 2, 1917.

[177]M. V. Ingram, "The Race Question from the Bible View," *Florida Baptist Witness,* Mar. 17, 1904.

[178]Editorial, "The Education of the Negro," *The Southern Witness,* Aug. 31, 1905; cf. *ibid.,* Jan. 31, 1907, p. 6.

[179]*Florida Baptist Witness,* Mar. 27, 1919, p. 7; Apr. 17, 1919, p. 15; and May 22, 1919, p. 18.

strained after the turn of the century than they had been previously. On numerous occasions, for example, Negro Baptist leaders were invited to address the Convention to represent the needs of their schools. The concern of Negro Baptist leaders for the education of their people is reflected in these addresses, and Florida Baptist Convention messengers usually responded with pledges of support.[180] How often these pledges were paid is not clear from the records, but it was never enough to meet the needs, for despite all efforts N. V. Collier, president of Florida Baptist Academy in Jacksonville reported in 1914 that of the 600 Negro Baptist ministers in Florida not more than a dozen had a high school education.[181] Clearly, the full story of the struggle by Negro Baptist leaders to keep their several schools going would be a story of sacrifice and frustration, if records were available to reconstruct the story. How many schools Negro Baptists in Florida had during this period is not clear from available records, but at least three are mentioned. These were (1) a training school at Fernandina,[182] (2) Live Oak Institute,[183] which appears to have been merged with Florida Normal and Industrial Institute,[184] and (3) Florida Baptist Academy at Jacksonville.[185] Though the Florida Baptist Convention gave very little help to these schools, one must remember the Convention's frequent financial distress. The Convention did encourage individual support by concerned members.

Also, during this period Florida Baptists became increasingly free of the prejudices of many of their ancestors who had approved slavery. They began to recognize the need the Negro and the white man had for each other.[186] A few leaders, moreover, were far ahead of many in recognizing the need for Florida Baptists along with Southern Baptists generally to re-examine their attitudes toward the

---

[180]Florida Baptist Convention, *Annual,* 1905, p. 83.

[181]*Ibid.*, 1914, p. 46. Collier asked for $1,000.00 of the amount the Convention had already pledged, but the Convention did not promise any action.

[182]*Ibid.,* 1905, p. 84.

[183]See Chapter III.

[184]Reid, *op. cit.,* p. 19. Cf. Coe Hayne, *Race Grit: Adventures on the Border Land of Liberty* (Philadelphia: The Judson Press), 1922, pp. 195 ff.

[185]Florida Baptist Convention, *Annual,* 1914, p. 46. In 1918, this school had 400 students, according to the Florida Baptist Convention *Annual,* 1918, pp. 64-67.

[186]*Ibid.,* 1911, p. 80.

Negro.[187] By 1918 the editor of the *Witness* was condemning all discrimination against the Negroes and heaping high praise on them for the great progress they were making against great difficulties.[188] Finally, and perhaps most significantly, the plan of cooperation between the Home Mission Boards of the Southern Baptist Convention and the National Baptist Convention, established before the turn of the century, was implemented in Florida during this period.[189] The general purpose of this plan was to bring Southern white Baptists and Negro Baptists closer together. Under this arrangement, Negro missionaries served jointly under the two boards. By 1912 this joint venture was affecting the thinking of Florida Baptists about race and was moving white and Negro Baptist leaders in Florida closer together.[190]

Despite the economic crises and conflicts experienced during this period, Florida Baptists made remarkable progress and laid strong foundations for greater progress to be achieved in the years to come. They came to the end of this period, moreover, not only with economic hope for the future, but also with a spirit of unity which was desperately needed. Finally, they were in the process of creating an organizational structure which would be needed to meet the challenges confronting them in the next two decades.

---

[187]*The Florida Baptist,* June 15, 1905, p. 9. Here the Woman's Missionary Union column quoted, with approval, the statement of J. M. Frost, who said that Negroes do not want to be wards but only want opportunity to help themselves.

[188]J. W. Mitchell, "Our Brother in Black," *Florida Baptist Witness,* June 27, 1918, pp. 2-3.

[189]Woman's Missionary Union page in *The Southern Witness,* June 7, 1906, p. 7.

[190]Florida Baptist Convention, *Annual,* 1911, p. 80.

Associational Development and Growth

1915

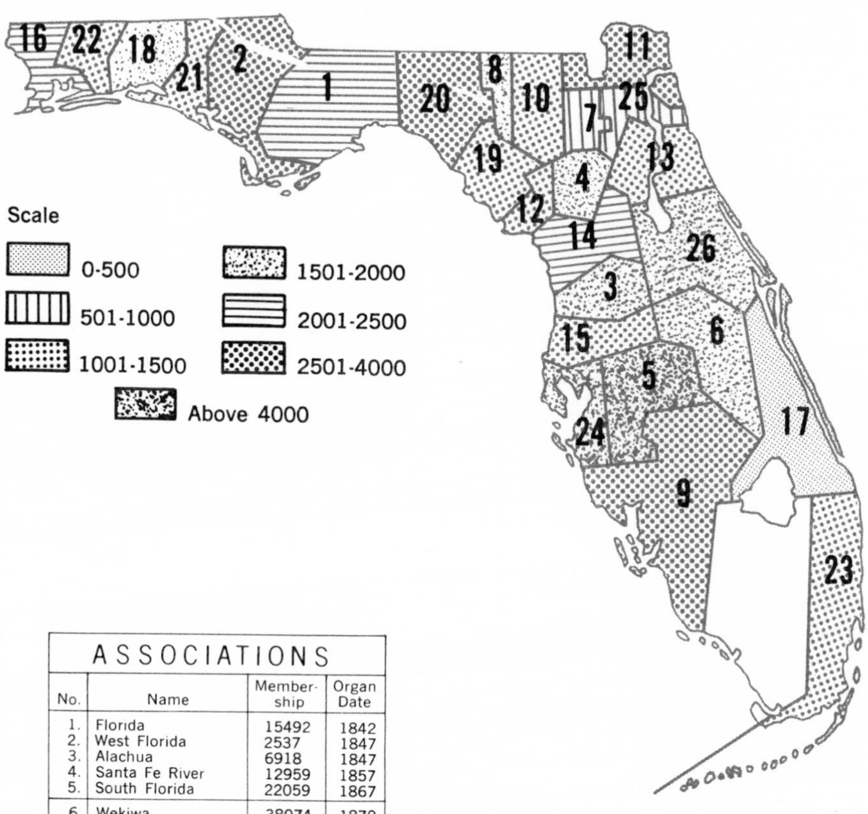

ASSOCIATIONS			
No.	Name	Membership	Organ Date
1.	Florida	15492	1842
2.	West Florida	2537	1847
3.	Alachua	6918	1847
4.	Santa Fe River	12959	1857
5.	South Florida	22059	1867
6.	Wekiwa	38074	1870
7.	New River	3715	1872
8.	Suwannee	6721	1873
9.	Peace River	3918	1876
10.	Beulah	6036	1879
11.	Jacksonville	67939	1879
12.	Harmony	3377	1879
13.	St. John's River	11314	1879
14.	Marion	11705	1885
15.	Pasco	5098	1885
16.	Pensacola Bay	31438	1887
17.	Indian River	10969	1889
18.	Graves	4425	1890
19.	Lafayette	2109	1891
20.	Middle Florida	4458	1900
21.	Holmes County	4523	1905
22.	Santa Rosa	6077	1907
23.	Miami	59975	1909
24.	Tampa Bay	46726	1911
25.	Black Creek	6856	1913
26.	Seminole	12436	1914

CHAPTER FIVE

Growth, Recession, and the Beginning of Recovery: 1921-1940

Although in this period Florida Baptists faced some of the same frustrations they had faced before, they also faced some new challenges, and in retrospect it seems clear that they were better prepared for them than before. They were better organized, and the resources they needed to meet the crises were provided in most instances.

It was a period of growth and change, with great increase in population, industry and wealth resulting in the growth of cities. Migration from rural areas to the cities, which accelerated during this period, marked the beginning of the transition from a predominantly rural to a predominantly urban state. Between 1920 and 1940 the total population almost doubled, growing from 968,470 to 1,897,414. The greatest increase came between 1920 and 1930 with 51.6 per cent. Between 1930 and 1940, when the effects of the depression were felt, percentage growth slowed to 29.2 per cent. The 1929 depression was of course the greatest crisis not only for the State but for Florida Baptists as well. However, they had known economic difficulties before, and despite the fact that they were plagued often with various financial crises throughout this period, they enjoyed remarkable growth in many ways. For example, the editors of the *Witness* pointed out in 1921 that although Florida Baptists were few compared to other Southern Baptists they were in a strong position compared to other denominations in Florida, claiming more than one-third of the State's religious population. Of a total denominational estimate of 324,856 in 1921 there were 24,650 Catholics, 114,821 Methodists, and 134,429 Baptists.[1] Moreover, during this period some of the

[1] *Florida Baptist Witness,* July 28, 1921, p. 10.

largest church buildings in the state were erected by Florida Baptists, and Sunday School attendance records were set which made all previous statistics seem insignificant. Cooperative Program gifts in 1920-1921 were $184,429, and reached a high for this period in 1925-1926, when the total reached $204,366. By 1933, reflecting the effects of the depression, gifts reached the lowest level in many years with a total of $63,661. By 1940, however, the churches were recovering from the financial crisis, and they gave $137,079 that year.[2] In 1921 there were 751 churches with a total membership of 155,965. The larger increase in membership than in total number of churches reflects the phenomenal growth in membership enjoyed by some city churches, and the rural-urban migration process mentioned above. Florida was fourth in the United States in per capita wealth, and awareness of this wealth probably contributed to an attitude of optimism even among many Florida Baptists who did not share in the wealth. They had hope for the future of Florida and for Florida Baptists. For example, editor Mitchell wrote in the *Witness* in 1922: "Certainly this is the greatest day from a religious point of view that this world has ever seen."[3]

The Convention: Problems and Response

While it is always risky and potentially misleading to generalize about the character of the Convention, it would appear that the character of the Convention changed in many ways during this period. The nature of these changes is difficult to define, but three illustrations may be helpful. For one example, in 1921, in contrast to earlier action, the Convention modified a resolution condemning inter-collegiate athletics so that it condemned only the gambling associated with them.[4] Second, the Convention gave more generously to Stetson than ever before and, though it was tempted again, it refused to repeat the educational tragedy of the preceding era.[5] Third, as the migration to the cities accelerated the process of urbanization and the growth of city churches, leadership of the Convention increasingly gravitated to the cities. The Convention focused its eyes quite naturally on the growing cities, for there was where the greatest needs were. Finally, the Convention came to include a wider variety of leadership with ten different presidents in twenty years. The executive secretary-treasurer

---

[2]Florida Baptist Convention, *Annual,* 1944, p. 150.

[3]*Florida Baptist Witness,* Mar. 16, 1922, p. 2.

[4]Florida Baptist Convention, *Annual,* 1921, pp. 13 ff.

[5]It refused to start an additional college that it could not support. This matter will be discussed in a later section.

never served as president. S. B. Rogers had suggested that change early in his administration. In short, the Convention became more sensitive to the changing times and the resources available.

The Convention of course faced some of the same problems it had known before. Perhaps the greatest problem which confronted the Convention during this period was the economic problem, aggravated in this period by hurricanes, by growth in size more than in economic resources, but most of all by the great depression of 1929. From the comments in the *Witness* it seems obvious that the immediate effects of the stock market crash of 1929 on most Florida Baptists were very slight. Its effects became more noticeable in the 1930's. The editor of the *Witness* argued that the real poverty of the land was not economic but spiritual.[6] Whether the depression was the cause or merely a contributing factor is not clear, but there was considerable unrest, especially in the city churches. W. L. C. Mahon observed in 1931 that the depression appeared to be lifting in the rural areas, but getting worse in the cities where there was more hunger and unemployment.[7] Remarkably, between 1921 and 1929 the number of churches reported increased from 751 to 908, but by the end of 1930 the number was back down to 751. Church membership in those 751 churches reported in 1930 was 115,705, a considerable increase over the 61,200 members reported in 1921. Apparently some rural churches closed while many city churches grew.

It appears that the depression had two quite different effects on the churches. In some cases it had a debilitating effect, creating or increasing tensions. In other cases it brought people into the churches and brought church members closer together. A graphic example of the latter effect was given to the writer in an interview with Dr. W. P. Brooks, who was pastor of the First Baptist Church of Sanford for 32 years beginning during the depression. The writer asked him which years of his long ministry in Sanford were the best years. Without a moment's hesitation, he replied that the depression years were best. When asked whether or not this was because Sanford escaped economic disaster, he said, "No." Then he described the exodus of people from the town and from the church because of the economic stress, and reported that people even tore down houses to avoid or lower taxes. Why, then, were they his best years? He answered that the people who were left were all poor, humble, more sensitive to each

---

[6]*Florida Baptist Witness,* Jan. 29, 1931, p. 6.
[7]Florida Baptist Convention, *Annual,* 1931, p. 24.

other's needs, and more open to the gospel.[8] Indeed, it appears to the writer that despite tensions that were intensified by the depression, the overall effect on the Convention was similar to effects Brooks saw on the Sanford church.

There was considerable desire for unity. The Convention could never have accomplished what it did without a spirit of unity. The Convention not only paid its pledge on the Seventy-five Million Campaign, but it showed gains in giving when other state conventions did not.[9] In addition, the Convention contributed heavily to the One Hundred Thousand Club of the Southern Baptist Convention, a plan which sought to enlist 100,000 persons who would give a dollar a month above their regular gifts so that debts of the Convention could be liquidated.[10] Between 1933 and 1943 Florida Baptists gave more than $150,000 through this program.[11] Considering the fact that many churches were in debt on buildings recently constructed and that some lost buildings, Florida Baptists indeed made amazing progress. Also, and again despite economic problems, many Florida Baptists continued to rise in social status. For example, they produced a Baptist governor again and recognized him at the Convention in 1928. He was Doyle E. Carlton, a deacon of the First Baptist Church, Tampa.[12]

The pastor's conference continued through the 1930's with much the same type programs with which it began. In 1938, the last year the pastor's conference program was published in the Convention *Annual,* the conference featured lectures and discussions on such topics as "Building and Beautifying our Public Worship." W. G. Stracener, then pastor of the First Baptist Church in Madison, read a paper on "The Sacrament of Silence."[13]

Finally, the Convention produced more foreign missionaries during this period than ever before. In 1930, the list of foreign missionaries from Florida included 14 persons: Mr. and Mrs. William Enete in Brazil, Mr. and Mrs. Cecil Moore in Chile, Mr. and Mrs. Frank Fowler in Argentina, Mr. and Mrs. A. J. Terry in Brazil, Mr. and Mrs. Martin S. Blair in Argentina, Mr. and Mrs. Chester Brand in

---

[8]Interview, Aug. 16, 1967.
[9]Florida Baptist Convention, *Annual,* 1932, p. 17.
[10]Barnes, *op. cit.,* p. 232; Florida Baptist Convention, *Annual,* 1934, p. 6.
[11]Florida Baptist Convention, *Annual,* 1944, p. 150.
[12]*Ibid.,* 1928, p. 76.
[13]*Ibid.,* 1938, p. 6.

Mexico, Mary Walters in Japan, and Albert Lee Davis in Argentina.[14]

THE STATE BOARD, ROGERS, AND BRITTAIN: GROWTH AND HARD TIMES

At the beginning of this period Florida Baptists in general and the State Board in particular were still enjoying the wise and able leadership of S. B. Rogers. Looking back over the past forty years of the Board's existence, Rogers observed in 1922 that whereas in 1880 the Convention had employed two missionaries and had an income of $150, in 1921 the Board employed 102 persons, received $204,770 for all causes, and reported 12,645 additions to the churches. In 1921 there were 826 Woman's Missionary Societies and auxiliaries, 111 Baptist Young People's Unions, and 428 Sunday Schools with an average attendance of 42,933.[15]

One of the first concerns of Rogers and the Board was for the payment of Florida's part in the Southern Baptist Convention's Seventy-five Million Campaign.[16] Rogers reminded Florida Baptists in 1923 of the deficits facing both the Home and Foreign Mission Boards, and of the significance of the campaign for erasing those deficits.[17] Florida Baptists responded generously, and by the end of 1923 Rogers was able to report that their quota of $1,300,000 was only $203,651.47 short of completion.[18] By the end of 1924 Florida Baptists had completed their part in the campaign.[19] In the Southern Baptist Convention as a whole, in contrast, the Seventy-five Million Campaign was a failure.

It was out of the failure of the Southern Baptist Convention's Seventy-five Million Campaign to erase the Southern Baptist Convention's deficit that the Cooperative Program was developed, involving a budgeted and percentage distribution of income received to various Convention causes.[20] E. D. Solomon, editor of the *Witness,* traced the idea of the Cooperative Program to Dr. M. E. Dodd, who was named chairman of a Southern Baptist Convention committee to fix amounts for each board and institution to receive from the Seventy-five Million Campaign. In 1923 Solomon, then state secretary of the

---

[14]*Florida Baptist Witness,* Mar. 27, 1930, front page.
[15]*Ibid.,* May 18, 1922, pp. 2-3.
[16]State Board, *Minutes,* Jan. 11, 1921.
[17]*Ibid.,* Apr. 25, 1923.
[18]Florida Baptist Convention, *Annual,* 1923-24, p. 20.
[19]*Ibid.,* 1924, p. 12.
[20]Barnes, *op. cit.,* p. 230.

Louisiana Baptist Convention, was asked to help Dodd on the committee. Solomon later reported that he and Dodd introduced the idea of percentages. If the whole amount was raised each board or institution would get what it requested. If not, then each one would get a percentage. The Southern Baptist Convention adopted the plan in Atlanta in 1924.[21] Many were not satisfied with the plan, however, and, according to Solomon, that is why the Southern Baptist Convention got in debt.[22] Apparently, Rogers was sold on the plan, however, and convinced Florida Baptists of its wisdom, for while the state conventions faltered and failed in their part of the campaign, thus increasing the Southern Baptist Convention deficit, Florida Baptists were among the first and the few to complete their pledge.

A second object of concern for Rogers and the Board during this period was for the erection of a building to house the denominational offices. Rogers conceived the idea of constructing a building larger than needed immediately, planning to rent the unused portion to provide revenue for payments on the building and to provide for future growth. The Board approved the plan, and created the Florida Baptist Building Corporation, which in turn had plans drawn up for the building construction, financing and rentals. The financial plan was to sell bonds bearing interest at seven per cent and maturing in from two to ten years.[23] The building corporation anticipated rentals amounting to $21,892 per year.[24] The building was completed in 1924 as planned. Unfortunately, however, the revenue received from rentals in the next few years fell short of expectations, partly because of the depression, and the State Board found itself plagued with debt and pressured by the bank.[25] It must have saddened Rogers, who was a good businessman and administrator, to have to leave the office at the end of 1925 with the debt unpaid and the pressures mounting. Though negotiations and progress made it possible to keep the building, the debt was not to be retired during the lifetime of Rogers who died in 1926, or during this period. However, in 1932 the building was named the Rogers Building in his memory.[26]

A third concern of Rogers during the last years of his administration was the creation of a loan fund to help many churches to con-

---

[21]*Florida Baptist Witness,* May 31, 1945, p. 4.

[22]*Ibid.*

[23]*Ibid.,* Aug. 9, 1923.

[24]Florida Baptist Convention, *Annual,* 1924, p. 87.

[25]*Ibid.,* 1928, p. 26.

[26]*Florida Baptist Witness,* Feb. 18, 1932, front page.

struct buildings. When he suggested that a centennial celebration be held in 1925, he hoped to raise $100,000 to create such a fund.[27] He did not reach the goal, but $12,353.52 was raised during the year, and he was influential in gaining additional help from various sources for church construction projects. For example, in 1924 the family of A. R. Jones gave $10,000 in his memory for the purpose of starting a building loan fund, and during the last year of Rogers' administration $47,811.61 was spent aiding building programs. The total number of churches receiving such aid during his administration was 496.[28]

Rogers understandably had mixed feelings about the boom in church building, however, because he observed in some cases that spending money on building enlargement created difficulties for the Board.[29] The Board report in 1925 indicated that at one time during the year the deficit was as high as $49,235.10. The situation improved somewhat the following year, but the report on foreign missions again suggested that the church building boom had lowered gifts to foreign missions also.[30] The report defended the building construction, however, observing that better equipped churches would ultimately give more to missions. In 1924 Rogers summarized the progress Florida Baptists had made in the past 15 years. Among the items he mentioned were $227,824 given for foreign missions, $219,465 for home missions and $282,645 for Christian education. Value of church property had increased from $705,371 to $14,002,872 or an increase of 567 per cent. Total church membership had grown from 37,027 to 77,846 or a net increase of 210 per cent.[31]

In 1926 Rogers resigned his position because of ill health. On December 8, 1926, Dr. Charles M. Brittain was elected executive secretary-treasurer. Having served as assistant secretary for six years before assuming the top office, he knew the problems of the Convention and gave good leadership. Immediately, he faced a new economic crisis affecting many areas because of a devastating hurricane earlier

---

[27]The centennial celebration took place on March 12, 1925. Rogers prepared a brief history to commemorate the event. At the Convention the next fall, he called for the writing and publication of a more complete history, and the Convention ordered that some person be appointed to do it. Florida Baptist Convention, *Annual,* 1925, p. 45. Apparently no one was immediately available to carry out the Convention's order.

[28]Rosser, *op. cit.,* pp. 99-100.

[29]Florida Baptist Convention, *Annual,* 1925, p. 15.

[30]*Ibid.,* 1926, p. 42.

[31]*Ibid.,* 1924, p. 37.

Charles M. Brittain, *Executive Secretary,*
1926 - 1941

in the year which had destroyed many churches in the Miami area and created economic disaster in many other communities.[32] In 1928 another hurricane struck, this time in the West Palm Beach area, killing 2500 people and inflicting property loss estimated at $75 million.[33] Churches in other areas gave much to help the hurricane victims, but even while help was still being sought to meet the needs constantly confronting the State Board, the greatest blow of all came. It was the stock market crash of 1929. The Board had already had to borrow money to meet obligations.[34] Then it was forced to cut its work back further. In 1930 the budget was $61,736, the smallest in many years.[35] Early in 1931 the State Board sent out letters asking advice on how to cut back. The executive committee met monthly,[36] seeking solutions to the financial crisis. At the March Board meeting President Hulley offered to return half of the money sent to Stetson University in order to help out in the emergency with the understanding that the old percentage would be restored at the December meeting. The Board accepted the offer and gave Hulley a rising vote of thanks.[37] Apparently the Board's efforts to cut back were not satisfactory to some, however, for in 1932 a resolution from the First Baptist Church of Orlando complained that the Convention had not adjusted sufficiently to the changing situation and suggested reduction of both staff and salaries. The resolution was referred to a committee,[38] and no further action was taken at the Convention. However, when the recommended budget of $100,000 was presented to the State Board at its January, 1933, meeting, it was reduced drastically to $53,249. Even that reduction was insufficient to some.[39] By such severe reduction in planned expenditures, the Board stayed in control of its debts, and did not lose its enthusiasm for planning for better things to come.

In 1931 the Board had appointed a committee on evangelism, and on recommendation of this committee, voted in January, 1933, to have a simultaneous evangelistic campaign in the month of April.[40]

---

[32]*Ibid.,* 1926, p. 45.
[33]Rosser, *op. cit.,* p. 103.
[34]State Board, *Minutes,* May 27, 1929.
[35]*Ibid.,* Feb. 3, 1931.
[36]*Ibid.*
[37]*Ibid.,* Mar. 24, 1931.
[38]Florida Baptist Convention, *Annual,* 1932, pp. 10-12.
[39]State Board, *Minutes,* Jan. 10-11, 1933.
[40]*Ibid.*

Considering the situation, it is amazing that in 1933 the State Board could report that Florida was the only state to report a gain in gifts to missions in 1932.[41] Moreover, the Board continued to enlarge its staff as the economic situation eased somewhat toward the end of the thirties, and responded to every genuine need its resources would allow. One of the last needs engaging the Board's attention was the need for a hospital, and the Board responded by appointing a hospital commission.[42] Another need to which the Board responded favorably was the request of the First Baptist Church of DeLand for help in its building program so that the church might accommodate the increasing numbers of Baptist students attending there. In January, 1931, the Board promised $5,000 for each of the following five years.[43]

Finally, in 1939, the State Board and the Convention voted to cooperate with the newly developed Southern Baptist Convention Ministers' Retirement Plan. It was a joint plan involving the minister, the churches, and the State Convention. Under this plan the minister put in three per cent of his salary, the local church, three per cent, and the Convention through the State Board, two per cent. The plan adopted by the Southern Baptist Convention made possible assistance to ministers then aged, but who had not been in the plan. Others would receive what they put in with interest.[44] In 1939, 211 Florida pastors and 233 churches were participating in the plan.[45]

By 1940 the budget of the State Board was $100,483, which was above what had been rejected a few years earlier, but the debt was also larger. The Board began the year 1940 with a deficit of $6,393 from the preceding year, and between January and May 1940, an additional deficit of $6,122 had accumulated.[46] On May 9, because of the debt the executive committee voted to cut salaries of Board employees ten per cent and to change the budget percentage to be used in the State from 55 per cent to 65 per cent. To save money Board approval was sought and received by mail.[47] Apparently, that move was not popular, for in September the Board received several resigna-

---

[41]Florida Baptist Convention, *Annual,* 1933, p. 17.
[42]State Board, *Minutes,* Jan. 23-24, 1939.
[43]*Ibid.*
[44]Florida Baptist Convention, *Annual,* 1939, pp. 28-31.
[45]*Ibid.*
[46]State Board, *Minutes,* May 9, 1940.
[47]*Ibid.*

tions.[48] By December the financial situation looked better, and salaries were restored to their earlier level.[49]

Departments and Work: Enlargement in Size and Scope

The First Big Sunday Schools

One of the most remarkable features of Florida Baptist church life in this period was the enormous increase in Sunday School enrollment and attendance. In 1922 when the Sunday School column in the *Witness* first began reporting Sunday School attendance each week, there were only three churches reporting 500 or more in Sunday School, three reporting between 400 and 500, and five having between 200 and 400 attending.[50] Before the end of the 1930's a number of churches were reporting between 900 and 1800 attending Sunday School. Main Street Church in Jacksonville was often the leading church in Sunday School attendance during the 1930's.[51]

This growth in Sunday School enrollment and attendance was probably due to several factors. First, it was the result of migration from rural areas to the cities, and migration from other states. Second, it was the result of the steady and effective work of W. W. Willian, who began serving as state Sunday School secretary in 1916. Between 1921 and 1940 under Willian's leadership the number of Sunday Schools grew from 428 to 1,649 and total enrollment grew from 34,273 to 117,343. In addition to writing and speaking, Dr. Willian promoted the work of the Sunday School through enlargement campaigns (beginning in 1926), church training schools and an annual assembly camp begun earlier at Columbia College in 1913 and continued at Stetson University after the closing of Columbia. During this period an additional assembly came to be held in West Florida at the assembly grounds of Bob Jones College, near Panama City. In 1933, the two assemblies were temporarily combined into one assembly at Tampa with an enrollment of 1,050 and with awards for studies in Sunday School work totaling 2,077.[52]

Also, standards of excellence came to be used, and summer workers were first employed during this period. One of the chief functions of

---

[48]*Ibid.,* Sept. 3, 1940.
[49]*Ibid.,* Dec. 3, 1940.
[50]*Florida Baptist Witness,* Mar. 19, 1922.
[51]*Ibid.,* June 23, 1938, p. 15; cf. *ibid.,* Jan. 11, 1939.
[52]Rosser, *op. cit.,* p. 138.

these summer workers was the promotion and demonstration of vacation Bible schools, another new feature of Sunday School work. The first mention of vacation Bible schools in Florida Baptist records appears to be in 1924 when three schools were conducted.[53] In 1926, eight schools were held with an enrollment of 1,753.[54] From this modest beginning the vacation Bible school movement grew steadily each year until it became a very significant part of Florida Baptist work.

To the Sunday School a great deal of credit must be given for the growth of the churches during this period, for strong emphasis was placed on teaching and evangelism. As the Sunday Schools grew, baptisms grew steadily also. Between 1921 and 1928 the number of baptisms rose from 3,813 to a record high for this period of 8,848.

In 1927, O. K. Radford and E. B. Evans were employed as field workers, reflecting the growth and vision of the Sunday School department.[55] Evans' employment was brief, but Radford continued as associate to Dr. Willian until 1938, when the work of the Sunday School and the Training Union was divided into separate departments. By mutual agreement Dr. Willian continued to promote Sunday School work and O. K. Radford worked with the Training Unions.[56]

Baptist Young People's Union-Training Union: "An Embarrassing Success"

Although the Baptist Young People's Union was an accepted part of Florida Baptist life by the 1920's, it was still a small movement compared to the Sunday School, even to the end of this period. It enjoyed remarkable growth during the Twenties, however, with the number of unions increasing from 581 in 1925 to 994 in 1930 and with enrollment increasing from 15,841 to 22,685 during that period. Before this period there were junior and senior unions only. In 1921, intermediate unions were added.[57] In 1925, adult unions were formed, and the name Baptist Young People's Union thus became a contradiction in terms. In all unions great emphasis was placed on training in individual Bible study, church membership, and missions.

What is most significant about the B.Y.P.U. during this period is the impact it made despite the small size of the movement. It is this

---

[53] *Ibid.*, p. 135.
[54] Florida Baptist Convention, *Annual,* 1926, p. 27.
[55] Rosser, *op. cit.*, p. 136.
[56] State Board, *Minutes,* May 2, 1938.
[57] Rosser, *op. cit.*, p. 235.

impact that caused Dr. Willian to describe assemblies held at Punta Gorda in 1924 as an "embarrassing success" when at the closing dedication services in these assemblies a total of 171 young persons volunteered for some kind of special service.[58]

Because of the addition of adult unions the name was changed in 1934 to Baptist Training Union.[59] The purpose of the Training Union was then defined to include (1) growth in Christian intelligence, (2) development of Christian character, (3) development in Christian efficiency, and (4) growth in church and denominational loyalty.[60]

In summary, the foundations were laid for the greater progress to be achieved in the 1940's by the division of the work of Sunday School and Baptist Young People's Union and by the election of O. K. Radford to give full time to the work of promoting the Training Union.[61]

Woman's Missionary Union: A Time of Sacrifice

The work of the Woman's Missionary Union grew during this period. Beginning with high hopes symbolized in the sending of Mrs. H. C. Peelman to the Baptist World Alliance in Stockholm, Sweden, in 1923,[62] the Union had to share in the despair which followed the catastrophes of hurricane and depression in the 1920's. The Baptist women of Florida were faithful to the point of sacrifice during the financial crisis, and only their faithfulness made possible some of Florida Baptists' greatest achievements in the field of foreign missions in this period. For example, when in 1927 the Foreign Mission Board announced that missionaries on furlough could not be returned to the field, the Lottie Moon Christmas offering in Florida brought in $3,757, and mainly because of the work of the W.M.U. all Florida's missionaries in foreign service were returned to their respective fields.[63]

In 1936, Mrs. Peelman retired as executive secretary of the Woman's Missionary Union. During her 25 years of service the organizations had grown from 211 in 1911 to 1,574 in 1936. Gifts of $5,465 had grown to $53,357 in 1936.[64] Miss Louise Smith, who had served

---

[58]*Ibid.,* p. 236.
[59]Barnes, *op. cit.,* p. 190.
[60]*Ibid.,* p. 191.
[61]State Board, *Minutes,* May 2, 1938.
[62]Lassiter, *op. cit.,* p. 61.
[63]*Ibid.,* pp. 64-65.
[64]*Ibid.,* p. 69.

since 1931 as young people's secretary, was elected to become the new executive secretary and assumed office on April 1, 1936.[65]

Among the notable achievements of the Woman's Missionary Union under Miss Smith's leadership were the assistance given by women of the Jacksonville association to their Negro sisters in preparing to entertain the W.M.U. of the National Baptist Convention in September 1936, and the organization in 1936 of the first Negro Young Woman's Auxiliary at Bethune-Cookman College in Daytona Beach.[66]

Student Work: Halting Beginning

One of the earliest discussions of the need for a special ministry to Baptist students occurred in 1920 when the possibility of establishing such a ministry at the University of Florida and Florida State College for Women was considered.[67] The matter was brought up again in 1921 at a State Board meeting, but nothing was done immediately because of lack of money.[68] In 1925, however, Miss Margaret Swern began a ministry to students at the University of Florida. In 1926, apparently the first ministry to students at Florida State College for Women was provided by the W.M.U., and the first state Baptist student convention was held.[69] S. H. Gresset was appointed in 1926 to serve at the University of Florida. These employees sought to contact Baptist students in their schools and to enlist them in the life and organization of the church. By 1928, plans were underway for buildings to house the activities of the student ministry at the two schools. In 1929, John Hall Jones was employed as student secretary at Gainesville with the additional responsibility of organizing and coordinating the work of ministering to students at other colleges, and planning a spring retreat each year.[70]

In 1930, following the stock market crash of 1929, the State Board was forced to consider every possible way of cutting costs. Since student work was a relatively new ministry, the Board agreed to drop it.[71]

---

[65]*Ibid.,* p. 76.
[66]*Ibid.,* p. 80.
[67]Rosser, *op. cit.,* p. 304.
[68]State Board, *Minutes,* Jan. 11, 1921.
[69]*Ibid.,* Dec. 12, 1929.
[70]*Ibid.*
[71]*Ibid.,* June 26, 1930.

The move was not popular, [72] and student work was restored in 1931 when economic conditions at the Board improved slightly.[73]

John Hall Jones continued as general secretary. By 1932, the Baptist Student Union had become a strong movement with a great deal of popular support in the Convention.[74] By 1933, Beatrice Priester was employed as student worker at Stetson, and the Baptist Student Union was a well established part of Florida Baptist life. In 1936, John Hall Jones resigned as state Baptist Student Union secretary, and J. Roy Robinson was employed to replace him.[75]

Brotherhood: The Layman's Movement Takes Shape

For many years before 1920 Florida Baptists had been aware of the interdenominational laymen's missionary movement. Between 1900 and 1920 the movement had been discussed and considered by several committees, but the Convention had taken no significant action. In 1925, a report on the movement was brought to the Convention, provoking considerable discussion of the need for such a movement among Baptist men. The result was the organization of committees in various regions of the State to coordinate the work of men's missionary unions already in existence. The movement was then called the Baptist Men's Movement.[76] The work grew, and in 1926 the committee on Baptist men's work reported many new organizations, now called Brotherhoods, in the State, and was calling for the employment of a state Brotherhood secretary.[77] In 1928, W. G. Upchurch was employed by the State Board as secretary of Brotherhood work. He sold his business and took up the work of promoting the work and organizing new Brotherhoods. When the depression hit, however, the Brotherhood work, like the student work, was dropped.[78] Convention minutes clearly indicate, nonetheless, that the work did not die,[79] and in 1936 when the pressure of the depression seemed to be lifting somewhat, the employment of a Brotherhood sec-

---

[72]W. A. Hobson, "Shall the Student Work Continue," *Florida Baptist Witness,* July 27, 1930, p. 8.

[73]State Board, *Minutes,* Jan. 6, 1931.

[74]*Florida Baptist Witness,* Oct. 27, 1932, pp. 4-5.

[75]State Board, *Minutes,* Dec. 10, 1936.

[76]Florida Baptist Convention, *Annual,* 1925, p. 48.

[77]*Ibid.,* 1926, pp. 81-82. The name Brotherhood was adopted to follow the action of the Southern Baptist Convention.

[78]Rosser, *op. cit.,* p. 315.

[79]*Ibid.,* p. 316.

retary was considered again, and Hugh Latimer was employed. Latimer began his work on February 1, 1936, and by the end of the year twenty-six new Brotherhoods had been formed. He served this work until 1939, and during his time in office the total enrollment of the state Brotherhoods almost doubled, increasing from 1,095 in 1936 to 2,097 in 1938. When Latimer resigned effective March 1, 1939, J. Harrison Griffin was elected to succeed him.[80]

Assemblies

Between 1920 and 1940, the annual summer assembly, begun at Columbia College in 1913 and continued at Stetson when Columbia closed, was greatly enlarged. A winter assembly ground was acquired at Umatilla,[81] and summer assemblies came to be held at Stetson and, in West Florida, at Bob Jones University.[82] These assemblies not only strengthened the work of the churches and all of their organizations, but also promoted interest in missions with great effectiveness. Combining elements of inspiration, teaching and sharing, the assembly program moved rapidly toward becoming a firmly established part of Florida Baptist life during this period.

The Beginning of a Bookstore

In a real sense the establishing of a bookstore was simply a new form of an old ministry of Florida Baptists, the work of colportage. Earlier a required part of the work of state missionaries had been the sale and distribution of good books. In January, 1922, the State Board discussed the possibility of establishing a bookstore to centralize and simplify this ministry, and in June purchase of property on Church Street in Jacksonville was approved for this purpose.[83] On May 4, 1925, S. B. Rogers announced in the *Witness* that the bookstore would soon be opened through a cooperative arrangement between the Southern Baptist Convention Sunday School Board and the Florida Baptist Convention.[84] Thus, another new significant work was begun by Florida Baptists.

Indian Missions: Action at Last

One mission enterprise among Florida Baptists which had a long

[80]*Ibid.,* pp. 317-318.
[81]State Board, *Minutes,* Jan. 4, 1923.
[82]*Ibid.,* Jan. 23, 1928.
[83]*Ibid.,* Jan. 10, 1922, and June 12, 1922.
[84]*Florida Baptist Witness,* May 4, 1925, p. 2.

history of interest without action but came to fruition in this period was a mission work among Florida Indians. Hindered heretofore by the hostility of the Seminoles to the white man because of earlier ill treatment, many Florida Baptists now saw their dream nearer realization when the subject was raised again in 1931. At that time the State Board appointed a committee to study the matter and to employ a missionary.[85] In September, 1932, the Board was still trying, but without success. It was in communication with an Indian Association in Oklahoma however, and pursuing the possibility of employing a Christian Seminole from Oklahoma as a missionary to the Florida Seminoles.[86] In January, 1934, negotiations were completed, and Willie King, a Seminole Indian from Oklahoma, was employed as missionary to the Seminoles in Florida.[87] As a result of his work the first Seminole Indian Baptist Church was organized in Dania on June 17, 1936, and Willie King was called as pastor.[88]

Evangelism

In 1934 Dr. T. O. Reese was employed as state evangelist. His employment was made possible by a memorial gift by W. C. Wells in honor of his wife. The gift guaranteed half of the salary of the evangelist, and the other half was underwritten by the State Board of Missions. This action was the forerunner of a regular Evangelism Department which was to be established later. By the end of the 1930's two other evangelists, C. L. Wattenbarger and R. D. Carrin, were employed. The work of these two evangelists symbolized the statewide growth of interest in evangelism and revival during the late 1930's.

Associational Growth

As population continued to increase and as transportation, both public and private, became more abundant and efficient, associational units continued to grow larger in number and smaller in size. Between 1920 and 1940, eleven new associations were organized. They included Okaloosa in 1923; Lake County, Holmes County and Southwest in 1924; Jackson County in 1926; Orange Blossom and Ridge in 1932; Pinellas in 1933; Northwest Coast in 1934; and Northeast Florida and Palm Lake in 1938. In most cases the new associations were formed from several churches in an association which was large geo-

---

[85]State Board, *Minutes,* Jan. 6, 1931.

[86]*Ibid.,* Sept. 29, 1932.

[87]State Board, *Minutes,* Jan. 1934; Florida Baptist Convention, *Annual,* 1934, p. 29.

[88]Lassiter, *op. cit.,* p. 81.

graphically and by new churches desiring to cut down the distance to associational meetings. The meetings themselves continued to play a significant role in the life of the denomination. The new associations also reflect significant growth in the number and size of Florida Baptist churches. Between 1921 and 1940, the number grew from 751 to 817. Total membership during that period grew from 61,200 to 155,965.

Florida Baptist Children's Home

In 1921, following the suggestion of the Southern Baptist Convention, the Florida Baptist Convention changed the name of its institution for homeless children from Florida Baptist Orphanage to Florida Baptist Children's Home. A basic reason for this change was the recognition that many children needing and receiving care were not orphans, but children from homes broken by separation, divorce, or other tragedies.[89] In 1922, a bequest of $3,836 made possible the construction of a new building which provided a steam laundry and dormitory space for fifteen girls. The Home was making progress in many ways then caring for 111 children. Unfortunately, it was also in debt, and the size of the debt increased steadily. The successful completion of Florida's part in the Seventy-five Million Campaign in 1924 eased the situation somewhat, reducing the indebtedness from $19,000 to $8,754. Special appeals brought in many special gifts. A boys' dormitory was built in 1926 to care for the growing number of children, almost 200 in 1927. The contributions never brought in enough cash, however, to reduce the indebtedness.[90] The Home's economic distress was complicated further by the rumors which continued to spread about the character of J. E. Trice, superintendent of the Home.[91] Although the State Board investigated the rumors in 1927 and finding no basis for them, reaffirmed confidence in Superintendent Trice, the rumors continued and probably affected contributions.[92] In any case the debt increased, and the Home situation was the subject of extensive discussion and debate at the convention of 1928.[93] By the end of 1929 the debt had increased to $16,875.[94]

---

[89]Rosser, *op. cit.*, p. 258.

[90]*Ibid.*, pp. 262-267.

[91]See Chapter IV.

[92]State Board, *Minutes*, Jan. 4, 1927.

[93]Florida Baptist Convention, *Annual*, 1928, p. 87; cf. J. E. Trice, "Baptist Children's Home in Arcadia in Great Need of Funds," *Florida Baptist Witness*, July 5, 1928.

[94]Rosser, *op. cit.*, p. 264.

During the same year the DeSoto County School Board took over the responsibility of operating the school for the Home, making possible a saving of $25,000 per year. Other costs, however, continued to increase the deficit. In 1931, Trice resigned and the situation appeared hopeless, but the trustees and the Convention, not willing to give up, asked Dr. J. Harrison Griffin to take a three-months leave of absence from his pastorate in Winter Haven and direct a campaign to raise money and pay off the debts. The campaign was given front page publicity in the *Witness,* and Griffin declared his intention to visit every section of the State. The debt then stood at $45,000.[95] Traveling over the State, Griffin soon raised over $30,000 and because of the depression, persuaded many of the creditors to settle for half of what was owed them. Thus, the Home was saved from what appeared to be certain disaster.[96] T. M. Johns was elected as superintendent in 1932, and the future looked very bright. He and Mrs. Johns were teachers and well qualified for the work. In 1938, the Home employed the first case worker, Miss Lora Baldwin, whose assistance in investigating applications made more efficient work possible.[97]

EDUCATION: THE JUNIOR COLLEGE ABORTION, AND STETSON UNIVERSITY

Although some of the old sources of tension still existed and new tensions developed, the relationship between Florida Baptists and Stetson University not only survived but reached a level of strength between 1920 and 1940 not known before.

Most of the tensions came between 1920 and 1930. It is difficult to expose the exact source however, for in 1921 the Convention had nothing but praise for Stetson. The report on Christian education indicated pride in Stetson's attendance and endowment, and the Convention increased its support of Stetson.[98] Moreover, public reaction to the controversy over the teaching of evolution in the public school increased and intensified the interest of Florida Baptists in denominational schools. A resolution in 1921, for example, called for the establishing of Baptist academies in all parts of the State. Another called on the legislature to protect the public school from teaching what would destroy the faith of boys and girls in the Bible. Also Wil-

[95] *Florida Baptist Witness,* Dec. 31, 1931, pp. 1 ff.
[96] Interview with J. Harrison Griffin, June, 1969.
[97] Rosser, *op. cit.,* p. 273.
[98] Florida Baptist Convention, *Annual,* 1921, p. 51.

liam Jennings Bryan addressed the Convention on the subject: "Law Enforcement, Christian Education and the Menace of Darwinianism."[99]

By 1924, when the Seventy-five Million Campaign was completed, tensions must have been developing anew because a Convention committee recommended that the State Board be instructed to negotiate for closer relations between the Convention and Stetson and that an annual financial statement and audit be requested of Stetson.[100]

In 1925, the report of the State Board to the Convention indicated that $14,325 had been given to Stetson during the year, and a strong statement was adopted which reaffirmed the relationship of Stetson University with the Convention.[101] The State Board also reported that consideration was being given to building a junior college, not to compete with Stetson, but to feed Stetson. Great interest developed in the junior college idea. Where the idea originated is not clear, but three events may have added to the enthusiasm for the project.

First, as hinted above, new tensions developed between Stetson and the Convention. Stetson's report to the Convention in 1926 clearly alludes to criticism which had been directed to Stetson concerning the tuition rates and the small number of Florida Baptist students attending Stetson. In the report President Hulley did not help matters by reporting that Northern friends had contributed five times as much as the Convention.[102] Immediately after Hulley's report a resolution was approved which called for a new Stetson-Convention relations committee, to report back before the end of the session. The committee was appointed and reported as instructed, recommending that a committee be appointed to make arrangements for bringing Stetson under more direct control by the Convention. The committee also recommended that if that could be done the Convention should raise one million dollars for Stetson in five years. In the meantime the committee recommended that budgeted funds be held in escrow.[103] After this threatening resolution, the Stetson band and choir played and sang, "Oh, The Touch of His Hand on Mine."[104] Since the committee recommendations were adopted, it is obvious that the tensions were strong. Tensions over Stetson are implied, moreover, in the discussion

---

[99] *Ibid.*, pp. 89-91.
[100] *Ibid.*, 1924, p. 65.
[101] *Ibid.*, 1925, pp. 18, 68.
[102] *Ibid.*, 1926, pp. 12-14.
[103] *Ibid.*, p. 68.
[104] *Ibid.*, p. 76.

of the specific proposal from the South Florida Association for a junior college to be established at Sebring.[105]

A second event which may have stimulated interest in the proposed junior college was the growth in the number of junior colleges in the country. Some Florida Baptists were simply tempted to "Keep up with the Joneses." W. D. Nowlin argued (1) that it would be better for Florida Baptists to have a first-rate junior college than a second-rate four-year college, (2) that of the 208 junior colleges in America 165 had been established in the last ten years, and (3) that the junior college would relieve the congestion at Stetson.[106] Lincoln Hulley challenged the proposed junior college idea, suggesting among other things that land speculators often encouraged such moves for business reasons. Further, he reminded the Convention of its 1919 agreement to work with Stetson.[107]

A third factor which perhaps contributed to interest in the proposed junior college was a general skepticism toward all long established schools,[108] a skepticism no doubt stimulated and encouraged by the evolution controversy.[109] Somehow it appears that a popular fallacy developed among Baptists, a fallacy which some Florida Baptists believed concerning the nature of their schools. Those schools that did not fit the ideal concept which these Baptists now had were assumed to have slipped from their moorings.[110] Actually, most of the early Baptist schools which had survived had probably changed very little, and the changes they had made were in the direction of a more denomination-centered emphasis. Nevertheless, this fallacy accounted for some false estimates of the character of Stetson and other denominational schools.

---

[105]*Florida Baptist Witness,* Oct. 28, 1926, p. 9. Here W. D. Nowlin gives reasons for the proposed college and the location. R. W. Thiot was designated as field representative for the junior college and associations which adopted the new college would be represented on the board of trustees according to the proposed charter. The associations, through their representatives on the board of trustees would have absolute control over it. *Ibid.,* p. 18.

[106]W. D. Nowlin, "Report of the Committee on Education and the Junior College," *Florida Baptist Witness,* Oct. 28, 1926, p. 9.

[107]Lincoln Hulley, "Stetson and a Junior College." *Florida Baptist Witness,* Sept. 11, 1926, pp. 9-10.

[108]Florida Baptist Convention, *Annual,* 1929, p. 71.

[109]Florida Baptist Convention, *Annual,* 1925, pp. 62-63; cf. O. K. Armstrong, "A Report of the Textbook Situation . . .," *Florida Baptist Witness,* Feb. 16, 1928, p. 9, and D. V. Pickern, "The Textbook Situation at Tallahassee," *Florida Baptist Witness,* Mar. 1, 1928, p. 10.

[110]Florida Baptist Convention, *Annual,* 1929, p. 71.

While interest in the proposed junior college continued through 1927,[111] the project never received Convention sanction and the movement eventually died for lack of sufficient support.

In the meantime, tensions between Stetson and the Conventions had been at least temporarily reduced by a new agreement reached between Stetson trustees and the Convention's committee in 1926. Briefly, the agreement involved: (1) changing the 1919 agreement to include more latitude for the Convention to nominate trustees until one satisfactory to the trustees could be found, (2) greater distribution of future elected trustees over the State, (3) occasional invitations to Southern Baptist ministers to speak to the students, (4) sending Stetson representatives to associational meetings to increase communication, and (5) the Convention's promise to raise $1,000,000 for Stetson in five years.[112]

The continued improvement of relationships between Stetson and the Convention was symbolized by the election of Lincoln Hulley as president of the Convention in 1928.[113] Although occasional sounds of discord were heard after that,[114] for the most part in the next few years there was peace and harmony between Stetson and the Convention. W. A. Hobson, long-time pastor of First Baptist Church, Jacksonville, known and respected over the State and a veteran trustee of Stetson, was employed to represent Stetson among the churches.

In 1934, Lincoln Hulley died and William Sims Allen was elected president of Stetson.[115] The new administration continued and increased the warm relationships in process, for Allen was warmly received by the Convention. With the help of W. A. Hobson, he greatly increased the amount of communication between Stetson and the State Board and the churches. Because of improved relationships, the Convention gave more money to Stetson between 1920 and 1940 than in all the preceding years combined, despite economic difficulties. Student enrollment also increased, from 671 in 1934 to 1,097 in 1940.[116] In addition, Stetson continued to build. In 1929, Hulley Gymnasium was constructed and an assembly hall for women, later named Stover

---

[111]*Florida Baptist Witness,* June 2, 1927, p. 3. Editor Mitchell reported that twelve associations had endorsed the idea. The trustees even set an opening date.

[112]Florida Baptist Convention, *Annual,* 1926, pp. 51, 68.

[113]*Ibid.,* 1928, p. 58.

[114]*Ibid.,* 1929, p. 71; cf. State Board, *Minutes,* May 9, 1932.

[115]Florida Baptist Convention, *Annual,* 1934, p. 12.

[116]Rosser, *op. cit.,* p. 203.

Theatre, was begun.[117] In 1934, Hulley Tower, already begun by President Hulley, was completed by his family after his death that year.[118] In 1935, a south wing was added to Chaudoin Hall at a cost of $54,000 to provide additional dormitory space for girls. In 1936, Conrad Hall was remodeled and enlarged at a cost of $40,000, and a dining hall costing $80,000 was added. In 1937, the Panhellenic Building was purchased and named Stevens Hall in honor of H. B. Stevens, who was manager of Mr. Stetson's enterprises for many years.[119] By 1939, plans were under way to raise a million dollars for Stetson, as pledged earlier by the Convention.[120]

The Florida Baptist Witness: Progress Toward Stability

The *Witness* continued to have the same financial troubles during this period it had always had, but during the 1930's the situation improved considerably. With the Convention headquarters firmly established in Jacksonville, the *Witness* found it easier to stay in one place and thus it continued to be published in that city. Also, the *Witness* achieved greater editorial stability with only three major editorial changes in twenty years.

In the beginning of the Twenties the paper was plagued with the old financial troubles, mainly resulting from overdue subscriptions.[121] Each year it operated at a greater loss, until in 1925 the deficit was $4,763.22,[122] and the State Board engaged in considerable discussion of the situation.[123] No action was taken, but fortunately the next three years saw some improvement. In 1928, editor J. W. Mitchell retired. He had been editor for ten years and despite economic problems, his record was impressive. Circulation of the *Witness* had grown from less than 3,000 to 7,500.[124]

P. L. Johnston, a Mercer graduate with long experience in newspaper work, became the new editor. Unfortunately, his illness and the stock market crash of 1929 increased the economic difficulties of the *Witness*. The State Board not only employed several temporary editors, including G. J. Rousseau, W. D. Nowlin, and L. M. White to

---

[117]Bowen, *op. cit.*, p. 14.
[118]*Ibid.*, p. 18.
[119]*Ibid.*, p. 16.
[120]State Board, *Minutes,* July 14, 1939.
[121]*Florida Baptist Witness,* Feb. 21, 1922, p. 4.
[122]Rosser, *op. cit.*, p. 155.
[123]State Board, *Minutes,* Jan. 22, 1925.
[124]Rosser, *op. cit.*, p. 155.

assist Johnston, but also paid the growing deficit each year. At the end of 1930, Johnston resigned. Then state secretary Brittain assumed the responsibility until the paper was leased on June 1, 1931, to Dr. E. D. Solomon. Coming immediately from Louisiana, where he had served as state secretary for some years, Solomon was well prepared for the job. The terms of the lease included a $6,000 annual subsidy which the Convention agreed to pay the *Witness*.[125] In exchange for that subsidy, Solomon agreed to give space in the paper for publicizing all the Convention's programs of work and to assume responsibility for the business affairs of the paper. The contract was to be reconsidered and renewed at the end of each five-year period.[126] Solomon agreed furthermore to share equally any profits the *Witness* might make.[127]

Solomon brought to the *Witness* a spice and wit not known before. His first editorials were short, pithy epigrams that caught attention and, by 1935, the State Board was no doubt glad to learn that the *Witness* was then operating on a much sounder financial basis.[128] In 1936, after some resolutions of differences between Dr. Solomon and the Board, the *Witness* printing press was sold to editor Solomon, the agreement was renewed,[129] and the steady progress already begun under Solomon continued. In the first decade of his career as editor, circulation doubled from 5,000 to 10,000.[130]

Theological Controversy

While theological debates at the beginning of this period were creating inner turmoil among some denominations and among some Baptists both Northern and Southern, Florida Baptists were calm. Florida Baptists were aware of the evolution controversy which was causing division and despair among others, but presumably they thought it would not come nigh them. At the beginning of this period the *Witness* editor disagreed with the claim of another writer that the church was losing its power and on the decline. On the contrary, the editor argued, the churches had never been so numerous or so effective before.[131]

---

[125]The annual deficit had often been more than $6,000.

[126]Rosser, *op. cit.,* pp. 156-157.

[127]*Florida Baptist Witness,* June 4, 1931, p. 6.

[128]State Board, *Minutes,* Jan. 22, 1935.

[129]*Ibid.,* May 4, 1936.

[130]Florida Baptist Convention, *Annual,* 1930, p. 68; also Florida Baptist Convention, *Annual,* 1941, p. 78.

[131]Editorial, "Can the Churches Be Saved," *Florida Baptist Witness,* Nov. 23, 1921, p. 2.

Two of the old controversies that had rent the churches in time past, footwashing and anti-missions, still mentioned, were really dead as organized movements.[132] Landmarkism also was dying as a movement. Interestingly, whereas, a former executive secretary, L. D. Geiger, had praised Landmarkism, in 1923 C. M. Brittain praised Lackawana church in Black Creek association, the church which expelled a Landmark preacher who had influenced the fellowship.[133] Brittain later scored the Landmarkers again, warning that (1) they were not really missionary as they claimed, (2) they were actually fighting organized mission work, (3) and they were ignorant and disgruntled, taking advantage of those less ignorant than they were. He further warned the Convention that Landmarkers were still working in the Lafayette and Rocky Creek associations.[134] It appears however, that although Landmarkism was dying as an organized movement among Florida Baptists,[135] it was not dead yet, and some of its ideas persisted among Florida Baptists. For example, a series of articles on Baptist history, by S. L. Loudermilk, came out in the *Witness* in 1940 defending the Baptist succession theory espoused by the Landmarkers.[136] Another example of Landmark influence is the tendency to dogmatic authoritarianism which affected the response of many Florida Baptists to the evolution controversy and those theological issues it touched.

The evolution controversy was also in the background of the fundamentalist-modernist controversy which divided many Northern Baptists, and although many Florida Baptists were aware of that controversy, they were kept from a direct clash over that issue partly because liberalism never got a strong foothold among Florida Baptists and partly because skillful Florida Baptist leaders avoided the issues. For example, editor Mitchell suggested in 1925 that Southern Baptists learn from the mistakes of Northern Baptists and stop talking about the evolution-modernist-fundamentalist controversy for a time.[137]

Florida Baptists were not able to avoid the controversy completely,

---

[132]C. W. Branch, "Footwashing," *Florida Baptist Witness*, Sept. 21, 1921, p. 22; cf. Florida Baptist Convention, *Annual*, 1939, p. 18.

[133]Editorial, *Florida Baptist Witness*, Aug. 23, 1923, p. 14.

[134]*Ibid.*, Sept. 28, 1928.

[135]By the 1920's many Landmarkers had left the Southern Baptist Convention and formed their own independent organizations.

[136]*Florida Baptist Witness*, Mar. 21, 1940, pp. 4 ff.

[137]J. W. Mitchell, editorial, "Why Not Learn from Others," *Florida Baptist Witness*, June 25, 1925, p. 4.

however, and its issues were specifically reflected in the debate over the 1925 Southern Baptist Convention statement of faith. The statement of faith itself appears not to have been questioned, but the unsuccessful attempt by S. P. Stealey to supplement it by including a statement which categorically condemned evolution, created considerable discussion. The discussion was immediately provoked by quotations in the *Witness* from an article published originally in *The Gospel Witness,* by a Canadian Baptist, T. T. Shields, which obviously were read by many Florida Baptists. Shields apparently condemned Baptist denominational machinery in general and Southern Baptist Convention leaders in particular. Editor Mitchell, referring to Shields' statement, defended the reputation of Southern Baptist Convention leaders in an editorial.[138] Immediately, Dean Adcock responded with a letter condemning what he called the "bureaucracy" of the Southern Baptist Convention. Soon others joined in the debate, but eventually the debate turned out to be no debate at all since most of the people commenting in the *Witness* agreed in supporting the view that a categorical rejection of evolution should have been included in the Southern Baptist Convention statement of faith.[139] They agreed therefore in upholding a minority position which the Southern Baptist Convention had rejected, at least as a part of its statement of faith.[140]

This reaction of Florida Baptist leaders to the Southern Baptist Convention's handling of the evolution controversy may have been in the background of the Florida Baptist Convention's refusal in 1927 to participate with other conventions in sub-budgeting a historical film to be prepared by E. Y. Mullins for the Southern Baptist Convention.[141]

Finally, it seems probable that the continued influence of Landmark ideas, combined with reactions among Florida Baptists to the evolution controversy, contributed to the kind of theological dogmatic authoritarianism which developed among Florida Baptists in 1932. During that year, for example, in response to complaints from ministerial students at Stetson, the State Board approved a motion that a

---

[138]"Choice Specimens," *Florida Baptist Witness,* June 18, 1925, p. 5.

[139]*Florida Baptist Witness,* July 2, 1925, p. 9; cf. Len G. Broughton, "The New Way," *Florida Baptist Witness,* May 28, 1925, pp. 8-11.

[140]Letter by J. D. Adcock, "Dr. T. T. Shields Again," *Florida Baptist Witness,* July 2, 1925, p. 9. Here Adcock says that in the future it would be recognized that Stealey had been the true hero of the Southern Baptist Convention and that his position would dominate Southern Baptists.

[141]Florida Baptist Convention, *Annual,* 1927, pp. 24-25.

statement of Christian principles be drawn up and signed by the president and faculty of Stetson.[142] Whether such a statement was ever drawn up is not clear, but the idea persisted, for in the next Convention a resolution from the New River Association was adopted which called for all employees of the Convention to sign a theological statement in which they acknowledged (1) the deity of Jesus, (2) His virgin birth, (3) the substitutionary atonement, (4) the bodily resurrection of Jesus, (5) salvation by grace, and (6) the inspiration of the Scripture.[143] However, the records give no indication that this requirement was ever implemented and enforced. It is certain that the requirement was not demanded by the Convention in later years.

Social Concern—Between 1920 and 1940

Florida Baptists shared in the growth of Southern Baptists generally in the area of social concern. The range of their interests continued to be broad and reflected their sensitivity to changing social conditions and to the thought of other Christians about those conditions. At the beginning of this period one finds continued interest in the same areas of concern which were uppermost in the minds of Florida Baptists during the last years of the 1900-1920 era. Chief among these were the problems of war, temperance, social legislation, and a ministry to the sick. Between 1920 and 1940, some of these problems came to be viewed from a new perspective, especially the problem of war. To these areas of concern was added one other problem, that of labor relations.

One of the social problems engaging the attention of Florida Baptists following World War I was war itself, their thinking on war providing the most significant example of the new perspective from which they viewed an old problem. At first, Florida Baptists simply joined others in passing resolutions in favor of disarmament and of those political candidates who promised to work for disarmament.[144] By the 1930's, however, Florida Baptists were readily approving statements opposing war rather categorically, statements indeed that bordered on pacifism.[145]

---

[142]State Board, *Minutes,* May 9, 1932.

[143]Florida Baptist Convention, *Annual,* 1932, pp. 12-13.

[144]*Ibid.,* 1921, p. 86.

[145]"Report of the Social Service Committee," Florida Baptist Convention, *Annual,* 1936, pp. 129-130, where the committee said: "War never settled any moral question" and "every war has been followed by a moral decline." Cf. editorial, *Florida Baptist Witness,* Apr. 29, 1937, p. 6.

Florida Baptists continued to support the temperance cause. They had rejoiced over the passing of the Eighteenth Amendment, which outlawed liquor, and they lamented efforts to get the law repealed.[146] When the law was repealed, their lamentations multiplied.[147] In an editorial in the *Witness* editor Solomon exposed one of the most profound incongruities in the manufacture of liquor in observing that while economic stress, hunger and starvation threatened millions, Americans approved the use of grain to make liquor.[148]

Their regret at the repeal of prohibition reflects the continued belief of many Florida Baptists in the use of legislation to enforce their understanding of ethical and moral propriety. Other issues for which they sought legislative control and law enforcement during this period were (1) the prohibition of government appropriations to sectarian schools,[149] (2) restriction of business and commercial amusements on Sunday,[150] and (3) the increase in crime, disorder, and immorality.[151]

A third area of continuing social concern, ministry to the sick, moved Florida Baptists in the direction of concrete action. Discussion of the possibility of establishing a hospital was brought up again at the State Board in 1938, and a committee was appointed to study the matter.[152] At the end of this period, however, nothing more was being done than the consideration of various proposals that were being made.[153]

Interest in social concerns came to include other issues and indeed evoked so much comment that some criticism was drawn. Florida Baptists were warned of becoming so preoccupied with social concern that they were in danger of neglecting solid evangelism and religious education.[154] It is doubtful whether Florida Baptists were guilty of this imbalance, but it is clear that their broadening social interests were not to be curtailed by such criticism. Social service committee reports indicated interest also in the problems of gambling, bad movies, and

---

[146]Florida Baptist Convention, *Annual,* 1926, p. 91.

[147]Editorial by J. L. Rosser, "Florida's Moral Crisis," *Florida Baptist Witness,* Aug. 23, 1934, p. 4.

[148]*Ibid.*

[149]Florida Baptist Convention, *Annual,* 1923, p. 83.

[150]*Ibid.,* 1927, pp. 78-79; cf. *Ibid.,* 1924, p. 39.

[151]Editorial by S. B. Rogers, "Christian World Taking Notice," *Florida Baptist Witness,* Feb. 15, 1923, p. 2.

[152]State Board, *Minutes,* Sept. 20, 1938.

[153]Florida Baptist Convention, *Annual,* 1939, pp. 156-157.

[154]*Florida Baptist Witness,* Feb. 9, 1928, p. 3.

the continued incidence of lynching. To each of these problems opposition was expressed.[155] However, on one relatively new issue, labor relations, Florida Baptists had difficulty finding a stance to defend. The rights of labor and management were each recognized, but the issues between them seemed not clearly understood. Child-labor legislation, for example, was opposed on the ground that it gave the control of children over to the federal government.[156]

Finally, while continuing to emphasize the control of public morals through legislation and public protest against all manner of improper behavior, including dress,[157] Florida Baptists gave less and less attention to the control of the behavior of church members through church discipline. The custom of listing statistics in the Convention annual reports on the number of people excluded for various reasons came to an end in 1925 when the last such report was published. During that year 1,416 were expelled, whereas only 305 were restored. Obviously, church discipline was losing its effectiveness. Thus in the 1920's church discipline not only largely ceased to be effective; it largely ceased to be.

Negro Baptists: A Bad Conscience and Improved Relationships

Between 1920 and 1940, Florida Baptists and their Negro Baptist brethren probably would have continued to drift apart had it not been for their shared common interest in education. Negro Baptist leaders continued to have a profound concern for the education of their people in general and their ministerial leadership in particular. They lacked resources to do all they knew needed to be done, however, and they had no recourse but to turn to their white Baptist brethren for help. Sometimes some help came and sometimes it did not come. In 1921, when help was asked from the State Board for Collier's colored school at Saint Augustine, the Board declined the request.[158] In 1924, help was promised for the Florida Memorial College at Live Oak,[159] and again in 1926.[160] Finally, in 1927 after much discussion the Board agreed to give $50.00 per month to Florida Normal and Indus-

---

[155]Florida Baptist Convention, *Annual,* 1936, pp. 129-130.
[156]*Ibid.,* 1938, pp. 14-15.
[157]*Ibid.,* p. 104.
[158]State Board, *Minutes,* May 24, 1921.
[159]*Ibid.,* Jan. 15, 1924.
[160]*Ibid.,* Jan. 5, 1926.

trial Institute in St. Augustine.[161] Also, in 1927, the State Board report to the Convention indicated a bad conscience on the subject of race. Executive secretary Brittain reported that several times recently he had been called into council on race problems. He did not indicate the nature of the problems, but he concluded that "while we are supporting missionaries in Africa we have neglected the African at our doors too long."[162] The report on Home Missions also reflected keen interest in closer relationships with Negro Baptists and a desire to help them.[163] It was not until the 1930's, however, that those promises came to be fulfilled with any regularity and then the help given was very small, including separated designated amounts for Florida Normal School at Saint Augustine for holding Negro institutes.[164]

In 1936, W. C. Sale, being given two months off from his church, volunteered to work with Negro Baptists as the Convention's representative receiving pay only for expenses. Two things Sale did were significant. First, he held Bible conferences for Negro church leaders. Second, he surveyed their educational institutions and needs. He found that Negro Baptists in Florida owned school property with an estimated value of one-half million dollars, including the property of four functioning schools: Florida Normal in Saint Augustine, Florida Memorial in Live Oak, an unnamed school in Orlando, and another in Lakeland.[165] Negro Baptist leaders expressed deep gratitude for the meager help the Florida Baptist Convention was able and willing to give.[166] In 1937, when Florida Negro Baptists were scheduled to entertain the National Baptist Convention in Jacksonville, Florida Baptist Convention leaders helped them to secure the Armory for a meeting place.[167]

Thus, toward the end of the 1930's relationships between Negro Baptists and white Baptists in Florida became increasingly friendly, with some white leaders recognizing the remarkable progress Negroes were making and expressing genuine desire to help them.[168]

---

[161]*Ibid.,* Jan. 4, 1927.

[162]Florida Baptist Convention, *Annual,* 1926, p. 17.

[163]*Ibid.,* pp. 78-79.

[164]State Board, *Minutes,* Jan. 22, 1935; cf. Florida Baptist Convention, *Annual,* 1934, p. 30; and for individual Negro members in need, State Board, *Minutes,* Jan. 6, 1931.

[165]Florida Baptist Convention, *Annual,* 1936, pp. 78-79.

[166]*Ibid.,* p. 83.

[167]*Ibid.,* 1937, p. 56; State Board, *Minutes,* Jan. 28, 1936.

[168]For example, an editorial by A. J. Moncrief, *Florida Baptist Witness,* Apr. 25, 1940, pp. 4ff.

In retrospect, it appears that the 1920's and 1930's proved to be two challenging and difficult decades for many Florida Baptists. They were difficult years because despite the optimism and enthusiasm with which Florida Baptists began this period, they had to face great problems. Having viewed the future in the early 1920's with hope, and enjoying a brief period of prosperity, toward the end of the 1920's they were threatened at the same time with symptoms of spiritual decline and economic disaster. Not only were some of their institutions and departments threatened with extinction by economic difficulties, but the unity of the Convention was sometimes threatened by theological controversies which had weakened Baptists in other parts of the country. Florida Baptists were also challenged by the problem of reaching a new generation of rural people now removed to the growing cities.

It is to the credit of Florida Baptists during this period that they not only survived the great depression and maintained their unity and their institutions, but they achieved modest success in reaching people in the rapidly growing towns and cities as well. However, as the churches succeeded, church discipline declined, at least in the traditional form. Organizational development reflected another kind of discipline, nonetheless, which prepared Florida Baptists for a successful ministry in the 1940's.

Associational Development and Growth

1940

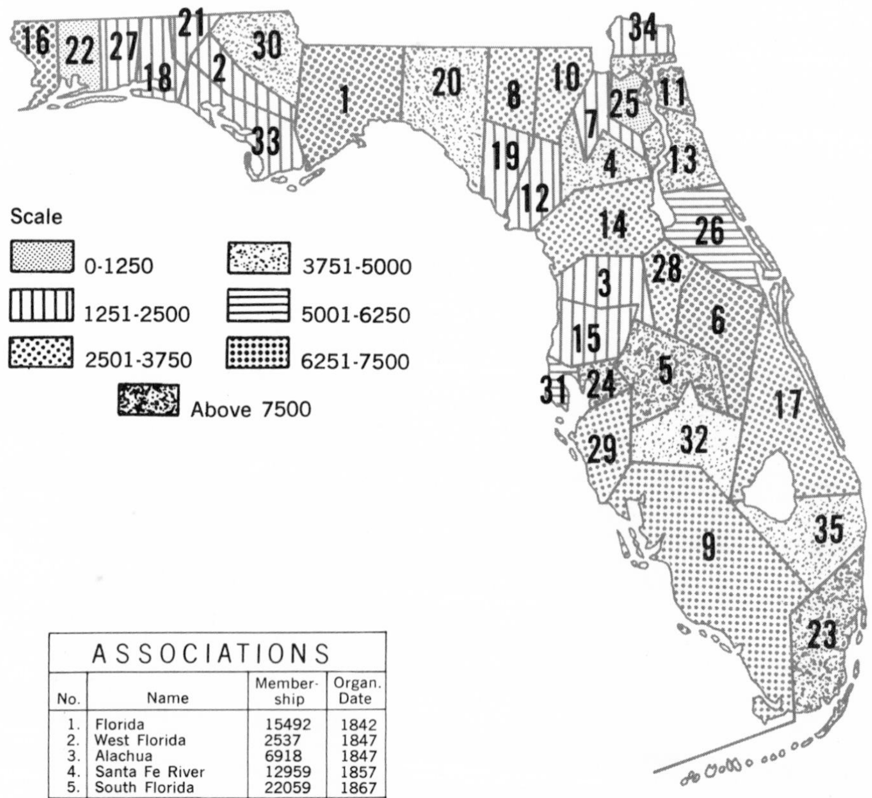

ASSOCIATIONS			
No.	Name	Membership	Organ. Date
1.	Florida	15492	1842
2.	West Florida	2537	1847
3.	Alachua	6918	1847
4.	Santa Fe River	12959	1857
5.	South Florida	22059	1867
6.	Wekiwa	38074	1870
7.	New River	3715	1872
8.	Suwannee	6721	1873
9.	Peace River	3918	1876
10.	Beulah	6036	1879
11.	Jacksonville	67939	1879
12.	Harmony	3377	1879
13.	St. John's River	11314	1879
14.	Marion	11705	1885
15.	Pasco	5098	1885
16.	Pensacola Bay	31438	1887
17.	Indian River	10969	1889
18.	Graves	4425	1890
19.	Lafayette	2109	1891
20.	Middle Florida	4458	1900
21.	Holmes County	4523	1905
22.	Santa Rosa	6077	1907
23.	Miami	59975	1909
24.	Tampa Bay	46726	1911
25.	Black Creek	6856	1913
26.	Seminole	12436	1914
27.	Okaloosa	4779	1923
28.	Lake County	8880	1924
29.	Southwest Florida	13825	1924
30.	Chipola	9287	1925

ASSOCIATIONS			
No.	Name	Membership	Organ. Date
31.	Pinellas	24107	1932
32.	Orange Blossom	10786	1932
33.	Northwest Coast	16025	1934
34.	Northeast Florida	7765	1938
35.	Palm Lake	20775	1938

CHAPTER SIX

Recovery from the Depression and New Problems: 1940 - 1950

Although Florida was well on its way to full recovery from the depression by 1941, Florida Baptist Convention leadership, long accustomed to economic difficulty, was very reluctant to expand. For example, an optimistic budget of $138,000, projected by the State Board late in 1940, was reduced to $86,705 upon the recommendation of a survey committee.[1] Those who planned the optimistic budget were perhaps more sensitive than they knew, for the Convention was to enjoy a freedom from economic difficulty in the next decade that was without parallel in all its previous history. The economic prosperity which came to the Convention in the 1940's was due mainly to the increase in population and industry which were both greatly accelerated by World War II. Population in Florida increased 46.1% between 1940 and 1950, from 1,897,414 in 1940 to 2,771,305 in 1950. Military camps and industrial plants established in or near the major cities and port towns joined with migration to create several burgeoning metropolitan areas, including Jacksonville, Pensacola, Tampa, and Miami.

The total number of churches was not significantly affected by this growth; indeed for several years the total number of churches reported represented a decrease over the preceding year. The overall increase between 1940 and 1950 was from 817 to 911 churches. It is worth noting for comparison that in 1929 the total number of churches was 908. Total membership shows a much more significant increase, from 155,965 in 1940 to 278,668, an increase of over 79%.

---

[1]State Board, *Minutes,* Jan. 27, 1941.

Thus, growth in total church membership more than kept pace with the population increase. The imbalance between the slow growth of the number of churches and the rapid increase in church membership means that many churches enjoyed great growth, particularly in the cities. In some cases, that growth probably resulted in the closing of some rural churches because of extensive migration to the cities and because of the shortage of ministers. A study reported in 1942 indicates that 396 of the 773 churches in the Convention were rural. Of these, 226 had preaching every Sunday. Moreover, the highest pastor's salary among these 396 rural churches was $1,540 and the average rural minister's salary was between $200 and $300 per year.[2]

During the late 1940's there were great increases in the income of the Convention and also in the demands on the Convention's budget. Cooperative program receipts grew from $137,079 in 1940 to $821,805 in 1950.[3] To further efficiency and equity, two practices became increasingly prominent and necessary. First, committees had to be relied on more and more to handle many detailed requests formerly handled directly either by the State Board or the Convention. Second, guidelines and policies for various departments and areas of work had to be developed. In short, the efficiency move, viewed earlier as a threat to spiritual life, came now to be regarded as a necessity.

The Convention and the Churches: Growth in the War Years

The move to committee efficiency, mentioned earlier, not only made the work of the Convention easier. It also reduced the amount of direct action the Convention in session could take. Thus, the Convention was like the State Board in moving increasingly and of necessity to a form of administration that came from the top down, through presiding officers, administrators, and committees. The Board, which met longer and more often, had to carry many more responsibilities, and the Convention assembled mainly to give sanction to the work of the Board, committees and administrators. On the other hand, in accordance with tradition, the State Board still received many general directions from the Convention through its actions in session and through committee appointments. For example, one of the first expressions of interest in some form of ministry to migrant laborers came from the Convention in 1941, and a ministry to migrants devel-

[2]Florida Baptist Convention, *Annual,* 1942, p. 111.
[3]*Ibid.,* 1952, p. 31.

oped in the 1950's and 1960's by the State Board in cooperation with the Home Mission Board.[4] Another example may be seen in the Convention's action in approving the recommendations of a survey committee in 1941 which included: (1) abolishing the evangelism department and placing the state evangelists under the direct supervision of the executive secretary-treasurer, (2) placing the Baptist Student Department under the direct supervision of the executive secretary-treasurer, (3) requiring the State Baptist Student secretary, then stationed in Gainesville, to spend one day or more each month in Jacksonville, and (4) reduction of the budget recommended by the State Board.[5]

The remarkable growth enjoyed by many town and city churches in the early 1940's contributed to a new spirit of optimism in the Convention, but it was an optimism that was different from that sometimes expressed earlier.[6] Despite the economic progress accompanying church growth, the optimism which now prevailed was more cautious, for it was combined with a spirit of realism, resulting from the shattering effects of the depression and the war. The goals adopted for the Centennial Crusade in 1945 (celebrating the organization of the Southern Baptist Convention in 1845) may appear to contradict this estimate of realistic optimism, for the 40,000 baptisms hoped for would have more than quadrupled the 8,336 baptized in Florida Baptist Convention churches the preceding year.[7] Lee Nichols, pastor of First Church, Daytona Beach, was chairman of a committee to promote the crusade, and great interest in the event was aroused.[8] Many, however, thought the goal was too high. According to the secretary-treasurer at the time, the unusually high goal created division in the Convention.[9] Whether the realism or pessimism contributed to or accounted for the failure of the crusade perhaps no one can say, but it was certainly a failure in a statistical sense, for the number of baptisms totaled only around 13,000. Nonetheless, it pushed the total number of baptisms above 10,000 for the first time, and the number has never fallen below that since 1946. Twenty-five years later the goal of 40,000 baptisms in a single year still has not been reached.

In 1950, when many Florida Baptist churches participated in the

---

[4]*Ibid.*, 1941, p. 42.

[5]*Ibid.*, 1949-50, pp. 21ff.

[6]Chapter V.

[7]Florida Baptist Convention, *Annual*, 1945, p. 69.

[8]Perhaps Lee Nichols' enthusiasm for state-wide success was inspired in part by his success in his own church. In 1945 his church reported 106 baptisms.

[9]Interview with Dr. John H. Maguire, August 27, 1968.

simultaneous revival efforts promoted by the Southern Baptist Convention, the results were more impressive, with a total of 18,460 baptisms reported.

One other significant event which captured the attention of the Convention during the 1940's was the million dollar campaign for Stetson. Although this campaign will be discussed in more detail later, it is worth mentioning here that, like the unrealistically high goal for the Centennial Crusade, the million dollar campaign at first appeared overly optimistic, for it moved slowly. The difference of course is that this goal was reached, despite the division which hampered the campaign. The Convention during the 1940's was divided also by two other sets of events. First, it was divided by the conflict between some younger men and the older leaders during and following World War II. A kind of generation gap developed which affected discussion of various issues.[10] Second, division was created over the cooperative program percentages adopted by the Convention. When John Maguire became executive secretary-treasurer in 1945, the division was 65% for state causes and 35% for South-wide causes. Carl Bates of Leesburg challenged the division, and although it was approved, 1945 was the last year such a large percentage of the budget went to state causes.[11] After 1945 the percentage moved and stayed nearer to a 50-50 division during the rest of the 1940's.

It is difficult to make broad generalizations with confidence as to what came nearest to dominating the attention of Florida Baptists during the 1940's. It seems clear, however, that only one event affected much of the thought and action of Florida Baptists during the 1940's the way the depression did during the 1930's. That event was World War II. No other event evoked the spontaneous over and above giving of Florida Baptists as did the relief campaign to help victims of war in 1946. Florida Baptists were asked for $155,000. They gave over $300,000.[12]

Finally, during the 1940's the Convention continued the tradition of varied leadership, being served by eight presidents, only three of whom served two terms. Because of growth in the size of the Convention, meeting places were gradually being restricted to the larger towns and cities. This restriction is significant as a symbol of an important change which began to take place in the late 1940's. The rural and

---

[10] *Ibid.*

[11] *Ibid.* Also, Florida Baptist Convention, *Annual,* 1948, p. 34.

[12] *Florida Baptist Witness,* September 9, 1954, p. 3.

C. H. Bolton, *Executive Secretary,*
1941 - 1944

small town churches which had been strong in the past were now in danger of being forgotten, in part because the Convention could no longer meet in the small towns as it had in the past, and in part because many small towns and rural churches were being shrunk by migration to the larger cities.

Freedom From Debt: The Coming of Bolton and Maguire

Having served as state secretary since 1926, C. M. Brittain resigned on May 6, 1941. He had served as executive secretary-treasurer for over fourteen years. Despite the fact that some of the greatest economic difficulties in Florida history were experienced during those years, Florida Baptists had done rather well under his leadership.[13] It is clear that Dr. Brittain was a mature, stabilizing force in a time of great crisis and difficulty.

Dr. Charles H. Bolton was elected to replace him.[14] A native of Alabama, Bolton had been in the printing business before entering the ministry, and had served churches in Alabama before coming to the First Baptist Church of West Palm Beach in 1927.[15] After a remarkable leadership of that church and service to the Florida Baptist Convention he became associate secretary of the Relief and Annuity Board in Dallas, Texas. From that work he answered the call of Florida Baptists to return to Florida, where he assumed office as executive secretary-treasurer on June 15, 1941. An energetic, able administrator and good business man, Bolton distinguished his brief administration with several significant actions. First, he improved finances. The Convention freed the Rogers Building from debt, becoming debt free for the first time in many years.[16] In addition Dr. Bolton led in establishing the financial policy of keeping a reserve fund to provide for emergencies. By 1945, $99,990 had been put into this reserve fund.[17] Also, under his leadership the State Board voted in 1943 to discontinue the One Hundred Thousand Club (mentioned in Chapter Five) and to pay the $38,972 on hand for that campaign to

---

[13]During his administration the number of churches had grown from 855 in 1926 to 973 in 1941 and church membership had increased from 109,444 to 115,675. However, his work, like that of the Convention during the depression, is not adequately measured by statistics. This fact is very apparent in a special address delivered to the 1942 Convention by Dr. John Rosser in appreciation of Dr. Brittain. Florida Baptist Convention, *Annual,* 1942, pp. 10-12.

[14]State Board, *Minutes,* May 7, 1941.

[15]Rosser, *op. cit.,* p. 108.

[16]Florida Baptist Convention, *Annual,* 1944, p. 14.

[17]*Ibid.,* 1945, p. 61.

Stetson toward the million dollar campaign commitment the Board had already made to the University.[18]

Second, Bolton led the State Board and the Convention in the inauguration of a city mission program involving a cooperative arrangement with the Home Mission Board by which expenses of the city missionaries would be shared equally by the State Board of Missions and the Home Mission Board. Under this arrangement, superintendents of city missions were established in four major cities, including H. M. Liechty in Jacksonville, Clifford Walker in Tampa, Theo Farr in Pensacola, and J. E. Johnstone in Miami.[19] The responsibilities of these missionaries included making surveys to determine need for new churches, organizing new churches, and assisting the established churches in their missionary work.

Third, under Bolton's leadership, the State Board employed in 1944, a stewardship secretary, Dr. B. C. Land, pastor of Riverside Church in Tampa. Mr. R. G. LeTourneau, the Texas philanthropist, offered to share equally with the Board in providing the salary and expenses of the secretary. Much like the efficiency and enlistment secretaries mentioned earlier, the stewardship secretary promoted stewardship, tithing, and evangelism in the churches.[20]

Finally, under Bolton's leadership the character of the state mission program began to change. Significant in this process of change was the gradual shift in emphasis from supporting missionary pastors as the main approach to employing area missionaries who would guide and encourage local churches to undertake the support of mission stations and mission pastors. Dewey Mann, for example, was stationed in Tallahassee in 1942 and was made field secretary to direct mission work in a district including eleven associations. Later in 1944 Mann was made assistant to the executive secretary. Under Mann's leadership four promotional workers were employed in West Florida.[21]

On July 1, 1944, Bolton resigned to become pastor of Riverside Baptist Church in Miami. To succeed him, Dr. Thomas Hansen and Dr. Wallace Rogers were nominated and elected, in succession, but each man declined to accept the position. For several months while the Convention was without a permanent executive secretary-

[18]State Board, *Minutes*, Dec. 10, 1943.

[19]Rosser, *op. cit.*, p. 111. Also see *Florida Baptist Witness*, Feb. 22, 1945, where the agreement is quoted in full.

[20]Rosser, *op. cit.*, p. 112.

[21]*Ibid.*, pp. 110-111.

John H. Maguire, *Executive Secretary,*
1944 - 1967

treasurer, Homer G. Linsday, Sr., served as acting secretary.[22] In December John H. Maguire was nominated and elected. He assumed his duties as the new state secretary on January 15, 1945.[23] A native of Oklahoma, Maguire grew up in Texas and was educated at Howard Payne College in Texas, George Washington University in Washington, D. C., and Southern Baptist Theological Seminary. He came to Florida as executive secretary-treasurer from the Calvary Baptist church in Birmingham, Alabama.

The most significant change brought about during the first five years of Maguire's administration was the further reorganization of the work of state missions. One of the first changes was the securing of an agreement with the Home Mission Board whereby the Home Mission Board would pay half the salaries of several regional missionaries. The State was organized into eight districts, and Dewey Mann was named field Secretary.[24] Later when Mann returned to the pastorate, further reorganization took place, and the name was changed from the Department of Missions, Evangelism, and Stewardship to Cooperative Missions Department, with Clifford Walker as secretary. To this department was assigned the task of promoting city missions, rural missions, evangelism, stewardship and schools of missions.

Another significant accomplishment of Maguire during the first five years of his administration was the establishing of a clear understanding of the executive-secretary's responsibilities and authority. This clarification came out of some minor tensions which developed between Maguire and employees of the Board, and it involved the right of censorship over the state paper and the power to determine who would be employed by the State Board. An example is the conflict which appears to have developed between Dr. Maguire and editor Solomon soon after Maguire began his work. Some conflict is clearly implied in a motion passed by the State Board in June, 1945, which instructed the chairman of the executive committee to advise Solomon that he was an employee of the Convention and that he should clear all articles and editorials dealing with the policies of the work and program of the Florida Baptist Convention with the executive secretary.[25] The exact issue in the editorials alluded to was not stated in the motion, but it appears to have been the hospital question. Dr. Solomon wanted the Convention to underwrite the construction of

---

[22]Florida Baptist Convention, *Annual,* 1945, p. 56.
[23]State Board, *Minutes,* Dec. 5, 1944.
[24]Rosser, *op. cit.,* p. 114.
[25]State Board, *Minutes,* June 5, 1945.

five hospitals and spoke frequently in support of the hospital venture in his editorials. The State Board and the Convention decided against such a venture. Thus, according to Dr. Maguire, Solomon was editorializing against Convention policy.[26] No executive secretary before him had had such authority, but then no executive secretary before him had carried such heavy responsibility as he was to carry.

During the 1940's the State Board's projected budget increased regularly and significantly, and after the reduction of the budget for 1941 from $138,000 to $86,705, the budget was rarely questioned or changed by the Convention. In 1950, the budget recommended for 1950-51 was $862,900.[27] As the budget increased and the staff of the state offices enlarged, the work of the Board increased. Fortunately, however, since the Board moved more and more in the direction of relying on committees and administrative leadership, it appears that the work of the Board really became less burdensome on individual members than in earlier years when it had less work to do.

One new object of special interest to which the State Board gave attention during the mid-1940's was helping churches in college centers. This need had first come to the attention of the Board in 1939.[28] Following World War II rapid growth in the number of Baptist young people in college placed severe strain on several churches near college campuses. It was necessary for those churches to provide additional facilities at a time when they were least prepared to provide them. Among the churches placed under special strain by the situation were First Church, DeLand; First Church, Tallahassee; and First Church, Gainesville. The State Board responded generously. In the year 1948, $6,000 was given for this purpose, $6,000 again in 1949, and $10,000 in 1950.[29]

In 1947 the Sally L. Yewell Memorial Chapel was constructed on the second floor of the Baptist Building with part of a legacy of $100,000 by Miss Yewell to the Florida Baptist Convention.[30]

Department Changes and Additions

As the financial resources of Florida Baptists increased substan-

---

[26]Telephone interview with Dr. Maguire, May 26, 1970. Also see State Board, *Minutes,* Dec. 5, 1944, June 5, 1945, and Dec. 9, 1947.

[27]Florida Baptist Convention, *Annual,* 1950, p. 41.

[28]State Board, *Minutes,* January 23-24, 1939.

[29]Florida Baptist Convention, *Annual,* 1948, p. 31, 1949, p. 44, and 1950, p. 35.

[30]*Florida Baptist Witness,* Apr. 3, 1947.

tially, the departments, agencies and institutions owned by or related to the Convention enjoyed great prosperity. In addition some new institutions and departments were created by Florida Baptists, some by the Convention itself, and others by local groups, which groups in some cases hoped for Convention support.

Thus, the Convention found it necessary to establish a tradition of distinction in thought about its agencies and areas of work. A careful distinction was therefore made between two kinds of aid. In the first category was that aid and support given to those agencies or institutions created, sponsored, controlled or otherwise directly related to the Convention. A second category of aid which came to be reflected in the Convention's pattern of support in the 1940's was temporary aid to local institutions which were expected to remain largely autonomous. Some examples are aid to local churches, hospitals, and, in some cases, children's homes. The primary attention of the Convention, however, was given to those agencies or areas of work directly related to the Convention.

Cooperative Missions, Evangelism and Stewardship

In January, 1940, the Convention voted to instruct the State Board to employ a superintendent of evangelism. Allen S. Cutts, who had been serving the Convention as promotion secretary, was assigned this task. His employment would have created a regular department of evangelism, except for the fact that before the year 1941 was out he accepted a pastorate in another state and was not replaced. Desire was expressed in 1942 by the Convention Committee on Evangelism for a department of evangelism, but no action was taken. Moreover, T. O. Reese, after serving nine years as state evangelist, resigned in 1943. Pat Wimberly, employed as state evangelist for only a few months, resigned the same year to re-enter the pastorate. Thus the work of evangelism still had no full-time direction and supervision.

In 1948, however, the Department of Cooperative Missions was created by reorganization and consideration of several areas of the work of state missions, including evangelism and stewardship. Before 1948 these areas of work had been under the direct supervision of the executive secretary-treasurer. This new department was placed under the direction of Clifford Walker, whose responsibility included the promotion of rural missions, city missions, schools of missions, evangelism and stewardship. The state was divided into five geographical districts, with superintendents over each district. In addition there were three city missionaries, one each in Jacksonville, the Tampa-St. Petersburg area, and in Miami.[31]

One of the first things Clifford Walker did was to arrange for the promotion of preacher's schools, which had been part of the work of state missions, to be transferred to the Department of Christian Education, where, under the direction of J. Harrison Griffin, these schools could be related to Stetson University.[32]

A second move that came from this newly created department was the creation of an annual state-wide evangelistic conference. The first of these conferences was held on March 8-9, 1949, and included on the program such well known personalities as R. G. Lee, renowned pastor of Bellevue Baptist Church in Memphis, Tennessee, J. B. Lawrence, executive secretary of the Home Mission Board, and C. E. Matthews, superintendent of evangelism for the Southern Baptist Convention.[33] This conference was to become a popular annual event among Florida Baptists.

Sunday School Growth, and January Bible Study

In 1946 Dr. W. W. Willian resigned as state Sunday School secretary. He had served the Convention for 30 years. Under his leadership the number of Sunday Schools had increased from 469 in 1915 to 803 in 1945, and enrollment had increased from 38,566 to 130,271. Vacation Bible schools had been introduced and had become an established part of Sunday School work and church life.[34] Moreover, much credit for growth in church membership from 59,931 in 1915 to 199,483 in 1945 must be given to the Sunday Schools and to Willian's leadership. In the 1940's the great growth of the town and city churches was dramatically illustrated in the great growth in Sunday School attendance. The large Sunday Schools reported in the 1930's were superseded by more and still larger schools in the 1940's. In 1944, for example, Main Street Church in Jacksonville was again leading the state in Sunday School attendance, averaging around 1200, but there were then 18 churches with 500 or more in Sunday School. In 1948 there were 36 churches with more than 400 in Sunday School, and Allapattah Church in Miami was the leading church with 1480.[35]

---

[31]Florida Baptist Convention, *Annual,* 1948, pp. 53-54.
[32]*Ibid.,* p. 85.
[33]*Ibid.,* 1948, p. 56.
[34]Rosser, *op. cit.,* p. 141.
[35]*Florida Baptist Witness,* Mar. 4, 1948, p. 9.

When Dr. Willian retired in 1946, Tom Collins, who had been serving as an associate in the Sunday School department, was elected to replace him.[36] He served for only a very short time, however, and at the 1947 Convention, Glenn Bridges was introduced as the new Sunday School secretary.[37]

One new feature of Sunday School work introduced in 1948 was the promotion of January Bible study in a special week in which the churches were asked to study one book of the Bible each year, using material provided by the Sunday School Board in Nashville. In 1948 the book studied was Ephesians, and 75 churches participated, earning 1579 awards.[38]

By the end of 1948 Bridges had resigned to become a missionary, and C. F. Barry was elected to replace him.[39] By 1950, Barry was setting ambitious goals for the future of Sunday School work in Florida, and could review the past decade with pride in the progress which Florida Baptists had made. He pointed out in his annual report of 1950 that during the last year Florida had led all other states in the Southern Baptist Convention in standard Sunday School units.[40] He reported that between 1940 and 1950 Sunday School enrollment had increased from 117,343 to 214,402.

Training Union: Beginning of "M" Night

Despite the able leadership of O. K. Radford, during the early 1940's the total enrollment in Training Union suffered greatly because of the number of young men entering military service.[41] Because the Training Union was still primarily a young people's organization and because of transportation problems many Training Unions died, and others declined in enrollment during World War II. However, when the war ended, the situation was greatly improved, so that by the end of the decade the total growth was impressive. Training Union enrollment grew from 37,778 in 1940 to 68,899 in 1950. Though still small compared to the Sunday School, the Training Union had become a well established part of Florida Baptist life. In addition to promoting annual assemblies at DeLand and West Florida, Radford and his staff promoted youth week and Christian home week in the

---

[36]State Board, *Minutes,* June 7, 1946.
[37]Florida Baptist Convention, *Annual,* 1947, p. 33.
[38]*Ibid.,* 1950, p. 48.
[39]*Ibid.,* 1948, p. 29.
[40]*Ibid.,* 1950, p. 52.
[41]*Ibid.,* 1944, p. 61.

churches and held district and state Training Union meetings to stimulate the growth of Training Union work.

Also in the 1940's the Florida Baptist Training Union department, in cooperation with the Southern Baptist Convention, began holding associational simultaneous mass meetings. In 1945, the first of these meetings, called "M" (Mobilization) night meetings, were held. The purpose of these meetings was to project plans for the work of Training Union for the coming year.[42] The meetings were held on the first Monday in December, and, although attendance reports are not available for 1945, the total attendance at the 1946 meetings was estimated at 10,000.[43] By the end of the decade every association was participating in this mass meeting.[44]

Brotherhood

Although statistical reports on Brotherhood enrollment were not printed in the *Annuals,* it is clear from the reports of secretary J. Harrison Griffin that the Brotherhood movement among Florida Baptists enjoyed significant growth under his leadership. Griffin worked diligently to enlist the men of the churches in the total life of their local churches and the denomination. In the early 1940's the Brotherhood department gave special attention to the Hundred Thousand Club, to the Million Dollar Campaign for Stetson, and to preparation for the Centennial Crusade. While the crusade was still in progress, however, Griffin resigned to become secretary of the new Department of Christian Education, in which he devoted full time to the Million Dollar Campaign for Stetson.[45] Under Griffin's leadership the number of Brotherhood organizations had almost quintupled from about 50 in 1939 to around 240 in 1944. Enrollment during that period had increased twenty-fold from around 240 to 4,800.[46]

Brotherhood-Music

In 1946 C. A. Holcomb was elected secretary of the newly created combination Brotherhood-Music Department.[47] Holcomb was a veteran of World War II, with previous experience as director of music and education in Louisiana and Texas, and was well qualified

---

[42]*Ibid.,* 1946, p. 51.
[43]*Ibid.*
[44]*Ibid.,* p. 55.
[45]State Board, *Minutes,* June 6, 1945.
[46]Rosser, *op. cit.,* p. 320.
[47]Florida Baptist Convention, *Annual,* 1946, p. 32.

to fill the dual role of secretary of a Brotherhood-Music Department.[48] In addition to sponsoring layman's rallies and a State Brotherhood Convention, Holcomb began planning activities to stimulate better music programs in the churches. Among the early activities he created were schools of music in the churches and music clinics held in several areas of the state; he also aided pastors in securing music and musicians for revivals. In 1948 Holcomb opened the Harmony Bay Youth Music Camp, a camp where 64 young people assembled for nine days of intensive music training. This camp was the beginning of a tradition and was symbolic of the great interest which was to develop in improving music programs for the churches. The most significant move, however, was probably the beginning of the annual state music festivals, the first of which was held in Gainesville in 1949.[49]

Woman's Missionary Union

During the last three years of Miss Louise Smith's administration as corresponding secretary, there were three significant accomplishments. First, the Florida Woman's Missionary Union became the first in the Southern Baptist Convention to reach its goal in the campaign to free the Southern Baptist Convention of debt by 1945. The southwide Woman's Missionary Union had agreed to raise $1,000,000 toward the campaign, and the Florida Union's part was $35,000, to be given through the Hundred Thousand Club and centennial offerings. Between 1941 and 1943 the total given to this campaign by Florida Baptist Women was $42,213.57. Second, during her tour of the mission fields in South America Miss Smith visited Mendoza, Argentina, where Florida's first foreign missionary, Frank J. Fowler, had served, and found a very crude church building which was scorned by the cultured people of the community. Despite their sacrifices the local members were not able to provide an adequate building. Upon returning to Florida, she displayed an adobe brick of mud and straw like those of the crude church building and challenged the women of the Florida Baptist Convention to build a better church at Mendoza. Under the direction of Mrs. Roy L. Lassiter, stewardship chairman, a special campaign to raise $15,000 for the project was begun. In a few weeks, with the help of the *Florida Baptist Witness* and a variety of friends, $19,145 had been raised. Although more than the goal, it was

---

[48]*Ibid.*, p. 8.
[49]*Ibid.*, p. 95.

not enough, but with additional help from the Lottie Moon offering the construction of the building was made possible. It was completed and dedicated in 1948.[50]

Third, Miss Smith helped to organize the first Inter-Racial Institute. The institute was a conference arranged by Baptist women leaders from the various Baptist conventions in Florida. The theme was missions, and proved to be a popular venture, held again in 1942, and 1943 when 500 persons attended. The program personalities included black and white missionaries.[51]

Other accomplishments under Miss Smith's leadership included the first Girls Auxiliary houseparty in April, 1942, and the first Royal Ambassadors conclave at Stetson the same year.

In October, 1943, when Miss Smith resigned to become Mrs. David Fair Boyd, Miss Elsie Renfroe, young people's secretary, was named acting secretary. While she was carrying this responsibility in 1944 a new project was adopted by the Florida Woman's Missionary Union. After hearing Mrs. M. E. Brantley, a Florida missionary to Nigeria, tell of the need and the anxiety of African youth for an education, and the lack of facilities, Florida Baptist women decided to raise $12,000 to establish a boys school in the Niger delta region. The sum of $14,711 was raised in 1944, and with $5,000 from the Lottie Moon Christmas offering, the new school was made possible.[52]

In December, 1944, Miss Josephine Jones was elected as the new executive secretary, and was presented to the Union at its annual meeting in January, 1945.[53] At the time the Florida Woman's Missionary Union had 1534 local organizations with a membership of 28,936. One of the first significant projects of the Union at the end of World War II was the World Relief and Rehabilitation Program adopted by the Southern Baptist Convention in 1946. Florida's portion was $150,850, of which the Woman's Missionary Union of Florida was asked to raise $50,000. Mrs. Roy Lassiter, stewardship chairman, directed this campaign also. A total of $51,125 was raised on schedule, which amount together with that raised by the Convention put the State well over its projected goal.[54] For several years Florida Baptist women continued to send money to similar relief efforts, pro-

---

[50]Lassiter, *op. cit.*, pp. 90-91.
[51]*Florida Baptist Witness,* July 22, 1943, p. 7.
[52]Lassiter, *op. cit.*, p. 94.
[53]*Ibid.*, p. 101.
[54]*Ibid.*, pp. 102-103.

viding food, clothing, and medicine to many who were the victims of the war.[55]

In 1946, after many years of holding its annual meetings in connection with the annual sessions of the Florida Baptist Convention, the Florida Woman's Missionary Union decided to hold its meetings at some other time of the year. Accordingly, the first separate meeting was held in March, 1947.

One of the special tasks long assumed by the Woman's Missionary Union was the education of the churches in the work of missions. One major means of accomplishing this task was the conducting of schools of missions in the churches. During the 1940's these schools became so popular and successful that they became too much for the Woman's Missionary Union to handle alone. Thus, after a peak year in 1946 when 143 such schools were arranged through the State office of the Woman's Missionary Union, the responsibility for these schools was transferred to the Department of Cooperative Missions of the State Convention.[56]

Finally, one of the most significant contributions of Florida Baptist women during the 1940's was the continuation of their interest and work in helping Negro Baptists in Florida. This work with Negro Baptists took two forms. First, inter-racial conferences were held in 1945 in several cities, including Tallahassee, Pensacola, Jacksonville, Tampa, Miami, and Orlando, and were repeated annually until 1950. In 1950 a small group of leaders from each of the three state Negro Baptist conventions met with Miss Josephine Jones to discuss more effective ways to promote racial understanding and harmony.[57] Second, Florida Baptist women became increasingly interested in the growth of Florida Normal and Industrial Memorial College, the only surviving Negro Baptist college in the state. Between 1942 and 1960 Florida Baptist Woman's Missionary Union gave the college a total of $86,657.18 for scholarships, current expenses and the development program.[58]

Baptist Student Union: Post-War Enlargement

Except at Florida State College for Women, the Baptist Student Union experienced a great loss in enrollment in the early 1940's because of the war. For example, Baptist enrollment at the University

---

[55]*Ibid.*
[56]*Ibid.*, pp. 107-108.
[57]*Ibid.*, p. 109.
[58]*Ibid.*

of Florida dropped from 750 to 110 in 1944.[59] However, the Union did not lose its effectiveness or decrease campus activity. For example, since 1941 a state spring retreat had been held each year.[60] In 1942 for the first time a fall retreat was held on every campus having a Baptist student organization. The purpose of these retreats was to plan for the beginning of the year's work. They became a tradition because they proved very helpful in launching an effective ministry among the students. Indeed, throughout the 1940's the Baptist Student Union was a most effective agency on several college campuses in keeping Baptist students close to the local churches. Great numbers of Baptist students were enlisted not only in the life of the local churches, but also in special religious activities on the campus sponsored by the Baptist Student Union. For example, in 1941 Billie Ruth Currin at Florida State College for Women reported that 78% of all Baptist girls at the college were involved in some aspect of Baptist activity.[61] Although numerous personnel changes took place on most college campuses, including the state Baptist Student office in Gainesville, student work maintained continuity and vitality because, once campus organizations were set up, the students themselves were very effective in enlisting other students. Roy Robinson resigned in 1940 and between 1940 and 1946 the office of state secretary was held successively by Sabin Landry, Jr. (1940-1942), Miss Billie Ruth Currin (1942-1943), Clyde B. Lipscomb (1943-1946), and Ray Koonce (1946-1956). Throughout the 1940's the state Baptist Student Union continued to promote fall retreats on each campus having an organized Union, an annual state student retreat each spring, and a state student convention.

When the war ended, Baptist veterans thronged the colleges and the Baptist Student Union had no difficulty in enlisting many of them in its activities.[62] The effectiveness of the B. S. U. in enlisting students in the life of local churches is reflected in the difficulties several churches in college centers had in providing facilities for the increasing numbers.

Also, after the war, the work of the B. S. U. took on new and enlarged dimensions. For example, the student summer missionary program had previously emphasized youth revival and vacation Bible

[59]Florida Baptist Convention, *Annual,* 1944, pp. 67-70.

[60]Spring retreats were held earlier, but the records do not indicate how regularly.

[61]Florida Baptist Convention, *Annual,* 1942, p. 65.

[62]*Ibid.,* 1946, pp. 83-85.

school work. After the war the B. S. U. began to send student missionaries during the summer to home and foreign mission fields in other states and countries around the world. One of the first such students was Miss Frances Horton, who was sent from Stetson as a 1947 summer missionary at Hawaii.[63] Later she went as a regular permanently appointed missionary to Japan.

By 1948 full-time student secretaries were working at Stetson University, the University of Florida, the University of Miami and Florida State University.[64] In addition some volunteer work was being done among the Baptist students at Florida Southern College and St. Petersburg Junior College.[65] By 1949 buildings for B. S. U. activities had

Baptist Student Center, University of Florida

been constructed or acquired and were in use on the campuses of Florida State University, the University of Florida, and Stetson University.

Stewardship Department Established and Consolidated

This new department was created by the State Board of Missions in 1944 and gave its first report to the Convention in 1945. B. C. Land was the first director, and his main responsibility was the promotion of stewardship and tithing.[66] In 1948 this department was consolidated with the Department of Missions and Evangelism under a new name, the Department of Cooperative Missions.[67]

---

[63]*Ibid.,* 1947, p. 89.
[64]*Ibid.,* 1948, p. 68.
[65]Rosser, *op. cit.,* p. 308.
[66]Florida Baptist Convention, *Annual,* 1945, pp. 52-55.
[67]*Ibid.,* 1948, pp. 53-54.

Christian Education

The Department of Christian Education, also a new department, was created in 1945 by the appointment of J. Harrison Griffin to the office of secretary of Christian Education. His major immediate work was the promotion of the million dollar campaign for Stetson.[68] Griffin served this office until the end of the decade, and under his direction the million dollar campaign was successfully completed.

Florida Baptist Foundation

The Florida Baptist Foundation was authorized by the Convention in 1946 and gave its first report to the Convention in 1947. The purpose of the Foundation was to receive, handle, or invest money or real estate from wills, bequests, or gifts, and to use these gifts as designated by the donor for any agencies of the Florida Baptist Convention. One of the first actions of the Foundation was to invest $100,000 which had been transferred from the Convention reserve fund to the Foundation in order that the income could be returned to the State Mission Board for mission causes.[69] By 1950 the Foundation was handling money received for the Stetson enlargement campaign, (the million dollar campaign) and for the W. M. U. scholarship fund.[70] For the first few years of its existence, the Foundation was not directed by an employee of the Board, but by trustees elected by the Convention.

Associational Growth

Associational growth slowed during the 1940's with only one new association, Gulf Stream, being formed in 1948. Geographical settlement did not change much since most of the increase in population involved migration into areas already settled. Also related to this stabilization of geographical settlement is the small increase in the number of churches, as indicated earlier. Little need was seen for the formation of new associations. The existing associations, however, began during the 1940's to be recognized by outsiders as a live force in Baptist life. During the early 1940's particularly, there were some very strong rural churches, and in associational meetings, judgments were formulated on critical issues that commanded the respect of denomina-

---

[68]Rosser, *op. cit.,* p. 320.

[69]Florida Baptist Convention, *Annual,* 1947, pp. 91-95.

[70]*Ibid.,* 1950, pp. 102-106.

tional and political leaders.[71] Thus, although the associations did not grow much in number during the 1940's, they did grow in influence.

Florida Baptist Children's Home

By 1940 the financial crisis of the late 1920's was forgotten, and the Florida Baptist Children's Home was enjoying better days. Although the home was still in debt, the debt was a manageable one, well within bounds, and by 1942 the mortgage debt was removed.

Because of local frictions between the administration of the Home and some of the citizens of the town of Arcadia, however, other problems developed. Some of the frictions stemmed from the earlier problems of the Trice administration, and the trustees, finding no way to remove them all, concluded that because of the frictions as well as the need for a larger location, it would be wise to move the Children's Home. Accordingly, a committee was appointed to consider new locations and plans were made to sell the property at Arcadia.[72] Since the Home had been in Arcadia for 40 years and since some local citizens had given generously to its support and valued it as an economic asset to the community, they naturally opposed the move. The trustees recommended it, however, and the Convention approved the move. Therefore, the old property at Arcadia was sold for $42,000, and after several offers and proposals were considered, the city of Lakeland was chosen as the new location for the Home. Through the help of the First Baptist Church and the Southside Baptist Church of Lakeland, and through donations from many friends, a 151-acre site was acquired, and the contract for the first buildings was let on May 6, 1947.[73] By the time the move was begun in 1948, six new buildings on the Lakeland property had been completed, and applications for admission were increasing.[74] The Home was then caring for 143 children in residence, and was giving aid to nine mothers outside the Home.[75]

Baptist Bible Institute

In the early 1940's a local group in Lakeland began a Bible School to supplement the meager theological education of older ministers who lacked education and qualifications or opportunity to attend college

---

[71]Article by an Episcopalian, Charles G. Hamilton, "What Makes Southern Baptists Tick," *Christian Century*, Oct. 3, 1951.

[72]Florida Baptist Convention, *Annual*, 1946, p. 96.

[73]Rosser, *op. cit.*, p. 278.

[74]Florida Baptist Convention, *Annual*, 1948, pp. 94-96.

[75]Rosser, *op. cit.*, p. 278.

and seminary for the normal ministerial preparation. Baptist Bible Institute was born in the minds of two ministers, Frank Faris, a rural minister and associational missionary for the South Florida Association, and T. S. Boehm, pastor of the First Baptist Church of Lakeland. With the encouragement and support of the South Florida Baptist Association and the First Baptist Church of Lakeland, these men moved to implement their conviction by opening the first session on September 7, 1943, using classrooms of the First Baptist Church. At first many of the classes were held at night and the teachers served without pay. No dormitory provisions were available; thus at first all students had to commute.[76]

After two years of operation in the First Baptist Church, individuals and churches in the Lakeland area raised money to acquire land and buildings for a campus. In 1945 Dr. J. C. Owen, a retired missionary to China, was elected temporary president and served one year.[77] During the third year of the institution's operation, the first building was constructed on the shores of Lake Beulah, in Lakeland, where the campus site had been acquired.[78] Forty students were enrolled in the fall of 1946, and Dr. Leon M. Gambrell was elected as the first permanent president.[79] In 1947-48 eleven barracks from Drane Field were moved to the campus to provide more space for students and their families. Before the 1946-1947 session was over more than 100 students were enrolled including representatives from eight states and four Indians from the Seminole reservation.[80]

Economic difficulty became the first problem. Help was sought and received from the Woman's Missionary Union and from various associations, and while it was enough for survival, more help was needed.

The Convention took little notice of this venture at its beginning in 1943, but before the end of the 1940's, the work of the little school had been called to the attention of the Convention, and by 1948 Baptist Bible Institute was included in the annual special offering for those State Mission enterprises not included in the regular budget.[81] It was to receive an apportioned section of the estimated budget, and the

---

[76] *Florida Baptist Witness,* Oct. 26, 1944, May 2, and July 25, 1946.
[77] *Ibid.,* Jan. 2, 1947.
[78] Baptist Bible Institute, *Catalogue,* 1969-70, p. 12.
[79] *Ibid.*
[80] South Florida Baptist Association, *Minutes,* 1945, p. 31, 1946, p. 23, and 1947, p. 25.
[81] Florida Baptist Convention, *Annual,* 1948, p. 31.

amount was set at $6,000.[82] Convention interest in the school was now established, an interest which was to grow in the future.

STETSON UNIVERSITY: NEW GROWTH AND THE MILLION DOLLAR CAMPAIGN

In the 1940's Stetson experienced the greatest growth and prosperity it had ever known. During the War there was a significant decline in enrollment, but increases following the War brought peak enrollments not to be equalled again until the late 1960's. From 1027 students in the 1940-41 session enrollment grew to 2,527 in the 1949-50 session.[83] At the beginning of this period Stetson was on good terms with the Convention and received systematic support from a stated percentage of cooperative program receipts, plus numerous special gifts. In 1941 the amount received was more than $25,000.[84]

The first crisis situation which Dr. Allen faced as president of Stetson in the 1940's came not from the Convention, but from the trustees. At the June, 1941, meeting of Stetson's trustees, John B. Stetson, Jr., chairman of the Board, presented a prepared statement to the Board, to the alumni, and to the newspapers. In this statement he accused President Allen (1) of acting hastily in doing away with football at Stetson, (2) of failing in his financial planning, (3) of failing as a leader of the alumni, and (4) of mishandling a delicate situation in the Law School, in which several faculty members were dropped. The trustees rejected Mr. Stetson's recommendations, however, and gave President Allen a vote of confidence.[85]

In 1943 when the State Board voted to discontinue the Hundred Thousand Club, it was decided that the money on hand would be paid to Stetson University on the commitments previously made to the University.[86]

At the Convention in 1944 President Allen described the decline in student enrollment from 900 to 300, not to be discouraging, but to call attention to the present need due to loss of tuition. The financial crisis was very real, and Stetson was saved from serious difficulty only by Convention help. In 1944 the Convention gave Stetson $20,000 for operating expenses.[87] President Allen also cited future needs

---

[82]State Board, *Minutes,* August 29, 1949.
[83]Florida Baptist Convention, *Annual,* 1950, p. 83.
[84]Garwood, *op. cit.,* pp. 198-199.
[85]*Florida Baptist Witness,* June 12, 1941, p. 6.
[86]State Board, *Minutes,* Dec. 10, 1943.
[87]Florida Baptist Convention, *Annual,* 1944, p. 26.

which would develop when veterans would be returning to school in great numbers, and stressed in particular the need for more buildings. At the conclusion of his address, C. H. Bolton, then executive secretary-treasurer, offered a resolution calling for the Convention to begin a campaign to raise one million dollars for Stetson in 1944.[88] The resolution called for a campaign committee consisting of J. Ollie Edmunds of Jacksonville (Chairman); Mrs. J. L. Rosser, State W. M. U. president; T. V. McCaul, Gainesville; Alphonse Pichard, Tallahassee; Dr. C. Roy Angell, Miami; Dr. David Gardner, St. Petersburg; and Dr. Wallace R. Rogers, Pensacola.[89] The resolution was approved and the campaign was begun. During the year the *Witness* gave great publicity to the campaign. At first the campaign went well and enthusiasm was high, with $535,000 being reported pledged by 298 of the 846 churches at the meeting of the Convention in January, 1945. At the height of the campaign the Jacksonville pastors' conference, for example, called for doubling the appropriation for Stetson.[90]

The goal of one million dollars was not reached in 1944. However, $200,000 was raised and Stetson, needing additional classroom space and dormitories, began immediate plans for enlargement. The increased enrollment anticipated soon called also for a corresponding increase in faculty. From a faculty of 35 in 1934 the teaching staff grew to more than 100 in 1945.[91] In 1945 with funds received from the million dollar campaign Stetson Lodge Hall was acquired for $30,000 and named Brittain Hall in memory of Charles M. Brittain, executive secretary-treasurer of the Convention from 1926 to 1941. In 1945 and 1946, Stetson Hall was rebuilt and enlarged, at a cost of $168,000, to serve as a woman's dormitory with a capacity of 168. Also, $25,000 was spent in redecorating several buildings and beautifying the campus. In 1946 through the city of DeLand and the Navy Department, the University acquired two surplus barracks to be used as men's dormitories; and it also leased two residences. Also in 1946, a small building was constructed to house the post office and a soda shop. This building was later to house the Gillespie Mineral Collection. Late in the 1940's also, Professor Harry S. Winters gave the University the J. F. Allen home, which now houses the alumni office.

---

[88]*Ibid.*, pp. 26-27.

[89]*Ibid.*

[90]State Board, *Minutes,* Sept. 12, 1944.

[91]Rosser, *op. cit.,* p. 203.

Finally, in 1948, a large residence was purchased to be the president's home.[92]

As indicated above, the million dollar goal was not reached in 1944, and by the end of the year enthusiasm appears to have waned. The campaign continued, however, and was made one of the special projects of the Brotherhood directed by J. Harrison Griffin.[93] In 1945, when Griffin was named secretary of Christian Education, he was given the special responsibility of continuing to direct the campaign.[94]

In 1946, the Florida Baptist Convention entered into a new agreement with the trustees of Stetson University which essentially did two things. First, it reaffirmed earlier agreements, and second, it defined arrangements for handling and using the money raised in the million dollar campaign.[95] By October 1, 1946, a total of $564,107 in cash and pledges had been raised. It seemed that Stetson-Convention relations could not be better. In the background, however, there developed several tensions, even while the million dollar campaign was still in process. The first factor causing these tensions may have been the efforts to get help from the Convention for Baptist Bible Institute, which efforts were frustrated at first because the State Board rejected the requests.[96] In response to the efforts of Baptist Bible Institute to gain support, the Convention established an Education Commission of fifteen members to consider the educational policy and program of Florida Baptists, and to receive all resolutions or requests coming to the State Board of Missions or the Convention concerning Baptist schools or Christian education in general. The Commission in turn was to report its findings and recommendations to the Convention.[97]

A second factor may have been the failure of a group in West Florida to get support for Chipola Baptist College, organized at Marianna Air Base in 1946 and 1947. Efforts to establish some kind of Baptist school in the area had been made in 1933, but the effort had failed. In 1946, a new attempt was made and Dr. B. C. Land was elected President. Plans were made to open the school on January 27, 1947, and aid was requested from the Convention.[98] Here too, how-

[92]Bowen, *op. cit.,* p. 21.
[93]State Board, *Minutes,* Mar. 24, 1944.
[94]*Florida Baptist Witness,* Sept. 20, 1945.
[95]Florida Baptist Convention, *Annual,* 1946, pp. 26-27.
[96]Garwood, *op. cit.,* p. 204.
[97]Florida Baptist Convention, *Annual,* 1946, pp. 42-43.
[98]Holmes County Association, *Minutes,* 1933, p. 8.

ever, the State Board refused aid, and voted a policy of supporting a single institution of higher learning only.[99] The Education Commission's first report to the Convention in 1947 reiterated the same policy. It also stated, as Convention policy concerning Baptist schools, that "ownership may inhere in the State Convention or in the trustees, but control by the Convention must be absolute" and that "the Florida Baptist Convention give financial support only to such educational institutions as it owns or controls."[100] These statements when compared with other statements made at the Convention concerning Stetson University, suggest that tensions were developing again. For example, a resolution from the Jacksonville Association referring to certain administrative policies of the University was sent by a committee to Stetson's trustees.[101] More specifically, Dr. Wallace Rogers, pastor of First Baptist Church, Pensacola, announcing his coming resignation from Stetson's board of trustees immediately after Dr. H. C. Garwood had brought the report on Stetson, stated, "I believe the Florida Baptist Convention should control Stetson."[102] It appears from this statement that the old charter controversy was about to rise again. It may be also that some of the supporters of the two schools which had been refused support by the Convention were beginning to look enviously at Stetson's privileged position.

In September, 1947, ill health forced Dr. Allen to resign as president of Stetson, and in December the Stetson trustees elected Dr. J. Ollie Edmunds as the new president. A native of Florida, a graduate of Stetson, an attorney for the Convention, a civic leader, and a prominent Baptist layman, Dr. Edmunds was an excellent choice. In February, 1948, after President Edmunds assumed office, the trustees adopted a set of resolutions which called for the erection of a building on the campus as a memorial to William Sims Allen.[103] In November the Convention approved a recommendation from the State Board and a Stetson planning committee that the building to honor Dr. Allen be a religious center and that a special offering be taken in Florida Baptist churches on January 30, 1949. The goal set for the special offering was $100,000.[104] The $39,192 collected from the special offering was not sufficient for construction of the building, but the

[99] State Board, *Minutes,* Dec. 9, 1947.

[100] Florida Baptist Convention, *Annual,* 1947, pp. 28-31.

[101] *Ibid.,* p. 76.

[102] *Ibid.,* p. 102.

[103] Garwood, *op. cit.,* pp. 209-210.

[104] Florida Baptist Convention, *Annual,* 1948, p. 73.

State Board of Missions provided additional funds in the amount of $46,367 and the building, named Allen Hall, was completed and dedicated in 1950 with Dr. and Mrs. Allen in attendance.[105]

Allen Hall

At the 1949 Convention, Dr. Earl Edington announced the completion of the Million Dollar Campaign.[106] Actually, only $352,-436.52 had been collected and given to the University for building purposes. In lieu of the remaining $650,000 pledged for the endowment, the Convention approved a decision by which the annual appropriation for Stetson was increased from 14% of the total Convention budget to 18%. The expectation was that the increased income for operating expenses would exceed what the amount pledged for endowment would have produced.[107]

---

[105]Garwood, *op. cit.*, p. 210; also Florida Baptist Convention, *Annual,* 1949, pp. 42-43.

[106]Florida Baptist Convention, *Annual,* 1949, pp. 19-20.

[107]*Ibid.*

In December, 1949, the State Board appointed a number of new committees, among which was an Institutional and Personnel Committee with the responsibility to study the work and needs of the Children's Home and the University and report to the Convention annually. Shortly thereafter, in February, 1950, Stetson's trustees approved a development program suggested by President Edmunds in the light of Stetson's needs and the Convention's increasing support. The enrollment then stood at 2,527.[108] Obviously the tensions described above had been buried in an avalanche of good will between Stetson and the Convention.

THE FLORIDA BAPTIST WITNESS: STABILITY AND SECURITY AT LAST

While no person, institution or agency should presume on lasting security in this world, after a long history of changes in name, location and management, and of economic insecurity, it appears that during the 1940's the Convention and the *Witness* management could believe that these problems were over. Sharing in the prosperity and growth of the state of Florida and the Convention during the 1940's, the *Witness* increased its circulation from 9,000 in 1940 to 25,400 in 1950.[109]

Editor E. D. Solomon visited the annual association meetings and many other meetings, promoting the *Witness* and persuading many churches to put the *Witness* in their budgets. Because of his warmth, wit, and enthusiasm, his eccentricities were usually tolerated. Often criticized for taking medical ads which made preposterous claims, Solomon defended himself by saying he had to take them to stay in business, and he often told a story of a woman who listened to the dogs howling outside while she rang the dinner bell for her farmer husband to come to lunch. Said she to the dogs, "What are you howling for? You don't have to eat it."

Solomon was a great editor in many ways, and a great deal of the credit for the progress and expanded ministry of the *Witness* must go to his personal sacrifices and his persistent and enthusiastic promotion of the church budget subscription plan. Toward the end of his career as editor, Dr. Solomon used many of his editorial columns to reminisce, telling many stories which are very interesting to read and which should provide excellent material for a biography, but which

---

[108]*Ibid.,* 1950, p. 83.
[109]*Ibid.,* p. 81.

hardly were appropriate for editorial pages. He retired in 1949. The August 11, 1949, issue of the *Witness* was the last issue under his editorial leadership.

W. G. Stracener was elected as the new editor and assumed office immediately on the retirement of Solomon. Stracener, a native of Louisiana, had attended Louisiana State University and had also done special study at Southwestern Y. M. C. A. School and Winona Lake School of Theology. A pastor in Florida since 1934, Stracener had served the First Baptist Church of Madison from 1934 to 1938, and Riverside Baptist Church in Miami, from 1938 to 1944. From Riverside he had gone to East Hill Baptist Church in Pensacola and was serving there when called to be editor of the *Witness* in 1949.

In his first editorial the word *gratitude* looms large, gratitude for the honor of serving Florida Baptists in this new responsibility. His first editorial also set forth his general editorial policy. In it he gave his pledge (1) to defend the faith, (2) to report denominational news faithfully, including news of local churches and associations, the Florida Baptist Convention, and the Southern Baptist Convention, (3) to publish feature articles of high quality, (4) to stimulate independent thought and cooperative action, and (5) to build on the foundation of E. D. Solomon.[110] The range of his editorials was very wide, covering many subjects from Sabbath-breaking to euthanasia. Thus, he gave promise of becoming a great editor in the years ahead. In 1950, Stetson University awarded him the honorary degree of Doctor of Divinity.[111]

Theological Discussion

Not much theological controversy is to be found on the surface among Florida Baptists during the 1940's. For the most part Florida Baptist thinking was dominated during this period by practical, social and political matters rather than by theological questions. Editorials and articles in the *Witness* were usually either devotional or journalistic news stories about the Convention or the work of the churches. In the few editorials and articles that did include theological discussion, the dominant theme during the early 1940's was the war. For example, in 1941, editor Solomon commented on the Christian attitude toward war. He declared that war was a judgment of God on wicked nations (other than our own) and that we were fighting to

[110]*Florida Baptist Witness,* August 25, 1949, p. 4.
[111]*Ibid.,* June 6, 1950, p. 5.

defend liberties our forefathers had gained.[112] J. L. Rosser, however, warned that in the midst of the war Americans should note that the same symptoms of national decay associated with the fall of ancient Rome were present in America.[113]

During the later 1940's four theological streams seem prominent. First, and predominantly, the main stream Christian doctrines that are shared by other groups than Baptists were emphasized, such as the doctrines of God, man, sin, Christ, and salvation by grace. Second, some of the traditional doctrines which identify most Baptists were stressed, including such teachings as believer's baptism by immersion, religious liberty, and the separation of church and state.[114] Third, Florida Baptists upheld that perspective which identifies them as Southern Baptists, specifically their unique participation in the world mission program of Southern Baptists. Fourth, some evidence of the continuation of Landmark influence in theology and polity is found among Florida Baptists during the 1940's. The main strength of Landmarkism as an organized movement was concentrated in independent Baptist churches not related to the Florida Baptist Convention. However, Landmark ideas appear among Florida Baptists despite the absence of the name. Examples are (1) the theological conservatism and fundamentalism characteristic of Landmarkism though not identified exclusively with it and (2) a theological exclusivism which suggests that only Baptists perpetuate a valid continuation of the Christian tradition. The Landmark type fundamentalism was defended by editor Solomon when he paid great tribute to J. R. Graves' *Seven Dispensations,* written in 1885, as the most up-to-date book of today on world conditions and prophecy.[115] The theological exclusivism reminiscent of Baptist succession theories was suggested in several articles in the *Witness* by L. O. Calhoun.[116] One article, for example, accepts a basic assumption of Landmarkers, that "Baptists can prove both historically and doctrinally that they are the only ones that can give New Testament Baptism."[117] No one published a challenge of

---

[112]*Ibid.,* Mar. 13, 1941, p. 6.

[113]J. L. Rosser, "A Stabilizing Faith," *Florida Baptist Witness,* Mar. 27, 1941, p. 5.

[114]For example, J. L. Rosser, "Keeping Our Heritage Unstained," *Florida Baptist Witness,* Dec. 20, 1945, p. 3.

[115]*Florida Baptist Witness,* Mar. 13, 1941, p. 6.

[116]For example, L. O. Calhoun, "The Danger of Accepting Alien Immersion," *Florida Baptist Witness,* Oct. 21, 1948, p. 3.

[117]*Ibid.*

these ideas. Elements of liberal theology which appeared among Florida Baptists at times between 1920 and 1940 do not appear in the 1940's. If they existed they did not appear in the usual records.

Social Concern

The practical interests of Florida Baptists covered many areas, but in addition to those related to institutions and work already established, the social concern of Florida Baptists during the 1940's was centered in four areas. First, it was focused on World War II and its horrible aftermath of suffering. After the U. S. had been attacked by the Japanese, Florida Baptists understandably shared the passions of many Americans, when they accepted a State Board of Missions report which quoted with approval the statement of someone who prayed concerning the war: "Oh God, help us to live like Jesus and fight like the devil."[118] When one compares this statement with Florida Baptists' anti-war statements of the previous decade, it is clear that social concern can easily change in substance as well as the form of its appearance. However, following the war, Florida Baptists were just as zealous in helping the victims of war as they had been in supporting the war effort.

Second, Florida Baptists continued to emphasize their concern for temperance and what they often considered related moral issues. Symbolic of this consideration is the combining of Social Service and Temperance reports which were a part of the Convention program in the 1940's. The first of these combined reports in 1944 expressed anxiety over the confusion, tragedy, violence, chaos, lawlessness, and uncertainty which prevailed during the war. It lamented the loss of values during war that are not easily regained, especially deplored the greed and race riots then prevalent and called for inter-racial missions.[119] In 1945 the Social Service and Temperance reports were combined again, but in 1946 they were separated.[120] The reason was probably that an organization which would concentrate on fighting alcohol was in process of development. Although it derived much of its support and leadership from Florida Baptists, it was to be composed of several denominations.

This organization was first called the Florida Cooperative Com-

---

[118]Florida Baptist Convention, *Annual*, 1942, p. 17.

[119]*Ibid.*, 1944, pp. 74-76.

[120]*Ibid.*, 1946, p. 100.

mittee for Narcotics Education,[121] then United Florida Drys.[122] In 1947 the Social Service and United Florida Drys reports were combined again.[123] In addition to listing as causes of the decay of civilizations such things as intemperance, immorality, and gambling, the report commended the recent Southern Baptist Convention statement on race relations.[124] By the end of the 1940's, United Florida Drys was a recognized organization among Florida Baptists and was receiving about half of its budget from them.[125]

A third area of social concern which caught the attention of Florida Baptists during this period was the concern for a ministry to the sick. For a long time before the 1940's, this need had been called to the attention of Florida Baptists, but little had been done beyond the occasional appointments of committees. In 1939 the Convention had established a hospital commission to study and evaluate proposals and possibilities for establishing a hospital. In the early 1940's E. D. Solomon, editor of the *Witness* and chairman of the hospital commission, stimulated new interest in the hospital venture by comparing Florida Baptists to the Catholics, who had five hospitals in Florida. He pointed out that the hospitals were not only healing the sick, but "were a veritable gold mine" in making money.[126] While the Convention eventually decided against building a hospital, it gave encouragement and help to several local Baptist groups working on such ventures. For example, by 1948, the Convention reported that three hospitals were in various stages of planning or construction. They included the Jacksonville Baptist Hospital, with more than $650,000 pledged to the building fund; the Pensacola Baptist Hospital with $250,000 on hand, and the Plant City Baptist Hospital, still raising money while the building was being constructed. During the 1940's the Convention gradually developed a policy that the Convention might approve the construction of hospitals and give some temporary help in raising money, but that the main support for hospitals was the responsibility of the local group beginning them.[127]

A fourth area of Florida Baptist social concern was the new social

---

[121] *Ibid.*, p. 103.
[122] *Ibid.*, 1947, pp. 72-75.
[123] *Ibid.*
[124] *Ibid.*
[125] *Florida Baptist Witness,* pt. 30, 1948. Also, Florida Baptist Convention, *Annual,* 1946, p. 182; 1948, p 31; and 1950, p. 35.
[126] Florida Baptist Convention, *Annual,* 1942, p. 94.
[127] *Ibid.*, 1948, pp. 75-76.

security legislation. The executive secretary-treasurer was instructed by the State Board in 1942 to write to Congress opposing the placing of church employees under social security. Apparently, the State Board was not opposed to social security itself, but feared an infringement of government on the religious liberty of individuals and of Baptist institutions.[128]

Finally, Florida Baptists came to share the concern of other Southern Baptists during the 1940's for the preservation of the separation of church and state. Two issues were viewed as potential threats to religious liberty and the separation of church and state. The first issue, the appointment of Myron C. Taylor as ambassador to the Vatican, raised the greatest objection. No doubt Florida Baptists had a part in the failure of Congress to approve this appointment.[129] The second issue was pending legislation which suggested various forms of limited aid to denominational institutions. Some Florida Baptists reiterated earlier statements of opposition to the use of tax money for sectarian ends.[130]

Race Relations and Negro Baptists

The relationship between the Florida Baptist Convention and Negro Baptists appears to have been a friendly one in the 1940's. Symbolic of this friendly relationship were the inter-racial conferences conducted by the Woman's Missionary Union and the meager financial aid given by the Convention to Negro schools. The amount of help given did increase during the decade, however. In 1940 only $160.00 was given to each of the two Negro Baptist schools then in operation, Florida Normal and Industrial Institute in Live Oak, and Florida Memorial College at St. Augustine.[131] In 1948 the total amount allotted to Negro work from the special state mission offering was $3,500, over twenty times as much as in 1940.[132]

In 1950 the Convention passed a motion made by Hal Hunter that the Negro Baptist Convention be invited to cooperate with the Southern Baptist simultaneous evangelistic crusade through their own organization and facilities.[133]

---

[128]State Board, *Minutes,* Mar. 3, 1942.

[129]Don Miley, "Separation of Church and State," *Florida Baptist Witness,* Oct. 23, 1947; also Florida Baptist Convention, *Annual,* 1945, p. 88.

[130]For example, J. L. Rosser, "Keeping Our Heritage Unstained," *Florida Baptist Witness,* Dec. 20, 1945, p. 3.

[131]Florida Baptist Convention, *Annual,* 1941, p. 22.

[132]State Board, *Minutes,* Feb. 24, 1948.

[133]Florida Baptist Convention, *Annual,* 1950, p. 18.

Little discussion of race relations occurred during the 1940's between Negro and white Baptists of Florida, although the series of inter-racial conferences sponsored by the Woman's Missionary Union probably revealed to Baptist women the need for such discussion. The typical attitude of many Florida Baptists on race relations at the time, however, was probably well represented by an editorial by E. D. Solomon in 1946. He clearly stated opposition to integration, and defended segregation, declaring that segregation was Biblically based. At the same time he condemned discrimination, and contended that the Negro must be given opportunity for education, equal wages, justice in courts and full citizenship. Moreover, he praised Northern Baptists for their contribution to Negro schools.[134] Like many Baptists and others, Editor Solomon failed to realize that the system of segregation in vogue in the 1940's reinforced some of the very types of injustice he condemned in his editorial. However, a much more constructive and positive statement on race relations was included in the combined Social Service and United Florida Drys Report. Among other things this report called for changes in attitudes and actions toward other races, putting both love and justice into practice in all human relationships.[135] Thus, among the leaders, real awareness of the race problem was developing.

In summary, by the end of the 1940's, Florida Baptists were over the excitement and crises associated with World War II, but were not yet prepared for the problems they would face in the 1950's. Nonetheless, they were stronger than they had ever been. The churches were growing and were sharing in the expanding economy of the State, the Convention had stable organization and mature leadership, and the future looked very bright indeed.

[134]*Florida Baptist Witness,* Feb. 28, 1946, p. 4.
[135]Florida Baptist Convention, *Annual,* 1947, pp. 72-75.

CHAPTER SEVEN

Unparalleled Progress: 1950-1960

In many ways the 1950's appear to be the one most fabulous period in Florida Baptist history. During this decade, Florida Baptists shared in the economic and population growth of the state of Florida and responded rather well to the challenges provided by that growth. Convention leaders observed early in this decade that Florida was the fastest growing state east of the Mississippi with a growth rate three times the national average, and 1,000 new people coming into Florida each week. Florida income increased from 635 million dollars a year in 1930 to over 3 billion in 1950, an increase of 400 per cent.[1] The population increased from 2,771,305 in 1950 to 4,951,560 in 1960,[2] an increase of 76.3 per cent. The process of urbanization, expanding in the 1940's, continued to increase in the 1950's until in 1960, 65.5 per cent of Florida's population was urban, and slightly over half the population was concentrated in the four metropolitan areas of Jacksonville, Miami, Orlando, and Tampa-St. Petersburg.

The Convention and the Churches

The Florida Baptist Convention not only responded to the challenge of Florida's growth, but they came to share in it as well. Church membership growth exceeded any other decade in previous Florida Baptist history as it increased from 278,668 in 1950 to 480,407 in 1960, not quite keeping pace with the population growth, but still

---

[1]Florida Baptist Convention, *Annual,* 1952, p. 21.

[2]*Encyclopedia Brittanica,* 1965 edition, Vol. IX, p. 473.

representing remarkable growth.[3] In 1957, the churches of the Florida Baptist Convention constituted 44.8 per cent of the Protestant church membership in Florida.[4] Moreover, they developed very early in the decade an awareness of the public importance of what they were doing, an awareness reflected in the creation of a public relations committee in 1951.[5] By 1955, the responsibility for directing a Baptist news service had become the assigned task of a Convention employee, Gus Johnson.[6] In 1959, a record was set in number of baptisms when 28,626 baptisms were reported. Cooperative Program receipts grew from $821,471 in 1950 to $1,321,380 in 1960.[7] Per capita giving increased from $2.95 in 1950 to $3.15 in 1952.[8] In 1952, Cooperative Program receipts reached over a million dollars for the first time when $1,122,863 was recorded. Total receipts handled through the state offices, including special offerings and designated gifts, made the total even larger. In 1950, the inclusive total was $1,149,748;[9] by 1960, the inclusive total had more than tripled to $3,887,390.[10] The total number of churches from which those gifts came grew from 911 in 1950,[11] to 1,257 in 1960.[12] In this remarkable growth Florida Baptists shared in the growing prosperity of churches in America rather generally, for the *Witness* reported in 1957 that United States church membership was at a new high with 62 per cent of the total population holding membership in some church, and that church gains doubled the population gains in 1956.[13] Statistics on Florida population growth in 1956 are not available for a comparison between Florida Baptist growth and the national church record during 1956. It is very clear, however, that when the whole decade of the 1950's is considered, Florida Baptists began, for the first time, to fall behind the population growth. It should be added, however, that much of the growth

---

[3]Slightly more than a 70 per cent increase, compared with population increase of 76.3 per cent.

[4]National Council of Churches, "Churches and Church Membership in the U.S.: An Enumeration and Analysis by Counties, States, and Regions," Series C, No. 39, 1957.

[5]Florida Baptist Convention, *Annual*, 1951, p. 105.

[6]*Ibid.*, 1955, p. 103.

[7]*Ibid.*, 1950, p. 218, and 1960, p. 306.

[8]*Florida Baptist Witness,* Mar. 26, 1953, p. 9.

[9]Florida Baptist Convention, *Annual,* 1950, p. 219.

[10]*Ibid.*, 1960, p. 309.

[11]*Ibid.*, 1950, p. 218.

[12]*Ibid.*, 1960, p. 306.

[13]*Florida Baptist Witness,* Sept. 12, 1957, p. 2.

in the 1950's was non-Baptist that is, from Northern states, where Baptist membership was relatively small.

As indicated above, nonetheless, Florida Baptists did enjoy phenomenal growth and did not fall far behind the population growth rate. One of the chief means of church growth during the 1950's was the many evangelistic crusades which occurred. The writer recalls reading while a college student in the 1940's that the age of great revivals was over, but the 1950's proved that judgment to have been wrong. During the 1950's the simultaneous evangelistic crusade, suggested originally by the Southern Baptist Convention, became popular and rather effective. Capitalizing on the publicity which was Southwide, local churches did their work well, and although they did not always reach the goal set, they boosted the annual records to new highs not to be exceeded in the 1960's.[14] A second means by which the phenomenal growth in church membership was achieved in the 1950's was closely related to the evangelistic campaigns; this was the Sunday School. With its dual emphases on teaching and evangelism, the Sunday School contributed greatly to the prosperity of the churches. Here again, records not to be surpassed in the 1960's were set. This growth in population and economy, moreover, was reflected in an amazing boom in church building. The building boom, begun in the 1920's and interrupted by depression and war, was not only resumed, but now assumed such proportions as to make the efforts of the 1920's seem modest by comparison. In the late 1950's, almost every issue of the *Witness* carried pictures of some new church building or buildings recently completed. The economy of Florida and of the nation was boosted, of course, during the early 1950's by the Korean War (1950-1953).

As Florida Baptists were enjoying their remarkable growth, few noticed or expressed alarm about the fact that for the first time in their history their own growth fell behind the growth of the State. Most people also took for granted the appropriateness of such extensive church building. Editor Stracener, therefore, was almost alone in having an uneasy feeling about the obsession for constructing new buildings. Early in the 1950's, he warned that great buildings may indicate interest in religion, but that this interest does not necessarily reflect vital commitment to Christianity. As evidence, he cited the construction of Europe's grand cathedrals during the time of shameful corruption in the church. Indeed, he debated the justification of very

---

[14]*Ibid.*, Mar. 22, 1951, p. 11.

large sums of money on fancy buildings, when this action is measured against the simplicity of Jesus' own life and against the great needs of the poor today. He made it clear that he was not against good buildings, but pleaded for simplicity and restraint.[15] It is doubtful, however, whether much heed was paid to his editorial, for the building emphasis continued and many churches created heavy debts that are still being paid.

Shifts in the concentration of churches, church membership and financial church strength reflected the continued and growing process of urbanization which took place during the 1950's. For the first time it became obvious that urban centers contributed the heaviest concentration of Baptist giving. For example, the six associations with the largest cities and membership contributed half the total given by Florida Baptists.[16] Many rural churches, once a main source of strength and influence in the past, now played a less prominent role, and most of the Convention leadership came from the larger towns and cities. Awareness of this fact prompted the creation in 1958 of a committee on the promotion of democracy in the Convention. The committee came into being as the result of Robert G. Witty's motion which called for a study of ways of enlarging participation in Convention affairs.[17] The committee found no easy answer to the problem, but it continued its study into the 1960's.[18]

The Convention's leadership became more varied, however, and demonstrated an awareness of the neglect of the rural churches. For the first time in any decade since the Convention was organized in 1854, not one Convention president succeeded himself. Thus in the 1950's, Florida Baptists experienced the greatest variety of presidential leadership in their history, with representation from virtually every section of the state. The executive leadership of the Convention, in contrast, saw less change at the top level during the 1950's, thus providing some real stability where increasingly the heaviest responsibilities for Convention affairs had to be concentrated. For example, there were no changes in the office of the executive secretary-treasurer or in the editorial office of the *Witness*. Changes became less frequent, moreover, in the department heads, such as state secretaries of the Sunday School, Training Union, and the Baptist Student Union.

---

[15]W. G. Stracener, "Buildings May Bless or Blight," *Florida Baptist Witness,* July 31, 1952, p. 4.

[16]*Florida Baptist Witness,* Jan. 12, 1956, p. 16.

[17]Florida Baptist Convention, *Annual,* 1958, pp. 26-27.

[18]*Ibid.,* 1960, p. 144.

The Convention's sessions in the 1950's were fairly calm, except for some restlessness whose source is difficult to identify but whose reality became apparent early in the 1950's. Editor Stracener commented on this nebulous dissatisfaction in 1952, calling attention to the desire for change apparent in the recent Convention. The nature of the desired change was not specified.[19]

Among the most significant Convention events in the 1950's was the Centennial Celebration. The 1954 Centennial Celebration, commemorating the organization of the Florida Baptist Convention in 1854 was planned as early as 1951 by the State Board centering around a historical pageant which would dramatize the story of the Convention.[20] In further preparation for the celebration, the *Witness* printed pictures of the historic monument at Madison, old Pigeon Creek Church in Nassau county, and other historic churches, and of the executive secretaries. A number of departments, the Sunday School and the Training Union, for example, published brief histories of their work in the *Witness*.[21] The historic pageant, written by Mrs. John A. Maguire and Mrs. Ruth Nemec, was presented at the 1954 convention as planned, with 150 Stetson students performing.[22] The convention that year broke all previous attendance records with 1,450 registered messengers and 2,043 visitors, making a total of 3,490 persons attending.[23]

Finally, the enlargement of the Florida Baptist Convention in size and stature during the 1950's was reflected by the increasing representation of Florida Baptist Convention leaders on boards, on committees, and on the program of the Southern Baptist Convention[24] and by the appointment by the Foreign Mission Board of thirty-three Floridians to mission fields around the world. The Florida Baptist Convention was now come of age.

The State Board and Administration

In the 1950's, the State Board of Missions continued to carry the heavy load of responsibility to which it had long been accustomed. Many of its meetings were given to routine requests for help from individuals, churches and missions, and to dealing with internal policies

[19]*Florida Baptist Witness,* Nov. 27, 1952.
[20]State Board, *Minutes,* Nov. 13, 1951.
[21]*Florida Baptist Witness,* Sept. 9, 1954, pp. 3ff.
[22]Florida Baptist Convention, *Annual,* 1954, p. 29.
[23]*Florida Baptist Witness, Dec.* 2, 1954.
[24]*Ibid.,* May 31, 1951.

of administration. The Board continued to operate several loan funds for church buildings, to give aid to numerous pastors of missions and small churches, and to make outright gifts to aid in the construction of buildings.[25] To further efficiency in dealing with increasing demands, the Board gradually developed guidelines and policies for the various departments and areas of work, thus reducing the amount of work handled directly by the whole Board.

The Board's work was not merely routine and heavy during the 1950's, however. It was also creative and visionary. One of the most creative and visionary things done by the Board between 1950 and 1960 was the development of the ten-year program under the leadership of John H. Maguire and the Institution and Survey Committee, chaired by Davis C. Wooley.[26] Approved by the State Board and the Convention,[27] the program called for a ten-year capital fund program in a special budgeting of monies received above and beyond the regular Cooperative Program budget. This capital fund budget would move progressively from the first year, when 95 per cent of the budget would go to state causes and five per cent to Southwide causes, with the percentages to change five per cent each year until a fifty-fifty ratio was reached in ten years. The purpose of the high percentage being given to state needs at first was to provide immediate needs for capital improvement funds for Stetson University, the Children's Home, camps and new work to be projected. This ten-year program was possible because in the 1950's the annual Convention budget was always a conservative one, and the churches unfailingly gave far more than was asked. It was out of this excess that the resources for this ten-year program were to come.

The program called for more than capital improvements involving money. In fact, most of the goals envisioned in the ten-year program did not directly involve money at all. For example, among the goals adopted were: (1) 250,000 baptisms, (2) 400 new churches, (3) an enrollment of 300,000 in Sunday School and 200,000 in Vacation Bible School, (4) a gain in Training Union in every church, (5) a Woman's Missionary Union in every church and an enrollment of 75,000 women, (6) 1,000 new Brotherhoods, with an enrollment of 30,000 men, (7) a Baptist Student Union organization on every college campus, (8) every Baptist becoming a tither, (9) a total gain of

---

[25]Florida Baptist Convention, *Annual,* 1952, pp. 34-37.

[26]*Florida Baptist Witness,* Sept. 11, 1952, pp. 8-9.

[27]State Board, *Minutes,* Sept. 4-5, 1952; also Florida Baptist Convention, *Annual,* 1952, pp. 34-40.

150,000 in church membership, and (10) an increase of 25,000 in the circulation of the *Witness*.[28]

Another creative and visionary decision of the Board during the 1950's was the decision to construct a new Baptist building in a better location in Jacksonville. The enlargement of the administrative responsibility taxed the capacity of the Rogers Building, and the increased traffic together with limited parking facilities in downtown Jacksonville made the old location on Church Street increasingly undesirable. Accordingly, on May 8, 1958, the State Board voted approval for the sale of the old Church Street property and the purchase of new property in south Jacksonville for the construction of the new facility.[29] On December 9, 1958, the Board broke ground for the new building, and construction was soon begun. By the end of 1959, the new building, located at 1230 Hendricks Avenue adjacent to the interstate highway, had been completed, and the Convention offices were moved in. It was a modern building with the bookstore on the first floor, ample room for expansion, and a spacious parking lot.[30]

Finally, on September 2, 1960, the Board approved a recommendation by the Education Commission for a study of long-range needs and problems of higher education in Florida with a view to planning twenty years in advance.[31] This very significant action will be described in a later section.

Convention Departments of Work: Administrative Changes, Adjustments, and Growth

Cooperative Missions

The Department of Cooperative Missions was created in 1948 by the consolidation of the Departments of Stewardship, Missions and Evangelism under this new name.[32] At the beginning of the 1950's, this Department continued in the promotion of these three areas of work. Headed by Clifford Walker, the Department had the additional responsibility of supervising both district and city missionaries. The state was divided into five geographical districts with missionaries serving in each district. In 1952, these five missionaries were Paul Mc-

[28]State Board, *Minutes*, Sept. 4-5, 1952; also Florida Baptist Convention, *Annual*, 1952, p. 41.

[29]State Board, *Minutes*, May 8, 1958.

[30]*Florida Baptist Witness*, Nov. 12, 1959, front page.

[31]State Board Minutes, September 2, 1960.

[32]Florida Baptist Convention, *Annual*, 1948, pp. 53-54.

Cullers, Waldo Wood, D. O. Alderman, John Pearce and B. D. Locke. Also, two city missionaries were serving, C. M. Coalson in Jacksonville and A. D. Dawson in Miami.[33]

By the middle of 1953, the Board was receiving reports of considerable dissatisfaction with the arrangement of the Department of Cooperative Missions. In brief, the arrangement was that the local group (the missions committee of the association or district) would employ the missionary desired, the State Board would pay his salary and the association would pay his travel expenses. A major complaint was that the uniformity of salary scale, determined by the State Board, resulted in some missionaries being paid more than local pastors in poor economic areas, while the pastors were expected to raise traveling expenses for the missionary.[34] Another complaint reported was that some of the missionaries promoted certain aspects of the work of the churches and neglected others. In the July, 1953, meeting of the Board, steps were taken to offset these complaints. First, the responsibilities of the associational and district missionaries were clarified. The missionaries were instructed to promote all aspects of the denominational program. Second, the distinction between rural and city missions was maintained and superintendents were added to supervise the work of the two types of missions. Third, the State Board assumed responsibility for the travel expenses of all full-time employees of the Board. The recommendations adopted by the Board also suggested the option that a local association desiring to employ its own missionary might have a subsidy of $125.00 per month from the State Board.[35]

The results of these moves by the Board were twofold. First, the Department of Cooperative Missions was greatly enlarged. By 1955, for example, the number of geographical districts had increased from five to thirteen. By the end of 1953, it had the largest staff of all departments and the largest portion of the budget for the department. Second, the associational and district missionaries were brought under more direct control by the State Board, once they were employed.[36]

In 1957, Dr. Paul A. Meigs was added to the Administration Department as director of evangelism and mission education. This action in a very real sense began a reorganization of the Department of Cooperative Missions because Meigs took over some of the work that had

---

[33]*Ibid.,* 1952, p. 60.

[34]State Board, *Minutes,* May 26, 1953.

[35]*Ibid.,* July 2, 1953.

[36]*Ibid.,* also Florida Baptist Convention, *Annual,* 1953, pp. 33-35, 43.

been done by the Cooperative Missions Department from its beginning. Specifically and most significantly, the responsibility for the planning and promotion of the evangelistic conference, an annual affair since 1949, was now removed from the Department of Cooperative Missions and given to Meigs.[37] In the course of the 1950's the evangelistic conference became an increasingly popular and successful venture. Outstanding speakers were secured and the attendance at the meetings in January of each year both reflected the growth of evangelistic interest among Florida Baptists and further stimulated that interest.

In 1958, Clifford Walker resigned as head of the Department of Cooperative Missions and the department was reorganized. The fifteen associational and district missionaries came to be called field secretaries and their work came under the direct supervision of the executive secretary-treasurer, John H. Maguire.[38] In a sense, the department of cooperative missions as a separate department with its own secretary was thus abolished. The work of course continued.

Sunday School: Growth Exceeds Population Rate

The Sunday School Department enjoyed the stability of having the same head throughout the 1950's, with C. F. Barry continuing to direct the work. In 1951, the first state leadership school for Sunday School workers was held in the First Baptist Church of Orlando, enrolling 2,000, 1,500 of whom were from churches in the Wekiwa Association. The leadership school became an annual activity of the Sunday School Department. Likewise, the January Bible study, begun in 1948, continued to be promoted by the Sunday School Department, and the number of churches participating grew steadily.[39] Also annual state Sunday School conventions were held throughout the 1950's, with attendance growing steadily, as in most other meetings.[40] C. F. Barry helped to make Florida Baptist Sunday School leaders aware of their relationship to other Southern Baptists and of the need for more training for meeting the challenges of Sunday School work in Florida's growing population. Nowhere is the growing alertness of the leaders more in evidence than in their attendance at Ridgecrest in

---

[37]Florida Baptist Convention, *Annual,* 1957, p. 59.
[38]*Ibid.,* 1958, pp. 52, 59.
[39]*Ibid.,* 1951, pp. 49-50.
[40]*Ibid.,* p. 50.

1951, when Florida, with 700 registered, had the largest representation of all states during the four Sunday School weeks.[41]

The alertness, dedication and work of these Sunday School leaders bore fruit, moreover, in the continued phenomenal growth of Sunday Schools, especially in the towns and cities. Between 1950 and 1960, total enrollment in Florida Baptist Sunday Schools increased from 214,402 to 397,771,[42] an increase of more than 80 per cent. Thus, while total growth in church membership could not quite keep pace with the population growth rate of 76.3 per cent, Sunday School growth far exceeded it. Also, some remarkable attendance records were set as many Sunday Schools, especially in the larger towns and cities, found themselves crowded beyond their wildest expectations. In February, 1951, Sunday School attendance reports published in the *Witness* indicate three churches with more than 1,000 in attendance. They were First Baptist Church, Jacksonville, Central Church, Miami, and the First Baptist Church, Saint Petersburg.[43] By April of 1951, thirteen churches reported 1,000 or more in Sunday School. Allapattah in Miami had over 2,000. Apparently, recent evangelistic crusades had greatly increased Sunday School attendance. In return, growing Sunday Schools had contributed to the success of the crusades.[44] In 1952, the reports were somewhat less spectacular,[45] but in 1953, new enthusiasm for Sunday School enlargement grew out of the promotion of the Southern Baptist Convention slogan, "A Million More in '54," in a campaign to add a million to the total Sunday School enrollment in the Southern Baptist Convention. Florida's part in the goal was 50,000.[46] Florida Baptist Sunday Schools did not reach their goal, but they did add 38,161 to their enrollment,[47] and they created a new spurt in attendance that continued into 1955, when, following another series of simultaneous evangelistic crusades, eighteen churches reported an attendance of over 1,000 in Sunday School.[48] Anyone who reads the growing Sunday School attendance statistics during the 1950's can easily understand why many churches felt not only justified but constrained to engage in rather ambitious building projects.

---

[41]*Ibid.*, p. 51.
[42]*Ibid.*, 1950, p. 218, and 1960, p. 306.
[43]*Florida Baptist Witness,* Feb. 15, 1951, p. 14.
[44]*Ibid.*, Apr. 12, 1951, p. 11.
[45]*Ibid.*, Sept. 11, 1952, p. 16.
[46]*Ibid.*, Mar. 26, 1953, p. 6.
[47]Florida Baptist Convention, *Annual,* 1953, p. 220, and 1954, p. 211.
[48]*Florida Baptist Witness,* May 5, 1955, p. 13.

Finally, the Sunday School Department continued in DeLand and other places the camps and assembly programs which grew rapidly during this period, promoting more effective ways of carrying on the work of the Sunday School.

Training Union: Unparalleled Growth

The Training Union Department, like the Sunday School Department, enjoyed stability of leadership, for it was directed throughout the decade by O. K. Radford until 1960, when he died. Under his leadership, the Training Union, again like the Sunday School, enjoyed remarkable growth. Between 1950 and 1960, enrollment in Training Union grew from 68,899 to 140,510, an increase of more than 100 per cent. Radford and his staff continued to participate in the summer camps and assemblies in DeLand and West Florida and continued to promote sword drills, speakers' tournaments and youth weeks in the churches. In 1955, he enlarged the number of district Training Union conventions from six to eight.

Perhaps the most spectacular event in Florida Training Union work during the 1950's was the great attendance at "M" (Mobilization) Night meetings. These meetings, begun in 1945, were held in each association simultaneously on the first Monday night in December, and projected plans for the coming year were dramatized, accompanied by an inspirational speaker. Attendance at these meetings doubled from a state total of 11,960 in 1951 to 23,904 in 1960.[49]

Radford's record as a denominational servant shows that he was outstandingly successful, as he ably served Florida Baptists for more than thirty-three years. When he became Baptist Young People's Union secretary there were only 635 unions in Florida with a total enrollment of 17,052. In 1938, when the name was changed from Baptist Young People's Union to Training Union and he became secretary of the separate department, only 500 of the 790 churches had Training Unions, with a total enrollment of 32,049. When he died in 1960, 1,217 of the 1,228 churches had Training Unions with a total enrollment of 134,410. C. J. Smyly was elected to succeed him as Training Union secretary.[50]

Woman's Missionary Union: Enlarging Influence and Service

Like the Sunday School and Training Union, the Woman's Missionary Union enjoyed the same continuity of leadership, with Miss

---

[49]Florida Baptist Convention, *Annual,* 1951, p. 20; 1960, pp. 27-28.
[50]*Ibid.,* 1960, pp. 27-28.

Josephine Jones continuing as executive-secretary throughout the 1950's. Also, like other Florida Baptist organizations during the 1950's, the Woman's Missionary Union of Florida enjoyed remarkable growth. Between 1950 and 1960, W. M. U. enrollment increased from 42,127 to 72,696.[51] The contribution of the Woman's Missionary Union to Florida Baptist life in the 1950's, however, is not adequately measured by this growth in enrollment. It is rather better measured by the support given to missions, and by the quality and variety of its forms of service to mission causes. As in the past the Union served very effectively as an auxiliary to the Florida Baptist Convention. While no accurate accounting is available of the total financial support given by the W. M. U. of Florida to various mission causes, it is clear that in 1959, the total of $464,179.14 was raised for three special offerings, for home missions, state missions, and foreign missions.[52] The quality and variety of forms of service by the W. M. U. of Florida can best be presented chronologically.

The distinctive work of the Woman's Missionary Union in the 1950's began with a camp for Seminole Indians at Dania, directed by Miss Elizabeth Provence. In 1953, similar camps were held at Dania, Brighton, and Big Cypress. All of these camps received a good response from the Indians, and they became annual events.[53]

In 1951, Miss Josephine Jones became a trustee at Florida Normal and Industrial College, thus bringing a significant honor to the Florida Woman's Missionary Union. Her election as a trustee also symbolized and recognized the interest and help given by Florida Baptist women to Negro Baptists in Florida. For one example, between 1942 and 1960, the Union gave to the Negro college a total of $86,657.18 for scholarship, current expenses and development.[54] Also, when the first Young Woman's Auxiliary camp was held in 1951, it was integrated, with two Negro girls from West Palm Beach included.[55] This integration was a small, but nonetheless significant extension of the communication between Negro and white Baptists in Florida. In 1955, the W. M. U. conducted the first camp for Negro boys and girls at Florida Normal and Industrial College in Saint Augustine. Thirty-five boys and girls came. In three years the attendance at camp grew

---

[51] *Ibid.,* 1950, p. 218; also 1960, p. 306.

[52] Lassiter, *op. cit.,* p. 134.

[53] Florida Baptist Convention, *Annual,* 1959, p. 96; also Lassiter, *op. cit.,* p. 131.

[54] Lassiter, *op. cit.,* p. 109.

[55] Florida Baptist Convention, *Annual,* 1951, p. 77.

to over 200. In 1959, with help from the Negro Baptist woman's conventions, a successful camp for Negro girls was conducted.[56]

The year 1953 brought another variety of work to Florida Baptist women, who in that year began providing a residence for Home Mission Board missionaries to migrant workers in the vicinity of Immokalee.[57]

Beginning in 1954, the Florida W. M. U. established the custom of providing an annual $1,000 scholarship to aid a foreign student in Florida. The first and only person to receive this scholarship during the 1950's was Samuel Ho from Hong Kong. (He was the only qualified applicant.) He graduated from Stetson University Magna Cum Laude in 1958 and later graduated from Bowman Gray Medical College in North Carolina. Also in 1954 the Union began providing a $450 annual scholarship for a foreign missions volunteer at Stetson. In 1958 the Union increased loans for missions volunteers. All told, a significant number of students were helped by these scholarship aids.[58]

In 1954 the first Royal Ambassador Congress in Florida was held in Ocala. Planned by Armand Ball, state Royal Ambassador director, the congress was attended by 700, including 27 Negro boys. This meeting became an annual event like the summer Royal Ambassador camps and contributed greatly to the Christian growth and dedication of hundreds of boys each year.[59] In October, 1957, following the suggestion of the Southern Baptist Convention W. M. U. and Brotherhood, the work of Royal Ambassadors was transferred from the Woman's Missionary Union to the Brotherhood Department.[60]

In January, 1958, the Florida W. M. U. joined with the Department of Student Work in Nashville and the Florida State Baptist Student Union in sponsoring the first International Student Retreat at Stetson University. This event, like many others which were begun in the 1950's, has continued to be held annually. By the end of the 1950's, students from more than thirty countries had attended these annual retreats.[61]

Because of its unique interest in missions, the Woman's Missionary Union of Florida has kept a careful record of Florida missionaries

---

[56]Lassiter, *op. cit.*, p. 131.
[57]*Ibid.*, p. 111.
[58]*Ibid.*, p. 110.
[59]*Ibid.*, p. 126.
[60]*Ibid.*, p. 127.
[61]*Ibid.*, p. 121.

serving in foreign countries. The Florida union uses a broader classification than the Foreign Mission Board, which classifies as state missionaries only those born in a particular state. Because of the growth of Florida residents through migration, the Florida Union includes also those having lived in the State at least seven years before their missionary service and those who were officially connected with the Florida Baptist Convention before going as missionaries. Using these criteria, the Florida Union established at the end of the 1950's that a total of eighty-two missionaries from Florida had served or were serving on foreign fields.[62]

Baptist Student Union: New Buildings and the International Retreat

Throughout the 1950's the Baptist Student Union continued to be very effective in ministering to the spiritual life of Baptist students on college campuses and strengthening the ties between them and their local churches. The State Baptist Student office enjoyed more continuity of leadership during the 1950's than in the 1940's with only one change in the State secretary's office. In 1951, under the direction of State Baptist Student Union secretary Ray Koonce, a definite ministry to Baptist students was provided on the campuses of Florida State University, the University of Florida, Stetson University, the University of Miami, and Florida Southern College.[63] The annual student retreat and the State Baptist Student Union Convention continued to be held each year. In 1951, 5,280 Baptist students were enrolled in the colleges of Florida. In 1951 also, 350 students attended the state B. S. U. convention and 180 attended the spring retreat at Camp O'Leno.[64] The increase in the number of Baptist students enrolled in college intensified the interest of the Florida Baptist Convention in a ministry to meet their needs, and the Convention readily responded to the requests of several churches adjacent to college campuses for aid to provide extra facilities for ministering to college students. A total of $25,000 each was pledged by the Convention to the First Baptist Church of DeLand and the First Baptist Church of Tallahassee.[65] In 1951 $15,000 was voted for Immanuel Baptist Church in Gainesville.[66]

---

[62] *Ibid.,* pp. 112-114.

[63] Florida Baptist Convention, *Annual,* 1951, pp. 78-79.

[64] *Ibid.*

[65] *Ibid.,* 1950, p. 35.

[66] *Ibid.,* 1951, p. 41.

In 1956, the State Board of Missions added $100,000 to the recommended budget for a Baptist Student Union house at Florida State University at Tallahassee.[67] This amount made possible extensive remodeling in 1957 of the old building, which had been constructed in 1937. Also in 1956 Ray Koonce resigned as State B. S. U. secretary and Joe Webb was elected to the post.

Baptist Student Center, Florida State University

In 1958 the first International Student Retreat was held on the campus of Stetson University, January 2-4, with students representing sixteen countries. The program leaders included J. Winston Pearce, pastor, First Baptist Church, DeLand, Carl Bahner, professor of chemistry at Carson-Newman College, and Frank Stagg, professor of New Testament interpretation at New Orleans Seminary.[68] This retreat was jointly sponsored by the Southern Baptist Department of Student Work at Nashville, the Florida State Baptist Student Department, and the Florida Woman's Missionary Union.[69] As indicated earlier, this retreat became an annual event.

Music—Brotherhood: Combined and Divided

At the beginning of this decade, C. A. Holcomb carried the responsibility of promoting the work of the Brotherhood and Music for

[67]*Ibid.,* 1956, p. 28.
[68]*Florida Baptist Witness,* Jan. 16, 1958, p. 1.
[69]Florida Baptist Convention, *Annual,* 1958, p. 90.

the Florida Baptist Convention. In 1950, a committee on camps and assemblies was elected, with nine members serving on a rotating basis, and Holcomb was designated as Assembly camp manager without additional remuneration. The committee on camps and assemblies promptly recommended that the Convention also take over the West Florida Assembly property valued at $65,000 from the local Board of Trustees and that the property be improved at a cost of $30,000. Finally, the committee recommended that three additional camp locations be established in different geographical areas of Florida.[70] Thus Holcomb carried three responsibilities at once. Moreover, he does not appear to have neglected any of them. In 1950 he reported that for 1951 there would be seven regional festivals preceding the customary state music festival, the purpose being to involve a great many more people. Plans were also projected for other areas of his responsibility.

Still, Holcomb was overburdened with responsibility, and was no doubt relieved to be able to introduce to the Convention of 1951 the new secretary of the Brotherhood, G. A. Ratteree, whose election again created a separate Brotherhood Department.[71]

Music, Camps, and Assemblies: Growth and Division of Responsibility

The Music, Camps, and Assemblies Department continued as a combination department for several years under the direction of Holcomb. In the meantime, in 1951, when the first year's report of the committee on camps and assemblies was presented to the Convention, it was obvious that needed plans and improvements were under way. With the approval of the State Board, $5,000 had been given to the Tampa Bay Association Assembly, plus a loan in the same amount, which had already been repaid. The committee spent $11,500 improving the West Florida Assembly. Also, development of an East Coast Assembly was under consideration at Stuart, where an assembly had been held in rented facilities for several years.[72] The need for additional and improved camp facilities grew out of the increased growth of the DeLand Assembly beyond the capacity of the facilities at Stetson.[73]

In 1953, C. A. Holcomb resigned, and W. G. Stroup assumed the

[70]*Ibid.,* 1950, p. 42. For further developments and decisions on camps and assemblies see Chapter VIII.

[71]Florida Baptist Convention, *Annual,* 1951, p. 19.

[72]Plans to establish a permanent State assembly at Stuart never materialized.

[73]Florida Baptist Convention, *Annual,* 1951, pp. 73-74.

responsibility for the Department of Music, Camps, and Assemblies.[74] The camps and assembly program continued to grow until, in 1958, Gus Johnson was given the responsibility of supervising the work of camps and assemblies, thus freeing W. G. Stroup to promote the work of church music exclusively.[75] By 1960, the greatest advance yet had been reached in the camping program with over 5,000 attending various camps. The taxed capacity of all the camps then led Tom Collins to introduce to the Convention of 1960 a resolution which cited the need for a central state camp site and called for the purchase of land to establish such a camp.[76]

Brotherhood: Record Convention Attendance

With G. A. Ratteree as the new secretary of the Brotherhood Department, the State Brotherhood convention at Winter Haven in 1952 smashed all previous records. The total number of Brotherhoods grew from 321 in 1950 to 836 in 1957. In 1957, the Brotherhood took over the work of Royal Ambassadors from the Woman's Missionary Union, and in 1959 the first Royal Ambassador Congress was held under the leadership of the Brotherhood. It met at Calvary Baptist Church in Clearwater with an attendance of 1,400.[77]

Christian Education and the Florida Baptist Foundation

The Department of Christian Education, established during the Million Dollar Campaign for Stetson and headed by J. Harrison Griffin, was continued after the million dollar goal was reached, and Griffin continued to promote Christian education. In the meantime, the work of the Florida Baptist Foundation, established in 1947, grew to the point where it was more than a lay committee of the Convention could handle adequately. For example, between 1947 and 1954, the Foundation received $434,949.78. Of this, $169,441.48 was distributed to designated agencies and institutions, leaving a balance of $265,507.29.[78] In 1951 some of the responsibility for the work of the Foundation came to be carried by J. Harrison Griffin. In 1952, however, Griffin retired, and the State Board of Missions voted to discontinue the Department of Christian Education.[79] After 1952 the work

[74]*Ibid.,* 1953, p. 66.
[75]*Ibid.,* 1958, p. 49.
[76]*Ibid.,* 1960, p. 38.
[77]*Ibid.,* 1959, p. 94.
[78]*Ibid.,* 1954, p. 44.
[79]State Board, *Minutes,* Sept. 4-5, 1952.

of the Foundation was handled for four years by the Foundation committee together with the executive secretary-treasurer, John Maguire. In 1955, the foundation entered into an agreement with Florida Industrial and Memorial College at Saint Augustine to manage their $300,000 endowment.[80] In 1956 the State Board approved the employment of G. A. Leichliter as executive secretary of the Foundation.[81] From 1956 to 1960, Leichliter directed the work of the Foundation, and during those years the volume of work done by the Foundation increased considerably as several different endowment funds were established for various institutions and causes of Florida Baptists such as Stetson University, the Children's Home, and Baptist Bible Institute. The financial reports are not complete and an accurate total of the amount handled by the Foundation between 1955 and 1960 would be difficult to determine, but a safe conservative estimate would be more than one million dollars.

Associational Growth

During the 1950's the growth in membership and new Baptist churches in many areas of the state resulted in developing interest in forming new associations. Thus, between 1950 and 1960, seven new associations were organized in widely separated geographical areas. They included Apalachee (1951), Brevard (1953), Ridge (1954), Big Lake (1955), Halifax (1958), Royal Palm (1958), Taylor (1958), and Choctaw (1959).

Florida Baptist Children's Home: New Buildings and a New Branch

The Home continued to grow and prosper in the 1950's under the stable leadership of T. M. Johns and Mrs. Johns. It continued to receive strong support through a stated percentage of the Convention's Cooperative Program receipts and through designated individual gifts which sometimes equalled or exceeded the amount received from the Cooperative Program. For example, in 1950 the Children's Home received 12 per cent of the Cooperative Program budget, which amounted to $45,585, whereas designated gifts that year totaled $56,917. By 1950, with additional land acquired at the new location in Lakeland, the Home owned 182 acres of land, 120 of which was in pasture, with the remainder in farm, grove, and campus. Also in 1950

---

[80]Florida Baptist Convention, *Annual,* 1954, p. 44.

[81]*Ibid.,* 1956, p. 53.

the Gaines vocational building and a chapel were constructed. The Home was caring for 157 children and had recently received license to place children in foster homes and to offer children for adoption in Polk, Hillsborough, and Hardee counties.[82]

On November 14, 1951, the new Florida Baptist Children's Home at Lakeland was formally dedicated. Services were held in the chapel of the Home and Dr. Earl Edington, president of the Convention, gave the dedication address. Dr. John H. Maguire gave the dedication prayer and benediction.[83]

In 1950 and 1951 efforts were made to consolidate the administration of the Florida Baptist Children's Home at Lakeland with the Baptist Children's Home in Jacksonville.[84] The suggestion to consolidate grew out of a study made at Florida State University under the direction of Dr. Doak E. Campbell. The intention of the suggestion was to coordinate the work of the two homes and to plan other centers. However, it appears that the trustees of the Florida Baptist Children's Home at Lakeland convinced the State Board, to which the proposal had been referred, that the problems of implementing the idea were too great to overcome, for the plan was never carried out.[85]

The publicity which accompanied the new home in Lakeland probably accounts for the remarkable increase in applications in 1951 and 1952. Despite the enlargement of the Home's facilities, the capacity of the home was taxed.[86]

In 1955, the State Board of Missions voted approval to establish in Miami a branch of the Florida Baptist Children's Home along with an adoptive agency.[87] In 1956 the Convention added $85,000 to the budget for the Children's Home to provide capital funds for this project.[88] The trustees proceeded to act immediately, and by 1958

---

[82]*Ibid.*, 1950, pp. 87-88.

[83]*Ibid.*, 1951, p. 30.

[84]The Home in Jacksonville was established in 1924 by a local Baptist group independently of Convention action. It was established and operated under a board of trustees elected by the Jacksonville Baptist Association. The Convention had contributed to its support since 1952, however, under a well-defined policy described earlier. See Chapter VI. The Home is now also sponsored by the Northeast Florida Baptist Association.

[85]Florida Baptist Convention, *Annual,* 1950, pp. 22-23, and *Annual,* 1951, p. 25.

[86]*Ibid.*, 1952, pp. 84-86.

[87]*Ibid.*, 1955, p. 55.

[88]*Ibid.*, 1956, p. 28.

the new branch in Miami was in operation.[89] The trustees and administration of the Home after investigating the problems involved in operating an adoption agency, however, concluded that such a venture would be unwise at the time. It would have needed to be related to a home for unwed mothers, and in view of other projected plans of Florida Baptists, the Convention committee agreed with the trustees and administration of the Home. Thus, the adoptive agency was not begun.[90]

Baptist Bible Institute Adopted and Moved

At the beginning of the 1950's Baptist Bible Institute at Lakeland was not owned by the Convention, but before the end of the decade, it became a Convention-owned institution. Directed by President Leon M. Gambrell, the Institute had gradually captured the sympathy of many Florida Baptists during the late 1940's, and by 1950 the Convention had acknowledged that the young institution, now enrolling more than 200 students, was qualified for aid from the special state mission offering in accordance with the Convention by-laws. Accordingly, Baptist Bible Institute received $6,000 annually from this offering for several years.[91] In 1951, request was made by the Institute for the Convention to take over full support, ownership and control.[92] The motion made to this effect was referred to the Education Commission, and although the matter was considered very seriously, the Commission did not recommend that the Convention take over at that time. President Gambrell resigned in May, 1952, and Dr. T. S. Boehm, who had been instrumental in founding the school, returned as acting head until Dr. Arthur House Stainback was elected president in October, 1952. Under Stainback's leadership, the very significant moving of the school to Graceville in west Florida occurred. The invitation for the move came from the First Baptist Church in Graceville in January, 1953. After visiting the proposed site, the trustees voted in March, 1953, to accept the invitation. The people of Graceville, in cooperation with the First Baptist Church, acquired a tract of 160 acres inside the city limits and gave it to the new school for a campus. The trustees proceeded immediately with building plans for the new campus.[93] The advantage of the new location was that it put

---

[89] *Ibid.,* 1958, p. 103.
[90] *Ibid.,* 1959, pp. 130-132.
[91] *Ibid.,* 1951, p. 35.
[92] *Ibid.,* p. 20.
[93] *Baptist Bible Institute Catalogue,* 1969-70, p. 13.

the Institute in the heart of the largest settled rural area in Florida where the greatest need for helping uneducated ministers existed. There it could serve sections of Florida, Georgia, and Alabama. In 1954 the Convention voted to ask the Southern Baptist Convention to take over the school, but the Southern Baptist Convention was not willing to do so.[94] In 1955, the Education Commission reversed its earlier position and recommended that Baptist Bible Institute be taken over by the Florida Baptist Convention.[95] The recommendation was approved, and the following year the second approval required for new work was given.[96] At a special meeting of the Convention in 1957 the details of the agreement by which the Convention would take over the school were worked out, and the Convention elected a new board of trustees.[97] In the meantime, Stainback had resigned, and George H. Gay, pastor of the First Baptist Church of Marianna, served as interim president until the new trustees elected Dr. James E.

Lee Chapel, Baptist Bible Institute

[94]Florida Baptist Convention, *Annual,* 1954, pp. 36-37.
[95]*Ibid.,* 1955, p. 26-27.
[96]*Ibid.,* 1956, p. 25.
[97]*Ibid.,* 1957, pp. 21-22, 46.

Southerland as president on December 1, 1957. A Florida native who had served pastorates in Florida and Mississippi, Dr. Southerland came to the presidency from the pastorate of the First Baptist Church of Oxford, Mississippi.[98] By the end of the 1950's the buildings constructed or acquired included a home for the president, the R. G. Lee Memorial Chapel, and an apartment for men. In 1960, 138 students were enrolled, and the school received $59,024, 6.5 per cent of the cooperative program budget of the Convention. Other designated gifts raised the total received through the state offices to $139,645.[99]

FLORIDA BAPTIST RETIREMENT CENTERS

In the Convention of 1957 the State Board was authorized to study the need for and possibility of establishing a home for the care of the aging.[100] A committee was appointed, and after considerable study and investigation, the Convention approved a charter with bylaws for a proposed facility for the aging. The charter named the institution "Florida Baptist Retirement Centers, Incorporated." Dr. J. Perry Carter was named general director, and 25 acres of land and a two and a half story home at Vero Beach were donated by Mr. and Mrs. Walter Buckingham. The property was valued at $125,000 and the Convention paid the Buckingham family $25,000 to build themselves a new home. Plans were adopted, and in 1959 five per cent of the Cooperative Program budget was allocated for the center.[101] In 1960, construction was begun on the first unit of the retirement center and interest in the project grew. During that year the center received the five per cent of the cooperative program budget, which amounted to $45,503. Other gifts received through the Convention offices raised the total amount of Convention support that year to $69,418.[102]

BAPTIST HOSPITALS IN FLORIDA

During the 1950's several hospitals begun by local Baptist groups were completed and became operative. None of these hospitals were owned by the Convention, but they were Baptist institutions ministering to the sick, and their existence was made possible by a great deal of Florida Baptist money. Also, the Convention itself had contributed to the building of several of them. Naturally, the *Witness* gave generous

[98]*Baptist Bible Institute Catalogue,* 1969-70, p. 13.
[99]Florida Baptist Convention, *Annual,* 1960, p. 45.
[100]*Ibid.,* 1957, p. 84.
[101]*Ibid.,* 1959, p. 51.
[102]*Ibid.,* 1960, p. 45.

publicity to the growth and progress of these hospitals. In October, 1951, the *Witness* carried on the front page a picture of the recently opened Pensacola Hospital.[103] On December 20, 1953, the new Baptist Hospital at Plant City, promoted for years by G. A. Leichliter, was opened.[104] In 1955, Jacksonville Baptist Hospital was opened. This hospital was owned by the Southern Baptist Convention, but several Florida Baptists, mostly in the Jacksonville area, were on the board of trustees.[105]

In the meantime, efforts were being made to establish another Southern Baptist Convention Hospital in the Miami area. The local group had requested and received Southern Baptist Convention approval in the convention of 1956.[106] However, the Southern Baptist Convention, like the Florida Baptist Convention, had a by-law requirement that new institutions be approved in two succeeding conventions before concrete action could be authorized. In 1957, the Miami group withdrew their request for Southern Baptist Convention support. One reason was that they did not wish to wait as long as the Southern Baptist Convention financial plan would have required. They regarded the need for the hospital as too urgent for waiting.[107] Thus the Baptist Hospital in Miami became a local institution.

Stetson University

Growth and Support

Stetson continued to be the largest single institution related to the Florida Baptist Convention. At the beginning of the 1950's relations between Stetson and the Convention, sometimes stormy in the past, were quite good. Indeed, many observers judged that the relationship was better than it had been in three decades.[108] Despite the crisis that did arise in 1956, the 1950's turned out to be one of the most significant decades in the history of Stetson and the Convention. For example, in the 1950's, Stetson received the largest percentage of the Co-operative Program budget in Florida Baptist history up to the present, with never less than 18 per cent being received in any year, and in 1954, the percentage went up to a high of 24 per cent.[109]

---

[103] *Florida Baptist Witness,* Oct. 25, 1951.
[104] *Ibid.,* Jan. 7, 1954.
[105] *Ibid.,* Sept. 1, 1955, pp. 1-2.
[106] *Ibid.,* June 14, 1956.
[107] Southern Baptist Convention, *Annual,* 1957, p. 55.
[108] State Board, *Minutes,* Sept. 2, 1951.
[109] Florida Baptist Convention, *Annual,* 1953, p. 36.

In 1950 a Reserve Officers Training Corps unit began operations on Stetson's campus.[110] During that year the student enrollment, still swelled by the influx of World War II veterans under the G. I. Bill, reached 2,527, and 613 were graduated. Prosperity in the University and Convention enthusiasm for the University had never seemed greater. In such an atmosphere, a ten-year capital-improvement program was launched on the recommendation of the Institutional and Survey Committee, chaired by Davis C. Woolley. The ten-year program was an ambitious one, including plans for a new law building, an addition to the library, a new music building, a fine arts building, a new men's gymnasium, a new women's gymnasium, a new biology wing on Science Hall, and considerable remodeling of old buildings.[111] In 1951 the veterans' boom was on the wane with enrollment down to 2,078, but there were 123 ministerial students and the University increased the requirement in religion from three to six hours for all students, and enthusiasm was sustained.[112]

Economic Difficulties and Convention Help

In 1952, however, the number of veterans and the total student enrollment declined further, to 1,189, and the school operated with a deficit of $133,170.79. The deficit continued in 1953, and had it not been for the Convention's generous support, Stetson's economic difficulties would have been extreme. The trustees and administration went on with development plans nonetheless, with the full support of the Convention. In March, 1954, ground was broken for a new dormitory, with Dr. Harold Sanders, Convention president, along with F. N. K. Bailey, president of Stetson's trustees, handling the shovel.[113] Special publicity was given to Stetson in the March 11, 1954, *Witness.*

As one way of dealing with the economic crisis, the State Board, on recommendation of President Edmunds, approved a policy change in the tuition of ministerial students. Because of the increased number of ministerial students and the resulting cost to the University, tuition grants to ministerial students were reduced from 100 per cent to two-thirds.[114] In September, this policy change was further defined by the provision that whatever tuition grants were given up to two-thirds would be on the basis of need and that the amounts given would be

---

[110]*Ibid.,* 1950, p. 83.
[111]State Board, *Minutes,* Sept. 2, 1951.
[112]Florida Baptist Convention, *Annual,* 151, pp. 80-82.
[113]*Florida Baptist Witness,* Mar. 11, 1954, front page.
[114]State Board, *Minutes,* Apr. 13, 1954.

shared on a fifty-fifty basis between Stetson and the Convention.[115]

The economic difficulties together with the tragic fire which burned the dining hall in December, 1954, made it difficult to maintain the optimism which had prevailed, but the Convention's response was immediate. By January, 1955, a list of committees for raising money for a new building had been named, approved and published in the *Witness.* Seven committees were organized with Harold Sanders as general chairman of the drive, assisted by James Parrish, Doyle E. Carlton, Sr., Earl Stallings and others as needed.[116] In February, 1955, Convention employees voted to fast for Stetson by giving the price of one meal to rebuild the dining hall,[117] and in April, a special Easter offering was taken in the churches to boost the drive.[118] In the meantime, a temporary kitchen and dining facility was set up in the

Emily Hall, Stetson University

[115]*Ibid.,* Sept. 2, 1955.
[116]*Ibid.,* Jan. 12, 1955.
[117]*Florida Baptist Witness,* Feb. 24, 1955, p. 3.
[118]*Ibid.,* Apr. 7, 1955, front page.

basement of the men's gymnasium.[119] During 1955, the Stetson Law School was moved to a new campus in St. Petersburg,[120] and a total of $175,000 was received from Convention efforts toward the food facilities building.[121] Also in 1955, a new women's dormitory was begun, later to be named Emily Hall, in honor of President Edmunds' wife, Emily Bryant Edmunds.[122] By 1956, the new building which would house the new dining hall and many other facilities was under construction. Also in 1956, construction was begun on three new men's dormitories later named Carson Hall, Gordis Hall, and Smith Hall in memory of three early teachers at Stetson, G. Prentice Carson, J. Archy Smith, and Warren Stone Gordis.[123]

Revival of Charter Controversy

Unfortunately, the year 1956 also brought new disturbance to the relationship between Stetson and the Convention. It is difficult to determine where the difficulties began, but early in 1956 Editor Stracener called attention to some of the problems. In an editorial entitled, "Considerations for Stetson Authorities," he raised three questions, two of which, he reported, had been suggested by the executive committee of the Miami Association. First, was the question of fraternities, and the suggestion was made that since they were undemocratic they should be disbanded. Second, he suggested that the trustees reconsider changing the charter to give the Convention control. Third, he suggested that the trustees reject further temptation to seek federal aid. Some complaints had been reported over surplus housing acquired by Stetson from the federal government.[124] The issue on which most attention was focused was the charter question. Many Florida Baptists, not knowing the history of the charter controversy, had to have it aired all over again. Thus, in the 1956 convention a resolution was introduced asking for changes in Stetson's charter to provide for a rotating board of trustees elected by the Convention and asking that the money for Stetson in the recommended budget be held in escrow until the charter was so changed.[125] After heated and lengthy debate, action

[119]Florida Baptist Convention, *Annual,* 1955, pp. 22-24, where other accomplishments in the Stetson ten-year program are summarized.
[120]Florida Baptist Convention, *Annual,* 1955, pp. 22-24.
[121]*Florida Baptist Witness,* Dec. 1, 1955, p. 4.
[122]Bowen, *op. cit.,* p. 16.
[123]Bowen, *op. cit.,* p. 16.
[124]*Florida Baptist Witness,* Feb. 23, 1956, p. 4.
[125]Florida Baptist Convention, *Annual,* 1956, p. 25.

on the resolution was postponed until the report of the State Board could be heard. Then a supplement to the State Board report was accepted as a substitute for the resolution. The supplement suggested that Stetson's trustees be asked to change the charter, but included no threats or penalties. After much discussion, the supplement, with the report was adopted.[126] A special Convention committee was appointed to consult with Stetson's trustees concerning the charter change. The State Board report, furthermore, not only reiterated its commitment to the ten-year program of building and endowment calling for $5,000,000, but it also doubled Stetson's percentage of Cooperative Program receipts above the operating budget for the coming year from 20 per cent to 40 per cent.[127]

New Agreement and New Plans

In 1957, after much consultation with Convention lawyers and among themselves the Stetson-Convention committee brought to the Convention a recommendation for a new agreement to be added to the agreements of 1919 and 1927, to wit, that the trustees should be elected by a joint Convention-Stetson trustee committee, and that the charter should remain unchanged.[128] The atmosphere was considerably improved, and the recommendation was approved.

In 1958, in response to suggestions by the State Board,[129] Stetson announced plans to open an Extension Department, directed by Dr. William H. McCammon.[130] The Extension Department began as scheduled, and within a year nine centers were in operation directed by E. C. Tyner who had served for many years as pastor of First Baptist Church, Dade City, Florida.[131] Also, in the fall of 1958 Stetson celebrated Homecoming and its Diamond Jubilee with a great convocation with noted special speakers, including Billy Graham, Harold Stassen, Brooks Hays, and J. D. Grey. The charter controversy having been settled, in 1960 Stetson received $259,189 from the Convention. Of that total amount, $164,926 came from Stetson's share of the Cooperative Program receipts, and the rest came from designated gifts, endowment income, and other sources.[132] At the same session, the

---

[126]*Ibid.,* p. 26.
[127]Garwood, *op. cit.,* p. 248.
[128]Florida Baptist Convention, *Annual,* 1957, pp. 44, 81.
[129]State Board, *Minutes,* May 4, 1956, and May 7, 1957.
[130]*Ibid.,* May 8, 1958.
[131]Florida Baptist Convention, *Annual,* 1959, p. 104.
[132]*Ibid.,* 1960, p. 45.

Education Commission recommended that the restrictions made earlier on capital funds for Stetson be lifted for 1959-60, and that the funds be freely used by Stetson's administration.[133]

Also in 1960, at the annual meeting of the Convention, the attention of the messengers was called to a report that Stetson University had received a contribution from the State Racing Commission, and Dr. Edgar R. Cooper moved that the State Board investigate the report and request Stetson to return the money if the charge was found to be true.[134] President Edmunds, apparently unaware of the facts, denied the report. Dr. Parrish, vice-president of Stetson, acknowledged uncertainty about the report. Stetson administrative authorities declared that to receive race track money was against Stetson's policy and promised that if the money had been accepted by mistake, it would be returned.[135] This incident appears to have cast a new pall over Stetson-Convention relationships just when they seemed to be improving.

During the last two years of this decade, in 1959 and 1960, the Education Commission, a standing Convention committee, studied the predictions concerning the number of students expected to be asking admission to college in the next few years. In 1959, before the study had gone very far, the first suggestion that Florida Baptists give consideration to establishing a junior college was made.[136] In 1960, the Education Commission recommended to the State Board that a study of long-range needs and problems of higher Christian education in Florida be made with a view to planning twenty years in advance.

The pall cast by the race track money question and other criticism plus the Education Commission's description of the need for more colleges in the future probably accounts for the ease with which the 1960 Convention approved the motion of O. E. Burton, pastor of Calvary Baptist Church in Clearwater, that the Convention accept an offer of eighty acres of land near Dunedin, at the junction of Highways 580 and 583, for building a college.[137] The motion was given only tentative approval, pending the acceptance of the Education

---

[133]State Board, *Minutes,* Sept. 2, 1960.

[134]Florida Baptist Convention, *Annual,* 1960, p. 38.

[135]Investigation shows Stetson did receive the money, and returned it. For further details on the incident, see Chapter Eight.

[136]Florida Baptist Convention, *Annual,* 1959, p. 102.

[137]*Ibid.,* 1960, p. 29.

Commission. The Commission, however, recommended further study before any action was taken.[138]

THE FLORIDA BAPTIST WITNESS

In the 1950's, the *Witness* continued to prosper under the able leadership of W. G. Stracener, with circulation more than doubling from 25,400 in 1950 to 57,442 in 1960.[139] The editorial page covered a wide range of subjects, including as examples morality, tithing, doctrine, news, evangelism, progress, missions, public relations, problems of urbanization, prayer, Christian education, and democracy. The *Witness* gave publicity to all major events as space permitted. It was not, therefore, surprising that the Convention of 1954 gave Dr. Stracener a standing vote of appreciation.[140] It is to the credit of editor Stracener, moreover, that he had the courage in 1959 to send out to his readers a questionnaire which gave them some opportunity to evaluate critically his work with the paper. He found that the *Witness* was read by all types of people and, surely to his good pleasure, that the page enjoyed most was the editorial page. Next in preference came the Sunday School lesson, then current events and news stories.[141]

Theological Discussion

During the 1950's, Florida Baptists did not engage in much theological discussion, at least so far as written records indicate. The most probable reasons for the scarcity of theological discussion are: (1) Florida Baptists during the 1950's were dominated by evangelism and practical considerations for which a very simple traditional theology was taken for granted, (2) Florida Baptists, like Southern Baptists generally, had not developed the kind of reflective attitude which produces much theological discussion, and (3) they took the theological tradition of Baptists for granted, thus assuming little need for further discussion. The few devotional and theological articles which appeared reflected traditional doctrine and said very little that was new. One series of articles on doctrine was published in the *Witness* during the 1950's by L. O. Calhoun, and W. E. Denham. The series reflects a conservative literal interpretation of the Bible and a rationalistic approach to its meaning for practical life and thought. Two of the

---

[138] *Ibid.*, pp. 115-116.
[139] *Ibid.*, p. 46.
[140] *Ibid.*, 1954, p. 28.
[141] *Florida Baptist Witness*, Apr. 23, 1959, p. 4.

articles provide examples that illustrate this approach. The first is an article by Calhoun on the doctrine of the Trinity. In it he equates belief in evolution with atheism. His argument is that religious truth is something that the church possesses absolutely and that if the people are properly indoctrined: (1) individuals will not be swept away by error, and (2) all church members will believe the same things.[142] The second article, by W. E. Denham, is on divorce, and in it the author equates remarriage with adultery.[143]

Social Concern

Social concern among Florida Baptists during the 1950's was expressed mainly in (1) economic support for such organizations as United Florida Drys and Protestants and Other Americans United for the Separation of Church and State, (2) committee reports calculated to inform the churches on social evils and (3) passing resolutions on issues of special interest. The most comprehensive summary of the areas and issues of interest to Florida Baptists is to be found in the Social Service report sometimes called the report on Social Service and Temperance.[144] The topics of social concern which caught the attention of Florida Baptist leaders during the 1950's were many and varied including war, race, temperance, gambling, drugs, family problems, church-state problems, commercial amusements, obscene literature and traffic violations. However, these issues did not all receive equal attention. In fact, some of the most important ethical issues which later became obviously paramount received very little attention —race and war, for example. Judging from economic support, resolutions, and repeated emphasis, it appears that Florida Baptists' major social concern in the 1950's centered in two areas.

First, they continued to be interested in preserving the separation of church and state. In addition to the continuation of their participation in the Southern Baptist campaign to nullify presidential efforts to establish an ambassador to the Vatican,[145] Florida Baptists passed a resolution in 1960 lauding President Kennedy for his stand on separation of church and state and aid to parochial schools.[146]

---

[142]L. O. Calhoun, "The Holy Trinity," *Florida Baptist Witness,* Apr. 5, 1951, p. 2.

[143]W. E. Denham, "Divorce and Remarriage," *Florida Baptist Witness,* Apr. 26, 1951, p. 2.

[144]Florida Baptist Convention, *Annual,* 1958, pp. 116-117.

[145]Florida Baptist Convention, *Annual,* 1951, pp. 23-24.

[146]*Ibid.,* 1960, p. 39.

Second, Florida Baptists continued to place strong emphasis on fighting the use of alcohol as a beverage. Judging from economic support and emphasis, it appears that this was their greatest concern. For example, between 1950 and 1960 Florida Baptists gave more than $50,000 to the support of United Florida Drys, an interdenominational organization dedicated to fighting the liquor traffic. In 1960, although eight other denominations contributed also, Florida Baptists were providing 66 per cent of the budget for that organization.[147]

During the 1950's Jack Eppes became the director of United Florida Drys and the organization began publishing a paper called *United Christian Action.*[148] The work and goals of this paper were centered in education, legislation, and rehabilitation. Among the activities used to achieve these goals were narcotics lectures in high schools, the promotion of local option elections, and the publication of literature on the evils of alcohol. Florida Baptists not only gave support to United Florida Drys, but they also passed resolutions favoring Sunday laws which would forbid the sale of liquor on Sundays. Interestingly, these laws were urged not on religious grounds, but on moral grounds.[149]

Two other major social problems, war and race, received considerable attention. The first issue, war, was raised by the Korean War which began in June, 1950, and came to some kind of an end in the truce signing in July, 1953. It provoked very little official comment among Florida Baptists despite the fact that 33,000 Americans were killed in the war. The Korean War does appear to have created a surge of renewed patriotism,[150] but produced very little discussion of the basic issues or the long-range significance of American involvement in Korea.

On the problem of race, although Florida Baptists approved traditional statements condemning racial prejudice and discrimination, the epoch-making 1954 Supreme Court decision on desegregation received very little official notice by Florida Baptists. One of the few references to the problem may be found in the Social Service and Temperance

[147]*Ibid.,* p. 48.

[148]*Ibid.,* 1954, p. 44.

[149]*Ibid.,* 1951, pp. 23-24.

[150]For example, J. Ollie Edmunds, "Stetson University and Military Training," *Florida Baptist Witness,* Jan. 25, 1951, p. 3; also G. A. Leichliter, "Christian Education," *Florida Baptist Witness,* Jan. 25, 1951, p. 2. The latter article reflects awareness of the war in its emphasis on education making young people strong in times of crisis.

Committee Report to the Convention in 1958 which reads as follows: "Most every group seems to suggest its answer to this question of race, but there is only one answer. It came two thousand years ago when Jesus elevated all men to the state of respect and dignity through himself. . . ."[151]

Negro Baptists and Race

Beyond reiterating statements on race prejudice, the Florida Baptist Convention did little for Negro Baptists beyond the small amounts given annually for Negro education from the special offering for state missions, which allotment for Negroes grew from the allotted $3,000 in 1951 to $5,000 in 1960.[152] In 1950, the amount given to Negro Baptists in Florida was broken down into designated amounts for ten student scholarships, two assemblies, part of a teacher's salary for eight months, and an emergency fund. All of these areas appear to stretch rather thin the $3,496 designated in 1950.[153] In 1951, the $3,000 allotted was simply designated for Negro education.[154] By 1960, the $5,000 allotted was designated to Florida Normal and Industrial College in Saint Augustine.[155] Beyond this support and the work done by the Woman's Missionary Union with Negro Baptists, such as the camps for Negro students mentioned earlier in this chapter, there was no significant contact between Florida Baptists and any of the Negro Baptist Conventions in Florida in the 1950's.

In retrospect, the 1950's appear to represent one of the most significant periods in Florida Baptist history. Not only was their growth in membership, income, and property values without parallel in their previous history, but their institutional growth was phenomenal as well. New hospitals, Baptist Bible Institute, and Florida Retirement Centers, are examples. Would this growth and prosperity continue in the 1960's? This question will be discussed in the next chapter.

---

[151] *Ibid.*, 1958, pp. 116-117.
[152] *Ibid.*, 1951, p. 35, and 1960, p. 46.
[153] *Ibid.*, 1950, p. 24.
[154] *Ibid.*, 1951, p. 35.
[155] *Ibid.*, 1960, p. 46.

CHAPTER EIGHT

Self Examination and Continued Expansion: 1960-1969

The State of Florida continued its growth momentum in people and economy throughout the 1960's. Spurred by industrial growth related to the war in Viet Nam, the Cape Kennedy space exploration center, the beginning of Disney World and many other forms of tourism, prosperity reigned. Towns became cities, cities became metropolitan centers, and the process of urbanization became the problem of urbanization. At the same time, despite the fact that Florida was the fastest growing state east of the Mississippi, several rural counties declined steadily in population for several years in succession. Between 1960 and 1968 the population grew from 4,951,560 to 6,160,000,[1] and the rural-urban imbalance increased, because not only did many rural people already in Florida move to the towns and cities, but many of those who came to Florida seeking economic opportunity settled in or near the industrial or metropolitan centers where most employment was available. Even retired people seeking a warmer climate for their last years tended to prefer areas near the cities or water in central and southern Florida.

The Convention and the Churches: Decline in Growth Rate

In 1963 executive secretary-treasurer John H. Maguire engaged in some reflection on gains made by Florida Baptists during the preceding ten years, and the statistics he reported show that some of the goals

[1]*Encyclopedia Brittanica Yearbook,* "States Statistical Supplement," 1969, p. 8.

set forth in the ten-year program adopted in 1952 had been reached.[2] He noted that the population of Florida grew from 3,118,000 in 1952 to 5,459,000 in 1962, a 75 per cent increase. During that period, Florida Baptists grew from 311,955 to 528,885 for a 69 per cent increase. Sunday School enrollment increased from 241,554 in 1952 to 418,088 in 1962, a gain of 73 per cent. Reflecting the continuation of church and economic growth, total gifts to all causes gained 229 per cent, or from $9,674,071 to $31,887,199. Gifts to missions through the State Convention offices almost tripled, increasing from $1,536,275 in 1952 to $4,334,190 in 1962. Maguire observed further that during the first five years of that period the Sunday School growth rate represented a seven per cent increase. In contrast, growth in world mission giving represented a 147 per cent increase.[3]

Between 1960 and 1968 the churches of the Florida Baptist Convention continued to grow in size and in number. The number of churches grew from 1,257 in 1960 to 1,433 in 1968. During these years, the churches reported the largest total number of baptisms ever recorded in any such brief period, averaging over 23,000 per year. During these years total gifts of Florida Baptist churches through the State Convention offices increased from $3,887,390 in 1960 to $5,715,837 in 1968. Total membership increased from 480,407 in 1960 to 614,900 in 1968. These statistics mean that much of the growth momentum developed in the 1940's and the 1950's was sustained in the 1960's. In contrast, when carefully scrutinized, they mean that while the growth rate in giving continued to climb, the growth rate in the number of baptisms and total church membership began to slow down. For example, despite continued increases in population and total church membership, the number of baptisms reported in 1968 (24,732) was smaller than the number reported in 1960 (25,621). Moreover, despite the special publicity for the Crusade of the Americas, which took place in 1969, that special campaign together with other evangelistic efforts of the churches resulted in 225 fewer baptisms than the preceding year. Also, despite the increase in total gifts, many individual churches reported increasing difficulty during 1969 in raising their budgets.

What accounts for this developing difficulty in maintaining growth rates in membership and church economics in keeping with the total

---

[2]Florida Baptist Convention, *Annual,* 1952, p. 41.

[3]John Maguire, "Gains and Trends in Florida for Ten Years," *Florida Baptist Witness,* May 2, 1963, p. 5.

growth of the state of Florida is hard to determine. Three factors appear to have contributed. First, economic inflation seems to have raised not only the standard and the price of living but also the social pressure on families to live on a high economic level. This social pressure increased the already large number of working wives and mothers. One result of this phenomenon, despite shorter hours, was to reduce the total amount of leisure the family had or was willing to give to the work of the church.

Second, and closely related, was the pressure of secularism which appeared to be increasing in the cities. This problem had many dimensions, two of which stood out. On the one hand, while many people moving from rural society to the cities had been liberated from some cultural elements in their background, the church being one of those elements, they had become enslaved by a combination of pressure systems which bore heavily in upon them. Among these pressure systems were the competitive economic pace set by others in an obsession for more and bigger homes, television sets, automobiles, boats and other fruits of a technological age, and the pressure for activism in work and leisure. On the other hand, the church in the secularized urban setting often found itself unable to reach and relate to people where they were. Some churches achieved some success by reproducing within the church something of the rural cultural ethos which gave transplanted rural people some contact with their roots and thus made life in the city more bearable for them. But it is debatable in 1970 whether those churches are touching those people at the center of their being in their everyday lives. Some mature leaders are now ready to confess that the churches are not reaching the people in the cities. The following interview the writer conducted with Dr. John H. Maguire shortly after his retirement in 1967 as executive secretary-treasurer is instructive on this point.

Question: During your work as executive secretary-treasurer Florida has made the transition from a predominantly rural to a predominantly city life. Are the churches reaching the people in the city?

Answer: No, they are not.

Question: Then this is one of the crises in church life, is it not?

Answer: Man alive, that is *the* crisis! That is where the water hits the wheel . . . I say emphatically that our churches in the cities are *not* reaching the people; and the people we are reaching are from a certain class structure.

Question: What class is most often reached?
Answer: Middle or upper middle, usually, though not always. Some churches have no professional people at all—think of it—a church with 1800 members and no doctor in it. Another church has 25 doctors in it.
Question: Do you think that is bad?
Answer: I think it is *very* bad.
Question: Well, what do you think our churches are going to have to do about this situation?
Answer: They are going to have to realize that they are going to have to take the church where the people are.
Question: You mean we are going to have to find new ways of reaching the people?
Answer: Yes, we do. We can't go home again. We can't follow the same pattern we have always followed. I've seen this change since I came.

A third factor which may help account for the slow down in the growth rate of Florida Baptists was the restlessness in the churches. In 1962 Stracener observed in the *Witness* reports of growing restlessness in many churches, reports that many churches and pastors were unhappy with each other. He speculated on the possible explanations of the restlessness and suggested three possibilities, though he did not feel certain of any of them. First, he suggested that the restlssness might indicate simple difficulties in adjusting to change. Second, he suggested that the restlessness might be a sign of spiritual sickness among some church members. Finally, he offered as a partial explanation the inability of some leaders to get along with people.[4] What Stracener did not say in this editorial is very much in harmony with what he did say. It is that people are not attracted to a church that is restless and unhappy for the reasons mentioned above.

A fourth and very significant factor in the failure of Florida Baptist growth to keep pace with Florida population growth undoubtedly is the fact that the bulk of people moving to Florida came from states where Baptists were not numerous, and, therefore, the proportion of Baptists among them was low.

The fact that in the slowing of their growth rate, Florida Baptists were reflecting nation-wide denominational trends did not make Flor-

---

[4]W. G. Stracener, "Disturbed Church-Leader Relationships," editorial, *Florida Baptist Witness,* Oct. 25, 1962, p. 4.

ida Baptist leaders any happier.[5] It appears from these figures that Florida Baptists were affected by the general national decline in church attendance. According to national polls, church attendance in the United States declined steadily from 1958 to 1966, from 49% to 44%. In 1967 the report shows a slight gain of 1%.[6] The national church membership ratio to the total population was of course higher, but it continued to decline from 64.4% in 1966 to 63.2% in 1969.[7] The polls also showed, however, that Baptists and Lutherans had the best record of attendance. Thus, the general United States statistics on attendance may not be representative of Baptists in general, or of Florida Baptists in particular. Not many answers or explanations of the decline were attempted by Florida Baptist leaders. One answer suggested was more emphasis on the Holy Spirit and less reliance on buildings.[8]

Upon reflection on the 1940's and 1950's it would appear that for a long time new life, excitement, and prosperity were brought to the city churches by the constant influx of people migrating from the country. In the 1960's, however, a significant sociological change took place. While the increase in the growth of cities continued and even accelerated, the migration from the country slowed. Three other factors now took significant places in the growth picture. One was a change in the city population process. When the writer was a college student in the late 1940's he was told by his sociology professor, Dr. Henlee Barnette, that no major city in the United States produced enough children to sustain itself. Quoting Walter Lippmann, he said the cities siphon off the cream of rural society and sterilize them. If, in fact, that was the case in the 1940's it is very apparent that after World War II, people in the cities had learned to have children. The second and most significant factor in the growth process was the influx of people from other states. This factor had always played a part in Florida's growth, but in the 1950's increasingly, and in the 1960's overwhelmingly, the migration from other states made the already growing cities of Jacksonville, Miami, St. Petersburg, Tampa, Pensacola, and Orlando into mushrooming giants. Moreover, current projections of population increase warn of continued city growth by

[5]"Churchgoing Portion of Population Shows First Decline in 90 Years," *Florida Baptist Witness,* Jan. 1963, p. 2.

[6]*Yearbook of American Churches,* 1969. (New York: Council Press) 1969, p. 205.

[7]*World Almanac,* 1969, p. 212.

[8]*Florida Baptist Witness,* Jan. 31, 1963, p. 4; also Mar. 21, 1963, p. 4.

migration.[9] Baptists among the mass of migrants from other states helped to continue the total growth of Florida Baptist Churches.

A third factor in the continuing growth of Florida Baptists is related to the migration mentioned above. It is the continued reliance of Florida Baptist Churches on the Sunday School and on special evangelistic meetings to reach new people. These two instruments continued to be effective throughout most of this decade. Toward the end of the 1960's, however, both these instruments appeared to lose some of their effectiveness.

The annual sessions of the Convention during the 1960's were presided over by the greatest variety of leadership. For the second time in the history of the Convention (the first time was 1950-1960), a whole decade went by without a single president serving more than one term of office. The variety this time was made necessary, of course, by a change in the by-laws of the Convention to provide variety of leadership. Of the ten presidents who served during the 1960's three were laymen. They all did a good job presiding over the annual sessions, and sometimes that was a difficult task, for despite the maturity of the leadership, several conventions during the 1960's had some stormy and tense sessions. The restlessness reported as observed in the churches was also reflected in the conventions, for although at times the issues which provoked controversy were significant, at other times exorbitant debate was engaged in over minor questions.

Debate and tension emerged sooner or later at most of the conventions, with discussion of problems of education and federal aid providing the main sources of conflict. In 1961 the debate arose over what amounted to a revival of the Stetson charter controversy.[10] In 1962 and 1963 the conventions were quiet, though tension was apparent in the voting over establishing a junior college and on the new Stetson-Convention agreement.[11] In 1964 conflict developed over committee nominations when Convention officers and Nominating Committee members were accused of recommending themselves for certain committees.[12] Considerable debate developed also over recommendations of the Education Commission concerning the proposed junior college.

---

[9]By 1980 the population of Florida is expected to reach 9,573,000 and by 1985 approximately 11,028,000. (*Florida Statistical Abstract,* 1967, Bureau of Business Research, College of Business Administration, University of Florida, Gainesville, 1967, pp. 14-15.)

[10]Florida Baptist Convention, *Annual,* 1961, p. 33.

[11]*Ibid.,* 1963, pp. 34-35.

[12]*Ibid.,* 1964, p. 23.

In 1965 the subject of argument again was the junior college-Education Commission report.[13] In 1966 the Stetson-federal aid controversy combined with the report on the proposed new junior college to create considerable discussion and warm feelings.[14] In 1967 the special session called to consider the articles of incorporation and by-laws of the junior college was very stormy.[15] By the time of the regular session in November, however, the atmosphere was quite different, and no major controversy developed. Most of the 1968 session was also peaceful. Near the end of the convention, however, a resolution on federal aid brought brief but heated debate.[16] The 1969 session was marred by stormy debate lasting several hours over discussion of a motion to delete Stetson University from the Convention budget.[17] The 1969 Convention ended its annual session and the decade of the 1960's with heated debate over theology in the Southern Baptist seminaries.[18]

The top level executive leadership of the Convention continued the stability developed in the 1950's with very few changes until near the end of the 1960's, and through the cooperation between the executive leadership and the officers of the Convention a great deal of progress was made in the 1960's despite the tensions.

The State Board of Missions and Executive Leadership

One significant reason the Convention was able to accomplish so much despite the tensions and conflicts of the 1960's was the creative leadership of the Convention's basic instrument, the State Board of Missions. With its widely distributed representative leadership, the State Board continued its work so effectively that throughout the 1960's the overwhelming majority of its annual recommendations to the Convention were adopted. In turn the State Board continued to implement directives received from the Convention, and in cooperation with the presidential and executive leadership it effected some very significant changes. Although these changes will be described in more detail later, it is worth mentioning here briefly that these changes included: (1) the purchase of land and the building of a new state

[13] *Ibid.*, 1965, pp. 26-28.

[14] *Ibid.*, 1966, pp. 29-30, 33-34.

[15] *Ibid.*, 1967, p. 24.

[16] *Ibid.*, 1968, pp. 38-39.

[17] *Florida Baptist Witness*, Nov. 20, 1969, p. 1.

[18] *Ibid.*, Dec. 4, 1969, p. 4. Further details on some of these controversies will be presented in a later section of this chapter.

assembly grounds at Lake Yale, (2) the beginning of complete reorganization of the associational missions program, (3) a change in the status of the Woman's Missionary Union from an auxiliary to a regular department of work like the Sunday School department and others, (4) the approval and release of a new junior college which became Palm Beach Atlantic College, (5) the construction and opening of a retirement center, (6) numerous top level personnel changes due to retirement and new programs, (7) extensive reorganization of the State Convention program of work, (8) development of a new agreement with the Home Mission Board, and (9) participation in the Crusade of the Americas.

During the periods of controversy the State Board often served as a stabilizing force and, as before, was heavily relied on by the Convention in the 1960's to work out problems that time did not allow solving on the Convention floor.

One major event which deserves special mention occurring during the late 1960's was the retirement of John H. Maguire, which became effective December 31, 1967. Having served Florida Baptists since 1945, the Convention and the State Board became aware of the significant progress made under his administration long before his retirement was announced. After Maguire suffered a heart attack in 1963 and was incapacitated for several months, plans developed during his recovery for a special pageant in his honor in the Convention of 1964. The pageant was directed by Agnes Pylant, and was performed in the sanctuary of the First Baptist Church of Tampa, where the session was held that year.[19] In 1966 the State Board minutes recorded a summary of progress made under Maguire's administration. Despite some repetition of statistics and information given elsewhere, the summary is worth presenting here because every detail is seen thereby in the total context. Between 1945 and 1966 the following accomplishments were made:

1. Membership increased from 184,140 to 581,956.
2. Churches increased from 826 to 1,400.
3. Income from the churches increased from $3,361,988 to $37,814,846.
4. World mission giving increased from $346,359 to $3,527,886.
5. Convention employees increased from 10 to 76.
6. Departments increased from four to ten.

[19]Florida Baptist Convention, *Annual,* 1964, p. 24.

7. Two children's home complexes were constructed, one in Lakeland and one in Miami.
8. Two complete camps and facilities were acquired and built, one at Lake Yale with 38 buildings and 200 acres and one in West Florida with 14 buildings and 8 acres.
9. Six Baptist Student Union buildings were completed at major colleges: the University of Florida, Florida State University, Stetson University, the University of South Florida, Jacksonville University, and the University of Miami.
10. A modern retirement center was constructed and opened at Vero Beach.
11. Baptist Bible Institute was taken over by the Convention and a new campus was built.
12. Three new commissions were set up:
    (1) *Florida Baptist Witness* Commission
    (2) Florida Baptist Foundation
    (3) Florida Baptist Education Commission.
13. A new work-revolving-fund was created which gave help to more than 400 churches.
14. A loan fund to help small and needy churches was established.
15. A new five-story office building on ¾ of a city block was constructed at a cost of over $1,000,000.
16. $5,578,981 was given to Stetson, $1,374,049 to Baptist Bible Institute, $419,301 to the Retirement Center, and $4,417,785 to children's homes.[20]

Since John H. Maguire announced his retirement well in advance, the State Board was able to employ Harold C. Bennett as the new executive secretary-treasurer before Maguire's retirement became effective. Thus, Bennett was introduced to the State Board as the nominee in August, 1967, assumed office on October 15, 1967, and the two men worked together for several months to make the administrative transition as smooth as possible. The State Board report to the Convention of 1967 was therefore a joint report prepared by the two men.[21] Bennett was born in North Carolina, graduated from Wake Forest College and Southern Baptist Theological Seminary, and came to his new responsibility from Texas, where he had served as director

[20]State Board, *Minutes,* Dec. 8-9, 1966.

[21]Florida Baptist Convention, *Annual,* 1967, pp. 58ff; also State Board, *Minutes,* Aug. 31, 1967.

HAROLD C. BENNETT, *Executive Secretary*
1967 -

of the Missions Division of the Baptist General Convention of Texas. Bennett was formally installed at Lake Yale Assembly on December 7, 1967.[22] He was awarded the Doctor of Divinity degree by Stetson University in the spring of 1968. Throughout his short term of service since October, 1967, Bennett not only continued to implement plans and programs already set in motion by the Convention and the State Board, but he also helped to initiate additional changes in the organizational structure of the state Convention offices. These changes will be described in a later section of this chapter.

Department Growth and New Areas of Work

Field Secretaries

As indicated in Chapter Seven, the work of associational missionaries came under the direct supervision of the executive secretary-treasurer in the late 1950's when the Department of Cooperative Missions was abolished and the associational missionaries came to be called field secretaries. In the early 1960's further changes were made in the associational mission program. First among these changes was the working out of a new agreement with the Home Mission Board. Formerly, the Home Mission Board of the Southern Baptist Convention had shared with the Florida Baptist Convention in the support of the associational mission program.[23] In 1961 the Home Mission Board proposed a new arrangement which would enlarge the area of cooperation in missions to include foreign language groups, National (Negro) Baptists, Jews, Indians, migrants, juvenile rehabilitation centers and other related mission work. Their proposal also included shared control and direction as well as financial support for these mission enterprises. On recommendation of a special committee, appointed to study the proposal, the State Board voted on May 6, 1961, to decline the invitation of the Home Mission Board. The reason given was that the Board's proposal was not in line with what had been recommended by the Southern Baptist Convention, which was that control should be retained by the State conventions. The State Board decided, moreover, that the dual control arrangement would be unwise and impractical, and that the Convention was not equipped to take on the enlarged program alone. Thus, the new agreement released the Home Mission Board from obligation for the Convention mission enterprises and pledged the State Board to take full responsibility for

---

[22]Florida Baptist Convention, *Annual,* 1967, pp. 58-59.

[23]Florida Baptist Convention, *Book of Reports,* 1960-61, p. 10.

the programs of evangelism, city missions and associational missions. Previously, the Home Mission Board had contributed $8,000 per year to these areas of work.[24] The Home Mission Board assumed support and direction of the other special mission programs.

A second change in the program of associational missions early in the 1960's was presented by John Maguire to the State Board and approved in April, 1963. It was a cooperative plan involving the church, the district (by associations) and the State Board. In brief, the field secretaries, formerly called associational missionaries,[25] were to be employed by an associational missions committee and a State Board personnel committee, and salaries were to be paid by the State Board, as before. The plan made it very clear that the employment of the field secretary was by the State Board, and that although the plan required associational and district missions committees, once the missionary was employed by the State Board the missionary then directed the missions committees rather than accepted instructions from them. Most of the responsibility for work, however, was in the hands of the missions committees. In this plan the field secretaries had ceased to be primarily servants of the associations and now became combination servants of the State Board and executives to the associations.[26] Later reports of the State Board to the Convention, however, indicate a more balanced view where the associational or district field secretary is described as responsible to and dependent on the associational or district missions committee for guidance.[27] Still later the field secretary is described as servant of the churches.[28]

In October, 1962, the field secretary program was expanded from ten to sixteen districts and, except for some geographic realignment of districts, maintained the same basic structure for several years. A certain ambiguity or lack of clarity in the dual responsibility of the field secretary to the State Board and to the local churches and missions committees accounted in part for some dissatisfaction which developed later in the 1960's over the field secretary program.

In March, 1967, the State Board, acting in response to requests from the Wekiwa and Seminole Associations for a study and evaluation of the field missions program, created a study committee jointly appointed by the president of the Convention and the chairman of the

---

[24]State Board, *Minutes,* May 6, 1961.

[25]Chapter VII.

[26]State Board, *Minutes,* Apr. 3, 1962.

[27]Florida Baptist Convention, *Book of Reports,* 1964-65, p. 8.

[28]*Ibid.*

State Board. A committee of fifteen was appointed, with Dr. Henry Allen Parker as chairman, and charged with the responsibility of making a thorough study of the total program of Florida Baptists, reviewing their commitments, their current programs and their future goals.[29] The study committee secured outside assistance in order to make the study more objective.[30] Undoubtedly the most significant person assisting Parker and the Committee of Fifteen was Dr. Albert McClellan, program planning secretary, Executive Committee of the Southern Baptist Convention. In the process of the study hundreds of people in all parts of the state were interviewed. One of the most common sources of dissatisfaction discovered was with the field secretary program. One statement in the report of the State Board to the Convention in 1967 suggested awareness of that dissatisfaction in the statement, "It is never the desire of your state office to place a person who would be undesirable to the district."[31]

At the Convention of 1968 the study committee of fifteen brought its report. Among other things the committee recommended that the field secretary program be changed from a system of State Convention support to a system of associational support with assistance from the Convention where requested.[32] This new arrangement was approved by the State Board and the Convention and is now in process of being implemented.

Sunday School Department

Throughout the 1960's the Sunday School Department continued to enjoy the stable mature leadership of C. F. Barry. Between 1960 and 1970 the total Sunday School enrollment grew from 397,771 in 1960 to 424,385 in 1968,[33] which represents a significant slow-down in the growth rate of the Sunday Schools especially when considered in view of the continued growth in population and even in Church membership. As the process of migration from rural areas continued, some Sunday Schools even suffered a decline in enrollment.[34] Furthermore, although comparative statistics on average attendance are

---

[29]Florida Baptist Convention, *Annual,* 1968, p. 45.

[30]*Florida Baptist Witness,* Aug. 1, 1968, p. 4. The outside assistance came generally from Baptist leaders in other states, including some from Southern Baptist Convention executive offices in Nashville, Tennessee.

[31]Florida Baptist Convention, *Annual,* 1967, p. 64.

[32]*Ibid.,* 1968, p. 46.

[33]*Ibid.,* 1960, p. 218 and 1968, p. 364.

[34]Florida Baptist Convention, *Book of Reports,* 1964-65, p. 20.

not available, many conversations the writer has had with church leaders would support the view that average attendance declined in many areas, even in comparison with enrollment. The Sunday School, however, continued to be one of the basic agencies of evangelism for Florida Baptists. Therefore, much of the credit for the growth in membership that was achieved has to go to the Sunday School. Moreover, while Florida Baptist Sunday Schools did not maintain the growth rate enjoyed in earlier years, they did become more efficient in their operations. For example, in 1963, the Sunday School column in the *Witness* noted that Florida led the Southern Baptist Convention in the total number of standard Sunday School units.[35] While goals set for increased enrollment were rarely achieved,[36] goals set for study course awards were sometimes exceeded.[37]

The record of Vacation Bible School enrollment in the 1960's exhibits an irregular pattern of growth and decline. Between 1961 and 1965 the total enrollment in the Vacation Bible Schools of Florida Baptists declined from 120,138 to 111,145.[38] By 1967, however, the record was up to 165,216,[39] only to fall back to 147,082 in 1968.[40] The record of the number of churches conducting Vacation Bible Schools follows a similar pattern.

The decline in the statistical progress of the Sunday Schools is sobering and not easily explained. Certainly no slackening in the promotional work of the state Sunday School Department occurred. On the contrary, the problem was recognized throughout the Southern Baptist Convention, and the promotion of the new theme, "Outreach for the Unreached," and the special "Adult Thrust" emphasis along with related efforts to reach more families, indicated acceleration in Sunday School promotional work. In addition, the Sunday School department continued to promote January Bible study week, Christian home week, various Sunday School clinics and such other meetings as were traditional. Toward the end of the 1960's moreover, the traditional emphasis on reaching new people came to be combined with a new emphasis on ministry to the people who had been reached al-

---

[35]*Florida Baptist Witness,* Apr. 4, 1963, p. 10.

[36]Florida Baptist Convention, *Book of Reports,* 1961-62, p. 2, and 1964-65, p. 20.

[37]*Ibid.,* 1960-61, p. 27.

[38]*Ibid.,* 1960-61, p. 31; cf. Florida Baptist Convention, *Annual,* 1965, p. 59.

[39]Florida Baptist Convention, *Annual,* 1967, p. 81.

[40]*Ibid.,* 1968, p. 91.

ready.[41] Also in 1967, the Sunday School Department participated in the total Convention promotion of the Crusade of the America's.[42]

In 1968 the State Board authorized the continued employment of C. F. Barry until February 5, 1970, at which time he reached 68 years of age.[43] By that time he had led Florida Baptists for 21 years in Sunday School work. A special banquet in his honor was held at the annual Sunday School convention which met in Winter Haven on February 23-25, 1970. At the beginning of C. F. Barry's ministry in 1949, there were 891 churches having Sunday Schools with a total enrollment of 180,000 members. At the end of his ministry as state Sunday School secretary, 1,445 churches had Sunday Schools enrolling a total of 414,478.[44]

Upon the retirement of C. F. Barry in 1970, James E. Frost was elected as the new director of the Sunday School Department. Educated at Hardin Simmons University and Southwestern Baptist Theological Seminary, he came to his new work with a background of experience as minister of Music and Education, as pastor, as consultant in the Training Union Department of Nashville from 1964 to 1968, and as Sunday School secretary of the Texas Baptist Convention from 1968 to 1970.

Training Union Department

The Training Union Department began the 1960's with a new secretary, C. J. Smyly. During the 1960's, the department continued to promote the traditional special emphasis of Training Union including: (1) regional and State Training Union conventions, (2) young people's speakers tournaments and intermediate sword drills, (3) youth week in the churches, (4) training courses in church membership, and (5) "M" night meetings. At the "M" night meetings the program and plans for the coming year continued to be outlined. However, despite the changes and flexibility introduced during the 1960's, the Training Union began to lose its appeal for many church members and in some cases for the entire church. This loss of appeal is reflected in the decline in attendance at the annual "M" night meetings. The meetings continued to attract large numbers, but it is significant and disturbing to observe the decline in attendance in view of the increases in church membership. Between 1962 and 1968 the total number of

[41]*Ibid.,* 1967, pp. 77-78.
[42]*Ibid.,* p. 77.
[43]State Board, *Minutes,* Oct. 11, 1968.
[44]Florida Baptist Sunday School Department, *Newsletter,* Winter, 1970, p. 1.

churches represented in the "M" night meetings declined from 1,130 to 997, and total attendance declined from 32,075 to 21,248.[45] Total enrollment in Training Union increased between 1960 and 1968 from 140,510 to 145,441, a rather slight increase in view of the total situation. However, Training Union attendance declined rather significantly in many churches, and in a few churches the Training Union died altogether.

Despite the importance of statistical reports on attendance at meetings as one criterion, adequate criteria for measuring the effectiveness of denominational institutions have not yet been devised. In some churches, nonetheless, the Training Union continued to be popular and strong with some modifications being made to meet changing needs.

In the 1960's the Training Union Department promoted and sponsored some new and creative activities which were very effective and should help to make the future work of training in church life more effective. Among these were: (1) a drama festival held at Stetson in February, 1962, (2) a special Training Union and Youth Assembly also at Stetson in 1962, with 814 enrolled and 89 life commitments being made,[46] (3) four area church administration conferences, (4) six learning improvement clinics,[47] and (5) the first state-wide conference on family life.[48] This conference on family life was very effective, with nationally known authorities participating along with 200 invited church leaders. Leaders of the conference included Dr. Evelyn M. Duvall, Dr. David R. Mace, Dr. Joe W. Burton, and Dr. John Drakeford. The writer took part in that conference, and his own reflection on its effectiveness has convinced him that, as indicated earlier, the influence of Training Union is not always adequately measured by the single criterion of total attendance at meetings.

In 1966 C. J. Smyly resigned as state Training Union secretary effective December 31.[49] E. L. Mixon served as acting secretary until 1969, when Dr. Robert S. Cook was elected to be the new secretary. Cook was educated at Hardin-Simmons University and Southwestern Baptist Theological Seminary, and served for 17 years as a consultant for adult work in the Training Union Department at Nashville before

---

[45]Florida Baptist Convention, *Annual,* 1963, p. 77; also, *Ibid.,* 1968, p. 92.
[46]Florida Baptist Convention, *Book of Reports,* 1965-66, p. 29.
[47]*Ibid.,* p. 32.
[48]Florida Baptist Convention, *Annual,* 1965, p. 29.
[49]State Board, *Minutes,* Mar. 30, 1967.

coming to his new position.[50] Also in 1969 the name of the Training Union Department was changed to Church Training Department.

Woman's Missionary Union

The Woman's Missionary Union enjoyed the continued capable leadership of Miss Josephine Jones through the early and middle 1960's. Between 1960 and 1968, the total Florida Baptist Woman's Missionary Union enrollment increased from 72,696 to 74,133, thus reflecting the same decline in growth rate experienced by other denominational organizations. The leaders of the Woman's Missionary Union did not slacken their efforts, however, but held more meetings than ever. Among the traditional activities continued during the 1960's were (1) annual Young Woman's Auxiliary conferences, (2) Girls' Auxiliary camps and house parties, (3) annual W. M. U. conventions, (4) providing scholarship aid to mission volunteers, and (5) various leadership conferences.

The Florida Baptist Woman's Missionary Union had revived its sense of history in the late 1950's, and in 1961 brought out the first published history of the W. M. U. in Florida to be published since 1913.[51] It was written by Mrs. Roy Lassiter, and entitled *On This Foundation.* Very quickly 2,000 copies were sold.

In September, 1967, Miss Josephine Jones retired as executive secretary and Miss Carolyn Weatherford was elected to fill the position. Also in 1967, the joint conferences held some years earlier between the women of the Florida W. M. U. and Negro Baptist women were revived and enlarged. A "Mission and Fellowship Conference," a cooperative venture between Florida W. M. U. and three Negro Baptist Women's Conventions, was held at Lake Yale, and attendance reached almost 200.[52]

In 1968 at its annual session the Florida W. M. U. approved a recommendation of the executive committee to move toward becoming a regular department of the Florida Baptist Convention rather than an auxiliary.[53] The State Board approved the move, which was to be completed by October, 1969.[54] In a real sense this action restored the Florida Woman's Missionary Union to something near its original relationship with the Convention. In 1881, when Mrs. N. A. Bailey was

[50]Florida Baptist Convention, *Book of Reports,* 1968, p. 41.
[51]Florida Baptist Convention, *Annual,* 1961, p. 62.
[52]*Ibid.,* 1968, p. 116.
[53]*Ibid.,* p. 115.
[54]State Board, *Minutes,* Apr. 23, 1968.

employed, she served as State secretary of Woman's Work. In 1894, the Convention made the W. M. U. an auxiliary rather than a department, and it retained that status until 1968, when it moved toward becoming a department again.

Also in 1968, the Woman's Missionary Union furnished and decorated a house at Stetson University to serve as a residence for a missionary and his family on furlough, so that they could be a part of the life of the University and of the churches of the Florida Baptist Convention. The house was named Lulu Sparkman Terry House in memory of Florida's first woman to be sent out as a foreign missionary. Finally, in 1968 the Woman's Missionary Union, in cooperation with the Home Mission Board and the Southern Baptist Convention, held a series of literacy workshops to train 42 people in the Laubach method of teaching adult illiterates to read.[55]

Evangelism and Vocational Guidance

In 1962 Dr. Paul Meigs was transferred from the Administration Department, where he had assisted Dr. Maguire, to become secretary of the newly created Department of Evangelism and Vocational Guidance. In addition to promoting evangelism in general his special responsibilities included the planning of the annual January evangelistic conference, which by 1962 had become a tradition among Florida Baptists. In addition he took the responsibility of planning the fourth annual church-related vocations conference, which met November 30 and December 1 at the First Baptist Church in Orlando.[56] Like the annual evangelistic conference, the church-related vocations conference was well attended each year by hundreds of young people. In 1964 Dr. Meigs' office recorded 3,700 names of young people committed to church-related vocations. These commitments included 658 for foreign missions, 188 for the pastoral ministry, and 200 dedicated to the church music ministry.[57]

Department of Church Music

The Department of Church Music continued throughout the 1960's under the leadership of W. G. Stroup, who had become state secretary of the Music Department in 1953. In many ways the 1960's turned out to be the greatest decade in the history of the Church Music Department. The number of choirs and total enrollment ex-

[55]Florida Baptist Convention, *Book of Reports,* 1969, p. 51.
[56]Florida Baptist Convention, *Annual,* 1962, p. 48.
[57]*Ibid.,* 1964, p. 82.

ceeded all past records. The highest record in the number of choirs was reported in 1965, when 3,223 choirs were reported.[58] The highest total enrollment was reported in 1968, when the record reached 63,289. Between 1965 and 1968 the number of choirs reported varied up and down from year to year, but generally recorded a decline from 3,223 in 1965 to 2,052 choirs in 1969.[59] Similarly, although total choir enrollment arose from 59,229 in 1965,[60] to 63,289 in 1968,[61] it fell back to 58,551 in 1969.[62] In short, a significant decline was reported in 1969 in both the number of choirs and total enrollment. Three possible factors may account for this decline. First, the decline may reflect the general decline in participation in church life. Second, it may reflect a weariness with statistical reports and therefore an inaccuracy in the total reports due to the unwillingness on the part of some churches to take the trouble necessary to report accurately. Third, the decline may reflect the increasing difficulty in finding trained leaders in church music. It is obviously difficult to maintain an effective choir program without trained leadership. Probably a combination of all these factors explains the reported decline. Nevertheless, statistical reports on the associational and state music festivals indicate a growing interest in the music ministry of the church. Total attendance at these festivals regularly exceeded 20,000 and in 1969 and 1970 several of these festivals the writer attended exceeded all expectations and taxed the capacity of the host churches.

The Department of Music continued to direct a number of other programs to promote interest in church music. First, the music and youth assemblies were continued and enlarged. The Harmony Bay Youth Music Camp, for example, enlarged its work in 1961 to include intermediates who had had little or no musical training.[63] In 1967 in addition to the music training at Harmony Bay, a similar camp was held at Lake Yale for ages 13-18, and during R. A. Camp Week at Lake Yale, music training was provided for a group of juniors.[64] Second, music leaders from the State Music Department participated in numerous other assemblies and in the annual church-related vocations conference. Third, numerous choral clinics and music training

---

[58]*Ibid.,* 1965, p. 70.
[59]Florida Baptist Convention, *Book of Reports,* 1968-69, p. 33.
[60]Florida Baptist Convention, *Annual,* 1965, p. 70.
[61]*Ibid.,* 1968, p. 81.
[62]Florida Baptist Convention, *Book of Reports,* 1968-69, p. 33.
[63]*Ibid.,* 1960-61, p. 37.
[64]Florida Baptist Convention, *Annual,* 1967, p. 88.

schools were held in churches and associations. Finally, a day of singing and praise was observed in many churches in 1965.[65]

During the 1960's two significant changes occurred in the music of many Florida Baptist Churches. First, the increased participation of many large and small churches in the associational and state choir festivals exposed many churches and choirs to a variety of types of church music that they would never otherwise have known. The exposure thus enriched their musical ministry. Second, many churches began to adapt their music ministry to the needs of young people. The form which this adaptation took was the clothing of both the traditional aspects of the Christian message and the longings and frustrations of young people in a new medium which was more attractive to the young people themselves: namely, a form of folk rock church music. The result was a surprising new interest and participation on the part of the youth in many churches. Notable examples were "Good News" and "Tell It Like It Is," gospel folk musicals which became very effective instruments of evangelism in the late 1960's.

Camps and Assemblies

Although the writer is prepared to defend the view that in some ways the 1960's represented a decline in growth rate, he is ready to confess that this statement is not an apt description of development in the area of camps and assemblies. Here the word "fabulous" is more in order, for the Florida Baptist program of camps and assemblies, continuing its long successful tradition, made the greatest strides ever in the 1960's. It was of course the decade of the birth of Lake Yale.

The background of the birth of Lake Yale lay in the fact that the camps and assembly programs of Florida Baptists had already become so popular that they were taxing the capacity of Stetson University, the West Florida Assembly and the East Coast Assembly. In 1960, over 5,000 people attended the various camps and assemblies. The newest assembly in 1960 was a Sunday School leadership assembly at Stetson enrolling 852 adult leaders. The Woman's Missionary Union leadership conference attracted 750 at Stetson and 354 at West Florida Assembly. The Brotherhood camp at west Florida enrolled almost 1,000, and the Harmony Bay music camp had a capacity enrollment of 120. In September 1960, the State Board received a request from the Woman's Missionary Union for the purchase of a

---

[65]*Ibid.,* 1965, p. 66.

state assembly ground. Out of this request came the first official move toward the establishing of a centrally located State assembly camp. It was made in the 1960 Convention when Tom Collins introduced a resolution from the camps and assemblies committee citing the need for a state camp and calling for the purchase of land for such a camp.[66] The resolution was approved, and after further committee investigation, the purchase of land on Lake Yale was authorized by the Convention in 1962.[67]

At the beginning of the 1960's, there was no separate department of camps and assemblies, and the work of coordinating these camps and assemblies was shared by several committees and departments. In 1964, as the result of the cooperative work of the committee on camps and assemblies, the State Board, and John Maguire, the first phase of a three-phase construction program began. The first two phases involved completing facilities for a Girls' Auxiliary camp and a Royal Ambassadors' camp. Both of these phases were completed and in use by 1965, when a total of 2,450 young people attended. The third phase, which called for adult facilities, was also authorized in 1965.[68] When the process of planning and developing Lake Yale got under way, however, it became obvious to the State Board and the Convention that the management of such a facility would require a full-time director and a separate department. Accordingly, in 1965, Paul Glore, who had been an associate in the Sunday School Department, was elected secretary of camps and assemblies,[69] and a loan of $500,000 was authorized for further development of the camp. By 1966 extensive building plans had been approved and construction had been begun on a large auditorium and administration building and two housing units.[70] In 1967 the new auditorium was completed and named in honor of John H. Maguire. The auditorium seated 1,200 and had two wings with space for a total of 900 people in study conferences. The administration building was completed also and named the S. O. Bean Administration Building in honor of the assistant executive secretary-treasurer.[71] In 1968, a staff building was completed which housed sixteen staff members plus an apartment for

---

[66] *Ibid.*, 1960, p. 38.
[67] *Ibid.*, 1962, p. 38.
[68] *Ibid.*, 1965, pp. 76-77.
[69] *Ibid.*, p. 76.
[70] *Ibid.*, 1966, p. 96.
[71] *Ibid.*, 1967, p. 104.

Maguire Auditorium, Lake Yale

house parents.[72] Other additions and improvements by the end of 1969 brought the total facilities to fourteen buildings on 210 acres of land.

S. O. Bean Administration Building, Lake Yale

Rapidly, as new facilities were made available, use by various Convention groups increased, so that from October 1, 1966, through Sep-

---

[72]*Ibid.*, 1968, pp. 72-74.

tember 30, 1967, 8,863 persons attended some conference or camp at Lake Yale, an increase of 5,239 over the same period the preceding year.[73] In 1968, the Camps and Assemblies Department reported feeding and housing 12,033 at Lake Yale during the preceding year and 4,569 at West Florida Assembly making a total of 16,602 at both assemblies.[74]

Baptist Student Union

Throughout the 1960's the State Department of Student Work continued under the leadership of Joe Webb. As the number of colleges in Florida grew and the number of Baptist students enrolled in them increased, the challenge and responsibility of ministry to these Baptist students on many campuses became tremendous. Many leaders both in areas near the growing universities and in the State Convention offices had observed the growing need in the 1950's and were in the process in 1960 of providing leadership and buildings on or adjacent to college campuses. When the newly constructed Student Center at Jacksonville University was given in August 1961 to the Convention by the First Baptist Church in Jacksonville, the total number of such centers on or near college campuses was brought to five. The other four were located on or near the campuses of Florida State University, the University of Florida, the University of Miami,

Baptist Student Center, Jacksonville University

[73] *Ibid.*, 1967, pp. 10ff.

[74] Florida Baptist Convention, *Book of Reports,* 1969, p. 24.

and Stetson University. Organized Baptist Student Unions were operating on twenty-one campuses with a total Baptist enrollment of more than 9,000.[75] In 1964, a new Baptist Student Union center was constructed adjacent to the campus of the University of South Florida.[76]

Baptist Student Center, University of Miami

Also in 1964 the first annual retreat for international married students was held, reflecting the sensitivity of the student leaders to special problems encountered by foreign families living in a new culture. By

Baptist Student Center, University of South Florida, Tampa

[75] *Ibid.*, 1960-61, p. 50.
[76] *Florida Baptist Witness,* Mar. 5, 1964, p. 1.

the end of 1969 the number of Baptist students on campuses with an organized B. S. U. had reached approximately 23,000.[77]

Throughout the decade, the Baptist Student Union continued to promote and participate in activities which by now had become traditional, such as (1) the annual retreat for international students, (2) the State Baptist Student Union Convention, (3) raising money to pay travel expenses for Florida Baptist Students to serve as summer missionaries on various mission fields at home and abroad, (4) organizing youth revival teams to serve churches as demanded throughout the year as well as during the summer, and (5) providing retreats for Baptist students.

In 1965, the report of the Department of Student Work to the Convention indicated a change in the interpretation of the function and purpose of the Baptist Student Union. This report indicated that whereas the Baptist Student Union in the past had been designed to meet the needs of Christian fellowship and enlistment, especially week-end enlistment in the churches of the college community, a reinterpretation of the function of the B. S. U. was in process which involved a rethinking of the traditional functions of the Baptist Student Union and a consideration of new functions that might be performed. One of these new functions was to enhance the academic and intellectual growth of Baptist students by relating academic matters more closely to spiritual growth. For example, dialogue and study groups were formed to discuss such subjects as "Science and Religion," "Christianity and Foreign Aid," "The Organized Church: Pro and Con," and "Man-Woman Relationships." Relevant books on these subjects were selected and studied and discussed as an extracurricular activity.

Closely related to this new approach to B. S. U. work was the effort to involve Baptist students in the issues and activities of campus life. The summer missions program was considered a part of the involvement effort, but in the late 1960's involvement came to be interpreted more broadly. Baptist students were encouraged to consider, upon graduation, such newly developed Baptist mission enterprises as the Journeyman program of the Foreign Mission Board or the US-2 program of the Home Mission Board.

A third aspect of the new approach in Baptist student work was an experiment, or pilot program, for a Chair of Bible at the University of South Florida. Approved by the State Board in 1965, with a budget

---

[77]Florida Baptist Convention, *Book of Reports,* 1968-69, p. 34.

of $2,000 to supplement the salary of a teacher, the program was implemented in January, 1966.[78] It was a joint project between the Department of Student Work and Stetson University. The teaching qualifications and standards met the requirements of Stetson University, which granted the credit, and the University of South Florida accepted transfer of the credit toward the students' degrees.[79]

In the report of the Student Department to the 1967 Convention, state secretary Joe Webb called attention to the enormous increase in the number of Baptist students, and special attention to the fact that 99 per cent of Baptist students were enrolled in non-Baptist colleges. This fact showed the need, he declared, for additional personnel to guide, counsel, and challenge Baptist students, especially in the non-Baptist universities.[80] There was indeed need for an increased and more effective ministry to Baptist students, particularly in view of the new community and regional colleges. In 1969, the State Board approved the addition of a campus ministry at the University of West Florida in Pensacola.[81]

Brotherhood Department

Like many other areas of work, the Brotherhood could not maintain a steady growth rate throughout the 1960's. Total enrolment grew from 19,263 in 1961 to 26,945 in 1965, and then steadily declined each year thereafter to 23,506 at the end of 1970. The decline in enrolment does not reflect reduced activity or effectiveness, however. On the contrary, the decline in total enrolment came despite accelerated activities, great successes and new ventures. Under the continuing leadership of G. A. Ratterree, the Brotherhood Department directed the first Brotherhood Camp at Lake Yale in 1967 with an attendance of 900, and R. A. Camps and Congresses at Lake Yale and Panama City attracted capacity crowds of boys throughout the 1960's. For example, the Brotherhood Camps conducted in 1969 had a total attendance of 1,450, and the R. A. Camps a total attendance of 1,217. The R. A. Congresses that year attracted 1,438.

---

[78]State Board, *Minutes,* Sept. 2-3, 1965; also Florida Baptist Convention, *Annual,* 1965, p. 81.

[79]Florida Baptist Convention, *Annual,* 1965, p. 81.

[80]*Ibid.,* 1967, p. 95.

[81]State Board, *Minutes,* Sept. 5, 1969.

Florida Baptist Foundation

In 1962, G. A. Leichliter retired as executive secretary of the Foundation. Gus Johnson was elected to replace him and the office was moved from Plant City to Jacksonville. Under Johnson's leadership the Foundation continued to administer trusts and endowment funds for various Florida Baptist institutions. One of the highlights of his work during the 1960's, was his assignment by the Convention as director of the special campaign to raise $1,500,000 for Stetson University and $500,000 for Baptist Bible Institute. During 1969 the Foundation assisted in preparing wills and administering funds involving over $1,000,000.

The Associations

Only one new association, the Florida Keys Association, was organized in the 1960's. It was organized on October 15, 1968, by six churches from the Miami Association.[82] Two associations, the Seminole Association and the Halifax Association, began discussion of the possibility of a merger. Faster transportation and communication facilities together with the smaller attendance at the annual association meetings were background factors in the proposed merger. Another factor was the need for larger fellowship among the pastors and other church leaders.

It appears that sometime in the 1950's and 1960's the annual association meeting had begun to lose something of its former effectiveness in some areas as migration to the cities and urbanization accelerated. The main evidence for this assertion is the decline in attendance compared with earlier periods, particularly in view of the large increase in membership.[83] The association meeting continues, however, to be an important event in the life of many associations, and still serves as an excellent opportunity for fellowship, communication and information on denominational affairs.

Stetson University

The 1960's brought storm and tragedy to Stetson University and to the relationship between Stetson and the Convention, yet the relationship survived the tragedy and the storm and Stetson ended the 1960's with the largest enrollment in its history. Near the beginning of the decade, the shadow which had been repeatedly cast over the rela-

---

[82]Florida Baptist Convention, *Annual,* 1968, p. 334, and 1969, p. 323.
[83]*Florida Baptist Witness,* October 30, 1969, p. 4.

tionship by the charter controversy was created once more. The question was raised by a resolution adopted in the 1961 Convention which asked that every effort be made to (1) transfer all Stetson's property to the Convention, (2) let the Convention alone elect the trustees, and (3) adopt a plan for the rotation of the trustees.[84] The report of the Education Commission to the 1961 convention clearly implied that differences between Stetson and its Baptist constituency still existed and called for reconciliation of those differences. The shadow was darkened further in 1962 when a report was brought to the State Board that, as reported in the 1960 Convention, the Stetson College of Law had accepted race track money. The *Minutes* record that Stetson agreed to return the money. However, legal complications frustrated the attempt to return the money, and as an alternative, the money was given to Florida Presbyterian College, which received it.[85]

In 1963, fortunately, the Education Commission and Stetson trustees brought a joint recommendation, which the Convention adopted, proposing (1) that the Convention accept the view of both Stetson's attorney and the Convention attorneys that it would be unwise to change Stetson's charter, (2) that all new trustees elected to Stetson's board be asked to agree to voluntary rotation, and (3) that every effort be made to strengthen the relationship beween Stetson and the Convention. The joint committee also reported that all but one of Stetson's trustees then serving had been nominated by the Convention under an earlier agreement.[86] Thus, the main cloud of misunderstanding was cleared once more, and in 1963 the Convention approved a special fund-raising drive to match a $1,500,000 grant by the Ford Foundation to Stetson.[87] The special fund drive approved by the Convention and the State Board was a joint campaign for Stetson and Baptist Bible Institute. Whatever amount was raised was to be divided between Stetson and Baptist Bible Institute, with Stetson receiving 75 per cent toward the Ford matching grant, and Baptist Bible Institute receiving 25 per cent.[88]

In 1965 the report of Stetson University to the Convention made reference to action being considered which was to create the next season of strife between Stetson and the Convention. The question con-

---

[84]Florida Baptist Convention, *Annual*, 1961, pp. 33-34.

[85]State Board, *Minutes*, Aug. 31, 1962; see Chapter Seven where this incident is first mentioned.

[86]Florida Baptist Convention, *Annual*, 1962, p. 33.

[87]*Ibid.*, 1963, p. 67.

[88]State Board, *Minutes*, Apr. 29, 1963.

sidered in the report was whether or not to accept federal funds for new construction made available by recent legislation. The trustees of Stetson were in the process of implementing segments of the long-range capital development adopted by the Convention in the 1950's and the projected building plans required even more than the generous contributions being made could provide. Thus, under great financial pressure, like other Southern Baptist Colleges, Stetson saw accepting federal aid as a temporary and partial solution to the building crisis.[89] At the conclusion of the 1965 convention, a resolution was approved which reaffirmed the Baptist tradition on separation of church and state and called for a committee of fifteen to study the implications of church-state cooperation in the light of that tradition. The committee was to bring report to its findings to the 1966 convention.[90]

In the meantime Stetson's trustees, pressed as they were with Stetson's building program, decided to accept a federal grant while it was still available. When report of their action came to the attention of the State Board in April, 1966, the Board approved a resolution asking the trustees to reverse their action.[91] The trustees, committed to completing the much needed science building and deeply involved in negotiations for the grant, declined to accept the State Board recommendation.[92] In November, 1966, the special church-state study committee appointed in response to the directive of the 1965 convention, brought its report to the Convention. The committee reported that much study had been given to the problem, but wished to reserve judgment, requesting additional time to study the problem and to await the findings of the Baptist Education Study Task, a Southern Baptist Convention committee studying the total problems of Southern Baptist educational institutions.[93] Some messengers, however, wanted decisive action on the issue immediately. Accordingly, a motion was made to cut Stetson out of the Convention's budget. The motion failed, but only after an extensive and heated debate.[94] However, the Convention passed a motion which called for excluding from Convention aid any agency or institution which received federal grants in the

[89]Florida Baptist Convention, *Annual,* 1965, pp. 94-96.
[90]*Ibid.,* pp. 34-35.
[91]State Board, *Minutes,* Apr. 7, 1966.
[92]*Ibid.,* June 8, 1966; and Sept. 6, 1966.
[93]Florida Baptist Convention, *Annual,* 1966, pp. 138-146.
[94]*Ibid.,* p. 29.

coming year.[95] Moreover, apparently anticipating the storm of opposition to the action taken by Stetson's trustees, the State Board had cut the budgeted amount recommended for Stetson in half compared to the preceding year, to 4.54 per cent or $149,820, which was the smallest amount and percentage given in many years.[96]

In September, 1967, Dr. Edmunds retired from his post as president of the University, and in November was invested as chancellor. He had served the University with great distinction for 20 years. He brought international recognition to the University through his travels and the many honors he won. Under his leadership the total assets of the University grew from $2,500,000 to $23,000,000, endowment grew from $500,000 to $4,775,000, and $15,000,000 was spent in construction of buildings. He was the first Florida college president to become President of the Association of American Colleges, and served as President of the Florida Baptist Convention in 1961. As announced in advance, Edmunds' retirement became effective on the election of his successor. Paul F. Geren was elected as the new president in September, 1967.

Dr. Geren had come to Stetson with an outstanding academic background including earned degrees from Baylor University, Louisiana State University, and Harvard University. He also came with a distinguished professional background as professor, soldier, author, college administrator and diplomat, having served as the first deputy director of the Peace Corps and as a Foreign Service officer for almost 20 years. Under Geren's leadership the trustees agreed to abide by the wishes of the Convention on the matter of federal grants for construction, and the November, 1967, Convention was a very harmonious one, especially in regard to Stetson-Convention relations. Thus, the cloud of controversy was lifted again.

In 1968, the trustees of Stetson sought to increase understanding and communication further by recommending a joint committee from the Convention and the trustees to draw up a statement of intents and purposes of the trustees of Stetson and the churches of the Florida Baptist Convention in the area of higher education.[97] Also in 1968 the Convention's Education Commission organized a series of dialogues in various sections of the state between Stetson representatives and local church groups to increase communication and understand-

---

[95]*Ibid.*

[96]*Ibid.*, p. 59.

[97]*Ibid.*, 1968, p. 105.

ing.[98] The Education Commission also called for increased support to Stetson.[99]

In 1968 and 1969 the University established and dedicated the Lulu Terry Sparkman House for a new missionary in residence program. Three missionary families, the Irvin Northcutt family, the William Hickman family, and the J. T. Owens family, have occupied the home. Also, the international dimension of the University was enlarged with acceleration in the number of study abroad programs.

In the spring of 1969, under pressure over some disagreement with the faculty, Paul F. Geren resigned his position as president. On Sunday, June 22, 1969, the day before his resignation was to take effect, he died in an automobile accident near London, Kentucky.[100] Because of the circumstances of President Geren's resignation and his tragic death, a great deal of feeling of hostility developed in the Convention toward Stetson. By the time of the Convention in November, the hostility had found other provocation in various rumors about social life at Stetson. A motion was made at the 1969 Convention that the amount designated to Stetson in the recommended budget be deleted and the money be redistributed to other causes. The only immediate reason given for the motion was that Stetson had been a thorn in the flesh of the Convention and that the Convention had been a thorn in Stetson's flesh, and that to continue the relationship would endanger the integrity of Stetson. No less than ten persons spoke on the motion, after which a move was adopted to cut off debate. The original motion to delete Stetson from the budget lost by five votes. Thus 1969 came to an end in a storm of controversy over Stetson University and the relationship was continued by a very close vote. A special committee was appointed to bring a recommendation to the 1970 convention as to what the future should be.

The paradox is that despite the difficulties in the relationship between Stetson and the Convention during the 1960's, Stetson not only made some of the most significant progress in its history and achieved some of the highest honors and recognition ever known, but it also received the largest support from Florida Baptists in all their long history. Therefore, the controversy may have obscured the deep common commitment that continued to exist between Stetson University and the Florida Baptist Convention.

---

[98]*Ibid.,* p. 106.
[99]*Ibid.,* p. 108.
[100]*Ibid.,* 1969, p. 113.

Stetson began the new decade with a total enrollment of 2,101 in 1961.[101] Although the enrollment dropped to 1,796 in 1962, by 1969 enrollment had reached an all-time record high of 2,921.[102] It was also a decade of unparalleled construction with the completion of five men's residence halls in 1961-62, the Dupont-Ball Library in 1964, a new business school building (Davis Hall) and a new men's dormitory in 1966, and another in 1967, a new science center in 1967

(Sage Hall), and a new school of music in 1969-70 (Presser Hall). Also, the University received as a gift from C. Aubury Stoudenmire a large brick residence which now houses the counseling center, and redecorated an old residence called the Taylor House to provide a home for the Chancellor Edmunds.[103] Also, in 1968 an old residence owned by the University was reconditioned to serve as a new style residence where a few men having special financial needs could obtain an education at a lower cost by sharing the preparation of their own meals and the maintenance of the residence. The House was named Wheeler House in honor of B. F. Wheeler, a Stetson trustee from Oviedo, Florida, who helped finance the repair of the building. All this construction and additions were made possible by many contributions from Florida Baptists and from other sources and by loans

---

[101]Florida Baptist Convention, *Book of Reports,* 1960-61, p. 57.
[102]*Ibid.,* 1969, p. 59.
[103]Bowen, *op. cit.,* pp. 18-20.

from the federal government. Although the percentage of the Convention's budget given to Stetson was smaller than that during the preceding decade by about half, because of the great increase in the size of the budget and income of the Convention in the 1960's the average annual support given to Stetson was actually larger than in the 1950's. Since Stetson's operating budget grew enormously during the 1960's, however, the larger annual support in dollars received during the 1960's provided a smaller percentage of the annual budget than had been the case in the 1950's.

Palm Beach Atlantic College

In 1959 the Education Commission brought a report to the Convention concerning the protected growth and future needs of higher education in Florida. In response to this report the suggestion was made that Florida Baptists needed to consider establishing a new college.[104] No action was taken immediately, but in 1960 concrete action was seriously considered when O. E. Burton, pastor of Calvary Baptist Church in Clearwater, presented a proposal to accept an offer of eighty acres of land to build a college in the vicinity of Clearwater, subject to the acceptance of the Education Commission.[105] With this last qualification the motion passed. In the same Convention, the Education Commission recommended more study before any action was taken on such a proposal.[106] In 1961 the State Board approved a recommendation of the Education Commission which included projection of a tentative plan for another Baptist college within ten years.[107] The Convention of 1962 moved toward concrete action by approving a resolution favoring the establishing of a junior college.

During the months which followed in 1963 considerable sentiment developed for the proposed college. The editor of the *Witness* summarized some of the reasons advanced for the college. Some argued that a new college was needed because of the population increase. Others called attention to the leavening that Baptist colleges created both in society and among other colleges. Still others called attention to the needs of Baptist young people.[108] The Convention of 1963 voted the second approval of the proposed junior college in accordance

---

[104]Florida Baptist Convention, *Annual,* 1959, p. 102.
[105]*Ibid.,* 1960, p. 29.
[106]*Ibid.,* pp. 115-116.
[107]State Board, *Minutes,* Sept. 1, 1961.
[108]Editorial, *Florida Baptist Witness,* Feb. 28, 1963.

with established policy.[109] The Education Commission was then instructed to bring a recommendation to the next Convention on location and other matters.[110]

After considering several proposals and offers of land, the Education Commission brought recommendation to the 1964 Convention that an offer made by the Palm Lake Association be accepted. The offer was for 200 acres of land to be given by Royal American Industries, Inc., with certain required provisions. The Convention approved a recommendation to advise Palm Lake Association that: (1) the college planned should be a two-year college, (2) at the beginning the student body goal should be 300, and (3) the trustees should be activated and the institution established as soon as $1,500,000 had been raised by Palm Lake Association.[111]

By September, 1965, the State Board appears to have developed second thoughts about establishing another college, for it approved a recommendation by the budget and allocations committee that the Board delay action on the Education Commission recommendation on the proposed college until further information became available from the Baptist Education Study Task report. The committee noted that the Education Commission's projected plans called for $1,000,000 per year to be allotted from Cooperative Program funds for one junior college. Since Palm Lake Association had not raised the $1,500,000 required by the 1964 Convention, the Board agreed not to recommend placing the junior college in the following year's budget.[112] Obviously, some differences existed between the State Board and the Education Commission, especially in the proposed financial plans.

Efforts to resolve these differences at the 1965 Convention resulted in warm and lengthy debate.[113] The State Board was instructed to meet with the Education Commission and bring a joint recommendation back to the Convention. After a joint meeting during the same session, a joint report was brought and approved by the Convention. The report indicated approval of (1) the Education Commission statement of objectives for the college, (2) the suggested list of trustees, and (3) the financial plan as amended. The amended financial plan for the new college called for (1) $75,000 to be added to the special state mission offering for the junior college and (2) working

---

[109]Florida Baptist Convention, *Annual,* 1963, pp. 34-35.
[110]*Ibid.*
[111]*Ibid.,* 1964, pp. 28-29, 92-93.
[112]State Board, *Minutes,* Sept. 2-3, 1965.
[113]Florida Baptist Convention, *Annual,* 1965, pp. 26-29.

financial goals including $200,000 for the college from the November, 1966, Convention budget, $250,000 in 1967 and each year thereafter, and (3) a State-wide campaign to raise $1,000,000, beginning in January, 1967. These working goals were not commitments, however, and were to be reviewed annually in conference among the State Board, the Education Commission and the Baptist college committee of the Palm Lake Association.[114] The Convention also approved the activating of the trustees at the direction of the State Board and the Education Commission.[115]

In the State Board meeting of April 7, 1966, the proposed junior college was a major item of discussion. The Education Commission had no recommendations, but asked numerous questions to which no conclusive answers were immediately given. The Baptist college committee of the Palm Lake Association reported that the financial campaign had slowed down because people were waiting until some building began or the school opened before they gave. Therefore, this committee made three recommendations to the State Board, First, the committee recommended that the college be established according to historic Baptist principles and that it abide by the New Testament. This recommendation was adopted. Second, the committee requested that the trustees be activated and a president be appointed and the college move toward a 1968 opening. This motion was lost. Third, the committee requested that the Palm Lake Association and the college committee be permitted to construct dormitories. This motion also was lost.[116]

At the 1966 convention a resolution was approved which called for activation of the trustees. The trustees were activated at a special joint meeting of the State Board and the Education Commission on December 8, 1966.[117] The 1966 session also approved the financial campaign recommended earlier. However, the request that $200,000 be placed in the budget was withdrawn by the college committee of the Palm Lake Association.[118]

Apparently, some pressure was brought later, however, to place the proposed junior college in the regular budget recommendations of the State Board. At the March 30, 1967, meeting, the Board heard, but took no action on resolutions presented by two strong churches,

---

[114]*Ibid.,* 1965, pp. 31-32.
[115]*Ibid.,* p. 31.
[116]State Board, *Minutes,* Apr. 7, 1966.
[117]Florida Baptist Convention, *Annual,* 1967, p. 118.
[118]*Ibid.,* 1966, pp. 32-34.

Main Street and Southside in Jacksonville, opposing inclusion of the new college in the regular budget until they met the requirements defined by the 1964 Convention.[119]

At a special called session of the Convention held in Jacksonville in March, 1967, a proposed charter and by-laws for the new college were approved after much discussion and some changes.[120] The trustees of the proposed college brought a recommendation to the November, 1967, Convention that plans for the new college be postponed in light of the reported interest of Billy Graham in establishing a college at West Palm Beach.[121] The trustees also reported plans to recommend that the Convention establish a four-year college if the Billy Graham college did not materialize.[122]

In 1968, the trustees of the proposed Baptist college, upon learning that Billy Graham had abandoned his plans to open a college in Palm Beach, proceeded on their own to name a president, Dr. Jess Moody, pastor of the First Baptist Church, West Palm Beach, and to open the college in September, 1968, using the facilities of the First Baptist Church of West Palm Beach. The college was named Palm Beach Atlantic College, and was opened in the Fall of 1968 with 225 students. On October 11, 1968, the State Board received a telegram from Jess Moody dated October 4, requesting on behalf of the executive committee of the college trustees that the Convention release the trustees. The State Board approved the recommendation.[123] The original trustees were released and Palm Beach Atlantic College came into being and became an autonomous institution controlled exclusively by a local board of trustees, all Baptists, in the Palm Lake Association.[124] Evaluating its status, Editor Stracener wrote, "as it is now being established, the cost of operating the new college will be the responsibility of the Palm Lake Association and not the Florida Baptist Convention."[125]

Nonetheless, Palm Beach Atlantic College was very much in evidence at the 1969 session of the Convention. Dr. Moody was president of the Pastors' Conference, and the Palm Beach Atlantic

---

[119]State Board, *Minutes,* Mar. 30, 1967.

[120]Florida Baptist Convention, *Annual,* 1967, pp. 24, 41.

[121]*Ibid.,* p. 48.

[122]*Ibid.,* pp. 118-119.

[123]State Board, *Minutes,* Oct. 11, 1968; also Florida Baptist Convention, *Annual,* 1968, pp. 100-101.

[124]*Ibid.*

[125]*Florida Baptist Witness,* Apr. 18, 1968, p. 4.

College choir sang. Probably no one, therefore, was surprised when a resolution was introduced asking for an amendment to the recommended Convention budget to include an amount to assist the new college. The motion was ruled out of order. However, after considerable debate and vain attempts to amend the by-laws and after involved parliamentary maneuvering, the Convention approved a recommendation that there be a special statewide offering with a goal of $150,000 for Palm Beach Atlantic College. The Convention also approved a motion by Joe Courson to instruct the State Board to appoint committees to bring recommendations to the 1970 Convention on the future relations of the Convention to Palm Beach Atlantic College and to Stetson University.

Baptist Bible Institute

The Baptist Bible Institute enjoyed the continued leadership of Dr. James E. Southerland throughout the 1960's, and with the control and support of the Convention it made the greatest progress in its history. In 1960, the institution received $59,024, six and one-half per cent of the Cooperative Program budget. Other Convention gifts to the school ran the total to $139,645. The enrollment stood at 189.[126] In 1969, the amount received from the Cooperative Program was $249,594, over four times the 1960 support. During the 1960's, the Institute widened its service to include students from as many as 27 states. In fact, by 1969 the majority of students enrolled at Baptist Bible Institute were from states other than Florida.[127]

During the current decade the faculty grew in number and strength and the school achieved a degree of academic recognition that is rare among similar schools when several colleges began to accept work done at Baptist Bible Institute for credit toward degree work.[128] Some students going to Baptist Bible Institute were discovered to have ability to do college work, and these students were encouraged to go to college when that was possible.

Also during the 1960's a number of building additions were made. In 1964, a seven room classroom building, and an administration building, were added. In 1965, the Frank Faris House, an apartment house for student families, was added.[129] In 1967 a library building

---

[126] Florida Baptist Convention, *Annual,* 1960, p. 45.

[127] Florida Baptist Convention, *Book of Reports,* 1968-69, p. 55; total enrollment is not given in the 1968 report to the Convention.

[128] Florida Baptist Convention, *Annual,* 1966, p. 108.

[129] Baptist Baptist Institute, *Catalogue* 1969-70, p. 15.

was completed, and the Convention authorized a loan of not more than $300,000 to construct a student center and two student houses.[130] As a result, in 1969 a student center was completed and put into use, and twenty-two houses and seven mobile homes were added for student housing.[131] The 1969 Convention approved a loan of $65,000 to build a new home for the president.

Florida Baptist Retirement Centers

The Florida Baptist Retirement Center at Vero Beach was approved and construction was begun on the first unit in the late 1950's. By the opening of the 1961 session of the Convention, the center was open with twelve single dwelling units and six cottage units for couples.[132] In 1962, Dr. J. Perry Carter retired as director and was replaced by Leo B. Roberts, who began work on January 1, 1963.[133] During 1962, the residents of the center increased from four to twenty-four, and seven more individual dwelling units and two duplex cottages were added.[134] By 1963, the center had 36 residents, five buildings, and a total property value of $450,000. The year 1964 brought to completion another duplex cottage, costing $18,000.[135] In 1965, the Convention approved a $200,000 loan to build a nursing home with twenty beds as an extension of the center.[136] By 1967, two other duplex cottages had been completed, making a total of five,[137] and a contract had been let and construction begun for the nursing home. The extended care unit was opened in 1968.[138] Also in 1968, Roberts retired, and Paul R. Adkins was elected as the new director. The center then had a three-phase program which included nursing care, custodial care, and residence in duplex apartments on the twenty-three acre campus at Vero Beach. On September 1, 1969, the center had 32 residents in the custodial center, 14 in the duplex apartments, and 16 in the infirmary, for a total of 62. The ages ranged from 66 to 96 years with an average of 82.8 years. In 1969 the centers had nine buildings with a total estimated value of $650,435.06.[139]

---

[130] Florida Baptist Convention, *Annual,* 1968, p. 56.
[131] Florida Baptist Convention, *Book of Reports,* 1968-69, p. 54.
[132] Florida Baptist Convention, *Annual,* 1961, p. 119.
[133] *Ibid.,* 1962, p. 42.
[134] *Ibid.,* p. 109.
[135] *Ibid.,* 1963, p. 105.
[136] *Ibid.,* 1965, pp. 103-104.
[137] *Ibid.,* 1966, p. 111.
[138] *Ibid.,* 1968, p. 102.
[139] Florida Baptist Convention, *Book of Reports,* 1968-69, p. 58.

The 1969 Convention approved a request of the trustees of the Retirement Centers that the operation of the Centers be taken over by the State Board of Missions and that the trustees be dismissed. The State Board has implemented this decision.

FLORIDA BAPTIST RETIREMENT CENTER, VERO BEACH

The Florida Baptist Children's Home continued in the 1960's under the leadership of Dr. T. M. Johns until 1969, when he retired after thirty-seven faithful and effective years of service to the Home. At the beginning of the decade 224 children received care in the Florida Baptist children's homes in Lakeland and in Miami. During the year 1960, 430 applications were received, and 78 new children were admitted.[140] In 1965, a new building was erected for the case work department.[141] In 1965, 397 applications for admission were received and 56 new children were admitted. In 1968, there were 162 children in residence in Lakeland and Miami, and the administrative staff conducted 1,451 interviews with children during the year and 541 with parents. The Home continued to render three main types of child care, namely, (1) group care in the institution, (2) a mothers' aid program, and (3) foster home care.[142]

---

[140]*Ibid.*, 1960-61, pp. 71-74.
[141]Florida Baptist Convention, *Annual*, 1965, p. 101.
[142]*Ibid.*, 1968, p. 99.

In 1969, Dr. and Mrs. T. M. Johns retired. Johns had been superintendent of the Home since 1932, and during his administration the Home had become free from crippling debt, moved from Arcadia to a new campus in Lakeland, and established a branch Children's Home in Miami. He had also served as president of the Convention in 1965.

Upon Johns' retirement, Roger S. Dorsett, who was then serving as manager of the South Florida Branch Home in Miami, was appointed superintendent.

Florida Baptist Witness

The *Florida Baptist Witness* continued through the 1960's under the editorial leadership of Dr. W. G. Stracener, who celebrated his twentieth year as editor in 1969. During those twenty years, circulation almost tripled increasing from 23,600 to 66,006. Stracener maintained a long tradition of faithful recording of Florida Baptist news.

Like many other aspects of Florida Baptist life, the growth rate in the circulation of the *Witness* declined in the 1960's. From a circulation of 57,442 in 1960,[143] an increase was made to 70,510 in 1967.[144] In 1968, however, the *Witness* experienced a rather severe readjustment because of unanticipated increases in the costs of printing and postage, and as a result wound up the fiscal year operating with a deficit. In January, 1968, the *Witness* Commission voted to increase the subscription price 25¢ per year on the three subscription plans to offset the deficit, but the new rates did not go into effect until October 1, 1968.[145] The total circulation, however, declined slightly over the preceding year even before the new rates went into effect (to 66,922). By 1969, the paper was again operating in the black, but the circulation total decreased still further to 66,006 on September 30, 1969. Two factors probably caused the decline. First was the increase in the subscription rates mentioned above. A more significant factor, however, was the increasing financial difficulty many churches began to experience in 1969. Because of inflation, stock market decline, increased unemployment, and loss of a proper sense of stewardship, many church's failed to make their budgets during the year, and the *Witness* subscription budget was often one of the first items to be removed.[146]

---

[143]*Ibid.*, 1960, p. 46.
[144]*Ibid.*, 1967, p. 125.
[145]*Ibid.*, 1968, p. 109.
[146]Florida Baptist Convention, *Book of Reports,* 1968-69, p. 64.

National Baptists and Race Relations

Except for the contribution the Convention made to Negro Baptist education through its annual gifts to Florida Normal and Industrial College, the most significant work among Florida Baptists in the area of black and white Baptist relations had been done by the Woman's Missionary Union before the 1960's. In 1967, the Convention endorsed the move of Florida Memorial College from Saint Augustine to Miami, the name having been changed in 1963.[147] In the 1960's regular aid was given to Florida Memorial College until 1969, when it was excluded from the recommended budget by action of the State Board.[148] The reason given for the exclusion was the pressure of more urgent requests and limitation of funds. Also the item was deleted with the understanding that consideration might be given to aiding Florida Memorial again in the future.[149] As indicated earlier, the Woman's Missionary Union enlarged its creative work with Negro Baptists in Florida. In 1968 for the first time a W. M. U. scholarship was given to a black mission volunteer, Willie Mae Andrews, a student at Stetson.[150]

In 1965, however, the most creative and promising move yet made by Florida Baptists in this area was executed when the Convention approved a motion made by Dr. Julius Avery, director of work with National Baptists in Florida. The motion called for the election of Dr. John Maguire, Charles Peterson, and James Monroe to serve on a joint committee with elected representatives of the three National (Negro) Baptist State Conventions in Florida. The function of the joint committee was to plan a program of cooperative work between Southern Baptists and National Baptists in Florida.[151]

Under the direction of Dr. Avery and the joint committee, the following year, 1966, and each year since, an inter-racial conference was conducted at Lake Yale for ministers and laymen of each of the Conventions represented. The effect of this experience in increased communication between black and white Baptist leaders is difficult to measure at this point, but it appears clear that the results were highly favorable. In the late 1960's an increasing number of churches opened their doors to all members of all races.

The Florida Baptist Convention in general made the greatest progress in its history, however, in changing its attitude on the subject of

---

[147]Florida Baptist Convention, *Annual,* 1967, p. 53.
[148]State Board, *Minutes,* Sept. 5, 1969.
[149]*Ibid.*
[150]Florida Baptist Convention, *Annual,* 1968, p. 117.
[151]*Ibid.,* 1965, pp. 30-31.

race. Nowhere is this change better symbolized than in the unanimous Convention approval in 1969 of an amendment to the report of the Florida Baptist Children's Home asking the trustees to consider changing the by-laws of the Home to approve considering every child on his merit without regard to race.

Social Concern

In the 1960's the social concern of Florida Baptists continued to grow and was expressed mainly in (1) the continuation of a standing committee on Christian life, (2) continued support of United Christian Action, and (3) the creation of a short-lived committee on public affairs which was created in 1962,[152] and abolished in 1967.[153] The committee on Christian life was something of a state counterpart to the work of the Christian Life Commission of the Southern Baptist Convention. The main work of this committee during the 1960's was to bring an annual report to the Convention, calling attention to various aspects of morality. Frequently condemned were drinking, gambling, drugs, sexual immorality, and corrupt politics, and an occasional statement was made condemning racial discrimination. The reports often abounded in praise for the work of United Christian Action, Incorporated, which covered many of the same areas as the committee on Christian life.

The Committee on Public Affairs was a Florida counterpart of the Baptist Joint Committee on Public Affairs of the Southern Baptist Convention. Created therefore to concentrate on areas of the problem of church-state relationships, it came to work also in areas which overlapped with the concerns of the committee on Christian life and United Christian Action. For example, in 1962, when the public affairs committee was created the committee sponsored the first statewide conference on public affairs. The program personalities reflect the wide interests of the conference. Included were C. E. Carlson of the Baptist Joint Committee in Washington, Glenn Archer of P.O.A.U.,[154] Irving E. Howard, writer for *Christian Economics,* Jack Eppes of United Christian Action, and Paul Meigs, director of evangelism for the Florida Baptist Convention.[155] Around 131 men at-

---

[152]*Florida Baptist Witness,* Apr. 5, 1962, p. 4.

[153]Florida Baptist Convention, *Annual,* 1967, p. 71.

[154]Protestants and Other Americans United for the Separation of Church and State.

[155]*Florida Baptist Witness,* Apr. 5, 1962, p. 4.

tended the first conference. An attempt was made to continue the conference as an annual affair. However, attendance declined so significantly in 1963 that the committee was forced in 1964 to abandon the effort.[156] In 1965, the Convention created a committee on church-state relations, and in 1967 the committee on public affairs was abolished.

A new area of social concern was brought to the attention of the State Board of Missions in 1961, when the great need for prison chaplains was reported. The Board learned that 40 per cent of the white prison inmates were Baptists. A recommendation was adopted which called for a committee to study the problem. Vernon Brown was asked to be chairman of such a committee.[157] The State Board *Minutes* do not indicate, however, whether or not the study was ever made.

The committee reports and activities described above do not provide an adequate picture of the growing sense of social responsibility experienced by many Florida Baptist churches. The picture will be supplemented, however, in a later section.

Theological Discussion

Theological discussion among Florida Baptists during the 1960's is not easy to discover and define. The records do indicate that three specific events in Southern Baptist life caught the attention of many Florida Baptists and precipitated some theological discussion and debate. The first of these events was the dismissal of Ralph Elliot, a professor at Midwestern Baptist Theological Seminary, after a heated controversy over the publication of his book, *The Message of Genesis,* by Broadman Press. Unfortunately, as Editor Stracener clearly implied in the *Witness,* the discussion began with theological issues raised in the book but degenerated into arguments over Professor Elliot's dismissal by people who in many instances had not read the book. Editor Stracener defended the action of the trustees in firing Elliot, but condemned those who judged the book without reading it.[158]

A second event which provoked some discussion among Florida Baptists was the publication of the *Baptist Faith and Message,* a new statement of faith framed in 1963 by a study committee of the Southern Baptist Convention. An editorial in the *Witness* encouraged care-

---

[156]*Ibid.,* Apr. 11, 1963, p. 4.

[157]State Board, *Minutes,* Aug. 31, 1961.

[158]*Florida Baptist Witness,* Nov. 4, 1962, p. 4; and Nov. 18, 1962, p. 4; see also E. Earl Joiner, "Baptist Tradition and Theological Controversy," *Florida Baptist Witness,* Sept. 13, 1962, p. 16.

ful study of the statement.[159] Most Florida Baptists apparently either ignored it or took it for granted, because very little comment was provoked for some years.

The third event, however, raised the 1963 statement of faith to new status. This was the controversy which followed the publication of W. A. Criswell's book, *Why I Preach the Bible Is Literally True,* by Broadman Press in 1969. In response to the publication of this book, a group of Southern Baptist professors roundly condemned the book and the publisher in an unsigned published statement. This action evoked an editorial in the *Witness* by Editor Stracener in which he challenged these professors, suggesting the following: (1) that they write a book giving their views, (2) that they produce an evangelistic record like Criswell's before they criticize him, (3) and that they sign their names if they were not ashamed of their views. Stracener wrote, "We grant the validity of the historical-critical approach (advocated by the professors) as a method of study," but added that "it is certainly not the only valid method." He said further that while he did not wish to judge whether that approach was inspired, he thought it might be judged by what it had produced.[160] No doubt this editorial and the issue were discussed by many Florida Baptists, but little comment was contributed by the readers of the *Witness.*

Later, reporting Criswell as suggesting that those who did not accept the Southern Baptist Convention statement of faith should leave the Convention, Stracener commented on the statement of faith, and suggested that the statement of faith be regarded as "the components of a statement of faith, not as items in a creedal statement carrying any mandatory authority, or even necessary as an adequate definitive test of beliefs which make one a good Southern Baptist."[161]

In the Convention itself very little theological discussion was engaged in, but decisive theological issues were in the background of many controversies that were debated on the Convention floor. Notable examples are the church-state controversy in the Convention of 1966 and a resolution passed in the 1969 Convention which admonished the seminaries to stay close to the Bible. The basic content of the latter resolution as adopted included three points. First, it stated that Southern Baptist educational institutions face infiltration by liberals and liberalism. Second, it affirmed Florida Baptist Convention sup-

---

[159] *Florida Baptist Witness,* Mar. 25, 1963, p. 4.
[160] *Ibid.,* Apr. 17, 1969, p. 4.
[161] *Ibid.,* Oct. 14, 1969, p. 4.

port of the 1963 Southern Baptist Convention statement of faith. Third, it urged the six Southern Baptist seminaries to (1) reject liberalism, and (2) become in reality and practice strong Bible-centered institutions. Editor Stracener expressed displeasure in seeing all six seminaries come under the category of the implied indictment of the word *become* in the last statement, because the statement implied that the seminaries had not been Bible-centered institutions in the past. Even so the statement as adopted was milder than the resolution originally submitted.[162]

It was rather striking that this resolution of the 1969 Convention came immediately after President Millard Berquist of Midwestern Baptist Theological Seminary delivered an address which aroused some critical comment among the messengers, who interpreted what he said as rather liberal. The resolution, furthermore, was adopted only after several changes and extensive debate. It seems clear, therefore, that Florida Baptists, though theologically generally conservative as they had been in the past, still reflected a theological diversity also similar to what they had displayed in the past.

Reorganization of the State Convention Administration

Toward the end of the current decade, Florida Baptists engaged in a period of reflective self study beginning in 1967 under the leadership of an appointed committee, which reported its findings and recommendations to the Convention in 1968.[163] Out of this study and out of the new administration of Dr. Harold C. Bennett came a rather extensive reorganization in 1968 and 1969 of the State Convention administration. State Convention employees were organized into these three divisions: (1) the Administrative Division, (2) the Missions Division, and (3) the Education Division. Each division appropriately reflects in a broad sense the earliest concerns of the Florida Baptist Convention.

The Administrative Division included (1) the office and work of the assistant executive secretary-treasurer, (2) business services, and (3) promotion. The duties of the assistant executive secretary-treasurer, S. O. Bean, were defined as assisting Dr. Bennett and the supervising of the department of camps and assemblies directed by Paul Glore.

The responsibility of the director of business services, Frank Rich-

---

[162]*Ibid.,* Dec. 4, 1969, p. 4.

[163]Florida Baptist Convention, *Annual,* 1968, pp. 45-50.

ardson, was defined as accounting for money handled by the state offices, supervising mail services, and printing.

The director of promotion, Charles E. Peterson, was declared responsible for publicizing the work of the Convention and promoting a regular program of stewardship. All persons in the administrative department are directly responsible to Dr. Bennett.

The Missions Division, directed by J. Woodrow Fuller, consists of the departments of the Brotherhood, Evangelism, and Woman's Missionary Union. The responsibility of this division included correlating its work with the mission programs of the Southern Baptist Convention. A unique new venture in this division is a cooperative arrangement with the Home Mission Board in developing language missions, work with National Baptists, weekday and Christian social ministries, migrant work and other similar or related programs.

The Education Division, directed by L. Keener Pharr, consisted of the Church Music, Student, Sunday School, and Church Training Departments. All the programs of the Sunday School Board of the Southern Baptist Convention were made the responsibility of this division also when these programs related to Florida. Finally, this division was made responsible for the promotion of church administration services.

The reorganization process mentioned above, and the decline in growth rate, combined with continued expansion of facilities, suggests a need to raise the question as to whether or not the churches of the Convention are moving forward in qualitative ways to meet current challenges. What may be needed and expected in the future? Some attention will be given to these questions in the concluding chapter.

Associational Development and Growth

1970

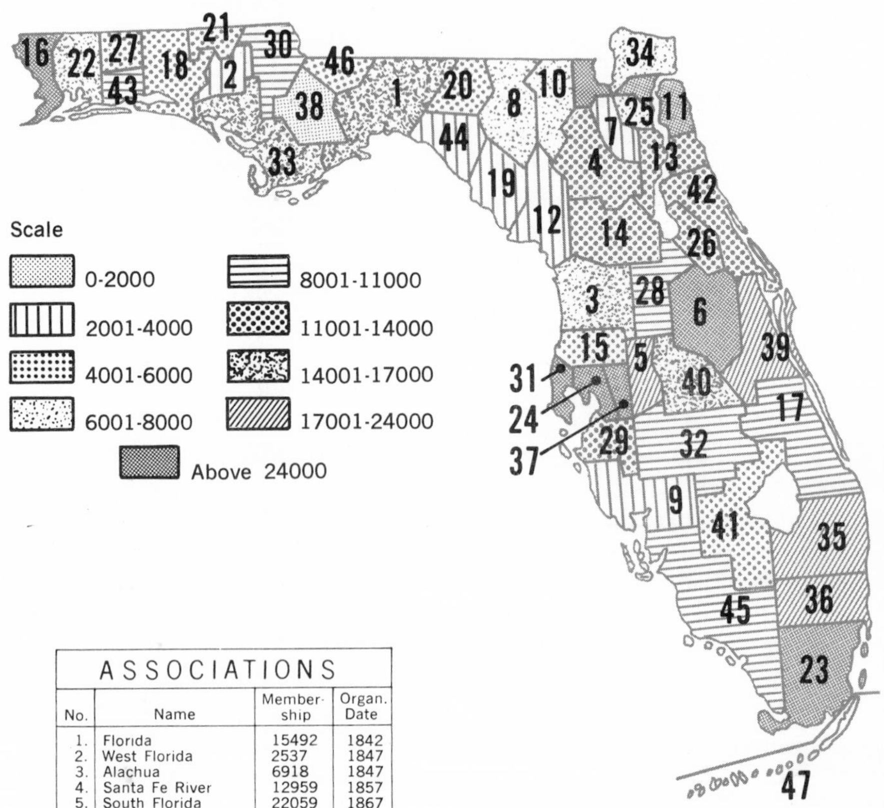

ASSOCIATIONS			
No.	Name	Membership	Organ. Date
1.	Florida	15492	1842
2.	West Florida	2537	1847
3.	Alachua	6918	1847
4.	Santa Fe River	12959	1857
5.	South Florida	22059	1867
6.	Wekiwa	38074	1870
7.	New River	3715	1872
8.	Suwannee	6721	1873
9.	Peace River	3918	1876
10.	Beulah	6036	1879
11.	Jacksonville	67939	1879
12.	Harmony	3377	1879
13.	St. John's River	11314	1879
14.	Marion	11705	1885
15.	Pasco	5098	1885
16.	Pensacola Bay	31438	1887
17.	Indian River	10969	1889
18.	Graves	4425	1890
19.	Lafayette	2109	1891
20.	Middle Florida	4458	1900
21.	Holmes County	4523	1905
22.	Santa Rosa	6077	1907
23.	Miami	59975	1909
24.	Tampa Bay	46726	1911
25.	Black Creek	6856	1913
26.	Seminole	12436	1914
27.	Okaloosa	4779	1923
28.	Lake County	8880	1924
29.	Southwest Florida	13825	1924
30.	Chipola	9287	1925

ASSOCIATIONS			
No.	Name	Membership	Organ. Date
31.	Pinellas	24107	1932
32.	Orange Blossom	10786	1932
33.	Northwest Coast	16025	1934
34.	Northeast Florida	7765	1938
35.	Palm Lake	20775	1938
36.	Gulf Stream	20974	1948
37.	Shiloh	13046	1950
38.	Apalachee	1005	1951
39.	Brevard	13237	1953
40.	Ridge	15957	1954
41.	Big Lake	4451	1954
42.	Halifax	11475	1957
43.	Choctaw	8194	1958
44.	Taylor	3693	1958
45.	Royal Palm	9623	1958
46.	Gadsden County	5463	1961
47.	Florida Keys	2705	1968

FLORIDA BAPTIST INSTITUTIONS

CHAPTER NINE

Conclusion and Reflection: Florida Baptists Look at the Present and to the Future

One of the most pressing questions confronting Florida Baptists is whether or not they can meet the challenges confronting them in the multi-faceted forms of urban problems. This question is important not only for the urban churches, but for small towns and rural churches as well because the whole of society is being affected by problems of secularism and urbanization in the cities.

Upon reflection, it would appear that for a long time in the 1940's and the 1950's, new life, excitement, and prosperity were brought to the city by the constant influx of people migrating from the country. As indicated already, however, in the 1960's, Florida Baptist leaders saw the necessity of taking a new look at themselves and the total situation in which they had been called to minister. Reflecting on the present and attempting to anticipate the future, require examination of several questions. The first question is whether or not there are churches in urban settings that are doing creative things to meet some of the challenges of urbanization. The second, closely related, is whether the churches in general are sensitive to the changing needs of people in the urban scene. The third question is whether or not the churches are preparing for the future. Finally, on the basis of the past and the current situation, what may be expected in the churches and in the Convention in the future? There is evidence for a qualified answer of yes to each of the first three questions raised above. Illustrations of the answers and the qualifications will be presented below. These illustrations will then be followed by an attempt to answer the question as to what may be expected in the future.

Varied Attempts to Meet Some of the Problems of Urbanization and Secularization by the Churches

As indicated earlier, the need for new approaches in keeping with today's times is keenly felt by many leaders in a wide variety of church settings. The form which the changed responses to these new needs take varies of course, according to the type church, but the variety is sufficient to give some indication of the future.

Institutional Churches

Although the term "institutional church" is inadequate to describe some of the new forms urban churches are taking and will take in the future, there are Florida Baptist churches now which bear enough resemblance to the institutional churches which developed in northern urban centers a generation or two ago to justify the use of the term. The characteristic which identifies a typical institutional church is social service. Increasingly, large churches in urban centers are taking on a new look which resembles the institutional church in some significant respects. Elements of this institutional church included (1) the creation of gymnasiums, bowling alleys and other facilities for organized forms of recreation in the church for youth, (2) sewing classes and related adult education activities for adults, and (3) day-care centers and week-day church schools, in some cases providing the same basic curriculum as the public schools. Examples of churches which provide some or all of these activities include the First Baptist Church of Daytona, First Baptist Church, Merritt Island, and First Baptist Church of Tampa. No doubt there may be other examples, and it seems safe to predict that the number will increase.

New Openness in Race Relations

That a new openness in race relations exists among Florida Baptists is nowhere more clearly symbolized than in the passing of the resolution without a dissenting vote in the 1969 convention requesting integration of the Children's Home.[1] A new openness in race relations may also be seen in numerous activities among the churches. These activities naturally take several forms which of course reflect the cultural setting in which a particular church resides. The first form which the new openness takes is the decision to open church membership to all members of all races. Although considerable attitudinal class consciousness probably still exists in most churches, a surprising

[1]See Chapter VIII.

number of churches have voted an open membership policy. Although relatively few of those adopting an open membership policy have actually received Negroes into their membership, an increasing number in urban settings have received members of the Negro race and other races. Examples of churches which have implemented a policy of accepting integration are Westside Church in Daytona, First Baptist Church in DeLand, Little River, Highland Park, Carol City, Central and Seventy-ninth Street in Miami, and Ballast Point and Old Fashion in Tampa.[2]

A second form of the new openness in race relations is seen in those churches which are not ready for integration, but which recognize the need for some movement toward other races. Some churches in rural areas, for example, have invited Negroes to worship in groups on special occasions, and have sent groups to conduct special services in Negro churches and other institutions.[3] A third form the new concern for Negroes has taken is the sponsoring of missions in predominantly Negro areas. At least two churches, First Baptist Church of Tampa and First Baptist Church, Sarasota, have taken such action recently.[4]

However, many churches have made little or no discernible progress in the area of race relations, and very little evidence could be found that any Florida Baptist churches are engaging in community action programs to end racial discrimination in areas of housing and employment. In general, the farther south one goes from the Georgia and Alabama line, the more openness one finds on the race question. The difference reflects the fact that where racial variety exists, sensitivity and responsiveness to changing needs appear to proceed slowly. Nonetheless, it seems safe to predict that in the future Florida Baptists will continue to change their attitude to other races as society continues to change. The annual inter-racial conferences directed by Julius Avery, mentioned in Chapter Eight, offer the hope of great progress to be made under the leadership of those groups toward the solution of many problems of race relations generally in Florida. However, a great deal of progress in this direction is yet to be made.

---

[2]Letters from William R. Moyle, May 22, 1970, and J. Roy Dobbins, May 28, 1970.

[3]Letter from John R. Wright, Superintendent of Missions, Chipola-Apalachee Associations, June 5, 1970.

[4]Letter from William R. Moyle, Superintendent of Missions, Tampa Bay Association, May 22, 1970.

New Forms of Ministry in the Churches

Recognizing the strains that urban living make on human life and aware of the broken, confused lives that often result, a number of Florida Baptist churches have sought to supplement and modify the traditional structures of Southern Baptist church life to create a more varied ministry to persons with special problems or needs. Special classes or schools are now being created for a wide variety of groups and individuals. The Central Baptist Church in Daytona has pioneered in efforts to help teen-agers struggling with drug problems. This church also has special classes for alcoholics and divorcees trying to reconstruct their lives.[5] The First Baptist Church of Merritt Island has what it calls a University of Christian Education which includes some functions of the Training Union, but includes also problems in the home and is far more complex and creative than the traditional Training Union as usually organized.[6] Specially creative work is likewise being done in the Training Union of the First Baptist Church of Jacksonville. Here, under the direction of Miss Frances Hendrix, the Training Union includes not only courses in Bible history and church history taught by ministers, but also courses in understanding children and teen-agers, taught by physicians.[7] Reportedly, Miss Hendrix directs the second largest Training Union in the Southern Baptist Convention. J. Ray Dobbins, Superintendent of Missions for the Miami Association, reports that 13 churches in Miami have day-care programs, and 45 have kindergartens.[8] Other churches conduct classes for the mentally retarded.[9] It seems very likely that such efforts to vary the church's ministry will increase.

Increased Ministry Beyond the Church

Perhaps the most unusual aspect of the work of many Baptist churches in the cities today is the new interest in varied forms of ministry beyond the church. One of the most challenging of these "beyond the church" ministries is a coffee house ministry which is being attempted in several urban centers. Notable among these is a house called "The Second Touch," sponsored jointly by the First Baptist

[5]Feature article, *Orlando Sentinel,* Sept. 14, 1969.

[6]Tom Clayton, Jr., "An Evaluation of the Ministry of the First Baptist Church, Merritt Island, Florida," unpublished paper, 1969.

[7]*Florida Times Union,* Sept. 13, 1969, p. A-20.

[8]Letter from J. Ray Dobbins.

[9]Letter from Thomas J. Draper, May 18, 1970.

Church of Daytona Beach, the State Board of Missions and the Southern Baptist Convention. This special work is directed by a minister, Robert Allen, who is assisted by volunteers from the First Baptist Church of Daytona Beach, from other churches and from Stetson University. Although it is a pilot project and some questions about its future and relationship to the church remain unanswered, it has proved to be successful in some ways in reaching hippies and other social drop-outs for Christ. For example, over 100 persons have accepted Christ through the "Second Touch" ministry during the past year.[10] A similar venture was begun recently in Orlando, sponsored jointly by the First Baptist Church and College Park Baptist Church. Born in the mind of Charles B. Brown, assistant pastor of the First Baptist Church, it is called "The Good Thief Coffeehouse." The director, Hugh Tarcai, is not an ordained minister, but is an evangelist nonetheless.[11] In addition to engaging in traditional forms of witness, these coffee houses give what help they can to rehabilitating hippies and social drop-outs who respond to their ministry.

A second form of ministry beyond the church is an alcoholic rehabilitation camp operated in District 12 by Mickey Evans.[12]

A third form of ministry being carried on beyond the churches is the good will center type service. For example, an institution called The Baptist Center, is operated in Panama City under the direction of the Home Mission Board, the Florida Baptist Convention and Northwest Coast Baptist Association. Though volunteers from local churches are utilized in this project, it is not considered a church or a regular mission expected to become a church. The program includes (1) Sunday school and worship on Sunday afternoon, (2) teenage fellowship on Friday nights, (3) sewing and cooking classes, (4) literary classes, and related activities to serve people in a lower economic area near a paper mill.[13]

A fourth form of "beyond the church" ministry, one which may become increasingly common, is illustrated broadly in the assistance given by 120 Florida Baptist churches and 67 individuals to victims of a recent hurricane in Mississippi. A total of $22,125.02 was given as of September 30, 1969. Also a group of young people from First Baptist Church of Pensacola, inspired by a suggestion by J. W. Brister,

---

[10]Interview with Dan Thomas, May 25, 1970.

[11]Rick Fleitas, "They're Rapping for God," *Orlando Sentinel Sunday Magazine,* May 10, 1970, p. 8.

[12]Letter from James R. Thompson, June 9, 1970.

[13]Letter from James K. Solomon, May 21, 1970.

chartered a bus and went to help restore the Beach Baptist Church building at Gulfport. More than fifty young people paid their own way, and the church provided $800.00 for supplies.[14]

A fifth type of ministry "beyond the church" is the ministry to students on college campuses. In the past, the Convention has sought to provide spiritual guidance and help to college students by helping churches in the vicinity of colleges to provide more buildings to make room for college students, and by placing campus ministers on college campuses having significant numbers of Baptist students. It now appears that the need probably can never be accomplished by Baptist student campus ministers alone. Great responsibility rests with the churches in the vicinity of college campuses. It is here, in the judgment of the writer, that great attention needs also to be given. The answer of simply providing additional facilities, given in the 1950's, is no longer adequate either, for it cannot any longer be assumed that if facilities are provided in the local churches Baptist students will flock to them and make full use of them. It may be that a different type of facility would help the situation. It is clear that the churches need to find new ways to minister to college students; they need also to find new ways for Baptist students in college to participate in the life of the local churches. One new approach to this problem that has developed in the last decade has been the utilization of Baptist student groups to perform folk musicals such as "Good News," and "Tell It Like It Is," in the churches.

Numerous other ministries being performed by churches, associations, the Convention and Home Mission Board include (1) high rise residence buildings for retirees, (2) ministries to migrant workers and their families, (3) help given to prisoners, ex-prisoners and their families, (4) counseling services to families and juvenile delinquents, (5) thrift stores for needy families, (6) Bible classes in low-rent housing areas and nursing homes and (7) special programs for retired persons.[15] In short, Florida Baptists can provide many examples of "outreach" ministry now in process. Others may be expected in the future.

Theological Conflict

Reflecting on the theological debate which ended the 1969 session of the Florida Baptist Convention and remembering the stormy debate

---

[14] *Florida Baptist Witness,* Oct. 9, 1969, p. 4.

[15] Letter from Thomas J. Draper, *op. cit.*

in the Southern Baptist Convention in 1970, the writer sees more conflict in the future for Florida Baptists. The same basic issue was at the heart of the debates in both Conventions, namely, interpretation of the Bible. Ralph Taylor, of Bowling Green, Florida, attending the Southern Baptist Convention was quoted as saying that he would use his strength and whatever money he could raise to organize those who agreed with him to see that the theological issues dividing the Convention are settled. Unfortunately, how he proposed to use money to settle a theological issue was not reported.[16] In the opinion of this author, it is a mistake to assume that theological questions are decided by majority vote in a Convention. All that is possible there is a measuring of majority opinion at a given time. If the same Baptists continued their Biblical and theological study, their opinion might be altered by that study. Equating differing opinion on a specific passage of Scripture with denying the inspiration of the Scripture is rather illogical reasoning. Nevertheless, present trends among Southern Baptists warn of more theological debate among Florida Baptists also.

Creativity and Conflict Over Education

The Local Church

As indicated earlier in another connection, new things being tried in education in the local churches promise much creativity in the future. The writer sees the possibility, however, that continued theological debate in the Convention may lead to difficulties in the educational program of the local church because, as the recent Southern Baptist Convention indicates, the debate may effect the resource materials used in the local churches. The creativity in methods now observed is likely to continue, nonetheless, despite the theological conflict.

Higher Education

The writer foresees increasing financial difficulty and continued competition for students among Florida Baptist educational institutions. The state of Florida appropriated $669 million for public schools in 1970, of which $152 million went to its colleges and universities. A small college like Stetson University seems to be at a great disadvantage in competing with institutions having such resources.[17] Thus, Stetson University will probably face increasing financial difficulty in the future. Its survival and growing strength will be assured

[16]*Florida Times Union,* June 8, 1970, p. A-7.
[17]*Collier's Encyclopedia Year Book,* 1969.

however, by continued and increasing spiritual, moral, and financial support from the Florida Baptist Convention. This strength and support will be made possible by constant close communication, cooperation, and faithful mutual stewardship between the Florida Baptist Convention and Stetson University. In addition, Stetson will need help from every honorable source possible.

Increasing Difficulty in Getting and Keeping Students for the Ministry

The problem of decline in students entering the ministry is likely to continue. Three factors may affect the problem. The first is the number of established pastors who are leaving the pastoral ministry for teaching, counseling, government, or other forms of service. While there is no accurate count of the number of Florida pastors who have left the active pastorate, the writer knows of quite a large number. The reasons vary widely, but a common complaint seems to be that the minister in the average church is not free to do his own thinking and to do his own acting in making his ministry socially relevant. Another factor may be the economic problem. Currently, the national family income average is $8,600 per year. The average for a Florida full-time Baptist pastor is $4,860. As editor Stracener says, "No wonder 266 pastors of full-time churches have to take employment apart from the church."[18] Florida's United Methodist ministers, in contrast, will be paid on scale ranging up from a minimum of $7,200 in the coming year. The minimum scale had been $6,000. A third factor in the problem of getting and keeping students for the ministry may be that the students receive inadequate guidance between the time the original decision for the ministry is made and the time they enter college. For example, in 1964, 3,700 Florida Baptist young people committed themselves to church-related vocations. In view of the well known decline in the number of college students preparing for church-related vocations, it would appear that, between the time of decision and entrance in college, something happens to many of these young people who make these commitments to church vocations early in their teens. Somewhere many must have changed their minds or lost their sense of commitment. Some serious study needs to be made of this problem.

---

[18] *Florida Baptist Witness,* Oct. 2, 1969, p. 4.

The story of Florida Baptists does not end here. It only comes to a pause for reflection and anticipation. Florida Baptists' ancestors left them noble examples of men who faced great problems with courage and dedication to Christ. In view of the rapid social, political, moral and spiritual changes taking place in Florida and the larger world, it seems clear that Florida Baptists face great problems in the future. These problems should not be viewed, however, as occasions for despair, but as challenges to their faith and courage. Florida Baptists should be able to learn from their past, and in the continued presence of the living Lord and the power of the Holy Spirit, the resources are at hand to meet every challenge they may confront. Furthermore, Florida Baptists today have many advantages their forefathers did not have in faster transportation and means of communication, and greater economic strength. Therefore, let them learn from their past, bring all the resources available to them into the service of God, continue to work together with one another, and with Him who is Lord of death, life, and history. If they do these things, Florida Baptists have a great future.

APPENDIX I

FIRST CONSTITUTION OF THE FLORIDA BAPTIST CONVENTION, ADOPTED IN 1854

1. This body is constituted upon the New Testament Scriptures as acknowledged and held, generally, by the Baptist denomination.

2. The constituents of this body shall be Baptist Associations of this State, and those adjacent in sister States; or as many of them as may accede to the terms of this Convention; and such auxiliary societies as shall contribute annually to our fund, according to the terms hereinafter prescribed, whose constitution shall be approved; and individuals who are regular members of Baptist churches, who shall contribute as hereinafter prescribed.

3. It shall be known by the name of "The Baptist Convention of the State of Florida."

4. Each Association shall be entitled to ten delegates, and to one additional delegate for every two hundred over the first thousand, provided the number shall not exceed twenty. Each auxiliary society, contributing annually fifty dollars to the funds of the Convention, shall be entitled to one delegate, and to one additional delegate for each fifty dollars contributed as aforesaid. Each individual contributing annually to the funds, as aforesaid, ten dollars, shall be a member. All delegates shall hold their appointments until others are elected to succeed them.

5. The officers of this Convention shall be a President, Secretary, Assistant Secretary, and Treasurer, who shall be chosen by ballot at each annual session.

6. An Executive Committee, consisting of at least seven members, shall be chosen by ballot at each annual meeting, whose duty it shall be to attend to the business of the Convention during its recess. This committee shall have power to fill vacancies which may occur, and also shall appoint a Treasurer in case of a vacancy in that office.

7. The Secretary shall enter in a book all the transactions of this body. The Assistant Secretary shall take charge of all distant communications to or from this body, and shall write all the letters which it may require.

8. The Treasurer shall take charge of all monies, specialities, and property of all kinds, belonging to the body, and give sufficient security for the amount in his hands, report the state of the funds from time to time as the Convention may direct, and hand over to his successor in office all monies, property, etc.

9. The acts and proceedings of this body shall be submitted from time to time, for inspections, to its constituents, and none of its decisions shall be binding on the associations or auxiliaries.

10. The following are the specific objects of the body, viz: 1st. To unite the influence and pious intelligence of the Baptists within its bounds, and thereby facilitate their union and co-operation. 2nd. To form and encourage plans for the revival of experimental and practical religion in the State, and elsewhere. 3rd. To aid in giving effect to useful plans of the several Associations. 4th. To afford an opportunity to those who may conscientiously think it to be their duty to form a fund for the education of pious young men who may be called by the spirit and their churches to the Christian ministry. 5th. And to promote pious and useful education in the Baptist denomination.

11. It shall have power to form rules, make arrangements, and appoint committees for the accomplishment of any and all the above objects. Provided, none of these rules and arrangements shall be inconsistent with the Scriptures and the known principles of the associations.

12. Two-thirds of the whole number of delegates present, shall form a quorum, and a majority shall decide a question.

13. When its funds will justify, this body may send delegates to the Southern Baptist Convention.

14. The above constitution shall be liable to amendment or alteration, by two-thirds of the delegates present at any of its annual meetings.

APPENDIX II

FLORIDA BAPTIST CHURCHES FOUNDED BEFORE 1860

Date	Name of Church	County
1821	Pigeon Creek	Nassau
1825	Bethlehem (Campbellton)*	Jackson
1825	Sardis	Jackson
1828	Ebenezer	Jefferson
1829	Indian Springs	Leon
1832	Providence	Columbia
1833	New River	Columbia
1834	Elizabeth	Jefferson
1834	Hickory Hill (Orange Hill)*	Washington
1838	Bethel (Jacksonville)*	Duval
1841	Sharon (Callahan)*	Nassau
1841	Concord	Madison
1841	Limestone	Holmes
1841	Monticello	Jefferson
1843	Providence	Gadsden
1843	Aenon	Leon
1844	Fellowship	Marion
1844	Key West	Monroe
1844	Union Academy	Jackson
1844	Ft. McCoy	Marion
1845	Lake Lindsey (Eden)*	Hernando
1845	Cluster Springs	Walton
1845	Greenwood	Jackson
1845	Ephesus	Nassau
1846	Ebenezer	Washington
1846	Econfina	Washington
1846	Liberty Hill (Camp Creek)*	Walton
1846	Holmes Valley	Walton
1846	New Hope	Walton
1846	Harmony	Holmes
1847	Pensacola	Escambia

Table 3—Continued

Date	Name of Church	County
1847	Milton	Santa Rosa
1847	Bethlehem	Jackson
1847	Mt. Pleasant	Columbia
1847	Rehoboth	Washington
1847	New Providence	Marion
1847	Holmes' Creek	Jackson
1847	Ft. Clark (Gainesville)*	Alachua
1847	Columbia	Columbia
1847	Bethlehem	(Old) Benton
1847	New Hope	Marion
1847	South Prong	Columbia
1848	Belleville	Hamilton
1848	Apalachicola	Franklin
1848	Harmony	Madison
1849	Tallahassee	Leon
1850	Beulah	Clay
1850	Flat Creek	Gadsden
1850	Mt. Gilead	Madison
1850	Mt. Pisgah	Jackson
1850	Hurrah (Alafia)*	Hillsborough
1850	Wacahoota	Alachua
1850	Ocala	Marion
1851	New Providence	Jackson
1852	Antioch	Gadsden
1852	Salem	Jackson
1852	Alagua	Walton
1852	Pine Barren	Jackson
1852	Hawthorne	Alachua
1852	Micanopy	Alachua
1852	Peniel	Madison
1853	Mount Besor	Wakulla
1853	Ucheeanna	Walton
1854	Thonotosassa	Hillsborough
1854	Peace Creek (Bartow)*	Polk
1854	Mt. Elon	Wakulla
1855	Lakeland	Polk
1855	New Hope	Jackson
1855	Chattahoochee	Gadsden
1856	Apopka	Orange
1856	Beulah	Duval
1856	Clay Landing	Levy
1856	Deep Creek	Nassau
1856	Paran	Putnam
1856	Perry	Taylor
1856	Half Moon Lake	Lafayette

Table 3—Continued

Date	Name of Church	County
1856	Pine Grove	Madison
1856	Oklawaha	Marion
1856	Midway	Columbia
1856	Brooksville	Hernando
1856	Mt. Pleasant	Columbia
1856	Ekaniah	Putnam
1856	Ft. McKee	Marion
1856	Friendship	Columbia
1856	Good Hope	Marion
1856	Lake Bryant	Marion
1856	Mossy Grove	Sumter
1856	Newmansville	Alachua
1856	New Hope	Marion
1856	Ocklawaha Bridge	Marion
1857	Fellowship	Holmes
1857	Friendship	Jackson
1858	Stafford's Pond	Marion
1858	Aucilla	Jefferson
1858	Williston	Levy
1858	Concordia	Gadsden
1859	Pine Barren	Jackson
1859	Tampa	Hillsborough
1859	Eliam	Putnam
1859	Shiloh (Greenville)*	Madison
1859	New Hope	Holmes
1859	Pleasant Grove	Leon
1859	Bethsaida	Wakulla
1859	Bethlehem	Wakulla
1859	New Port	Wakulla
1860	Bethpage	Jefferson
1860	Lake Jackson	Leon
1860	Mt. Gilead	Jefferson
1860	Oak Grove	Leon

*Present name of the church

APPENDIX III

LIST OF ASSOCIATIONS AND DATES ORGANIZED

1835	Suwannee (extinct)
1842	Florida
1847	Alachua
1847	West Florida
1857	Santa Fe River
1867	South Florida
1869	Wekiwa
1872	New River
1873	Suwannee
1876	Peace River
1877	St. Johns River
1879	Beulah
1879	Harmony
1879	Jacksonville
1885	Pasco
1885	Marion
1887	Pensacola Bay
1889	Indian River
1890	Graves
1891	Lafayette
1900	Middle Florida
1907	Santa Rosa
1909	Miami
1911	Tampa Bay
1913	Black Creek
1914	Seminole
1923	Okaloosa
1924	Lake County
1924	Holmes County
1924	Southwest Florida
1925	Chipola
1932	Orange Blossom
1933	Pinellas
1934	Northwest Coast
1938	Northeast Florida
1938	Palm Lake
1948	Gulf Stream
1950	Shiloh
1951	Gadsden
1951	Apalachee
1953	Brevard
1954	Ridge
1955	Big Lake
1958	Halifax
1958	Taylor
1958	Royal Palm
1959	Choctaw
1968	Florida Keys

APPENDIX IV

HISTORICAL TABLE

Year	Place	Presidents	Vice-Presidents
1854	Parlor R. J. Mays, Madison County	R. J. Mays	Organized at this time
1855	Concord Church		
1856	Greenwood		
1857	Thomasville, Georgia	F. Fleming	
1860	Monticello		
1866	Madison	W. B. Cooper	
1867	Lake City	K. Chambers	
1868	Madison	B. S. Fuller	
1869	Monticello	H. Z. Ardis	
1870	Jacksonville	P. P. Bishop	
1871	Madison	P. P. Bishop	
1872	Lake City	W. B. Cooper	
1873	(Nov. 21) Providence Ch.	J. H. Tomkies	
1875	(Feb. 11) Jacksonville	J. H. Tomkies	
1876	(Feb. 11) Gainesville	J. H. Tomkies	
1876	(Dec. 10) Madison	W. B. Cooper	
1877	Gainesville		
1878	Madison		
1879	Tallahassee		
1880	Madison	W. N. Chaudoin	
1881	Ocala	W. N. Chaudoin	Whitfield Walker
1882	Lake City	W. N. Chaudoin	T. W. Getzen
1883	Lake City	W. N. Chaudoin	T. W. Getzen
1884	Orlando	W. N. Chaudoin	H. M. King
1885	(Dec.) Jacksonville	W. N. Chaudoin	H. M. King
1886	(Nov.) Gainesville	H. M. King	Walter Gwinne
1888	(Jan.) DeLand	H. M. King	S. V. Marsh
1889	Ocala	W. N. Chaudoin	H. M. King
1890	Monticello	W. N. Chaudoin	H. M. King
1891	Pensacola	W. N. Chaudoin	C. H. Nash
1892	Kissimmee	W. N. Chaudoin	C. H. Nash
1893	Lake City	W. N. Chaudoin	R. H. Whitehead
1894	Plant City	W. N. Chaudoin	R. H. Whitehead
1895	Leesburg	W. N. Chaudoin	R. H. Whitehead
1896	Pensacola	W. N. Chaudoin	L. D. Geiger
1897	St. Augustine	W. N. Chaudoin	L. D. Geiger
1898	(Jan.) Tampa	W. N. Chaudoin	Samuel Pasco
1898	(Nov.) Madison	W. N. Chaudoin	S. Pasco, G. T. Leitner
1899	DeLand	W. N. Chaudoin	W. S. Jennings
1900	Arcadia	W. N. Chaudoin	W. S. Jennings
1901	(Nov.) Marianna	W. N. Chaudoin	W. S. Jennings
1903	(Jan.) Lake City	W. N. Chaudoin	W. S. Jennings, J. F. Forbes
1904	Kissimmee	S. B. Rogers	G. T. Leitner, C. A. Carson
1905	Jacksonville	S. B. Rogers	G. T. Leitner, C. A. Carson
1906	Bartow	S. B. Rogers	G. T. Leitner, C. A. Carson

HISTORICAL TABLE—(Continued)

Year	Place	Presidents	Vice-Presidents
1907	(Special) Lake City	W. S. Jennings	G. T. Leitner, C. A. Carson
1907	Live Oak	S. B. Rogers	C. A. Carson
1908	Plant City	S. B. Rogers	J. L. Jones, W. S. Jennings
1909	DeFuniak Springs	S. B. Rogers	J. L. Jones, W. S. Jennings
1910	Gainesville	C. A. Carson	J. L. Jones, W. A. Hobson
1911	DeLand	C. A. Carson	J. L. Jones, Lee MacDonell
1912	Ocala	C. A. Carson	J. L. Jones, Frank Bentley
1912	(Dec.) Lakeland	C. A. Carson	J. L. Jones, N. A. Blitch
1913	Arcadia	C. A. Carson	N. A. Blitch, W. D. Nowlin
1914	(Dec.) Pensacola	N. A. Blitch	A. J. Holt, E. D. Beggs
1916	(Jan.) Live Oak	N. A. Blitch	E. Sanford, Ira J. Carter
1917	Orlando	Frank Bentley	O. K. Reaves, J. H. Tucker
1918	Tallahassee	Frank Bentley	C. A. Hardee, J. T. Sanders
1919	Tampa	O. K. Reaves	G. W. Scofield, W. C. Hodges
1920	Jacksonville	O. K. Reaves	J. H. Griffin, C. H. S. Jackson
1920	Kissimmee	C. W. Duke	Bunyan Stephens, J. D. Adcock
1921	Miami	C. W. Duke	B. B. Tatum, R. A. Rasco
1922	Gainesville	A. A. Murphree	W. T. Hundley, B. F. Ezell
1923	DeLand	A. A. Murphree	Lincoln Hulley, S. B. Cole
1924	Lakeland	J. L. White	A. M. Bennett, L. G. Broughton
1925	Tampa	J. L. White	Lincoln Hulley, Doyle Carlton
1926	Lake City	W. L. C. Mahon	J. H. Griffin, E. A. McCloskey
1927	Bradenton	W. L. C. Mahon	F. N. K. Bailey, L. W. Kickliter
1928	Miami	Lincoln Hulley	R. H. Ferrell, G. J. Rousseau
1929	Jacksonville	Lincoln Hulley	E. C. Collins, J. E. Martin
1930	Tampa	Wm. D. Nowlin	W. A. Hobson, J. Dean Adcock
1931	Orlando	Wm. D. Nowlin	W. A. Burns, W. R. Lambert
1932	Daytona Beach	E. C. Collins	T. V. McCaul, L. T. Wilson
1933	Pensacola	E. C. Collins	E. R. Gaston, T. M. Johns
1935	DeLand	J. Dean Adcock	W. S. Allen, S. B. Cole
1936	Arcadia	J. Dean Adcock	W. S. Allen, S. B. Cole
1937	Ocala	J. Dean Adcock	Claude Jones, W. S. Allen
1938	Jacksonville	T. V. McCaul	W. A. Burns, A. Pichard
1939	West Palm Beach	T. V. McCaul	E. D. McDaniel, D. F. Sebastian
1940	Lakeland	J. H. Griffin	J. W. Jelks, J. M. Lee
1941	Gainesville	W. S. Allen	J. W. Jelks, A. W. Mathis
1942	Panama City	W. S. Allen	C. R. Angell, D. M. Gardner
1943	Jacksonville	J. E. Martin	Thos. Hansen, E. D. McDaniel
1944	Bradenton	J. E. Martin	Thos. Hansen, J. C. Sims
1945	Jacksonville	Thomas Hansen	Wallace R. Rogers, A. J. Burrell
1946	(Jan.) Jacksonville	Thomas Hansen	A. W. Reaves, Preston B. Sellers
1946	(Nov.) Tampa	C. H. Bolton	Don Waldon, T. O. Baldwin
1947	Orlando	W. R. Rogers	J. A. Sawyer, H. C. Meador
1948	Miami	Doak S. Campbell	J. P. Tucker, W. J. Norton
1949	Daytona Beach	C. Roy Angell	A. L. Carnett, A. M. Herrington
1950	Ocala	M. J. Berquist	Lee Nichols, John R. Martin
1951	Winter Haven	E. B. Edington	J. R. White, Jr., M. B. Knight
1952	Ft. Lauderdale	A. L. Carnett	D. I. Carlton, J. P. Rodgers

HISTORICAL TABLE—(Continued)

1953	Tampa	J. W. Parrish	E. C. Tyner, J. H. Avery
1954	Daytona Beach	H. G. Sanders	C. A. Howell, J. Earl Tharp
1955	Lakeland	C. B. Carroll	Lee Nichols, R. P. Tomlinso
1956	Orlando	P. B. Sellers	D. C. Crawford, L. D. Calhc
1957	Jacksonville (Special)	J. E. Stallings	F. L. Hall, Carson Brittain
1957	Pensacola	J. E. Stallings	F. L. Hall, Carson Brittain
1958	Miami	J. H. Avery	Vaughn M. Johnson
1958	Tallahassee	Carl A. Howell	H. F. Folsom, W. C. Brumbe
1960	St. Petersburg	W. Hal Hunter	D. E. Carlton, Jr., J. A. Ban
1961	Orlando	J. Ollie Edmonds	D. K. Simmons, Mrs. J. H. Lockhart
1962	Daytona Beach	M. B. Knight	H. A. Parker, M. D. Durran
1963	Jacksonville	Henry A. Parker	C. Norman Bennett, Jr., Jo L. Pelham
1964	Tampa	Homer G. Lindsay, Sr.	A. P. Minshew, J. R. Thomps
1965	Ft. Lauderdale	T. M. Johns	Harry C. Elrod, Joe M. Bamberg
1966	Pensacola	James Monroe	James F. Graves, Joseph C. Abernathy
1967	Sarasota	Edgar R. Cooper	Fred B. Chance, C. H. Kiser
1968	Daytona Beach	Conrad R. Willard	Mrs. Clyde B. Lipscomb Girod H. Cole, Jr.
1969	Miami	Doyle I. Carlton	Don H. Houser Girod H. Cole, Jr.

HISTORICAL TABLE—(Continued)

Year	Secretaries	Preacher of Convention Sermon	Text
1854	D. G. Daniel, S. C. Craft		
1855	D. G. Daniel, S. C. Craft		
1857	D. G. Daniel, S. C. Craft	Alex Smith	Phil. 2:16
1860			
1866	C. D. Campbell	R. W. Whidden	Dan. 2:44
1867	C. D. Campbell	J. H. Tomkies	
1868	J. H. Tomkies	B. S. Fuller	
1869	P. P. Bishop	H. Z. Ardis	Mark 11:22
1870	H. B. McCallum	P. P. Bishop	
1871	H. B. McCallum		
1872	H. B. McCallum	J. H. Tomkies	
1873	E. Sarle, N. A. Bailey	L. W. Simmons	John 17:22
1875	H. B. McCallum, R. W. Whidden	S. French	Heb. 5:9
1876	H. B. McCallum, R. W. Whidden	K. Chambers	
1876	W. C. Barkley	K. Chambers	
1877			
1878			
1879			

HISTORICAL TABLE—(Continued)

Year	Secretaries	Preacher of Convention Sermon	Text
1880	Paul Willis		
1881	Paul Willis, N. A. Bailey	A. H. Robinson	Zech. 3:9
1882	Paul Willis, N. A. Bailey	Basil Manley	I Sam. 1:27, 28
1883	Paul Willis, N. A. Bailey	H. M. King	Rev. 22:17
1884	Paul Willis, N. A. Bailey	T. E. Langley	I Tim. 1:11
1885	N. A. Bailey, A. P. Ashurst	N. A. Bailey	Isa. 53:11
1886	N. A. Bailey, A. P. Ashurst	S. K. Leavitt	Jno. 4:35
1888	N. A. Bailey, Paul Willis	J. L. Underwood	Heb. 7
1889	N. A. Bailey, Paul Willis	L. T. Lynch	Rev. 3:21
1890	N. A. Bailey, Paul Willis	W. B. Dye	Jno. 15:5
1891	N. A. Bailey, Paul Willis	W. C. McCall	Col. 2:9
1892	N. A. Bailey, F. C. Waite	J. H. Curry	II Cor. 5:14
1893	N. A. Bailey, E. H. Rennolds, Sr.	M. M. Gregor	Jude 3rd Verse
1894	N. A. Bailey, E. H. Rennolds, Sr.	C. S. Farris	Jno. 17:3
1895	N. A. Bailey, E. H. Rennolds, Sr.	A. P. Pugh	Heb. 11:26
1896	N. A. Bailey, E. H. Rennolds, Sr.	L. D. Geiger	Matt. 6:9
1897	N. A. Bailey, E. H. Rennolds, Sr.	W. A. Nelson	Dan. 6:10
1898	L. D. Geiger, E. H. Rennolds, Sr.	J. J. Parsons	Isa. 60:7
1898	L. D. Geiger, E. H. Rennolds, Sr.	C. H. Nash	II Cor. 5:19
1899	L. D. Geiger, E. H. Rennolds, Sr.	W. T. Hundley	Luke 17:20
1900	L. D. Geiger, E. H. Rennolds, Sr.	J. F. Forbes	I Peter 1:18-19
1901	L. D. Geiger, E. H. Rennolds, Sr.	F. W. Cramer	Acts 1:8
1903	E. H. Rennolds, Sr., F. C. Edwards	O. J. Frier	Ex. 14:15
1904	E. H. Rennolds, Sr., F. C. Edwards	W. A. Hobson	I Pet. 1:11
1905	E. H. Rennolds, Sr., F. C. Edwards	F. C. Edwards	Jno. 14:12
1906	E. H. Rennolds, Sr., F. C. Edwards	W. C. McCall	
1907	E. H. Rennolds, Sr., F. C. Edwards	C. A. Ridley	Hagg. 2:7; Col. 2:9
1908	E. H. Rennolds, Sr., W. C. Foster	C. W. Duke	Matt. 17:17, 18
1909	E. H. Rennolds, Sr., W. C. Foster	C. C. Carroll	Acts 2:17
1909	E. H. Rennolds, Sr., C. W. Foster	None Preached	
1910	E. H. Rennolds, Sr., W. C. Foster	C. E. W. Dobbs	Eph. 5:27
1911	E. H. Rennolds, Sr., R. L. Turner	J. B. Pruitt	Matt. 28:19
1912	E. H. Rennolds, Sr., R. L. Turner	J. J. Cloar	Matt. 28:18
1912	R. L. Turner, F. C. Edwards	A. J. Holt	Phil. 1:6
1913	C. L. Collins, S. R. Skinner	W. L. C. Mahon	John 1:29
1914	C. L. Collins, J. W. Senterfitt	W. B. Parshley	Matt. 7:21
1916	C. L. Collins, J. W. Senterfitt	E. R. Pendleton	Matt. 24:14
1917	C. L. Collins, J. W. Senterfitt	Wallace Wear	Isaiah 26:3
1918	C. L. Collins, J. W. Senterfitt	E. T. Poulson	Matt. 28:20
1919	C. L. Collins, J. W. Senterfitt	J. Dean Adcock	Phil. 3:10, Heb. 12:2
1920	C. L. Collins, J. W. Senterfitt	R. E. Reed	Phil. 3:5
1920	C. L. Collins, J. W. Senterfitt	S. B. Cole	Phil. 3:13-14
1921	C. L. Collins, J. W. Senterfitt	Lincoln Hulley	Luke 23:33
1922	C. L. Collins, J. W. Senterfitt	Bunyan Stephens	John 3:16
1923	C. L. Collins, J. W. Senterfitt	A. J. Moncrief	Eccles. 7:10
1924	C. L. Collins, J. W. Senterfitt	J. L. White	Heb. 6:1

1925	C. L. Collins, J. W. Senterfitt	W. D. Nowlin	John 3:16
1926	C. L. Collins, J. W. Senterfitt	F. D. King	John 3:16
1927	C. L. Collins, J. W. Senterfitt	T. V. McCaul	Ps. 40:16
1928	C. L. Collins, J. W. Senterfitt	J. E. Martin	Rev. 14:6
1929	J. W. Senterfitt, C. L. Collins	W. Raleigh White	John 3:30
1930	J. W. Senterfitt, C. L. Collins	Thomas Hansen	II Tim. 1:8
1931	J. W. Senterfitt, Ray Y. Walden	E. H. Jennings	Heb. 13:8
1932	J. W. Senterfitt, Ray Y. Walden	D. M. Gardner	Rom. 8:18
1933	J. W. Senterfitt, Ray Y. Walden	G. J. Rousseau	Matt. 16:18
1935	J. W. Senterfitt, Mac Senterfitt	J. H. Griffin	Matt. 13:33
1936	E. C. Bostick, J. M. Anderson	D. F. Sebastian	Acts 16:10
1937	E. C. Bostick, R. Y. Walden	F. C. McConnell	Phil. 1:3-5
1938	E. C. Bostick, A. J. Gross	A. E. Calkins	Matt. 28:18
1939	E. C. Bostick, J. W. Senterfitt, Jr.	A. W. Mathis	I Pet. 2:34
1940	E. C. Bostick, M. D. Jackson	C. R. Pittard	Phil. 3:13-14
1941	E. C. Bostick, M. D. Jackson	A. C. Abney	Acts 4:11-12
1942	C. M. Brittain, M. D. Jackson	W. T. Halstead	John 10:10
1943	M. D. Jackson, Hawley Ridenour	W. G. Stracener	Matt. 17:20
1944	M. D. Jackson, R. P. Tomlinson	J. A. Inman	Matt. 28:18-20
1945	M. D. Jackson, R. P. Tomlinson	H. H. Shirley	Psalms 8:3, 4
1946	M. D. Jackson, C. L. Crissey	J. P. Tucker	Acts 4:12
1946	M. D. Jackson, C. L. Crissey	W. P. Brooks, Jr.	Micah 6:8
1947	M. D. Jackson, C. L. Crissey	A. M. Parker	Rom. 1:16
1948	M. D. Jackson, W. A. Robinson	M. J. Berquist	Matt. 27:33-54
1949	M. D. Jackson, W. A. Robinson	E. D. Solomon	Matt. 10:6
1950	M. D. Jackson, W. A. Robinson	T. S. Boehm	John 1:1-36
1951	M. D. Jackson, W. A. Robinson	R. Kelly White	Luke 22:31, 32
1952	M. D. Jackson, W. A. Robinson	Lee Nichols	Matt. 16:16
1953	M. D. Jackson, W. A. Robinson	T. O. Baldwin	Prov. 29:18; Acts 26:19
1954	W. A. Robinson, M. D. Jackson	C. H. Bolton	Hab. 3:17-19
1955	M. D. Jackson, H. V. Adams, Jr.	P. B. Sellers	Heb. 2:8, 9
1956	M. D. Jackson, H. V. Adams, Jr.	E. C. Abernathy	Mark 16:15
1957	M. D. Jackson, H. V. Adams, Jr.	Special	
1957	M. D. Jackson, H. V. Adams, Jr.	H. G. Lindsay, Sr.	Matt. 28:18-20
1958	M. D. Jackson, H. V. Adams, Jr.	E. C. Tyner	Jno. 9:4
1959	M. D. Jackson, H. V. Adams, Jr.	J. A. Sawyer	Esther 4:14
1960	M. D. Jackson, H. V. Adams, Jr.	Frank T. Anderson	Luke 22:19
1961	M. D. Jackson, H. V. Adams, Jr.	Vaughn M. Johnson	Acts 4:7, 12
1962	M. D. Jackson, H. V. Adams, Jr.	Fred T. Laughon, Jr.	Matt. 28:16-20
1963	M. D. Jackson, H. V. Adams, Jr.	Arthur W. Rich	Rev. 3:14-22
1964	M. D. Jackson, H. V. Adams, Jr.	Edgar R. Cooper	John 1:6
1965	M. D. Jackson, G. H. Gay	Homer G. Lindsay, Jr.	I John 2:5, 6
1966	M. D. Jackson, G. H. Gay	R. Wilbur Herring	Exodus 3:1-10
1967	G. H. Gay, W. C. Roebuck, Jr.	Conrad R. Willard	Phil. 3:13-14
1968	W. C. Roebuck, Jr.	C. Earl Cooper	Esther 4:14
1969	Truett Smith, W. C. Roebuck, Jr.	Earl B. Eddington	Luke 7:19-28 Gen. 11:31

APPENDIX V

LIST OF EXECUTIVE SECRETARIES, DEPARTMENT HEADS AND OTHER OFFICERS

I. Executive Secretaries

1. W. N. Chaudoin—1880-1901.
2. L. D. Geiger—1901-1909.
3. S. B. Rogers—1909-1926.
4. C. M. Brittain—1926-1941.
5. C. H. Bolton—1941-1944.
6. John H. Maguire—1944-1967.
7. Harold C. Bennett—1967-

II. Woman's Missionary Union Executive Secretaries

1. Mrs. N. A. Bailey—1881-1886.
2. Mrs. L. B. Telford—1886-1893.
3. Miss Jennie L. Spalding—1894-1911.
4. Mrs. H. C. Peelman—1911-1936.
5. Miss Louise Smith—1936-1943.
6. Miss Josephine Jones—1944-1967.
7. Miss Carolyn Weatherford—1967-

III. Sunday School

1. Louis Entzminger—1910-1911.
2. George Hyman—1912-1913.
3. T. F. Hendon—1914-1916.
4. W. W. Willian—1916-1946.
5. Tom Collins—1946-1947.
6. Glenn Bridges—1947-1948.
7. C. F. Barry—1948-1970.
8. James E. Frost—1970-

IV. Training Union

1. O. K. Armstrong—1920.
   (1921-1938 work promoted by W. W. Willian in addition to his work as Sunday School Secretary)
2. O. K. Radford—1938-1960.
3. C. J. Smyly—1960-1966.
4. E. L. Mixon (Acting)—1966-1969.
5. Robert S. Cook—1969-

V. Brotherhood

1. W. G. Upchurch—1928-1931.
   (1932-1936—no one employed)
2. Hugh Latimer—1936-1939.
3. J. Harrison Griffin—1939-1945.
4. C. A. Holcomb—(Brotherhood music)—1945-1951.
5. G. A. Rattaree—1951-

VI. Baptist Student Union

1. John Hall Jones—1929-1936.
2. J. Roy Robinson—1936-1940.
3. Sabin Landry—1940-1942.
4. Billie Ruth Currin—1942-1943.
5. Clyde Lipscomb—1943-1946.
6. Ray Koonce—1946-1956.
7. Joe Webb—1956-

VII. Editors of Florida Baptist Witness

1. F. B. Moodie— (W. N. Chaudoin and
2. A. P. Ashurst—1884-1885. N. A. Bailey—Associate editors)
3. W. N. Chaudoin—1885.
4. C. C. Hill—1885.
5. S. M. Provence—1885.
6. J. H. Griffith—1886.
7. N. A. Bailey—1886.
8. L. B. Plummer—1887. (Bailey and Chaudoin—Assoc. editors).
9. P. C. Drew—1888.
10. W. J. Turnley—1888.
11. C. H. Nash—1888. (served as editor with Turnley).
12. M. F. Hood—1888.
13. J. C. Porter—1890-1893. (also E. C. Hood, M. F. Hood, S. H. Blitch, L. D. Geiger, and C. A. Nash).
14. C. S. Farris—1893-1895.
15. J. C. Porter—1895-1904.
16. W. A. Hobson—1904-1905.
17. F. C. Edwards—1905-1909.
18. J. H. Warp—1906-1909.
19. C. M. Brittain—1909-1911.
20. F. C. Edwards—1909-1911.
21. E. Z. Golden—1911-1912.
22. W. D. Nawlin—1912-1914.
23. A. J. Holt—1914-1918.
24. J. W. Mitchell—1918-1928.
25. P. L. Johnston—1928-1930.
26. C. M. Brittain—1930-1931.
27. E. D. Solomon—1931-1949.
28. W. G. Stracener—1949-1970.
29. E. R. Cooper—1970-

VIII. Stetson Presidents

1. J. F. Forbes—1885-1904.
2. Lincoln Hulley—1904-1934.
3. William Sims Allen—1934-Sept., 1947.
4. J. Ollie Edmunds—Dec., 1947-1967.

5. Paul F. Geren—1967-1969.
6. John Johns—Acting President—1969-1970. President—1970-

IX. Florida Baptist Children's Home

1. B. M. Bean—1904-1912.
2. J. E. Trice—1912-1931.
3. T. M. Johns—1932-1969.
4. Roger S. Dorsett—1969-

X. Baptist Bible Institute—Presidents

1. Leon Gambrell—1946-1952.
2. A. H. Stainbach—1952-1957.
3. James S. Southerland—1957-

XI. Florida Baptist Retirement Center—Directors

1. J. Perry Carter—1959-1962
2. Leo B. Roberts—1963-1968
3. Paul R. Adkins—1968-1970
4. William H. Lord—1970-

APPENDIX VI

STATISTICAL TABLES

Membership—Population Statistics—1870-1970

Year	Population	Church Membership	Percent of Population	Sunday School Membership	Percent of Church Membership	Training Union Membership	Percent of Church Membership
1870	187,748	4,740	2.527	—	—	—	—
1880	269,493	17,180	6.375	—	—	—	—
1890	391,422	13,792	3.524	3,241	23.499	—	—
1900	528,542	23,136	4.377	10,127	43.772	—	—
1910	752,619	39,017	5.184	19,577	50.176	—	—
1920	968,470	57,078	5.894	34,702	60.798	4,741	8.306
1930	1,468,211	115,705	7.881	84,843	73.327	18,312	15.826
1940	1,897,414	162,396	8.559	117,995	72.659	37,978	23.386
1945	2,420,000*	184,140	7.609	116,765	63.410	1,795	.975
1946	2,431,000*	201,480	8.288	133,841	66.428	2,337	1.160
1947	2,540,000*	224,884	8.854	159,811	71.063	43,915	19.528
1948	2,606,000*	242,804	9.317	180,016	74.140	52,062	21.441
1949	2,679,000*	261,527	9.762	193,499	73.988	58,561	22.391
1950	2,771,305	278,668	10.055	214,402	76.938	68,899	24.724
1951	2,966,000*	296,704	10.004	224,927	75.808	76,298	25.715
1952	3,118,000*	311,955	10.004	241,574	77.438	76,851	24.635
1953	3,284,000*	330,220	10.055	259,903	78.706	86,449	26.179
1954	3,462,000*	369,294	10.667	298,064	80.711	99,750	27.010
1955	3,670,000*	371,807	10.130	319,533	85.940	105,945	28.494
1956	3,941,000*	388,487	9.857	333,684	85.893	111,165	28.614
1957	4,245,000*	411,145	9.685	353,078	85.876	119,888	29.159
1958	4,571,000*	429,871	9.404	365,084	84.928	125,704	29.242
1959	4,790,000*	455,175	9.502	382,224	83.972	134,410	29.529
1960	4,951,560	480,407	9.702	397,771	82.799	140,510	29.248
1961	5,205,000*	507,881	9.758	412,460	81.212	149,029	29.343
1962	5,392,000*	528,885	9.809	418,088	79.051	151,498	28.645
1963	5,532,000*	543,626	9.828	421,074	77.450	153,493	28.232
1964	5,654,000*	557,031	9.852	426,800	76.621	154,037	27.653
1965	5,802,000*	570,614	9.835	431,667	75.650	152,157	26.665
1966	5,914,000*	581,956	9.840	426,817	73.342	155,558	26.730
1967	6,035,000*	600,836	9.956	430,419	71.637	152,971	25.460
1968	6,210,000*	614,900	9.902	424,385	69.017	145,441	23.653
1969	6,354,000*	632,780	9.959	414,478	65.501	137,773	21.773
1970	6,789,443	638,906	9.410	406,650	63.648	127,967	20.029

*Estimated population from the U. S. Department of Commerce, Bureau of the Census

Mission Gifts and Property Expenditures—1900-1970

Year	Total Gifts	Mission Gifts	Percent of Gifts	Property Value	Yearly Increase in Prop. Value	Comparative Percent of Gifts
1900	$ 55,029	$ 5,615	10.203	—	—	—
1910	252,130	34,206	13.567	—	—	—
1920	467,403	92,773	19.849	—	—	—
1930	1,356,212	168,438	12.420	—	—	—
1940	1,572,260	231,615	14.731	—	—	—
1945	3,361,988	585,383	17.411	$ 10,308,032	$ 657,769	19.564
1946	5,497,539	816,373	14.849	12,283,822	1,975,790	35.939
1947	6,524,111	893,118	13.689	15,086,555	2,802,733	42.959
1948	6,967,707	1,045,928	15.011	20,717,750	5,631,195	80.818
1949	8,062,219	1,170,000	14.512	26,920,041	6,202,291	76.930
1950	9,423,025	1,350,204	14.329	29,214,329	2,294,288	24.348
1951	9,978,676	1,348,872	13.517	33,788,394	4,574,065	45.838
1952	11,230,347	1,536,276	13.679	38,481,655	4,693,261	41.790
1953	13,282,230	1,766,150	13.297	44,104,646	5,622,991	42,334
1954	14,819,219	1,947,094	13.138	50,903,129	6,798,483	45.876
1955	17,282,924	2,302,857	13.324	60,380,961	9,477,832	54.839
1956	20,158,928	2,495,126	12.377	71,230,194	10,849,233	53.818
1957	21,496,715	3,163,802	14.717	79,079,097	7,848,903	36.512
1958	22,716,150	3,684,065	16.217	91,210,122	12,131,025	53.402
1959	25,931,907	4,059,766	15.655	106,177,697	14,967,575	57.718
1960	28,778,183	4,131,649	14.357	121,570,050	15,392,353	53.486
1961	29,168,051	4,091,574	14.028	130,525,505	8,955,455	30.703
1962	31,887,199	4,601,212	14.430	149,110,145	18,584,640	58.282
1963	32,374,844	4,502,233	13.907	158,870,661	9,760,516	30.148
1964	35,264,809	4,824,052	13.680	167,216,507	8,345,846	23.666
1965	37,813,846	5,206,632	13.769	178,230,339	11,013,832	29.126
1966	39,285,537	5,612,374	14.286	190,616,739	12,386,400	31.529
1967	41,884,919	5,933,213	14.166	203,193,988	12,577,249	30.028
1968	45,394,886	6,424,575	14.153	214,105,070	10,911,082	24.036
1969	48,975,856	6,801,662	13.888	237,848,624	23,743,554	48.480
1970	55,577,803	6,983,785	12.566	236,864,732	–983,892	–1.770

Gains/Losses in Total Gifts, Mission Gifts and Property Values of Florida Baptists, 1945 to 1970

Year	Total Gifts	Net increase/ decrease	% increase/ decrease	Mission Gifts	Net increase/ decrease	% increase/ decrease	Property Value	Net increase/ decrease	% increase/ decrease
1944	$ 2,866,171	—	—	$ 532,834	—	—	$ 9,650,263	—	—
1945	3,361,988	$ 495,817	1.730	585,383	$ 52,549	9.862	10,308,032	$ 657,769	6.816
1946	5,497,539	2,135,551	63.520	816,373	230,990	39.460	12,283,822	1,975,790	19.167
1947	6,524,111	1,026,572	18.673	893,118	76,745	9.401	15,086,555	2,802,733	22.816
1948	6,967,707	443,596	.680	1,045,928	152,810	17.110	20,717,750	5,631,195	37.326
1949	8,062,219	1,094,512	15.708	1,170,000	124,072	11.862	26,920,041	6,202,291	30.901
1950	9,423,025	1,360,906	16.880	1,350,204	180,204	15.402	29,214,329	2,294,288	8.793
1951	9,978,676	555,651	.590	1,348,872	–1,332	–.099	33,788,394	4,574,065	15.657
1952	11,230,347	1,251,671	12.543	1,536,276	187,404	13.893	38,481,655	4,693,261	13.890
1953	13,282,230	2,051,883	18,271	1,766,150	229,874	14.963	44,104,646	5,622,991	14.612
1954	14,819,219	1,536,989	11.572	1,947,094	180,944	10.245	50,903,129	6,798,483	15.414
1955	17,282,924	2,463,705	16.625	2,302,857	355,763	18.271	60,380,961	9,477,832	18.619
1956	20,158,928	2,876,004	16.641	2,495,126	192,264	8.349	71,230,194	10,849,233	17.968
1957	21,496,715	1,337,787	6.636	3,163,802	668,676	26.799	79,079,097	7,848,903	11.019
1958	22,716,150	1,219,435	5.673	3,684,065	520,263	16.444	91,210,122	12,131,025	15.340
1959	25,931,907	3,215,757	14.156	4,059,766	375,701	10.198	106,177,697	14,967,575	16.410
1960	28,778,183	2,846,276	10.976	4,131,649	71,883	1.771	121,570,050	15,392,353	14.497
1961	29,168,051	389,868	1.355	4,091,574	–40,075	–.970	130,525,505	8,955,455	7.366
1962	31,887,199	2,719,148	9.322	4,601,212	509,638	12.456	149,110,145	18,584,640	14.238
1963	32,374,844	487,645	1.529	4,502,233	–98,979	–2.151	158,870,661	9,760,516	6.485
1964	35,264,809	2,889,965	8.927	4,824,052	321,819	7.148	167,216,507	8,345,846	5.253
1965	37,813,846	2,549,037	7.228	5,206,632	382,580	7.931	178,230,339	11,013,832	6.587
1966	39,285,537	1,471,691	3.892	5,612,374	405,742	7.793	190,616,739	12,386,400	6.950
1967	41,884,919	2,599,382	6.617	5,933,213	320,839	5.717	203,193,988	12,577,249	6.598
1968	45,394,886	3,509,967	8.380	6,424,575	491,362	8.282	214,105,070	10,911,082	5.370
1969	48,975,856	3,580,970	7.888	6,801,662	377,087	5.869	237,848,624	23,743,554	11.090
1970	55,577,803	6,601,947	11.878	6,983,785	182,123	2.677	236,864,732	–983,892	–.414

Gains/Losses in Church, Sunday School and Training Union Membership of Florida Baptists, 1945 to 1970

Year	Church Membership	Net increase/ decrease	% increase/ decrease	Sunday School Membership	Net increase/ decrease	% increase/ decrease	Training Union Membership	Net increase/ decrease	% increase/ decrease
1944	176,688	—	—	110,826	—	—	1,790	—	—
1945	184,140	7,452	4.218	116,765	5,939	5.359	1,795	–5	–.003
1946	201,480	17,340	9.417	133,841	17,076	14.624	2,337	542	23.192
1947	224,884	23,404	11.616	159,811	25,970	19.404	43,915	41,578	1779.119
1948	242,804	17,920	7.969	180,016	20,205	12.643	52,062	8,147	18.552
1949	261,527	18,723	7.711	193,499	13,483	7.490	58,561	6,494	12.483
1950	278,668	17,141	6.554	214,402	20,903	10,803	68,899	10,338	17.653
1951	296,704	18,036	6.472	224,927	10,525	4.909	76,298	7,339	10.652
1952	311,955	15,251	5.140	241,574	16,647	7.401	76,851	533	.725
1953	330,220	18,265	5.855	259,903	18,329	7.587	86,449	9,598	12.489
1954	369,294	39,074	11.833	298,064	38,161	14.683	99,750	13,301	15.386
1955	371,807	2,513	.680	319,533	21,469	7.203	105,945	6,195	6.211
1956	388,487	16,680	4.486	333,684	14,115	4.417	111,165	5,220	4.927
1957	411,145	22,658	5.832	353,078	19,394	5.812	119,888	8,723	7.847
1958	429,871	18,726	4.555	365,084	12,006	3.400	125,704	5,816	4.851
1959	455,175	25,304	5.886	382,224	17,140	4.695	134,410	8,706	6.926
1960	480,407	25,232	5.543	397,771	15,547	4.068	140,510	6,100	4.538
1961	507,881	27,474	5.719	412,460	14,689	3.693	149,029	8,519	6.063
1962	528,885	21,004	4.136	418,088	5,628	1.364	151,498	2,469	1.657
1963	543,626	14,741	2.787	421,074	2,986	.714	153,493	1,995	1.317
1964	557,031	13,405	2.466	426,800	5,726	1.360	154,037	544	.354
1965	570,614	13,583	2.438	431,667	4,867	1.140	152,157	–1,880	–1.236
1966	581,956	11,342	1.988	426,817	–4,850	–1.124	155,558	3,401	2.235
1967	600,836	18,880	3.244	430,419	3,602	.844	152,971	–2,587	–1.691
1968	614,900	14,064	2.341	424,385	–6,034	–1,402	145,441	–7,530	–4.923
1969	632,780	17,880	2.908	414,478	–9,907	–2.334	137,773	–7,668	–5.272
1970	638,906	6,126	.968	406,650	–7,828	–1.889	127,967	–9,806	–7.118

BIBLIOGRAPHY

A. BOOKS

Barnes, W. W. *The Southern Baptist Convention.* Nashville: Broadman Press, 1954.

Campbell, Doak S. *The Florida Baptist Association: The First Hundred Years, 1842-1942.* Florida Baptist Association, n.d.

Campbell, Jesse H. *Georgia Baptists: Historical and Biographical.* Richmond: H. K. Hilyson, 1847.

Davis, William W. *The Civil War and Reconstruction in Florida.* New York: Columbia University: Longmans Green and Co., 1913.

Douglas, Marjory S. Florida: *The Long Frontier.* New York: Harper and Row, 1967.

Freeman, Edward A. *The Epoch of Negro Baptists and the Foreign Mission Board.* Kansas City, Kansas: The Central Seminary Press, 1953.

Gannon, Michael V. *The Cross in the Sand: The Early Catholic Church in Florida.* Gainesville: University of Florida Press, 1965.

Garwood, H. C. *Stetson University and Florida Baptists.* DeLand, Fla.: Florida Baptist Historical Society, 1962.

Hayne, Coe. *Race Grit: Adventures on the Border Land of Liberty.* Philadelphia: The Judson Press, 1922.

History of the Baptist Denomination in Georgia. compiled for the *Christian Index.* Atlanta, Ga.: The Index Publishing Co., 1881.

Holt, A. J. *Pioneering in the Southwest.* Nashville: Sunday School Board, 1923.

Johns, John E. *Florida During the Civil War.* Gainesville: University of Florida Press, 1963.

Lassiter, L. B. *On This Foundation.* Jacksonville, Florida: Convention Press, 1961.

Lincoln, C. Eric. *The Negro Pilgrimage in America.* New York: Bantam Books, 1967.

Mead, Frank S. *Handbook of Denominations in the United States.* Nashville: Abingdon Press, 1965.

Mercer, Jesse. *A History of the Georgia Baptist Association.* Washington, Ga.: 1838.

Nelson, P. V. *Forty Fruitful Years: A History of Lake County Association of Baptist Churches, 1924-1964.* n.d., n.p.

Olmstead, Clifton E. *History of Religion in the United States.* Englewood Cliffs, N. J.: Prentiss-Hall Inc., 1960.

Osborn, C. George. *The First Baptist Church, Gainesville, Florida, 1870-1970.*

Pegues, A. W. *Our Baptist Ministers and Schools.* Springfield, Mass.: Willey & Co., 1892.

Rosser, John L. *A History of Florida Baptists.* Nashville: Broadman Press, 1949.

Rogers, S. B. *A Brief History of Florida Baptists, 1825-1925.*

Sweet, William Warren. *The Story of Religion in America.* New York: Harper and Brothers, 1950.

B. PERIODICALS

Adcock, J. D. "Dr. T. T. Shields Again," a letter, *Florida Baptist Witness* (July 2, 1925).
"Another Deadly Amusement," and editorial, *Florida Baptist Witness* (Nov. 26, 1920).
Armstrong, O. K. "A Report of the Textbook Situation . . . ," *Florida Baptist Witness* (Feb. 16, 1928).
"Blood Money in Education," *Florida Baptist Witness,* (March 2, 1911).
"Bro Carlton Opposes the New College," *The Southern Witness* (July 18, 1907).
Broughton, Len G. "The New Way," *Florida Baptist Witness* (May 28, 1925).
Caddin, R. T. "Unbroken Succession of the True Church," *Florida Baptist Witness* (Jan. 5, 1898).
Calhoun, L. O. "The Danger of Accepting Alien Immersion," *Florida Baptist Witness* (Oct. 21, 1948).
———. "The Holy Trinity," *Florida Baptist Witness* (Apr. 5, 1951).
"Can the Churches Be Saved," an editorial, *Florida Baptist Witness* (Nov. 23, 1921).
"Caught in a Trap," an editorial, *Florida Baptist Witness* (June 7, 1910).
Chaudoin, W. N. "Origin of the Witness," *Florida Baptist Witness,* (Jan. 9, 1893).
"Choice Specimens," *Florida Baptist Witness* (June 18, 1925).
"Churchgoing Portion of Population shows First Decline in 90 Years," *Florida Baptist Witness* (Jan. 3, 1963).
"Concerning Unionism," an editorial, *Florida Baptist Witness* (Feb. 20, 1919).
Crutcher, G. H. "Why Florida Baptists Should Build a Hospital in Tampa," *Florida Baptist Witness* (Jan. 5, 1970).
Denham, W. W. "Divorce and Remarriage," *Florida Baptist Witness* (Apr. 26, 1951).
"Dogma and Fidelity," *Florida Baptist Witness* (Mar. 9, 1911).
"Dr. Whitsett Denies the Charge," an editorial, *Florida Baptist Witness* (Aug. 19, 1896).
Duke, C. W. "General Funston and Religious Liberty," *Florida Baptist Witness* (Nov. 30, 1916).
———. "The Unit System for Florida," *Florida Baptist Witness* (Nov. 7, 1916).
"The Education of the Negro," an editorial, *The Southern Witness* (Aug. 31, 1905; Jan. 31, 1907).
Edwards, F. C. "The War Renewed," *The Southern Witness* (Nov. 21, 1907).
Farris, C. S. "A Divided House," *Florida Baptist Witness* (Jan. 30, 1895).
"The Final Word," an editorial, *Florida Baptist Witness* (June 5, 1919).
Fleitas, Rick. "They're Rapping for God," *Orlando Sentinel Sunday Magazine,* (May 10, 1970).
Florida Times Union, (July 6, 1968).
———. (Sept. 13, 1969).
"Florida Association," *Christian Index* (Dec. 14, 1854). Article signed "G."
Geiger, L. D. column on "Missions," *Florida Baptist Witness* (Nov. 15, 1903).
"The God of War," an editorial, *Florida Baptist Witness* (Nov. 4, 1902).
Hamilton, Charles G. "What Makes Southern Baptists Tick," *Christian Cen-*

tury (Oct. 3, 1951) reprinted *Baptist and Reflector* (Oct. 11, 1951).
Hamlin, A. G. a letter, *The Gospel Herald* (May 23, 1903).
————. "Reply to George T. Leitner and Others," *Florida Baptist Witness* (June 14, 1906).
Hayman, J. M. a letter. *Florida Baptist Witness* (July 30, 1885).
Hobson, W. A. "Baptist Efficiency," *Florida Baptist Witness* (Feb. 4, 1915).
Hobson, W. A. "Shall the Student Work Continue," *Florida Baptist Witness* (July 27, 1930).
————. "The Trice Trouble," *Florida Baptist Witness* (Dec. 16, 1915).
————. "The Unit System in Florida," *Florida Baptist Witness* (Dec. 7, 1916).
Hulley, Lincoln, "An Open Letter to Florida Baptists," *Gospel Herald* (Nov. 14, 1907).
————. "Florida Baptist Convention Issue," *Gospel Herald* (Jan. 30, 1908).
————. "Real Estate Values," an editorial, *Gospel Herald* (Oct. 31, 1907).
————. "Stetson and a Junior College," *Florida Baptist Witness* (Sept. 11, 1926), pp. 9-10.
————. "The Stetson University Charter," *Gospel Herald* (Apr. 25, 1907, May 16, 1907).
————. "Who Will Pay the Bill," *Gospel Herald* (Nov. 14, 1907).
Ingram, M. V. "The Race Question from the Bible View," *Florida Baptist Witness* (Mar. 17, 1904).
"Inter-church World Movement," *Florida Baptist Witness* (Apr. 22, 1920), p. 7.
Joiner, E. Earl. "Baptist Tradition and Theological Controversy," *Florida Baptist Witness* (Sept. 13, 1962), p. 16.
"The Layman's Movement," editorial, *Florida Baptist Witness* (Mar. 4, 1909).
"Liberty, Unity, Fraternity," an editorial, *Florida Baptist Witness* (Aug. 2, 1917).
Maguire, John. "Gaines and Trends in Florida for Ten Years," *Florida Baptist Witness* (May 2, 1963), p. 5.
Mahon, W. L. "Origin of Cuban Baptist Missions," *Florida Baptist Witness* (Mar. 2, 1898).
Marion Association Column, *Florida Baptist Witness* (Nov. 12, 1885).
Masters, Victor I. "The Board and Florida Baptists," *The Southern Witness* (July 28, 1907).
McPherson, R. P. "The Union Meeting Menace," *Florida Baptist Witness* (May 8, 1919).
Miley, Don. "Separation of Church and State," *Florida Baptist Witness* (Oct. 23, 1947).
Moodie, F. B. editorial, *Florida Baptist Witness* (Sept. 3, 1890).
"Ministerial Education," an editorial, *Florida Baptist Witness* (Mar. 10, 1904).
Mitchell, J. W. "Our Brother in Black," *Florida Baptist Witness* (June 27, 1918), pp. 2-3.
————. "Our Labor Troubles," an editorial, *Florida Baptist Witness* (Dec. 4, 1919).
————. "Why Not Learn from Others," an editorial, *Florida Baptist Witness* (June 25, 1925), p. 4.
Moncrief, A. J. An editorial, *Florida Baptist Witness* (Apr. 25, 1940), pp. 4 ff.

Moodie, F. B. "The New Baptist University at Lake City and What It Aspires to Be," *The Southern Witness* (July 4, 1907).
Muse, Thomas. Letter in *Florida Baptist Witness* (Mar. 26, 1925).
"No North and No South," editorial, *Florida Baptist Witness* (June 1, 1888).
Nowlin, W. D. "Report of the Committee on Education and the Junior College," *Florida Baptist Witness* (Oct. 28, 1926), p. 9.
"Our Brother in Black," an editorial, *Florida Baptist Witness* (Nov. 8, 1906).
Patterson, W. G. "More about Landmarkism," *The Southern Witness* (Feb. 21, 1907).
Patterson, C. R. "What Do the Baptists of Florida Need in Their Educational Institutions?" *The Southern Witness* (Nov. 8, 1906).
Pickern, D. V. "The Textbook Situation at Tallahassee," *Florida Baptist Witness* (Mar. 1, 1928), p. 10.
Queen, P. T. L. "Jacksonville Union Meeting," *Florida Baptist Witness* (Feb. 9, 1911), p. 3.
———. "Sunday School Convention," *Florida Baptist Witness* (May 18, 1911), p. 4.
"Render Unto Caesar the Things that are Caesar's," *Florida Baptist Witness* (Apr. 26, 1917), p. 6.
Rennolds, E. H. "Religious Census of the Legislature," *Florida Baptist Witness* (Apr. 6, 1911), p. 10.
Rogers, S. B. "Christian World Taking Notice," *Florida Baptist Witness* (Feb. 15, 1923), p. 2.
———. "Efficiency in the Country," *Florida Baptist Witness* (Apr. 29, 1915).
Rosser, J. L. "A Stabilizing Faith," *Florida Baptist Witness* (Mar. 27, 1941), p. 5.
———. "Florida's Moral Crisis," *Florida Baptist Witness* (Aug. 23, 1934), p. 4.
———. "Keeping Our Heritage Unstained," *Florida Baptist Witness* (Dec. 20, 1945), p. 3.
"The Sheldon Experiment," an editorial, *Florida Baptist Witness* (Mar. 28, 1890).
"The South and the Independent," an editorial, *Florida Baptist Witness* (Nov. 1, 1906), p. 6.
"State Aid to Colleges," editorial, *Florida Baptist Witness* (Mar. 25, 1896).
Stracener, W. G. "Disturbed Church-Leader Relationships," an editorial, *Florida Baptist Witness* (Oct. 25, 1962), p. 4.
———. "Buildings May Bless or Blight," *Florida Baptist Witness* (July 31, 1952), p. 4.
"Three Acts of Injustice," an editorial, *Florida Baptist Witness* (Apr. 5, 1899).
Trice, J. E. "Baptist Children's Home in Arcadia in Great Need of Funds," *Florida Baptist Witness* (July 5, 1928).
Tucker, letter to editor of *Index* (Feb. 28, 1845), in *Christian Index* (Mar. 21, 1845).
Ware, G. W. S. article in *Florida Baptist Witness* (Feb. 15, 1906).
Warren, L. B. "Florida's First Missionary," *Southern Baptist Witness* (Aug. 4, 1904), p. 6.
Weaver, R. W. "Centennial Address," *Florida Baptist Witness* (Mar. 19, 1925).
"What Makes a Christian," *Florida Baptist Witness* (Mar. 2, 1911), p. 6.

C. DENOMINATIONAL JOURNALS, ANNUALS AND MINUTES

Baptist Home Mission Monthly
Florida Baptist Associational *Minutes*
Florida Baptist Churches, *Minutes*
Florida Baptist Convention *Annuals*
Florida Baptist State Board of Missions, *Minutes*
Report of the American Baptist Home Mission Society
Southern Baptist Convention, *Annuals*
Southern Baptist Missionary Journal

D. UNPUBLISHED WORKS

Bowen, Olga. "Buildings on Stetson Campus." Unpublished manuscript, 1968, Stetson University Library.

Browning, Edwin B. "The Early History of Concord Missionary Baptist Church, 1841-1868," mimeographed, 1946, Garwood Baptist Historical Collection, Stetson University Library.

Crouch, Kenneth, "State Songs," Unpublished manuscript, University of Virginia Library, 1970.

Dalton, Jack P. "A History of Florida Baptists." Unpublished Doctoral dissertation, University of Florida, 1952.

Garwood, H. C. "Baptist Beginnings in Education," a monograph, Garwood Baptist Historical Collection, Stetson University Library. (Mimeographed.)

History of First Baptist Church, Fernandina. Printed, no author, n.d.

Peaslee, Mrs. Herbert R., Jr. *A Century of Witnessing in South Florida Baptist Association 1867-1967*. South Florida Baptist Association, 1967.

Plant City: First Baptist Church, History, A Century of Service 1866-1966.

Reeves, Gordon C. "A History of Florida Baptists." Unpublished Masters thesis, Stetson University, 1938.

Reid, Ira D. "The Negro Baptist Ministry: An Analysis of its Profession, Preparation and Practices," a report of a survey by the Joint Survey Commission of the Baptist Inter-Convention Committee, 1951. (Mimeographed.)

Semple, James H. "A History of the Florida Baptist Convention, from 1865 to 1918." Unpublished Doctoral dissertation, Southwestern Baptist Theological Seminary, 1962.

Sheffield, I. C. S., *et al. History of Harmony Baptist Association Since Organization, Comprising Parts of Levy, Gilchrist and Alachua Counties* (n.d.) Garwood Historical Collection, Stetson University Library.

Simpkins, G. E. "History of Eden Baptist Church (1845-1961)." Mimeographed, Garwood Historical Library, Stetson University.

E. ENCYCLOPEDIAS

Collier's Encyclopedia Year Book, 1969. New York: Crowell-Collier Educational Corporation, 1969.

Encyclopedia Britannica Yearbook, 1969. Chicago: Encyclopedia Britannica, 1970.

Encyclopedia Britannica. Chicago: Encyclopedia Britannica, 1965, V. IX.

Florida Statistical Abstract, 1967, Bureau of Business Research, College of Business Administration, University of Florida, Gainesville, Florida, 1967.

World Almanac. New York: New York World-Telegram and the Sun, 1969.

Yearbook of American Churches, 1969. New York: Council Press, 1969.

INDEX